FIFTY KEY ANTHROPOLOGISTS

Fifty Key Anthropologists surveys the life and work of some of the most influential figures in anthropology. The entries, written by an international range of expert contributors, represent the diversity of thought within the subject, incorporating both classic theorists and more recent anthropological thinkers. Names discussed include:

- Clifford Geertz
- Bronislaw Malinowski
- Zora Neale Hurston
- Sherry B. Ortner
- Claude Lévi-Strauss
- Rodney Needham
- Mary Douglas
- Marcel Mauss.

This accessible A–Z guide contains helpful cross-referencing, a timeline of key dates and schools of thought, and suggestions for further reading. It will be of interest to students of anthropology and related subjects wanting a succinct overview of the ideas and impact of key anthropologists who have helped to shape the discipline.

Robert Gordon is Professor of Anthropology at the University of Vermont, USA, and Research Associate at the University of the Free State, South Africa. He is the author of *The Bushman Myth* and *Going Abroad: How to Travel Like an Anthropologist*.

Andrew P. Lyons is Professor Emeritus of Anthropology at Wilfrid Laurier University, Waterloo, Canada, and current editor-in-chief of *Anthropologica*.

Harriet D. Lyons is Professor of Anthropology at the University of Waterloo, Canada.

ALSO AVAILABLE FROM ROUTLEDGE

Anthropology: The Basics
Peter Metcalf
9780415331203

Archaeology: The Basics, second edition
Clive Gamble
9780415359757

Sociology: The Basics
Ken Plummer
9780415472067

Social and Cultural Anthropology: The Key Concepts, second edition
Nigel Rapport and Joanna Overing
9780415367516

Archaeology: The Key Concepts
Edited by Colin Renfrew and Paul Bahn
9780415317580

Fifty Key Thinkers on History, second edition
Edited by Marnie Hughes-Warrington
9780415366519

Fifty Key Sociologists: The Formative Theorists
Edited by John Scott
9780415352604

Fifty Key Sociologists: The Contemporary Theorists
Edited by John Scott
9780415352598

FIFTY KEY
ANTHROPOLOGISTS

Edited by
Robert Gordon, Andrew P. Lyons,
and Harriet D. Lyons

Routledge
Taylor & Francis Group

LONDON AND NEW YORK

First published 2011
by Routledge
2 Park Square, Milton Park, Abingdon, Oxon, OX14 4RN

Simultaneously published in the USA and Canada
by Routledge
711 Third Avenue, New York, NY 10017 (8th Floor)

Routledge is an imprint of the Taylor & Francis Group, an informa business

Typeset in Bembo by Taylor & Francis Books

British Library Cataloguing in Publication Data
A catalogue record for this book is available from the British Library

Library of Congress Cataloging in Publication Data
Fifty key anthropologists / edited by Robert Gordon, Andrew Lyons,
and Harriet Lyons.
p. cm. – (Routledge key guides)
Includes index.
1. Anthropologists–Biography. I. Gordon, Robert J., 1947–II. Lyons,
Andrew P. (Andrew Paul) III. Lyons, Harriet.
GN20.F54 2010
301.092'2 – dc22

ISBN 13: 978-0-415-46104-7 (hbk)
ISBN 13: 978-0-415-46105-4 (pbk)
ISBN 13: 978-0-203-83879-2 (ebk)

CONTENTS

ALPHABETICAL LIST OF CONTENTS

CHRONOLOGICAL LIST OF
CONTENTS

CONTRIBUTORS

Thomas S. Abler is Professor Emeritus at the Department of Anthropology at the University of Waterloo in Ontario. His research has focused on the ethnohistory of the Iroquois, particularly the Seneca Nation. His books include *Chainbreaker: The Revolutionary War Memoirs of Governor Blacksnake* (1989), *Hinterland Warriors and Military Dress: European Empires and Exotic Uniforms* (1999), and *Cornplanter: Chief Warrior of the Allegany Senecas* (2007).

Andrew Bank is an Associate Professor in History at the University of the Western Cape. His current research interest is the history of anthropology in southern Africa. He is the author of *Bushman in a Victorian World: The Remarkable Story of the Bleek-Lloyd Collection of Bushman Folklore* (2006) and co-author of *An Eloquent Picture Gallery: The South African Portrait Photographs of Gustav Theodor Fritsch, 1863–5* (2008).

Stanley R. Barrett earned a BA in English and philosophy at Acadia University, an MA in comparative sociology at the University of Toronto, and a PhD at the University of Sussex. He has published books on a West African Utopia, racist and anti-Semitic organizations in Canada, class and ethnicity in rural Ontario, as well as theory and methods texts. He currently is University Professor Emeritus at the University of Guelph.

John M. Cinnamon teaches anthropology and African studies at Miami University (Ohio). He has worked extensively in Gabon and Cameroon and has published on the historical anthropology of equatorial Africa, the rain forest environment, and the influence of missionary ethnographers on professional anthropology. Currently he is studying the history of the late colonial and post-colonial religious imagination in Gabon.

John W. Cole is Professor of Anthropology Emeritus at the University of Massachusetts in Amherst. He is past president of the Society for the Anthropology of Europe, the Northeastern Anthropology Association, and the Massachusetts Society of Professors. He received an honorary doctorate in political economy from the University of Trento in 2002.

Regna Darnell is Distinguished University Professor of Anthropology and First Nations Studies at the University of Western Ontario. Books include: *Invisible Genealogies* (2001), *Historicizing Canadian Anthropology* (co-ed. 2006), *Continuity and Revolution in Americanist Anthropology* (2000), and *Edward Sapir: Linguist, Anthropologist, Humanist* (1990). She is founding editor of *Critical Studies in History of Anthropology* and *Histories of Anthropology Annual*, both from the University of Nebraska Press. She is a member of the Royal Society of Canada and a former president of the Canadian Anthropology Society.

Gregor Dobler is Lecturer in Social Anthropology at Basel University. He specializes in political and economic anthropology and has published work on France and on Southern Africa.

Benjamin Eastman is Assistant Professor of Anthropology at the University of Vermont. His research focuses on politics, sports, and cultural change in contemporary Cuba and Latin America. He is a co-editor of *America's Game(s): A Critical Anthropology of Sport* (2008).

Jeffrey David Ehrenreich is Professor of Anthropology at the University of New Orleans. He has conducted ethnographic research among the Awa (Ecuador), and the Piaroa and Warao (Venezuela), and he has published numerous articles, books, and edited volumes, including *Political Anthropology of Ecuador; Reading the Social Body* (with Catherine Burroughs); and *Politics and Religion in Amazonia* (with Javier Ruedas). He is the founding editor of *TIPITI*, the Journal of the Society for the Anthropology of Lowland South America.

Brian Joseph Gilley is an Associate Professor of Anthropology at the University of Indiana in Bloomington. He is the author of *Becoming Two-Spirit* from the University of Nebraska Press and Co-editor of *Critical Interventions in Queer Indigenous Studies* from the University of Arizona Press.

Michael Goldsmith is Associate Professor of Anthropology at the University of Waikato, Hamilton, New Zealand. His research interests include Pacific Christianity, history and politics (particularly in Tuvalu) as well as cultural identity and ethnicity in New Zealand. Publications include the co-authored book *The Accidental Missionary: Tales of Elekana* (2002), a co-edited special issue of the *Journal of the Polynesian Society* (2003), and articles in *American Anthropologist, Anthropological Forum*, and *Journal of Pacific History*.

Robert Gordon is Professor of Anthropology at the University of Vermont and Research Associate at the Free State University. Some of his books include *Law and Order in the New Guinea Highlands* with Mervyn Meggitt and *The Bushman Myth*.

Patrick Harries is Professor of History at the University of Basel. He is an expert on Swiss linkages to Africa.

David L. R. Houston is a PhD Candidate at McGill University, studying tourism and the informal economy, as mediated by Information and Communications Technology. Along with this research, he pursues teaching opportunities and research into ICT, sexuality and gender, and complex systems in a diverse array of geographical locations.

Virginia Kerns, Professor of Anthropology at the College of William and Mary, earned a PhD at the University of Illinois. She is the author *of Scenes from the High Desert: Julian Steward's Life and Theory* (2003, Urbana: University of Illinois Press) and *Journeys West: Jane and Julian Steward and Their Guides* (2010, Lincoln: University of Nebraska Press).

Richard Borshay Lee received his MA from the University of Toronto and his PhD from Berkeley. He is University Professor Emeritus of Anthropology at the University of Toronto. His research interests include human rights and indigenous peoples, ecology and history, AIDS, and the politics of culture. He is known for his studies of the Ju/'hoansi-!Kung San of Botswana. His books include *Man the Hunter* (1968), *Kalahari Hunter-Gatherers* (1976), *Politics and History in Band Societies* (1982) (with Eleanor Leacock), *The Dobe Ju/'hoansi_*(third edition 2003), and *The Cambridge Encyclopedia of Hunters and Gatherers* (1999).

Andrew P. Lyons is Professor Emeritus of Anthropology, Wilfrid Laurier University, Waterloo, Ontario. He is currently Editor-in-Chief of *Anthropologica, Journal of the Canadian Anthropology Society*. His research interests include the history of anthropology, ritual, and symbolism, and the anthropology of mass communication. He has done fieldwork in West Africa. His publications include *Irregular Connections: A History of Anthropology and Sexuality*, co-authored with Harriet Lyons.

Harriet D. Lyons is Professor, Department of Anthropology, University of Waterloo, Ontario. Her research interests include the anthropology of sexuality and gender, ritual and symbolism, and the interface between literature and ethnographic writing. She has done fieldwork in West Africa. Her publications include articles on West African mass media and film, the female circumcision controversy, as well as *Irregular Connections*, co-authored with Andrew Lyons.

Judith Macdonald is a Senior Lecturer at Waikato University, New Zealand. She carried out fieldwork in Tikopia, Solomon Islands in 1979–80 and again in 2006. Her areas of research interest are medical anthropology and research methodology.

William E. Mitchell trained with Margaret Mead, has authored several books including *Mishpokhe* and *Bamboo Fire*, and edited a book on clowning. He lives in Vermont where he hikes and travels to New York to attend the opera.

David Price is a professor at St. Martin's University in Lacey, Washington where he teaches courses in anthropology and social justice. His research uses the Freedom of Information Act, archives, and interviews to document historical interactions between anthropologists and intelligence agencies. He is the author of *Threatening Anthropology* (Duke, 2004) and *Anthropological Intelligence: The Deployment and Neglect of American Anthropology During the Second World War* (Duke, 2008).

Harald E. L. Prins is a Dutch anthropologist who taught comparative history at the University of Nijmegen before coming to the US as a List Fellow at the New School for Social Research. Now a Distinguished Professor at Kansas State University, he did ethnographic fieldwork in North and South America and remains active in native rights advocacy. He has made several documentary films and authored over a hundred publications, including *The Mi'kmaq: Resistance, Accommodation, and Cultural Survival*.

Judith (Modell) Schachter is Professor of Anthropology and History at Carnegie Mellon University. Her research interests include: adoption and kinship; the history of anthropology;

Hawai'i and the US. Publications include *Ruth Benedict* (1983); *Kinship with Strangers* (1994); *A Town without Steel: Envisioning Homestead* (with Charlee Brodsky, 1998); *A Sealed and Secret Kinship* (2002); 'Constructing Moral Communities: Pacific Islander Strategies for Settling in New Places' (2002); 'Changing Interpretations of Fosterage and Adoption in Pacific Island Societies' (2008); 'Writing Lives: Ruth Benedict's Journey from Biographical Studies to Anthropology,' forthcoming in *Pacific Studies*.

Rina Sherman left South Africa for exile in Paris during the last years of the apartheid regime. She is a writer, ethnographer, and filmmaker who studied and worked with Jean Rouch. She obtained her doctorate with distinction from the Sorbonne. An acclaimed film-maker with over twenty films to her credit, she is also a novelist and currently is completing a long-term visual anthropology project with the Himba in Namibia.

Parker Shipton received his PhD from Cambridge. He is a professor of anthropology and research fellow in African studies at Boston University. Among his books are *The Nature of Entrustment* (Herskovits Award, African Studies Assn.), *Mortgaging the Ancestors*, and the forthcoming *Credit between Cultures* (all from Yale University Press). He is the Series Editor of the Blackwell Anthologies in Social and Cultural Anthropology, Co-editor of the *On the Human* forum (Nat. Humanities Center), and a former president of the Association for Africanist Anthropology.

Karen Sykes is Professor of Anthropology at the University of Manchester. She is the author of *Arguing with Anthropology: An Introduction to Critical Theories of the Gift* (Routledge, 2005), and has conducted research in Papua New Guinea since 1990.

Amy B. Trubek is a cultural anthropologist focusing on food and culture and cooking as a cultural practice. She is the author of *Haute Cuisine: How the French Invented the Culinary Profession* (2000: University of Pennsylvania Press) and *The Taste of Place, A Cultural Journey into Terroir* (2008: University of California Press).

Luis Vivanco is a cultural anthropologist whose research focuses on the culture and politics of environmentalism, ecotourism, and environmentally focused media. He is author of the book *Green Encounters: Shaping and Contesting Environmentalism in Rural Costa Rica* (Berghahn Books, 2006), and co-editor of *Tarzan was an*

Ecotourist ... And Other Tales in the Anthropology of Adventure (Berghahn Books, 2006). He has conducted ethnographic research in Costa Rica and Oaxaca, Mexico, and is currently writing an introductory textbook for cultural anthropology students.

Aram Yengoyan is Distinguished Professor of Anthropology at the University of California, Davis. His research interests are in cultural theory; the analysis of ideologies, cultures, and national cultures; the history of anthropological theory and the enlightenment(s); the relationship between language and culture; and the epistemology of cultural and linguistic translation. He has done extensive field-work in Southeast Asia and Australia. His recent publications include *Modes of Comparison: Theory and Practice*, which he edited for the Comparative Studies in Society and History Book Series.

Rosemary Lévy Zumwalt is Vice President and Dean at Agnes Scott College. The author of several prize-winning books including *Franz Boas and W. E. B. Du Bois at Atlanta University, 1906* (2008); *Ritual Medical Lore of Sephardic Women: Sweetening the Spirits and Healing the Sick* (2002); *American Folklore Fellowship: A Dialogue of Dissent* (1988); *The Enigma of Arnold van Gennep (1873–1957): Master of French Folklore and Hermit of Bourg-la-Reine* (1988); and *Wealth and Rebellion: Elsie Clews Parsons, Anthropologist and Folklorist* (1992).

INTRODUCTION

The world is truly a topsy-turvy place that continues to surprise. The same applies to social or cultural anthropology. In the late sixties and early seventies several prominent anthropologists and social theorists were confidently predicting the end of anthropology. How wrong they were! Anthropology is thriving. If one understands the story told by all the articles in this volume one can appreciate some of the reasons why this might be. It is because of the engrossing and crucial questions anthropologists ask and the way they approach them.

The editors of this volume were intrigued when Routledge asked them to edit a volume on fifty key anthropologists. What or who is *significant*? One is reminded of the famous quote attributed to Mao when a French journalist asked him what he thought was the significance of the French Revolution and he replied that it was too soon to tell! The issue then is problematic: what exactly constitutes a key thinker in *anthropology*? When, where, and for whom is such a distinction recognized? When we discussed the notion of fifty key thinkers with colleagues, there was an interesting consensus about the top twenty or thirty individuals. Beyond that point there was less of a consensus, although certain names did recur with frequency despite the fact that we and our colleagues represent a variety of traditions and theoretical orientations.

The three editors teach in Canada and the United States, but one of us was born in England, another in what is now Namibia, and a third in the Bronx, New York. In the past three or four decades we have witnessed some convergence of national traditions in anthropology which were formerly more distinct.

This is not merely because many anthropologists have moved back and forth across the Atlantic. Rather it may reflect the worldwide problems of postcolonialism, gender and class inequalities, globalization in production, consumption, ideology, and religion. These realities affect the way we do our fieldwork and they also affect the way we view our own past and our predecessors.

The writers we discuss are now part of a variegated hybrid tradition in anglophone anthropology. We actually selected fifty-one people, because John and Jean Comaroff often work as a team. Twenty-five of them are American, six are French, one is Swedish, another Norwegian, and the remainder come from or have taught in different parts of the British Commonwealth, including five South Africans, one Indian, a New Zealander, and eleven British. In fact the picture is more complicated. Franz Boas was born in Germany, Bronislaw Malinowski and Paul Radin were born in Poland, and Robert Lowie and Eric Wolf were born in Austria. Victor Turner, A. R. Radcliffe-Brown, Bronislaw Malinowski, Paul Radin, the Comaroffs, Mary Douglas, Fredrik Barth, F. G. Bailey, Rodney Needham, and Claude Lévi-Strauss taught or researched for substantial periods on both sides of the Atlantic and also in other parts of the world. At least eighteen of our group were or are Jewish, although few of them were devout. While only nine of the fifty-one are women, this is a higher number than one would find in most disciplines over a similar time frame. We have included six French nationals in our group, because French anthropology has had a major impact on anthropology everywhere in this new century and the last one, and elements of it have been thoroughly incorporated into anglophone anthropology. Our contributors reflect a similar range and diversity, coming as they do, apart from the United States and Britain, from Canada, New Zealand, the Netherlands, France, Germany, Switzerland, and South Africa.

In debating and discussions about whom one should include in a list of key anthropologists we have opted for a group broadly representative of the diverse movements and currents in the world of socio-cultural anthropology. Certain names are almost synonymous with important theoretical movements, such as Malinowski with functionalism, Lévi-Strauss with structuralism, and Marvin Harris with cultural materialism. Many of them, but not all, taught at major universities where they trained graduate students who became leading figures in their own right. Some of our group never received the recognition their work deserved during their lifetime. This was especially true of Arnold van Gennep and Zora Neale Hurston. Whatever the case, they have been true to the discipline. Already in 1910 A. C. Haddon, the pioneer English anthropologist, observed that anthropology thrived on controversies because it was an anarchical subject advocating views which frequently challenged both Church and State.

The significance of some of our key thinkers depends on an ability to forge original ideas that can be used by other scholars.

Sometimes their influence may transcend the bounds of anthropology. This has been true of Hurston in literature, folklore, and Afro-American studies, of Lévi-Strauss and Geertz throughout the Arts and Social Sciences, of Turner in religious and drama studies, of Douglas in religious studies and organizational studies, of Rubin in gender studies, queer and poststructural theory, and of Appadurai in cultural studies.

Edward Tylor once wrote that 'anthropology is a reformer's science.' Anthropology indeed has a reputation as a radical discipline, but the scholars included in this collection represent a variety of political perspectives. The centrality of fieldwork has tended to imbue anthropologists with a concern for subject peoples, though they have differed in the way this was expressed. A central problematic for the discipline has been the attempt to define an appropriate response to 'otherness' and subjection.

The articles in this book are written for students and teachers of anthropology as well as lay people who wish to understand a little more about social anthropology. For readers wishing to further explore our fifty key anthropologists, as well as the many others who have made important contributions to the discipline, there are several valuable sources including the excellent *Biographical Dictionary of Anthropology*, edited by Vered Amit, Routledge, New York (2004). Other useful sources include the University of Wisconsin's series on the History of Anthropology, founded by George Stocking and currently edited by Richard Handler, and the University of Nebraska's series, *Critical Studies in the History of Anthropology*, edited by Regna Darnell and Stephen Murray. Regna Darnell also edits the journal *Histories of Anthropology Annual*, published by the University of Nebraska Press. The quarterly *History of Anthropology Newsletter*, edited by Henrika Kuklick, contains much useful information and a regularly updated bibliography. Books which can be consulted include Henrika Kuklick's *The Savage Within* (1991, Cambridge: Cambridge University Press) and her excellent, recently edited *A New History of Anthropology* (2008, Malden, MA: Wiley Blackwell). Adam Kuper's readable *Anthropology and Anthropologists: The Modern British School* has been republished in several revised editions, most recently in 1996 (London: Routledge). Marvin Harris's *Rise of Anthropological Theory* is an informative but opinionated classic (1968, NewYork: T. Crowell). Thomas Hylland Eriksen and Finn Sivert Nielsen's *A History of Anthropology* is a concise insightful book written from an Scandinavian perspective (2001, London: Pluto). Sydel Silverman's *Totems and Teachers* is a collection of longer essays by well known scholars about the famous anthropologists who taught them. A delightful recent history of Social Anthropology is David Mills's *Difficult Folk?* (2008, New York: Berghahn) while Thomas Patterson's *A Social History of Anthropology in the United States* (2001, New York: Berg) provides a Marxian analysis. A valuable overview by Barth, Gingrich, Parkin, and Silverman examines *One Discipline, Four Ways: British, German, French and American Anthropology* (2005, Chicago: University of Chicago Press). For a useful survey of the history of anthropology outside of the Anglo-American canon consult Aleksander Boskovic's (ed.) *Other People's Anthropologies* (2008, New York: Berghahn). Now in its third edition, Paul Erickson and Liam Murphy's *A History of Anthropological Theory* (2009, Toronto: University of Toronto Press) is a useful, popular, and accessible undergraduate text, More recent theoretical developments are discussed in Sherry Ortner's *Anthropology and Social Theory* (2006, Durham: Duke University Press).

ROBERT GORDON, ANDREW P. LYONS, HARRIET D. LYONS

Note on cross-referencing in the text

Names marked in **bold** make reference to key figures who have their own individual entries. Terms in SMALL CAPS are explained further in Appendix 1, which contains a number of key anthropological terms for reference.

FIFTY KEY
ANTHROPOLOGISTS

ARJUN APPADURAI (1948–)

Arjun Appadurai was born and raised in Mumbai, India. He initially came to the United States after attending Elphinstone College in Mumbai, earning his BA from Brandeis University in 1970 and then obtaining his MA (1973) and PhD (1976) from the University of Chicago. As a student at Chicago he worked closely with both anthropologists and historians at the innovative and interdisciplinary Committee on Social Thought. His geographic area of focus from then till now has been South Asia, and during his graduate studies he worked closely with renowned scholars of South Asia including the anthropologist, Bernard Cohn. He went on to teach and do research in Anthropology departments at the University of Pennsylvania, University of Chicago, and Yale University between 1979 and 2003. He then became the Provost and the John Dewey Distinguished Professor of Social Sciences at the New School of Social Research. As of January 2009 he became the Goddard Professor of Media, Culture and Communication at New York University. He is a fellow of the American Academy of Arts and Sciences and the recipient of numerous scholarly fellowships and awards.

The personal and intellectual impact of both his experiences as an immigrant and his interdisciplinary training are revealed consistently throughout Appadurai's fecund intellectual career. His scholarly publications on India have traversed various cultural terrains, including religion, colonialism, agriculture, cuisine, public culture, and urbanization. His earliest intellectual project was to question the tendency to characterize South Asian culture as static rather than exploring the importance of change to this region. His first book, *Worship and Conflict under Colonial Rule: a South Asian Case* (1981), a revision of his dissertation, was a fine-grained study of a South Asian Hindu temple, Sri Partasarati Svami Temple, a Sri Vaisnava shrine. Using a specific place of worship as his field-site, Appadurai combined archival and ethnographic methodologies to re-examine assumptions in both anthropology and history as to what defines 'traditional' Hindu worship practices.

Appadurai has committed himself to question and re-examine received wisdom regarding the best and most appropriate ways to investigate the material and symbolic organization of social life. This commitment is readily apparent in a special issue of *Cultural Anthropology* edited by Appadurai called 'Place and Voice in Anthropological Theory' (1988). Here Appadurai questioned the tendency of academic disciplines to rely on certain 'territories of knowledge' to demarcate social reality in particular ways, thus shaping conceptual and theoretical frameworks and ultimately the organization of the disciplines themselves. Other essays that reconsider how the geography of South Asia has been anthropologically traversed, relying on certain gateway concepts, include 'Center and Periphery in Anthropological Theory' (1986a) and 'Is Homo Hierarchicus?' (1986b).

His introductory essay in *The Social Life of Things: Commodities in Cultural Perspective* (1986) re-examines the notion of a commodity by considering the process by which value becomes attached to things. Appadurai proposed that commodities themselves, as much as or more than the larger exchange systems within which any individual commodity is embedded, have powerful stories to tell about social organization. These stories can not be well documented unless multiple disciplinary perspectives are embraced. A theory of the social life of things became a powerful tool for analyzing the social and material conditions involved in exchange systems. This essay as well as the edited volume has been widely used in anthropology, history, and other allied disciplines.

He has continued to publish essays interrogating the epistemological and ontological foundations of disciplinary knowledge in the social sciences, focusing on the discipline of anthropology and the geographic region of South Asia. Recent examples include 'The Geography of Canonicity' (1993), 'Diversity and Disciplinarity as Cultural Artifacts' (1996a), and 'Grassroots Globalization and the Research Imagination' (2000a).

By the late 1980s Appadurai also began to incorporate theories of migration and globalization into his scholarship, further moving his thinking away from the classical anthropological strategy of linking a geographic locale with a bounded community and culture. The fluidity of symbolic and material life, both across time and through space, which had been articulated in *The Social Life of Things*, moved to the center of his scholarly work. In collaboration with his late wife, the historian Carol Breckenridge, he commenced a new intellectual project on the notion of 'public culture,' that was a novel recasting of former, spatially demarcated definitions of culture, a necessary task given the increasingly economically and culturally connected social realities of modernity. With public culture, groups of people can share values, beliefs, and practices (for example relationships to mass media) but not share a geographic locale. In 1988 they founded the renowned scholarly journal *Public Culture* which created a forum for scholars interested in pursuing the construction and movement of cultural ideas, practices, and formations across national, linguistic, class, race, and gender boundaries. Although Appadurai's published record on globalization and public culture is notable, he has also been heavily involved in creating intellectual environments for other scholars to further explore interdisciplinary projects on culture and globalization, first with the journal, and subsequently as the founding director of the Chicago Humanities Institute at the University of Chicago and as director of the Center for Cities and Globalization at Yale University.

The book *Modernity at Large, Cultural Dimensions of Globalization*, first published in 1996, compiled his scholarship on culture and globalization, creating new analytic frameworks for understanding all manner of endeavors, including watching television, playing cricket, and counting people. In this collection, Appadurai addressed debates in social theory as to the possibilities of human agency in the face of social and economic constraints, particularly consumer capitalism, examining closely the role of mass media in creating new globalized arenas for values, practices, and beliefs. His view was generally optimistic: 'consumption in the contemporary world is often a form of drudgery, part of the capitalist civilizing process. Nevertheless, where there is consumption there is pleasure, and where there is pleasure there is agency' (1996b: 7). For Appadurai, anthropologists must address the role of consumption in modern societies, deploying the ethnographic gaze to focus on the role of consumption practices in people's everyday lives. At the same time, his analysis of economic forms of consumption is mediated by his investment in the power of symbols and signs in people's everyday lives. The essay, 'Disjuncture and Difference in the Global Cultural Economy,' reprinted in *Modernity at Large*, was particularly influential because Appadurai, among the first anthropologists to problematize the concept of culture in the context of globalization, created a case for future scholarship focusing on what he defined as global cultural flows. He called for scholars to look at what he calls disjunctures in the global system, with a focus on landscapes based not on territories but rather on 'perspectival constructs.' These are: ethnoscapes, mediascapes, technoscapes, financescapes, and ideoscapes. For example, members of a given ethnic group may form distinctive enclaves or temporary communities throughout the world as immigrants, guest workers, refugees, tourists, and businessmen (global ethnoscapes). The environmental movement spreads to many different cultures, adapting to each environment (global ideoscapes). Television and computers have taken over the world, but the technologies and media products have to some degree been indigenized (global technoscapes and media-scapes). The focus on such constructs, Appadurai argues, allows scholars to identify the emergence of an integration of material and symbolic actions, now global in scope but still culturally inflected. His own theoretical perspective works to more fully reconcile the economic system of capitalism into the emerging academic corpus connecting all aspects of globalization by fully engaging material conditions with systems of meaning.

Recently Appadurai has extended his commitment to creating communal intellectual spaces to understand globalization by investing in research that involves greater civic engagement. He is the founder of the non-profit PUKAR (Partners for Urban Knowledge, Action, and Research) in Mumbai. He is also the co-founder and co-director of ING (Interdisciplinary Network on Globalization). His current research focuses on the effects of globalization, particularly in the South Asian context, by looking at ethnic violence, urbanization, and new forms of grass-roots activism. The recently published *Fear of Small Numbers: An Essay on the Geography of Anger* (2006) chiefly concentrates on the connection between globalization and con-temporary ethnic conflicts.

Appadurai has always embraced anthropological preoccupations as powerful ways of informing understandings of the human experience. For example, he has recently discussed the importance of the dis-cipline's long engagement with magic, which he defines as 'what people throughout the world do when faced with uncertainty, cata-strophic damage, injustice, illness, suffering or harm.' He then calls it a 'universal feeling that what we see and feel exceeds our knowledge, our understanding and our control,' a universal feeling that has allowed, for example, Americans to accept certain banking practices that could be seen as magical (*Immanent Frame*, November 2008). In an interview, Appadurai uses **Mary Douglas**'s seminal ideas in *Purity and Danger* to help explain modern tensions between the middle classes in Bombay and their slum-dwelling neighbors (*Perspecta34*, 'The Illusion of Permanence,' June 2003.)

Appadurai's version of navigating 'traditional' and 'modern' ideas within the discipline of anthropology created exciting new intellec-tual paths. His ideas helped shape the anthropological research of many scholars and students, leading to contemporary ethnographic inquiries considering movement, imagination, consumption, and media in the contemporary construction of culture. As Appadurai asserts in *Modernity at Large*, 'I view locality as primarily relational and contextual rather than as scalar or spatial' (1996b: 178). His efforts to articulate and elucidate this alternative definition of place, geography, and culture, as well as the implications for individuals, communities, and the formation of knowledge, has allowed several generations of anthropologists to cross intellectual boundaries and discover new scholarly frontiers just as many thought that world had, once again, become flat.

Selected readings

Appadurai, A. (1981) *Worship and Conflict under Colonial Rule: A South Indian Case*, Cambridge: Cambridge University Press.

——(1984) 'How Moral is South Asia's Economy? – A Review Essay,' *Journal of Asian Studies* 43(3): 481–97.

——(1986a) 'Center and Periphery in Anthropological Theory,' *Comparative Studies in Society and History* 28(2): 356–61.

——(1986b) 'Is Homo Hierarchicus? – A Review Essay,' *American Ethnologist* 13(4): 745–61.

——(1988) 'How to Make a National Cuisine: Cookbooks in Contemporary India,' *Comparative Studies in Society and History* 30 (1): 3–24.

——(1993) 'The Geography of Canonicity,' in *What is Fundamental?* The Committee on Social Thought, Chicago: The University of Chicago: 3–12.

——(1995) 'Playing with Modernity: The Decolonization of Indian Cricket,' in *Consuming Modernity: Public Culture in a South Asian World*, C. A. Breckenridge (ed.), pp. 23–48, Minneapolis: University of Minnesota Press.

——(1996a) 'Diversity and Disciplinarity as Cultural Artifacts,' in *Disciplinarity and Dissent in Cultural Studies*, C. Nelson and D. Gaonkar (eds.), pp. 23–35, New York: Routledge.

——(1996b) *Modernity at Large: Cultural Dimensions of Globalization*, Minneapolis: University of Minnesota Press.

——(1999) 'Disjuncture and Difference in the Global Cultural Economy,' *Public Culture* 2(2): 1–24.

——(2000a) 'Grassroots Globalization and the Research Imagination,' *Public Culture* 12(1): 1–19.

——(2000b) 'The Grounds of the Nation-State: Identity, Violence and Territory,' in *Nationalism and Internationalism in the Post-Cold War Era*, K. Goldmann, U. Hannerz, and C. Westin (eds.), pp. 129–42, London: Routledge.

——(2000c) 'Spectral Housing and Urban Cleansing: Notes on Millennial Mumbai,' *Public Culture* 12(3): 627–51.

——(2004) 'The Capacity to Aspire,' in *Cultural and Public Action*, V. Rao and M. Walton (eds.), 59–84, Stanford, CA: Stanford University Press.

——(2005) 'Materiality in the Future of Anthropology,' in *Commodification: Things, Agency and Identities* (The Social Life of Things

Revisited), W. van Binsbergen and P. Geschiere (eds.), pp. 55–62, Hamburg: LIT Verlag.

——(2006) *Fear of Small Numbers: An Essay on the Geography of Anger*, Durham, NC: Duke University Press.

Appadurai, A. (ed.) (1986) *The Social Life of Things: Commodities in Cultural Perspective*, New York: Cambridge University Press.

——(1988) 'Place and Voice in Anthropological Theory,' Special Issue of *Cultural Anthropology* 3(1).

——(2002) *Globalization*, Durham, NC: Duke University Press.

Appadurai, A. and. Breckenridge, C. A. (1995) 'Public Modernity in India. Introductory Essay,' in *Consuming Modernity: Public Culture in a South Asian World*, C. A. Breckenridge (ed.), Minneapolis: University of Minnesota Press.

AMY B. TRUBEK

FREDERICK G. BAILEY (1924–)

Not many scholars have the audacious foresight to launch their careers with a research program rather than a research project. From 1952 through 1959 Bailey focused on a set of inter-related problems and topics in India resulting in three splendid monographs. In addition he published a further fifteen books and forty scholarly papers, almost all of them concerned with political anthropology. His work can be divided into three categories: the early Indian phase, his theoretical volumes, and his eventual turn towards anthropology at home (Britain and the United States).

His Indian monographs should be treated as a trinity, because together they constitute a comprehensive portrait of political activity in one part of the country. The second category also includes three books, but the focus here will be entirely on one of them, *Stratagems and Spoils* (1969). This is because it was the capstone study in an intellectual movement which provided the discipline with a new perspective. Several of Bailey's books published in the 1970s and 1980s reflect his interest in his own society, especially formal organizations. *Morality and Expediency* (1977) is representative, because it was his first full-scale monograph in the genre, and because it represented anthropology at home: an analytic examination of political interaction in universities.

Frederick George Bailey was born into a lower-middle-class family in Liverpool and went to Oxford to study Classics on an Open Scholarship in 1942, but left the following year to join the British Army. After the War he returned to Oxford, leaving with the degrees of MA and BLitt in 1950. He then enrolled for a doctorate in social anthropology under **Max Gluckman** at Manchester University and received his PhD in 1955. After teaching at the University of London's School of Oriental and African Studies he moved in 1964 to found the anthropology program at the University of Sussex. He accepted a Professorship at the University of California at San Diego in 1971, where as Emeritus Professor he continues to write books at a pace that leaves younger colleagues breathless.

Work in India

The Indian research program focused first on a village, then on a region, and finally on the modern system of representative democracy. Along the way tribe, caste, the mercantile economy introduced by British colonialism, and the administrative machinery of the modern state were treated as interdependent but contradictory political structures generating significant social change.

Caste and the Economic Frontier (1957) is a study of Bisipara, a village located in an isolated and poverty-stricken part of Orissa state. Bisipara was home to about 700 Oriya-speaking Hindus whose forebears had settled in the area some 300 years earlier. Bailey's focus was on the impact of external factors on political activity in the village, particularly the caste system. His rich ethnography enabled him to explain how the encroaching mercantile economy affected the capacity of peasants to retain control and ownership of their land, and how two Untouchable Distiller castes were able to gain sufficient wealth to become prominent landowners themselves, which led to their attempts to elevate their positions in the caste hierarchy.

Tribe, Caste and Nation (1960) dealt with a village of about 500 people less than an hour's walk from Bisipara, called Baderi. Both villages were dependent on irrigated rice cultivation for subsistence, but otherwise were quite different. Bisipara was a multi-caste settlement. Baderi was dominated by a single caste called Konds, formerly labelled Animists or Tribalists, who spoke the Kui language. Unlike Bisipara, the fulcrum of political action and social change in Baderi was not the village, but instead the dispersed clan system. Presumably that explains why Bailey focused on the wider region. He examined the power struggles between the Aboriginal Konds and the Hindu settlers, and introduced the term 'bridge-actions' to capture the manner individuals pursued their interests by mobilizing support across competing political structures such as tribe, caste, and the modern state.

FREDERICK G. BAILEY (1924–)

Tribe, Caste and Nation is sometimes regarded as the best of the three Indian monographs. This is not only because of the scope of the study, but also because of its methodology and theoretical sophistication. Taking the position that disputes and conflicts are 'diagnostic' of the causes and directions of social change, Bailey organized the study around 38 such cases. While the analytic focus was on social structure the author's discussion of antinomies such as static versus dynamic and synchronic versus diachronic advanced the discipline's capacity to deal with social change.

In *Politics and Social Change* (1963) Bailey focused on the system of representative democracy in the State of Orissa, aiming to discover what impact parliament had on the older political structures of tribe and caste, and what it meant to people in their everyday lives. He began by interviewing about 50 State Assemblymen and then shifted the inquiry to the level of constituencies and villages. Bailey candidly presented this challenging project as an experiment in methodology, testing whether the tools of social anthropology can cope with the complexity of a modern state.

Transactionalist theory: politics, power, and self-interest

The Indian volumes were a hard act to follow, but *Stratagems and Spoils* surpassed expectations. Drawing on the work of several prominent predecessors, especially **Fredrik Barth, Raymond Firth, Edmund Leach**, and **Bronislaw Malinowski**, Bailey sketched out the nuts and bolts of what became known as the TRANSACTIONAL or interactional model, and sometimes action or agency theory. It opens with a comparison between the Mafia and violent interaction among Swat Pathans, arguing that both the Mafia and the Swat Pathans arrange their politics in much the same way and claiming that, beneath the veneer of cultural variation, political activity everywhere, whether in advanced Western states or in tribal and peasant societies, exhibits a common set of principles.

Bailey distinguishes between normative and pragmatic rules of behavior. Normative rules are general guides to conduct, consisting of public, formal, or ideal rules of society. Pragmatic rules are deviations from the ideal rules; they consist of the tactics and strategies that individuals resort to in order to effectively achieve their goals. While not denying that duty and altruism exist, his message is that human interaction is dominated by pragmatic rules manipulated by choice-making actors capable of rational calculation. In everyday life most of us, guided by self-interest, thread our way between the norms, seeking the most advantageous route. This is no less true of politician, who 'are all caught up in the act of outmanoeuvring one another, of knifing one another in the back, of tripping one another up. ... No statesman is effective unless he knows the rules of attack and defence in the political ring' (Bailey 1969: xi, xii).

On one level *Stratagems and Spoils* is a study of politics and power, but on another level it provides a theoretical perspective for the entire discipline. People are not puppets controlled by the institutional framework; they are active agents locked in competitive struggle. Nor is the social structure unified and static; it is a dynamic entity, continuously being reshaped by the shifting transactions, alliances, coalitions, competitions, and choices that characterize human inter-action. The transactional model pushed the image of the social world so far away from **Radcliffe-Brown**ian STRUCTURAL-FUNCTIONALISM as to render a paradigmatic shift.

Morality and Expediency is an expanded version of the Louis Henry Morgan Lectures delivered at the University of Rochester in September and October, 1975. Its subject matter is the university as an organization which struggles between the contradictory goals (or 'myths' as Bailey labels them) of scholarship, collegiality, and ser-vice to society. This book picks up the scent of the self-interested, manipulative actor which permeates *Stratagems and Spoils*, and pursues it into even darker corners. The focus is on the unprincipled side of human interaction, on 'institutionalized facades, make-believe and pretence, lies and hypocrisy' on what 'every public figure pretends does not exist' (Bailey 1977: 2)

Bailey distinguishes between public and private interaction. Public arenas are where principles, goals, and slogans flourish, and are the locus of non-rational debate. As principles and beliefs are devoid of criteria of ultimate worth, they can be proclaimed but not demon-strated. The private arena, uncontaminated by the urge to play to an audience, is where things get done. This is because under the pro-tection of privacy, principles can be relaxed and compromise prevails. To the extent that this occurs, the private arena is where rationality takes over. Yet the public arena is not merely an irksome ideological screen. It is there where people persuade each other that the world is orderly and therefore meaningful – what Bailey labels the basic lie, without which we might all go mad.

One chapter is devoted to committees. As part of the bureaucracy, they should be guided by rationality and impersonality, not collegiality, since bureaucracies ideally only consider that part of an individual pertinent to the task under consideration. Communities, in contrast, deal with the full, rounded person. Bailey shows how in reality the community dimension always invades committee deliberations. Through casual remarks and gossip, committee members exchange personal information about the individuals under discussion. Indeed, 'such committees cannot work effectively unless they use such information, without formally admitting that it exists' (ibid: 66).

Bailey reduces the political faces of his colleagues to ten analytic constructs or 'masks' that stand mid-way between role and personality. There is Reason, a 'technician of the intellect,' who is unconcerned with first principles, believes that every problem has a solution, and questions the sanity of anyone who fails to see things his way (ibid: 128). Another mask is Baron, 'the man with moustaches, with testicles. ... ' for whom intimidation is the weapon of choice (ibid: 134). Despite the book's insights into the workings of universities, and other types of formal organizations, it never had the same impact as his previous books, largely because anthropology at home still cannot compete with the discipline's traditional focus on the (increasingly elusive) exotic 'Other.'

Not everyone has been enthusiastic about Bailey's approach to politics or to the wider discipline. A criticism aimed specifically at the Indian monographs is that social change is assumed to be externally generated. That may be a fair comment with regard to *Caste and the Economic Frontier*, but misses the mark if the other two books are also the targets. Some have contended that Bailey ignored the politics of the powerful. But his books covered such illustrious figures as Gandhi and de Gaulle, and in later years Lyndon Johnson and Hitler. *Stratagems and Spoils* has been criticized for promoting an overly cynical view of the human condition, and for focusing so narrowly on the micro level of interacting individuals that sight is lost of the broader historical and structural forces that arguably shape human conduct. Yet it has been translated into French, Italian, Spanish, and Japanese and praised as the modern successor to Machiavelli's *The Prince*. Many anthropologists, indeed, would regard it as the field worker's model *par excellence*.

Bailey excelled in all dimensions of academic life: administration, research, and, not least of all, teaching. At Sussex the graduate program in anthropology, which focused on peasant communities in southern Europe, was almost a one-man show, and he edited several volumes of his students' work. Little wonder that those who studied under him during that era have remained so loyal.

Over the years Bailey has changed his position regarding some of the fundamental issues in anthropology, most obviously the shift from social structure to the transactional model. In later years Bailey began to treat ideas and their influence on behavior, as the analytic starting point. In a later book (*Treason, Stratagems and Spoils*, 2001) rational calculation partly gave way to an emphasis on emotion, spontaneity, and unanticipated consequences, and duty was allowed alongside self-interest. As Bailey's conception of the actor and the social realm became more complex, it appeared that his faith in underlying order, and thus in science, became less certain. Yet he never gave up on the comparative method, or his fascination with politics, and that has been a good thing. That is why he has made so great a contribution to the anthropological analysis of the political process.

Selected readings

Bailey, F. G. (1957) *Caste and the Economic Frontier*, Manchester: Manchester University Press.
——(1960) *Tribe, Caste and Nation*, Manchester: Manchester University Press.
——(1963) *Politics and Social Change*, Berkeley: University of California Press.
——(1969) *Stratagems and Spoils*, Oxford: Blackwell (reprinted 2001, Boulder, CO: Westview Press).
——(1977) *Morality and Expediency*, Oxford: Blackwell.
——(2001) *Treasons, Stratagems and Spoils*, Boulder, CO: Westview Press.
——(2003) *The Saving Lie*, Philadelphia: University of Pennsylvania Press.
——(2008) *God-Botherers and other True Believers*, New York: Berghahn.

STANLEY R. BARRETT

GEORGES BALANDIER (1920–)

In a highly productive administrative, academic, research, and writing career that has spanned over six decades, Balandier has made vital contributions to French anthropology, African Studies, and social theory. It is possible to identify three key, interrelated phases in Balandier's career. First, in his early anthropology of the colonial situation, he announced his departure from classic 'timeless' anthropology and in this work he gave priority to cities, a dynamic colonial present and its historical roots. Second, in the 1960s, he shifted toward political anthropology and 'social dynamics,' drawing on general anthropological and sociological theory. Third, since the 1980s, Balandier has focused on the contemporary world, on the sociology of the present, and on the ruptures of modernity and overmodernity (*surmodernité*).

Born in a small town, Balandier grew up in a France rent by antagonistic currents that in neighboring countries gave rise to Nazism, Italian fascism, and the Spanish civil war. A childhood visit to the 1931 Paris Colonial Exposition made a strong impression and contributed to a lifelong interest in other societies. Balandier studied philosophy and literature at the Sorbonne as well as ethnology at the Institut d'Ethnologie in Paris before finding employment at the Musée de l'Homme. During World War II, he left Paris to return to his home region partially to avoid the 'Service of Obligatory Labour.' There he served in the French resistance. Back at the Musée de l'Homme after the War he worked under his mentor and friend, Michel Leiris, who introduced him to Sartre and Camus, then at the peak of their influence. He wrote a 'furious' autobiographical novel, *Tous Comptes Faits* (1947), and in 1946, with the help of Leiris and Denise Paulme, traveled to Dakar, Senegal to join the Institut Français d'Afrique Noire (IFAN).

In Dakar, he befriended Senegalese intellectuals like Alioume Diop and Léopold Senghor and collaborated with Paul Mercier on a study of Lébou fishing people near Dakar, who were subjected to colonial domination, cultural mixing, and the proximity of the colonial capital. These experiences led him away from the then dominant atemporal anthropology toward the study of the dynamics of power relations, contestations, and change.

After Senegal, Balandier became director of the local IFAN in Guinea-Conakry. As in Dakar, he aroused the suspicions of the colonial establishment by associating with African, pro-independence intellectuals and politicians including Sékou Touré, whose messianic Marxist fervor led Guinea to a precipitate independence and later to what Balandier (2003: 79) called 'nepotistic predation' and 'a sort of tropical totalitarianism.' He came to realize that up to the moment of the 'colonial freezing,' the political history of Africa had been 'more inventive and thus more diversified than that of Europe' (Balandier 1977 :62).

In 1948 Balandier was assigned to Brazzaville (Moyen-Congo) to create a sociology section at the Institut d'études centrafricaines. He began to study social and cultural change among Kongo-speakers in Brazzaville and later, among Fang villagers in northern Gabon. He wanted to compare Kongo society, 'with its long history, hierarchies, former kingdoms, and inequalities' to the 'more egalitarian,' less territorially rooted Fang, 'who gave form to their modernizing initiatives in the framework of a re-composition of tribes and clans' (Balandier 1997: 280). As a hierarchical society, pre-colonial Kongo was stratified with nobles, religious experts, warriors, commoners, and slaves. The more egalitarian Fang, with informal bigmen, village heads, and warriors, but no nobles and few slaves, were much less stratified. Balandier's emphasis (1977: 231–32) on 'foreign impositions,' subterranean autonomy, the 'religious imagination,' 'the birth of peasant national-ism,' and 'the critique of the colonial situation,' departed significantly from the then dominant STRUCTURAL-FUNCTIONALIST anthropology.

In 1951, he published his seminal article on 'The Colonial Situation' that prefigured the anthropology of colonialism. This arti-cle treated the colonial situation as a complex totality that linked colonizing and colonized societies in an ongoing dynamic of power relations, coercion, conflict, ideological mechanisms, and crisis. In 1952, Balandier returned to France, where he prepared two doctoral theses (at the Sorbonne and the École des Hautes Études), defended in 1954 and published in 1955 as *Sociologie actuelle de l'Afrique noire* (Eng. tran. 1970) and *Sociologie des Brazzavilles Noires*. The first developed his comparative study of colonial crises among Congolese Ba-kongo and Gabonese Fang. The second was one of the first anthropological studies of an African city as a product of colonialism.

Following his thesis defense he was elected to the École Pratique des Hautes Études (EPHE) in Paris where he created the Centre for African Studies, which he directed until 1984. At the EPHE and later at the Sorbonne he trained a generation of prominent Africanist anthropologists, including Claude Meillassoux, Emmanuel Terray, Marc Augé, Jean Copans, and Jean-Loup Amselle. In his long teaching career, he also taught in Africa, the United States, England, Japan, Canada, Mexico, and Iran. Throughout, Balandier retained an intellectual restlessness, a desire to undertake the greatest number of activities, create openings for his students, and to enable them to continually renew their research.

In the late 1950s, Balandier turned his attention from the colonial situation to emerging concerns of development, underdevelopment, modernization, urbanization, and industrialization and, with Alfred Sauvy, initiated the concept of the 'Third World' (*Tiers Monde*). His African experiences sensitized him to European depredation of Africa's and Asia's human and material wealth and the disorganization, ruptures, and chronic crises brought about through sustained relations with the West. In 1956, he wrote, 'Asia and Africa were first modernized in function of European interests, without possessing the political auton-omy affording them the capacity to define their future. Disequilibrium and predations accumulated, without any solutions beginning to compensate for the destructive impact' (Balandier 2003: 275).

In 1957, Balandier published his most widely read book, *Afrique Ambigüe* (Eng. tran. 1966), a rich, reflexive, philosophical memoir based on his years in post-war Africa. Meanwhile, he continued to explore social dynamics, the sociology of mutations, tradition and modernity, development, dependency, and the social costs of progress. From 1961 to 1966, he taught at the École Normale Supérieure in Paris. While continuing to teach sociology and ethnology at the Sorbonne, he served from 1963 to 1973 as director of the department of Human Sciences at the Overseas Research Office (ORSTOM). He also edited a prominent book and co-edited a number of academic journals, including *Présence Africaine*, *Tiers Monde*, *Cahiers d'études africaines*, *Cahiers internationaux de sociologie* and the *Journal of Modern African Studies*.

In *Anthropologie politique* (1967, Eng. tran. 1970), Balandier undertook a systematic overview of the anthropological study of politics. When attempting to define and formalize 'politics,' one must, he argued, consider a broad range of political systems and practices, emphasize power rather than decision-making and employ a dynamic perspective.

In *Sens et Puissance* (Meaning and Power) (1971), Balandier developed his theory of social dynamics, in which society is an ever-moving, approximate order in constant formation subjected both to internal and external forces including events, ruptures, crises, and confrontations. In *Anthropo-logiques* (1974) Balandier extended his analysis of 'society,' arguing that society as such does not exist. Societies are aggregates of antagonistic groups: men and women, adults and youths, dominant and dominated, and 'societies within societies' that must be regulated. He also spelled out his differences from the STRUCTURALISM of **Claude Lévi-Strauss** who had differentiated between modern societies that were changeable, 'hot,' and subject to historical forces, and the 'cold,' post-Neolithic societies that were amenable to structural analysis. Balandier argued that that there were no 'cold' societies and that all societies were dynamic systems of tensions, more complex than the dualistic class tensions proposed by Marxists (freemen and slaves, patricians and plebeians, lords and serfs, the bourgeoisie and the proletariat).

During the 1980s, Balandier turned to a sustained analysis and critique of modernity, 'overmodernity' (*surmodernité*), galloping economism, and the impact of rapid growth of science and technology. In *Le détour* (1985), he argued that the detour by way of the anthropological study of Others opened the possibility of seeing ourselves as we have become and of identifying the major categories that organize us: the political body, the division of sexes, the techno-imaginary, and emerging logics of information and communication. He characterized the late twentieth century as an era of erasures, ruptures, crises, and uncertainties, both product and producer of the conquests of science, economic failures, weakening powers, and institutions. At the same time, destruction and destructuration have given rise to the new and the unprecedented – transitions that have shaken values, hierarchies, laws, justice, and the security of people and goods.

In *Le désordre: Eloge du mouvement* (1988), Balandier continued his comparative examination of the coherences and dysfunctions of modernity by way of tradition. He argued that all societies are confronted by disorder – order and disorder are inseparable; people create order from disorder. Modernity combines movement, heterogeneity, and uncertainty, which heighten awareness of disorder. Current figures of disorder include brutal events, epidemics and evil, violence and terrorism, weakened politics. He laid out a range of insufficient responses including totalitarian ideologies, exploitation of fear, sacralization of individual action, the cult of money and entrepreneurship, and the quest for religious certainty.

The title, *Le Dédale: Pour finir avec le XX siècle* (1994), draws on the classical myth of Daedalus, the Minotaur, and the labyrinth. In some versions, Daedalus built the labyrinth so cunningly that he himself was barely able to escape. This myth served as a metaphor to explore the unprecedented paths our era has led us on; paths characterized by expanding powers, ambivalence, blind alleys, and traps. In this world, order dissolves order, growing complexity discourages straightforward logic. We meet new Daedaluses, masters of technical power at the crossroads of the imaginary, who seek the detours of the sacred, and who interrogate exploded democracy.

In *Le Grande Système* (2001), Balandier focused on 'new, New Worlds,' worlds that are not territorial but that have emerged through advances in science, technology, and conquering economism. A logical memory links these emerging worlds, that of an expanding, worldwide Grand System that imposes itself, revealing the true face of globalization.

Fenêtres sur un nouvel âge: 2006–2007 (2008), argues that rupture is no longer a choice but a product of perpetual movement, pushed ahead by unceasing technological invention, exploited and accelerated by conquering economism and giving birth to the 'new New Worlds' where we already live, without knowing what they are or where they are leading us. How, he asks, can one master a disorientation that renders us strangers to ourselves?

Although deeply versed in social theory, Balandier is perhaps less well known to Anglophone audiences because of his resistance to grand theorizing or, as he puts it, 'partisan dogmas' and in-vogue 'intellectual systems that offer ease of occupation,' be it Marxism, 'excessive structuralism,' or post-structuralism. Indeed for much of his career, Balandier worked in the shadow of **Claude Lévi-Strauss**, whose work he greatly admired, but which he characterized as 'an almost decontextualized anthropology … that treats from a distance systems of action and even more systems of historicity.' In contrast, Balandier characterized his own work as situated 'at the heart of turbulences' and attentive to 'immediate history' and to 'crises as revealing moments in societies and cultures' (Balandier 2003: 9, 25, 70, 60, 62).

Selected readings

Balandier, G. (1955) *Sociologie des Brazzavilles Noires*, Paris: A. Colin.
——(1966 [1951]) 'The Colonial Situation: A theoretical approach,' in *Social Change: The Colonial Situation*, I. Wallerstein (ed.), pp. 34–81, New York: Wiley.
——(1970 [1955]) *The Sociology of Black Africa: Social Dynamics in Central Africa*, New York: Praeger.
——(1966 [1957]) *Ambiguous Africa; Cultures in Collision*, New York: World Publishing.
——(1968 [1965]) *Daily Life in the Kingdom of the Kongo from the Sixteenth to the Eighteenth Century*, New York: Pantheon Books.
——(1970 [1967]) *Political anthropology*, New York: Pantheon Books.
——(1974) *Anthropo-logiques*, Paris: Presses universitaires de France.
——(1977) *Histoire d'autres*, Paris: Stock.
——(1980) *Le pouvoir sur scènes*, Paris: Balland.
——(1994) *Le Dédale: Pour finir avec le XX siecle*, Paris: Fayard.
——(1997) *Conjugaisons*, Paris: Fayard.
——(2001) *Le Grand Système*, Paris: Fayard.
——(2003) *Civilisés, dit-on*, Paris: Presses Universitaires de France.
——(2005) *Civilisations et puissance*, Paris: Editions de l'Aube.
——(2008) *Fenêtres sur un nouvel âge: 2006–2007*, Paris: Fayard.

JOHN M. CINNAMON

FREDRIK BARTH (1928–)

If anthropologists were ranked solely on the basis of the sheer number and variation of their ethnographic projects, Fredrik Barth would have few peers. He has conducted fieldwork in Iraq, Iran, Pakistan, Sudan, New Guinea, and Norway. Yet there is much more to his reputation than volume and variation. His monographs are ethnographic gems, reflecting a remarkable talent for fieldwork and language acquisition, and some have made major contributions to theory.

Three of Barth's books are representative: *Political Leadership among Swat Pathans* (1959), *Ethnic Groups and Boundaries* (1969), and *Ritual and Knowledge among the Baktaman of New Guinea* (1975). The first laid the groundwork for a new perspective: the TRANSACTIONAL model. The second significantly shifted the direction of ethnic studies, both in anthropology and generally. The third monograph is selected because it marked a dramatic new ethnographic setting and problem focus, and dealt with a rare example of a culture virtually untouched by the modern world.

Barth was born to Norwegian parents in Germany. His geochemist father eventually took up a position in Chicago. Graduating from the University of Chicago in 1949 with an MA in anthropology, specializing in palaeontology and evolutionism, Barth joined an Iraq-bound research team as a physical anthropologist. While there he discovered that it was living, 'exotic' people who interested him. He wrote a PhD dissertation, based on his experiences in Iraq, for the University of Oslo. It was rejected because **E. E. Evans-Pritchard**, on consultation, judged the duration of the fieldwork insufficient. Ironically, Barth later demonstrated that splendid research can be done in less time.

Barth then decided to enrol at the London School of Economics to study under **Raymond Firth**, but, as Firth was on leave, he had to work with **Edmund Leach**, who several years earlier had spent five weeks in Iraqi Kurdistan. When Leach left for Cambridge in 1953, Barth followed. After doing fieldwork in Pakistan and obtaining his PhD in 1957 he returned to Norway and was recruited by the University of Bergen, where the Department of Anthropology that he founded became internationally renowned for its political and ecological perspective. He also taught at the University of Oslo, Harvard, and Emory. Subsequently, Barth and his anthropologist wife, Unni Wikan, joined the Department of Anthropology at Boston University where he concluded his teaching career. On retirement he returned to Oslo as a research fellow at the Ministry of Culture and has held a number of visiting professorships.

Fieldwork among Pakistan's Swat Pathans in 1954 only lasted several months but Barth had studied the Pashto language and was able to soon dispense with interpreters. He was equally quick to realize that Swat political life bore little resemblance to the formal authority structures enshrined in the literature on political anthropology. There was, in fact, no institutionalized leadership in Pathan society. This did not mean there were no leaders. Indeed, there was fierce competition among leaders, but those who followed did so voluntarily rather than having allegiance ascribed through birth or group affiliation. Barth described the relationship between leaders and followers as a transaction reflecting choice. Leaders offered individuals gifts and protection in return for allegiance and a willingness to bear arms. To some degree, leaders had a hold on their followers because the latter were often their tenants and in debt to them. However, the position of leader was tenuous. If a man could not maintain his wealth or defend his honor followers would switch support to a more powerful leader.

Pathan society had two kinds of leader. Secular leaders emerged entirely from the Pashtun or landowning caste. Land was accumulated through inheritance, purchase, and conquest, and was the main source of political authority. Yet a successful leader had to have more than land and wealth. He had to be courageous in battle, violent, revengeful, and even mercurial. The other type of leader was the Saints. Their political authority was largely derived from their reputation for morality and holiness and from their service as mediators between feuding Pashtun factions. However, they too were landowners, obtaining land as gifts stemming from their role as mediators. They also inherited and purchased land, and sometimes seized it by force. The Pashtun landowners and the Saints, whose land also gave them political clout, occupied complementary roles. The former engaged in brutal competition; the latter's mediator role reduced the threat of anarchy intrinsic to such competition. Structural features such as caste and descent groups (called 'frameworks' by Barth) limited the range of choices available to the actor, but did not determine political allegiance. Two strands of action theory, and two models of social processes were developed by Barth in his Pathan ethnography: although self-interested, calculating actors exercising choice in a competitive arena capture the essence of political behavior among Pathans (the TRANSACTIONAL MODEL), Barth pushed the analysis further, arguing that the aggregate choices constituted processes which unintentionally generate new structural forms in society (the generative model). To Barth's regret it was the transactional model which was elaborated by subsequent action theorists such as **F. G. Bailey**. He later acknowledged that he and others overemphasized the self-interested, choice-making individual competitor, underplaying the processes which generated structural forms.

If *Political Leadership among Swat Pathans* was a path-breaking study, the same was true of *Ethnic Groups and Boundaries*, probably

Barth's best-known work despite being an edited volume. Its goal was to explain how ethnicity persists. Barth distanced himself from notions of cultures as bounded groups, and separated culture from ethnicity, rejecting the long-established assumption that ethnicity is created and maintained by primordial bonds. He argued that rather than being weakened by contact between ethnic groups, ethnicity is actually strengthened, including, critically, the boundaries between ethnic groups. Added to the above was a phenomenological element: ethnicity is self-ascribed and involves identity and meaning.

Barth made no attempt to construct a typology of ethnic groups, attempting instead to apply a generative model to the processes that create and maintain ethnic groups. The key to the process was the ethnic boundary and its maintenance, not the internal make-up of an ethnic group. These boundaries, which may or may not be territorial, not only persisted in the face of interethnic contact and interdependence, but were strengthened by it. Indeed, a dramatic reduction of cultural differences between ethnic groups does not necessarily reduce ethnic identity or the saliency of ethnic boundaries.

While ethnic groups take culture into account, there is no one-to-one relationship between ethnicity and culture; thus, to trace the history of an ethnic group is not to trace the history of a culture since ethnic groups only select a limited set of features from culture – features useful in reinforcing their boundaries. Despite considerable regional variation, Pathans maintained a self-identity as a distinctive ethnic group with a clear social boundary, because the basis of that identity was a set of key values deemed peculiar to Pathans as a people.

Barth gave fresh impetus to ethnic studies, not least of all by explaining how ethnic ties have persisted into the modern world. Inasmuch as he stresses the manner in which ethnicity is negotiated and labeled through interactions with other groups, hints of his earlier transactional analysis are evident. What was novel was the emphasis on self-ascription and identity, and therefore on meaning. This concern with subjectivity and meaningful interaction reflects the influence of the great sociologist, Max Weber.

Few anthropologists today employ the term 'primitive' outside quotation marks, yet when a previously unknown and unstudied group in New Guinea called the Baktaman made the headlines, the antennae of anthropologists tingled. Enter Barth. Following a brief scouting trip, he took up residence among the Baktaman in January, 1968, remaining for 11 months. This project marked a dramatic shift in both geographical setting and problem focus. In *Ethnic Groups and Boundaries* Barth's emphasis on self-identity and meaning had signaled a partial move away from his previous political and ecological perspective. *Ritual and Knowledge among the Baktaman of New Guinea* completed the move. His new focus was on ritual, symbolism, knowledge, and communication – especially non-verbal communication. Barth treated ritual as a tradition of knowledge, reflecting the worldview of the Baktaman and analyzing ritual as a set of modes of communication and thought.

Fieldwork centered on the secret male initiation cult, the gateway to manhood, social recognition, and sacred knowledge. All men had to pass through it to achieve the status of full human beings. Barth discovered there was a paucity of myths or other genres of indigenous interpretive material to help him understand the ritual and that his best hope was to undergo initiation himself. After much negotiation, he was accepted as an initiate and discovered a world rich in symbols with multiple referents. These non-verbal symbols were embedded in the male initiation rite whereby Baktaman expressed and gained knowledge of the world. Barth then pointed out an enormous problem for the investigator: how to capture the essence of and put into words a ritual that can only be understood when one participates in its performance. He contended that Baktaman had no exegetical (explanatory) tradition of their own. Informants' explanations of the symbolism in the initiation ritual would have been an artifice of the fieldworker, not a faithful expression of Baktaman thought. While recognizing that some cultures possess traditions of exegesis, Barth raised the possibility that native explanations may have been artificially created and thus contaminated by the questions posed by researchers. Whether Barth is right or wrong, his efforts to avoid imposing an outsider's explanatory framework on the data display his skill as a fieldworker at its best.

Barth depicted his experiences in New Guinea as an 'anthropological treat.' Yet the Baktaman were not entirely untouched by the outside world. They initially came into contact with Europeans in 1927 when two adventurers entered their village. Apparently the next contact was with a Patrol Officer in 1964. But the villagers already possessed considerable knowledge by then about Europeans and their pacification policy as a result of interaction with their neighbors. By the time Barth had entered their community, there were steel axes and knives, and salt was readily available. Barth lived a simple and frugal existence among the Baktaman, trading salt for local food items. He candidly admitted that he found the fieldwork challenging, never achieving linguistic fluency and relying on an interpreter/assistant. Yet because the Baktaman only numbered 183 people, he was able to interact with virtually everyone.

Barth usually eschews discussions of general theory, preferring to let his data and interpretations speak for themselves. Yet it would be interesting to hear what he has to say about the concept of culture in the context of the Baktaman community. Does it constitute a distinctive way of life and are culture and ethnicity synonymous? Then, too, we only have Barth's judgment that the key to Baktaman society is the male initiation cult. Might another fieldworker have seen things differently, and produced a different ethnography?

Barth was not the first to challenge STRUCTURAL-FUNCTIONALISM, with its rigid social structure resting in a state of equilibrium, and its coercive normative order denying agency and choice to human beings. Leach (1954), had already set the critique in motion, yet Barth nudged it in a new direction, in laying the foundation for the transactional model.

Barth almost single-handedly put Scandinavian anthropology on the map. In recent years his influence there seems to have diminished. He has been charged with ignoring the macro-structural and historical forces that arguably created the rough-and-tumble politics of the Pathans, in an area which is currently a Taliban stronghold. Moreover, his conception of power as a contest between equals conceals the differential advantage related to class position. It might be added that the only voice heard in his work is that of the authoritative author. That style, along with his overwhelming interest in 'exotic' peoples, might suggest that his work is now out of step with contemporary anthropology. Yet even if his various monographs consisted entirely of low-level description, his high reputation would be assured. The fact that they are packed with analysis of general theoretical importance leaves no doubt about his stature in the discipline.

Selected readings

Anderson, R. (2007) 'Interview with Fredrik Barth,' *Revista de Antropologia Iberoamericana* 2(2): i–xvi.

Barth, F. (1959) *Political Leadership among Swat Pathans*, London: Athlone Press.

——(1966) *Models of Social Organization*, Occasional Paper No. 23, London: Royal Anthropological Institute.

——(1969) *Ethnic Groups and Boundaries*, Boston, MA: Little, Brown.

——(1975) *Ritual and Knowledge among the Baktaman of New Guinea*, New Haven, CT: Yale University Press.
——(1993) *Balinese Worlds*, Chicago, IL: University of Chicago Press.
Leach, E. (1954) *Political Systems of Highland Burma*, London: Athlone Press.
Vincent, J. (1990) *Anthropology and Politics*, Tucson: The University of Arizona Press.

STANLEY R. BARRETT

RUTH FULTON BENEDICT (1887–1948)

Ruth Fulton Benedict was one of the founders of the CULTURE AND PERSONALITY school of American anthropology. The books for which she is famous, *Patterns of Culture* and *The Chrysanthemum and the Sword*, offer descriptions of contrasting cultures that laid the foundation for an analysis of the links between individual personality and cultural norms. Benedict insisted that the findings of anthropology reach a wide audience and that anthropologists confront the political issues of the day.

Ruth Fulton was born in 1887, in Norwich, New York. Her father died when she was two years old, leaving her mother immersed in mourning. In a life story, Benedict attributed her persistent fascination with dichotomy to the childhood experience of the 'calm' of death juxtaposed to wild outbursts of grief.

Early on Ruth seemed absorbed in her own world. An eventual diagnosis of deafness explained her withdrawal, but a habit of hesitancy and restraint continued for the rest of her life. Her childhood was nomadic, following her mother's career as a librarian and a teacher. In 1905 Ruth and Margery, a year younger, entered Vassar College, following in their mother's footsteps. At Vassar, Ruth discovered the power of writing to integrate her experiences, observations, and emotions.

After she graduated, she returned to Buffalo, New York, to live with her mother. She took a job as a social worker, and encountered the poor, struggling, and often failed immigrants of an industrial city. Impatient with the little she could accomplish, and hampered by deafness, in 1911 she moved to California to live with Margery and her husband. Ruth taught in a private school in Pasadena, and she met Stanley Rossiter Benedict, a chemist, whom she married in 1914.

World War I intensified her commitment to contributing 'meaningfully' to the world. Chemical detective stories, written with Stanley, failed to satisfy her and she turned to biography as a contribution in a time of chaos. Benedict drafted essays on three 'pioneering women' (Mary Wollstonecraft, Margaret Fuller, and Olive Schreiner), developing a theme that characterized her later anthropology: the impact of social conditions on creativity, self-fulfilment, and individual freedom. The biographical studies also extended Benedict's engagement with feminism. She argued that 'feminism is not a system but a passionate attitude' and that her three subjects attained heroic status through the *adventure of living*. In the portraits, Benedict applied techniques she later used in anthropology, extracting 'character' from myriad details and using distance to expose the lineaments of the familiar.

When Houghton-Mifflin rejected the biographical project, Benedict turned to academia. In 1919 she enrolled in courses at the New School for Social Research. Her teachers, Elsie Clews Parsons and Alexander Goldenweiser, opened different doors to the discipline, the closely empirical and the broadly theoretical. Parsons encouraged Benedict to pursue a PhD in anthropology and in 1921 introduced her to **Franz Boas**, head of the anthropology department at Columbia University. Father of American cultural anthropology, Boas became Benedict's mentor, training her in the CULTURAL RELATIVISM and the liberal tolerance that shaped his anthropological work. In 1923 she completed her dissertation, 'The Concept of the Guardian Spirit in North America,' which was based on library research not fieldwork. 'Guardian Spirit' marshaled abundant details in an exploration of the 'diffusion' of traits across a culture area, in the Boasian tradition. At the same time, an inquiry into spirituality suited Benedict's intuition that non-material aspects of life provided the clues to a culture's deepest preoccupations.

PhD in hand, she began a career in teaching, first as Boas's assistant and then on her own. Over the next 25 years Ruth Benedict trained generations of anthropologists, inspiring students despite her perceived aloofness. She gave special attention to women, encouraging fieldtrips, the pursuit of a career, and confidence in the face of continuing sexism, even in anthropology – a discipline that accepted women relatively early. By 1930, her marriage to Stanley Benedict had ended.

In 1923 Benedict met the student whose impact on her anthropology and her life would be profound. **Margaret Mead** began in psychology, but was soon persuaded to shift to anthropology. Exchanging ideas, manuscripts, and letters, the two developed theoretical approaches to the discipline they shared, and an emphasis on socialization, broadly defined, provided a scheme for comparing cultures in terms of the benefits for individuals. The pliability of the human being, the relativity of presumed human universals, and the boundless capacity for transforming social conditions became central principles in anthropology. In the 1920s the two also wrote poetry, and they drew another poet-anthropologist into their circle, the linguist **Edward Sapir**. For nearly a decade, Benedict and Sapir debated the value of poetry against the clear illumination of a science.

Eventually Benedict replaced the poetry of Anne Singleton (her pseudonym) with anthropological pieces. Articles based on fieldwork (the Serrano in California, the Zuni in the Southwest) alternated with examinations of the concept of culture. By the early 1930s, Benedict contemplated bringing her material into a full-length book. 'Psychological Types in the Cultures of the Southwest' (1930) and 'Configurations of Culture in North America' (1932) provided the organizing themes. Data came from her fieldwork, Boas's Kwakiutl studies, and Reo Fortune's *The Sorcerers of Dobu*. She puzzled over *configuration* and she submitted the manuscript with the word *pattern* instead. Published by Houghton-Mifflin in 1934, *Patterns of Culture* instantly became, and has remained, a classic in anthropology.

Benedict's choice of 'pattern' reflected a move from earlier pieces, in which she posited a theory of the integration of cultures. Pattern suggested a dynamic, continually emerging arrangement, intrinsic, creative, and adaptive. The word also emphasized the aesthetic dimension of integrity, an outcome in elegance that she transformed into a comparative method. Cultures could be compared according to the degree and the elegance of configuration. She borrowed pattern from art, poetry, and her view of an individual's life trajectory – and it provided the grounding for a later inquiry into the impact on self-fulfilment of diverse 'designs for living.'

Remembered for the phrase 'culture is personality writ large,' *Patterns* argues that every culture selects along an 'arc of traits,' choosing from a universal span pieces that at once fit together and create a distinct character: the Apollonian Pueblo Indian, the para-noiac Dobu Islander, and the megalomaniac Kwakiutl. Her own society constituted the fourth character, subject of a stern critique for rampant greed and overweening ego, and intolerance of the indivi-dual who lacks those traits. The last chapters of *Patterns* offer a brilliant analysis of the relativity of 'abnormality' and the production of deviance through the imposition of rigid demands on conformity. 'Abnormality,' she wrote, is a label applied to 'those who are not supported by the institutions of their civilizations' (Benedict 1934: 258). She expanded the thesis in a 1934 article, 'Anthropology and the Abnormal,' published in *The Journal of General Psychology*. The growing field of social psychology provided support for her inquiry into the personal and social effects of discordance between individual and culture.

During the 1930s, Benedict edited the *Journal of American Folk-Lore*. The appointment recognized her contribution to studies of myth and folklore, and the significance of her analysis of the links between imagination and behavior. In 1935, she published a compilation of myths in the two-volume *Zuni Mythology*. Under her editorship, the *Journal* achieved prominence, and folklore moved from a marginal to a central place in anthropology.

Events of the decade pressed heavily: the Great Depression at home and the rise of fascism in Europe. Benedict responded by applying disciplinary insights to economic and political breakdown, addressing her fellow citizens in a variety of media, from the *New York Herald Tribune* to the *American Anthropologist*. In every instance, Benedict mounted a severe critique against the United States. She criticized her country for wasting the resources of its population, for discriminating against particular groups, and for nurturing neuroses in its citizens.

Benedict expanded her interpretations of personality and culture with ideas from Karen Horney and Harry Stack Sullivan. 'Continuities and Discontinuities in Cultural Conditioning' appeared in *Psychiatry* in 1938, and confirmed Benedict's rejection of Freudian theory. Asserting the significance of childrearing, she pointed to the failures in the United States: children learned nothing that fit them into an adult world. Discontinuity between childhood and adulthood created a dysfunctional American character. Moreover, Americans treat their methods as *natural* and thus 'overlook the possibility of developing social institutions which would lessen the social cost we now pay' (Benedict 1953 [1938]: 531). Acknowledging custom, she reiterated, permits the 'conscious direction of the life course.' The frequently reprinted piece has entered the canon of American childrearing literature.

Benedict always admired Boas for his 'actions in the world of affairs' (Benedict 1943: 15). In the 1930s she used anthropological techniques to elucidate the rise of fascism in Europe and the evident racism at home. In 1940, she published a short book, *Race: Science and Politics*. In it, she dismantled scientific claims of different intellectual endowments among racial groups. In a widely distributed pamphlet version, Benedict exposed the political uses of a presumed 'science' of race. The same year (1940) she delivered a series of lectures at Bryn Mawr College, reprinted in 1970 as 'Synergy: Some Notes of Ruth Benedict.' The lectures explored the processes through which harmony between social institutions, religious beliefs, and individual personalities can be achieved without enforcing conformity, suppressing creativity, and arresting change.

In 1941 the United States entered the war, and two years later Benedict accepted a position in the Federal Government's Office of War Information. Her decision reflected her commitment to the role of anthropologist as citizen. Like her colleagues (Mead, Geoffrey Gorer), she applied theories of childrearing and adult personality to gauge the behavior of both allied and enemy nations (Thailand, Rumania, Burma). Then, in 1944, she was 'assigned' to Japan, 'our most alien enemy' (Benedict 1946: 1). She prepared reports for the OWI, drawing on films, interviews, and secondary sources in order to get at the character of the Japanese. Two years later, she transformed bureaucratic prose into her last book, *The Chrysanthemum and the Sword*.

The book is a model of *national character* studies, beautifully written and persuasive. For Benedict, Japan exemplified a 'high synergy' society, in which institutions fit together coherently and personality coincides with culture. Benedict indicates the methods by which 'integrity' comes about, the details of behavior that reinforce the pattern, and the methods of childrearing that guarantee successful integration of individuals into social institutions. She maintains the crucial tenet of her anthropology: bringing contrasting cultures into illuminating relation, in this case Japan and the US. The contrast was explanatory: one culture was driven by shame, the other by guilt. A book written to help the US understand its enemy established a comparative approach in the discipline premised on the diversity of emotional drives across cultures.

Chrysanthemum offers a program for enlightened change in Japan and at home, and the book satisfied Benedict's commitment to contributing 'meaningfully.' The American military used the book in peace negotiations with Japan (honoring the Emperor), and millions of readers in the US acquired a compassionate view of the 'alien.' Readers in Japan appreciated the book's penetration into the sources of their culture and, alert to cultural values, acquired the potential to engineer the direction of life after total defeat. As in all her writings, Benedict referred to the terms and conditions of her own culture, exposing the arbitrariness of arrangements and advocating the conscious redesign of pattern.

After the war Benedict returned to Columbia University, where she participated in comparative studies of childrearing practices through UNESCO and the Studies of Cultures at a Distance project. In 1946 the American Anthropological Association elected her president, and her farewell speech, a year later, summarized the strands in her anthropology and set a template for the future.

Benedict reminded her audience that the goal of social science, and anthropology in particular, is to improve human lives in all societies. Yet, while putting *man* at the center of studies of society, anthropologists exclude 'emotion, ethics, rational insight and purpose' (in Mead 1959: 461). In anthropological writings the person becomes simply a mechanical cog in the social system. To move the person beyond this spiritless position as a research object, Benedict told her audience, anthropologists must follow the great humanists. Philosophy, literary criticism, and literature should guide the discipline in its insights, its principles, and its commitment to diffusing interpretations beyond the ivory tower of academia. The 'common man,' his concerns, hopes, and creativity, is the subject of and audience for anthropology.

Ruth Fulton Benedict died in September 1948, 61 years old. Obituaries testify to her importance in the discipline as scholar and citizen, scientist and writer. She had bequeathed to anthropology her conviction that the only subject worth studying was 'man' and the conditions for self-fulfilment, freedom, and passionate living. In insisting that any scholar must address the pressing concerns of the day, she showed that CULTURAL RELATIVISM did not absolve the anthropologist from clear-eyed judgments. And last but not least, Ruth Benedict instructed her fellow anthropologists in the importance of *writing* as an aspect of inquiry and a route to the understanding and tolerance it was anthropology's duty to implement.

Selected readings

Benedict, R. F. (1934) *Patterns of Culture*, Boston, MA: Houghton Mifflin.
——(1953 [1938]) 'Continuities and Discontinuities in Cultural Conditioning,' in *Personality in Nature, Culture, and Society*, C. Kluckhohn and H. Murray (eds.), pp. 515–21, New York: Knopf.
——(1940) *Race: Science, and Politics*, New York: Modern Age.
——(1943) 'Franz Boas,' *The Nation* 156: 15–16.
——(1946) *The Chrysanthemum and the Sword*, Boston, MA: Houghton Mifflin.

——(1970 [1940]) 'Synergy: Some Notes of Ruth Benedict,' selected by Abraham H. Maslow and John J. Honigmann, *American Anthropologist*, New Series 72(2): 320–33.

Mead, M. (1959) *An Anthropologist at Work*, Boston, MA: Houghton Mifflin.

Modell, J. Schachter (1983) *Ruth Benedict: Patterns of a Life*, Philadelphia: University of Pennsylvania Press.

JUDITH (MODELL) SCHACHTER

FRANZ BOAS (1858–1942)

Franz Uri Boas, the central figure in twentieth century American anthropology, was born in Minden, Germany on July 9, 1858, into a prosperous Jewish family. His father was a textile merchant. His mother passed on to him the political ideals of the abortive 1848 revolution. Beginning in 1877, Boas studied at the Universities of Heidelberg, Bonn, and Kiel. He moved from physics to geography, receiving his doctorate from Kiel in 1882. His dissertation was on laboratory studies of the colors of sea water, but his interests went beyond this, as he sought to understand subjective perceptions of color differences, which differed from their objective qualities.

After compulsory military service, Boas spent 1883–84 among the Baffin Island Eskimo, working on cartography and investigating Eskimo perceptions of the color of water and ice. Living on the land and enduring the frigid climate in their company, Boas responded to the richness of Eskimo culture. One might think that such extreme conditions might determine every aspect of Eskimo life, but Boas found that their culture had many unique features, such as religious beliefs, games, ceremonies, and folklore, that the environment could not explain. His ideas concerning the wholeness and distinctiveness of cultures and, consequently, CULTURAL RELATIVISM may have developed from this experience. Boas returned to the Royal Ethnological Museum in Berlin and worked with the anthropologist, Adolph Bastian. He completed a habilitation degree in geography and began to teach. His ethnographic interest shifted to the Northwest Coast of North America after 1885. Boas decided that career opportunities were greater in America because of European anti-Semitism. In 1887, he moved to New York as an assistant editor for *Science* and married Marie Krackowizer whose family had settled in New York. They helped Boas to establish his career.

From 1889 to 1892, Boas taught at Clark University in Massachusetts, where the first American PhD in anthropology was awarded to A. F. Chamberlain. Clark's President was G. Stanley Hall, a prominent psychologist and expert on adolescence. Boas's experiments measuring Worcester, Massachusetts school children in order to determine their relative rates of growth caused controversy, when parents protested at the strange measurements performed on their offspring by a foreigner with duel scars on his face. In 1892, most of the faculty resigned in protest against interference from Hall and benefactor Josiah Clark. Boas moved to Chicago where, as assistant to Frederick Ward Putnam, he oversaw physical anthropology and Northwest Coast ethnology for the Chicago World's Columbian Exposition in 1893. The newly established University of Chicago had already employed its single anthropologist, Frederick Starr, and did not offer Boas a job. For a while he worked at Chicago's Field Columbian Museum, but failed to obtain a permanent position. In 1896 he returned to the American Museum of Natural History in New York, again under Putnam's direction. Putnam cobbled a position for Boas, which became permanent in 1899, between Columbia University and the Museum.

With a solid institutional base, Boas began to consolidate his vision of Americanist anthropology. He persuaded museum patron Morris K. Jesup to sponsor a North Pacific Expedition exploring ties between Asia and the New World. Considerable ethnographic work was accomplished but the promised synthesis never appeared. Boas intended the Museum to fund fieldwork for anthropology graduate students so he could produce a cohort of professional anthropologists. By 1905, however, his relations with the Museum had deteriorated and he accepted full-time employment at Columbia.

In 1898, Boas conspired with WJ [sic] McGee of the Bureau of American Ethnology to found a new series of the *American Anthropologist* as a national journal. His revival of the long-dormant American Ethnological Society in New York provided a geographical base to balance against the Bureau in Washington DC and Putnam at Harvard. The American Anthropological Association was founded in 1902. Boas served as its third president, following McGee and Putnam.

During World War I, Boas's pacifism and foreign background engendered strong resentment. He was censured by the AAA in 1919 for an article in *The Nation* accusing four anthropologists of spying in Mexico (thereby perverting their science). Boas became an activist, moreover, in opposing both the rise of National Socialism in

Germany during the 1930s and increased anti-Semitism at home. These years established his reputation as a public intellectual outside anthropology, still widely understood as restricted to study of the 'primitive.'

Boas retired from Columbia in 1938 but continued to be active in New York anthropology and public life. He died December 21, 1942, collapsing into the arms of **Claude Lévi-Strauss**, while discussing racism at a luncheon at the Columbia Faculty Club.

Boas's writings were crucial to the professionalization of anthropology, linguistics, folklore, and education. His technical publications in American Indian ethnology and linguistics form a 'six-foot shelf' of texts collected from native speakers of a variety of Northwest Coast languages. Boas advocated collecting such texts not only to preserve what are now referred to as 'endangered' languages but also to provide a unique window into the spirit of a people, what he called 'the native point of view.' He investigated expressive forms in folklore and art as well as language. Throughout his career, Boas returned to the field whenever possible. In his absence, he trained local informants to record texts for him on his instructions and in response to specific questions, particularly George Hunt for the Kwakiutl (now known as the Kwakwala) and George Teit for the Tsimshian. These texts were published with minimal translation and commentary.

Boas collaborated with the Bureau of American Ethnology to produce a *Handbook of North American Indian Languages* to capture the variety of 'psychological types' found across the continent. The grammatical sketches (with accompanying short texts) that appeared in 1911 and 1922 were written largely by Boas's first generation of Columbia students. The linguistic differences defied interpretation if one were using categories of Greek and Latin grammar, but made sense in their own terms. Boas intended these sketches to provide a model for future scholars. During the same period, he worked to provide a standard orthography for the languages of the Americas, targeted for untrained recorders but simultaneously facilitating comparison across languages.

Boas devised a method to reconstruct the history of interconnections among peoples without pre-contact writing systems. His geographical logic revealed the past borrowing of elements of both culture and language throughout a culture area. The Northwest Coast was ideally suited to such a model because it encompassed many independent linguistic families whose speakers had become remarkably similar in culture through their interactions over time. Initially Boas had been enthusiastic about interpreting local histories through genetic classification of linguistic relationships from the distant past, but he retreated to a more conservative position that the effects of borrowing and prior historical relationship were indistinguishable at great time depth (in contrast to the position of his most distinguished linguistic student, **Edward Sapir**).

The historical patterns of group relationship that Boas postulated were not accessible for contemporary Native Americans. They became visible only through convergent evidence from physical anthropology (largely anthropometry), archaeology (albeit in a fledgling state during most of Boas's career), linguistics, and cultural anthropology. These are the four sub-disciplines of anthropology that Boas enshrined at the core of Americanist anthropology. He contributed to all four.

His anthropometric work with European and Jewish immigrants which began in 1897 demonstrated that head form, which had been regarded as virtually immutable, and was considered a major indicator of racial differences in character, changed slightly in one generation, between parents and their children. This established the plasticity of racial types and initiated anthropological deconstruction of the concept of race, recognizing 'race' as a primarily social phenomenon. Because later physical anthropology drew heavily on emerging developments in genetics, Boas has rarely been credited for the innovative character of this work. He spurred the development of archaeology, particularly in Mexico, despite the centering of archaeological work at Harvard rather than Columbia.

Boas's mentalist and anti-racist anthropology is best represented in his 1911 manifesto *The Mind of Primitive Man* which reflected his strengths as a four-field anthropologist. He argued for the fundamental unity and equal capacity of the human species. Differences of culture were attributable to cultural background and historical circumstances rather than innate abilities. Like many of Boas's key theoretical positions, this now seems obvious because it has been so thoroughly absorbed into the anthropological paradigm that arose from it. Boas's devastating critique of evolution is based in this insistence on the legitimacy of all cultures. The peoples studied by anthropologists were not 'primitive' survivals of the ancestors of civilized modern cultures. Boas's ethnographic work, by providing concrete counterexamples, demonstrated that unilinear sequences of human progress were not universal. Complex settled societies existed on the Northwest Coast without farming, dependent on maritime and riverine resources. Matrilineal kinship might succeed as well as precede patrilineal. He insisted that race, language, and culture, although they often were correlated, must be treated as independent variables. Boas's anthropology was an empirical as well as a mentalist science. Careful fieldwork and cross-cultural comparison alone could lead anthropology to valid laws of human nature and culture. Despite his debunking of premature generalizations, which included those of Marxists and Freudians as well as evolutionists, Boas believed that rigorous methods would produce such laws.

Boas was an organizational as well as an intellectual leader. Beginning with his first Columbia PhD, **Alfred Kroeber**, in 1901, Boas placed his students in key universities, occasionally museums. This cohort included **Robert Lowie**, **Paul Radin**, Alexander Goldenweiser, Leslie Spier, and Clark Wissler. By the end of World War I, Boas's former students controlled publications, held major academic appointments, and trained their own students to implement the Boasian program.

In 1917, Boas founded the *Journal of American Folklore* which he edited for 17 years. He encouraged anthropologists to publish alongside European folklorists based in literature departments and facilitated contributions from Quebec French, American Black, and Caribbean folklore. **Zora Neale Hurston** was an early protégé in the latter field, as was Ella Cara Deloria for the Sioux and Assiniboine. Both women were members of the groups they studied. Boas's folklore work was assisted by the financial and editorial contributions of Elsie Clews Parsons, a post-PhD convert from sociology, south-western ethnographer, and philanthropist. The anthropology program at Columbia was the only one in North America where women were welcomed as students. **Ruth Benedict** and **Margaret Mead** are best known, but these women also included Ruth Bunzel, Gladys Reichard, and Esther Goldfrank.

Boas's anti-racism became more prominent over his career. He established warm relations with African American scholars, particularly W. E. B. DuBois, and encouraged Black anthropologists to enter anthropology. This work arose not from the physical anthropology of Boas's early career, but rather from his critique of American society, grounded in his experience of anti-Semitism. He assisted European intellectuals stranded in Nazi Germany to emigrate to the United States and obtain academic positions. **Claude Lévi-Strauss**, several members of the Frankfurt School, and a number of European linguists were among the beneficiaries of Boas's practical activism.

Assessing the reputation of Boas has been a recurrent preoccupation of American anthropology. In the post-war years, anthropology turned away from the study of the American Indian and attempted to constitute itself as hard science. Evolutionism was revived by **Leslie White** and **Julian Steward**. Boas's would-be successors were dismissive of his contributions, particularly in the realm of theory. More recently, however, Boas's theoretical achievements have been re-acknowledged and restored to their central place in the Americanist tradition, if not for all anthropology carried out in North America. Perhaps most important, however, is his role as a public intellectual in the area of anti-racism, his advocacy of the relevance of the social sciences in the public sphere, and of the importance of tolerance for diversity to life in a democratic society.

Selected readings

Boas, F. (1911) *The Mind of Primitive Man*, New York: Macmillan.
——(1940) *Race, Language and Culture*, New York: Free Press.
Cole, D. (2000) *Franz Boas: The Early Years, 1858–1906*, Vancouver: Douglas & McIntyre.
Darnell, R. (1998) *And Along Came Boas: Continuity and Revolution in Americanist Anthropology*, Amsterdam: John Benjamins.
——(2001) *Invisible Genealogies: A History of Americanist Anthropology*, Lincoln: University of Nebraska Press.
Stocking, G. W., Jr. (ed.) (1974) *The Shaping of American Anthropology, 1883–1911: A Franz Boas Reader*, New York: Basic Books.

REGNA DARNELL

PIERRE BOURDIEU (1930–2002)

Pierre Bourdieu, sociologist and anthropologist, was part of a generation of famous French intellectuals including Jacques Derrida, Jean Baudrillard, and Michel Foucault, who were shaped by a double heritage: studies at elitist Parisian institutions at a time when philosophy was at the center of French intellectual life as well as the 1968 student unrest which turned their interest to questions of power and politics. While Derrida and Baudrillard turned philosophy towards an intellectual skepticism which continuously criticizes the foundations of our knowledge, and Foucault built on STRUCTURALISM to explore the anonymous powers shaping a society's form, Bourdieu, as a social theorist and as a public intellectual, turned to *practice*. His major writings serve a twofold aim: to analyze social inequality, and to understand the link and overcome the dichotomy between human agency, the ability of individuals to make free choices, and the structures of society which may limit choice.

Bourdieu grew up in a village at the foot of the Pyrenees. His father had turned from a peasant into a postal clerk, 'a renegade' in the rural world. His early years shaped his keen eye for social differentiation and marginalization, and his constant and programmatic attempt to bridge the gap between the Parisian intellectual he became and the 'ordinary people' who were the subject of many of his studies.

After attending the Lycée in Pau, he won a scholarship to the Lycée Louis-le-Grand (1948–51) in Paris, and the elite École Normale Supérieure while studying at the Sorbonne. Among his peers in the ENS were Derrida and historian Emmanuel Le Roy Ladurie; his teachers included Althusser, Bachelard, and Canghuilhem. Studying philosophy, Bourdieu read Husserl and Merleau-Ponty, two phenomenological philosophers whose focus was the constitution of knowledge, personality, and sociability in everyday life, and Marx, who impressed him for privileging real-life change over mere intellectual inquiry and provided him with the concept of *practice*. Reflecting on these years, Bourdieu saw himself as an angry outsider in the world of a Parisian intellectualism centered on existential philosophy. This did not stop him from advancing to one of the most prestigious positions the system had to offer. After passing his philosophy aggrégation in 1954, he taught for a year at a provincial Lycée – and was conscripted into the army.

The three years he served in Algeria during the liberation war were intellectually defining. After conscription, he remained for two years to teach at the University of Algiers. He returned to France in 1960 as Sorbonne sociologist Raymond Aron's assistant before teaching at the University of Lille from 1961 to 1964. In 1964, he became Directeur d'Études at the École Pratique des Hautes Études in Paris (and after 1975 at the École des Hautes Études en Sciences Sociales, founded as an offshoot of the EPHE). In 1982, he was appointed as Chair in Sociology at the Collège de France in Paris, a post he held until his death.

In Algeria, Bourdieu turned from philosophy to anthropology and sociology. The experience of the colonial war and fieldwork in Kabyle brought him into contact with a world outside academia, a world that seemed much closer to his own roots in rural France. In his anthropological work on Kabyle, Bourdieu developed his most important theoretical concepts and found his own distinct perspective as a social scientist, which he later applied to different fields.

His insistence on sound empirical inquiry, his stress on practice, and focus on the formation of inequality through culture can be traced back to this double exposure to a peasant world and to late colonial society.

His early Kabyle studies were still very much in the STRUCTURALIST mode, struggling to make it more complex and better adapted to everyday life. 'The Kabyle House' which originally published in the *Festschrift* for **Lévi-Strauss**, who had been instrumental in EPHE's employment of Bourdieu, is a good example. It describes the spatial organization of the Kabyle house in structuralist terms of dyadic homological opposition: Fire–water, cooked–raw, light–shadow, male–female, culture–nature, and so on. These oppositions, Bourdieu argues, shape the perception of space in the wider social world and in Kabyle cosmology, and the way people make sense of their world is constructed in the interplay between these different levels. Bourdieu was already struggling with structuralism's objectivism and started to anchor meaning in practice – even if he still starkly privileged ritual practices as more meaningful than everyday life.

Lévi-Strauss's influence can be perceived in many of Bourdieu's writings, but Bourdieu soon turned towards a programmatic insistence on practice. He uses 'practice' and 'strategy' to re-introduce human agency, which structuralism had excluded from social theory in the name of an objectivist analysis. For Bourdieu, society is the outcome of individual strategies, but these strategies are neither freely chosen nor based on rational calculations. They are shaped by a practical sense which individuals acquire in their socialization. When social actors choose a way of dealing with a given situation, they do so with knowledge of the aims they should achieve, with a sense of possible ways to reach them, and with a feeling for the specific actions necessary to do so. All this is acquired in the individual's socialization and mostly taken for granted, not consciously evaluated.

The notion of *habitus*, Bourdieu's most famous concept, describes how society manages to shape individual strategies. As humans grow up in a specific society, they learn to be individuals according to the rules of that society's game. Often without conscious reflection, they learn to perceive the world and act in it in a way that makes sense in relation to their society. By living in a house built according to the cultural patterns within which its builders perceived the world, for example, we acquire a practical notion of what the world is like; by playing children's games that mimic how one should act in order to become successful in the real world, we learn the rules of meaningful strategy. The society we grow up in shapes our individuality, our habitus. Little of this is consciously learnt in a reflective way. Even in the most 'intellectual' domains, such as art or philosophy, most of our convictions are formed in practically and bodily dealing with the world.

With habitus as the link between society and individual, Bourdieu tries to trump the choice between subjectivism (social theories based on the agency of free individuals) and objectivism (social theories only interested in the objective structures of a society). Habitus is thus 'structured structure' and shapes how we express our individuality. But habitus is also 'structuring structure.' Once we have developed a certain habitus, we apply it in our practice, and thus reproduce society so that it continues to fit our specific habitus. By structuring individuals' habitus, society creates the preconditions for its own reproduction through human agency.

Habitus does not solve the problem of structure and agency but provides a concise formula to designate their link, and opens up possibilities for an empirical analysis of its inner workings. Its iridescent character between society and individual marks Bourdieu's position as standing between actor-oriented approaches and theories interested in systems and eliminating individual agency.

Bourdieu's interest in a critical theory of power and inequality finds its expression in a concept linked to habitus: that of cultural (or symbolic) capital and symbolic domination based on it. Bourdieu sees three forms of capital at work in any society: economic capital, social capital (an individual's ability to rely on social networks and to mobilize social relations for his or her own aims), and symbolic capital (the capacity to influence interpretations of the world). In the struggle over power within a society, economic and social capital are important, but cannot be effectively sustained without symbolic capital. Symbolic domination is the control over the meaning people convey to their world. It is mediated through culturally bounded knowledge and through the symbolic dimensions in public life. Hidden in cultural knowledge, symbolic domination masks its effects much more efficiently than economic and political domination do. Like Marx's concept of ideology and Gramsci's hegemony, symbolic domination serves to explain why the powerless only rarely revolt against the existing social structures. They have all too often internalized symbolic domination without realizing how power-laden the cultural domain is. Cultural, economic, and social capital position people within their society, and simultaneously form their subjectivities. By shaping the habitus of future social actors, societies thus also reproduce their power relations.

With this differentiation of forms of capital, Bourdieu fragments economic concepts of class and provides a means to analyze 'vertical' struggles between different segments of society. *Distinction* (1984) is a complex description of the workings of the three forms of capital in French society. Predominance, he argues, is not only negotiated in economic or political terms; symbolic capital as expressed in taste (in music, art, or everyday consumption) is one of the most efficient markers of social distinction and means of social differentiation. 'Legitimate culture' – the dominant taste of people with a high amount of cultural capital – in Western societies typically privileges highly encoded cultural expressions which stress form, not function. Abstract painting or most twentieth century classical music, for example, cannot be understood by reference to everyday life, but only through a close familiarity with the codes involved: connoisseurship, which, according to Bourdieu, is socially acquired, is nonetheless perceived as a personal attribute by the cultural elite. This turns cultural capital into an effective means of social inclusion and exclusion.

Bourdieu's concept of symbolic capital is certainly shaped by his own experiences with the mandarins of French intellectual life. Against this background, his insistence on empirical data, questionnaires, diagrams, and numbers expresses a different way of directing one's regard toward practices, and a reaction against the free floating rhetoric of intellectualism he criticized in some of his teachers and colleagues. In spite of his impressive empirical apparatus and his interest in breaking up class boundaries, however, his descriptions of the working class and their 'taste of necessity' are not free from negative evaluations based on his own habitus anchored in 'legitimate' culture. Some traces of this can also be found in the massive and ethnographically fascinating collective work, *The Weight of the World* (1999), a collection of interviews with lower class French. Here, the paradoxes of his attempts to demystify scientific objectivity while keeping an analytical distance that enables 'objective' social criticism become visible. Bourdieu's work is driven by a discomfort about injustice and inequality, not least in relation to his own position in society – a discomfort that necessarily leads to a partisan standpoint.

Bourdieu authored over 35 books and more than 400 scholarly articles. In this oeuvre, he applied the fundamental concepts first developed from his ethnographic work in Algeria to a wide range of areas, from nineteenth century art to linguistics, and from the education system to marriage rules. Later in his life, he became the most important left wing intellectual in France and perhaps in Europe. He was an advisor to the labour union CFDT, co-organizer of the International Parliament of Writers in Paris, and finally a founding and leading member in the anti-globalization movement Attac. In addition to his scholarly work, he had a life-long interest in photography, and his photographic work on Algeria has been exhibited worldwide.

Bourdieu's work has left many traces in anthropology. His focus on practice and everyday life has resonated with a generation of anthropologists moving away from both structuralism and classical Marxism while grappling with deconstructivist questions to anthropological theory; it has also heavily influenced the study of material culture by providing a clear connection between social practices and the material things we live with. The concept of habitus has found ample usage in anthropological studies to describe the link between society and individuals. The most crucial influence Bourdieu has had on anthropology, however, stems from his insistence on the symbolic dimensions of power – and correspondingly on the political dimension of culture. Anthropology's move towards a more critical understanding of culture and its consequences for societal differentiation has been shaped by Bourdieu's work.

Selected readings

Bourdieu, P. (1961) *The Algerians*, Boston, MA: Boston Press.

——(1977a) *Reproduction in Education, Society and Culture*, London: Sage.

——(1977b) *Outline of a Theory of Practice*, Cambridge: Cambridge University Press.

——(1979) 'The Kabyle House,' in *Algeria 1960, Essays by Pierre Bourdieu*, pp. 133–53, Cambridge: Cambridge University Press.

——(1984) *Distinction. A Social Critique of the Judgment of Taste*, London: Routledge.

——(ed.) (1999) *The Weight of the World. Social Suffering in Contemporary Society*, Cambridge: Polity Press.

——(2007) *Sketch for a Self-analysis*, Cambridge: Polity Press.

GREGOR DOBLER

JEAN (1946–) AND JOHN COMAROFF (1945–)

Undoubtedly one of the most distinguished partnerships in the history of anthropology, Jean (born 1946) and John (born 1945) Comaroff met while undergraduates at the University of Cape Town where they studied with **Monica Wilson**. After graduating in 1966 and

1968 respectively, both moved to the London School of Economics to work with Isaac Schapera, where they completed their doctoral dissertations in 1974 and 1973, based on fieldwork among Tswana-speakers, in particular the Barolong, in what is now the North-west Province of South Africa.

After several years at Swansea University College and Manchester University they moved to the University of Chicago in 1978 and rapidly made their way up the academic hierarchy. Jean was appointed to the Bernard E. & Ellen C. Sunny Distinguished Professorship and John to the Harold Swift Distinguished Service Professorship in 1996. Unlike many senior anthropologists, they are still engaged in fieldwork and are renowned for their careful mentoring of students, whose work they have sometimes published in several significant collected volumes. Among students who have worked with them, several are prominent, including Judith Farquhar, William Hanks, Anna Alonso, Loic Wacquant, Brad Weiss, Rosalind Morris, Randy Matory, and Adeline Masquelier.

The Comaroffs' theoretical contributions can be broadly located within three phases. The first entails a rethinking of African political processes with a focus on talking political language (John) and ritual as signifying practice (Jean). This is followed by the multiple volumes on *Revelation and Revolution* in which they interrogate the history of the locales in which they did fieldwork, using in particular the concepts of Practice, Materialism, and Hegemony to develop a conceptual framework of structure, power, and agency. Most recently they have worked on the new political economy wrought in the main by neo-liberalism. They have utilized such keywords as 'occult economies' and 'millennial capitalism' in their rethinking of dominant economic and political paradigms.

With her first book, *Body of Power, Spirit of Resistance*, Jean made a major contribution to medical anthropology and religion by emphasizing how embodiment and ritual were signifying practices that produced a 'collective will' and by demonstrating how African Zionist beliefs and rituals embodied resistance to apartheid. John's initial interests, epitomized by *Rules and Processes* (co-authored by Simon Roberts) emphasized a more traditional concern: how disputes were embedded in the socio-cultural order. He rejected the dominant rule-centred approach in legal anthropology by arguing that the dynamics of disputes and the 'laws' which are applied are constantly being negotiated verbally. Issues that would lead to conflict, such as marriage payments and kinship, were built into the system and thus predictable. Even the meaning of such traditional anthropological concerns as marriage payments and kinship were dynamic and changing.

It was however the two volumes of a projected three volume series entitled *Of Revelation and Revolution* that drew the most attention, with numerous symposia and review essays devoted to these books by anthropologists and historians. In these volumes they use extensive archival and ethnographic material to re-examine the Tswana response to Christianity and European ways of life. They seek a broad canvas to display this 'long conversation,' showing how even 'traditional' kinship and ritual practices have been impacted and articulated with regional practices. Indeed their work attempts to develop an anthropology of colonialism and modernity itself. Developing insights from Marx (especially the dialectic), Gramsci (hegemony), and **Bourdieu** (practice), they treat colonization as both a matter of coercion and a struggle over meaning or consciousness. Colonization occurs less at the ideological level than at the unconscious hegemonic level where ideology infiltrates and permeates mundane practices and representations, such as notions of hygiene, architecture, and time. Indeed it is by regulating bodily regimes through clothing and hygiene that commodities meet the self. This is what hegemony is about: ideologies that are so naturalized that they do not appear to be ideology at all.

According to the Comaroffs, missionaries are some of the most important agents of colonization because of their long and sustained personal interactions with local people. The colonial situation also provides Europeans with an opportunity for experimentation, and many ideas developed here are carried back and impact in the metropole as part of the dialectical relationship with industrial capitalism. Indeed for them colonization is a two-way process in that there is reciprocal determination, albeit tilted and decidedly unequal in terms of power. Modernity is not some monolithic artifact imposed upon weak people but the product of this conversation.

'The long conversation' is the key metaphor they use to explain how both sides generate their own forms of cultural hybridity. Local agency resides in how people interpret and change the meaning of European cultural practices. They show how insights can emerge from the study of mundane practices at the everyday level. The colonial era is not over but continuing to shape various modernities.

The unit of analysis is problematic for the Comaroffs. The idea of an extended case method can, they feel, short-change history as it might artificially cut off the event. Instead one wants a free-ranging dialectic between local and wider systems, both in time and in space.

In both *Revelation and Revolution* and their essays in *Ethnography and the Historical Imagination* the Comaroffs argue persuasively that anthropology needs to think historically and that history needs to be addressed ethnographically. It would be wrong however to simply see this turn to history as a fashion stimulated in part by the recent work of Edward Said and **Eric Wolf**. Both their major teachers, **Monica Wilson** and Isaac Schapera, were heavily involved in historical research when they were students, and from Schapera they learnt the importance of analyzing Africans and Europeans within the same social system and of giving equal weight to the magician and the missionary (an idea Schapera derived in turn from his teacher **A. R. Radcliffe-Brown**). This perspective was further developed in dialogue with a group of anti-apartheid academics located in Britain, and was necessitated by the very fact that they could not understand their field data without recourse to history. They are acutely self-conscious of their craft and continually question whether ethnography, the basis of good anthropology, is simply a colonial gaze or a humanistic art.

Sometimes erroneously categorized as POSTMODERNISTS, the Comaroffs are better viewed as empirically grounded anthropologists who are rather concerned about neo-modernity and its contradictions. Their current focus is on the 'Neo World Order.' Neo-modernity refers to newer forms of sociability characterized by network formation, informationalism, and globalization. It is closely associated with neo-liberalism, which gives primacy to consumerism above production as the prime source of value. While producing desire and expectation, neo-liberalism decreases security through deregulation, privatization, outsourcing, and new forms of social exclusion, which chip away at that edifice known as the State, transforming it into an ensemble of bureaucratic institutions and a licensing office. Capitalism is still a vast ensemble of dialectical processes grounded in socially embedded local challenges. However, a key for this dramatic change to millennial capitalism was the transnationalization of primary production which made traditional class conflicts obsolete by transforming internal classes to countries as a whole. Thus decontextualized, capitalism made organized local protests difficult as the market has replaced society, which is now largely a universe of aggregated transactions.

This new form of free market, or Milton Friedmanesque capitalism, characterized by growing inequalities and grounded in consumerism, has messianistic qualities in the belief that, if properly enacted, all will be transformed. The Comaroffs have elaborated on a number of features concerning millennial capitalism. They have shown how it is an occult economy in which wealth is created by techniques that defy conventional explanation. These magical actions produce a thriving alternative modernity, seduced by the allure of accruing wealth from nothing. Gambling, Ponzi-like schemes, and speculation are characteristic activities, especially when coupled in various complex ways to a near pervasive sense of risk and threat. Scams open up spaces of mystery in which supernatural agents ply their trades. They note the close parallels with new religious movements. Occult economies are a response to a world gone awry with enchantment. This consumeristic messianism is approached from the perspective of postcoloniality, looking at the emerging situation from the perspective of Southern Africa where they have done, and continue to do, sustained fieldwork. Their concern is how social order is maintained and created in such conditions.

Lawlessness is directly related to neo-liberalism and privatization, as the state has privatized and outsourced many of its services and states have surrendered their claim to monopolizing the means of coercion, as evidenced by the rise in private security companies, vigilantes, and paramilitaries. Deregulation has provided opportunities, some legal and some illegal. They talk of twilight economies operating in the interstices of legality and illegality.

Occult economies inevitably arise when the state is seen as being ineffective, indeed incapable of meeting the needs of its citizens, who are gradually transformed into denizens. The state's response in such situations is often by way of magical rituals and ceremonial enactments and use of legal fetishism. A good example is the notion of 'civil society,' a highly ambiguous term that is 'good to think' and is presented as the ultimate magic bullet for its promise of providing a meaningful social existence. The fetishism of the law is manifested in the rise of new constitutions. Such documents are frequently part of the transition to a neo-liberal model that gives primacy to the rule of law but which can be manipulated by dictators who disguise their nefarious activities in a cloak of constitutionality, which is part of the emerging culture of legality. A situation of 'lawfare' has emerged in which law is used to coerce and negotiate. As civil law becomes less effective in the Neo-world there is increasing recourse to lawfare as part of the horizontal 'tapestry of partial sovereignties.'

One aspect of the empire of the market and its interfacing with law that the Comaroffs have recently analyzed is the way in which culture is turned into property: the corporatization of ethnic identity and the commodification of culture by 'ethnopreneurs.' They note again the dialectical contradictions of the situation which simultaneously excludes and creates a new moral economy, enriching and deepening inequalities.

The nation-state for them, especially in Africa, is always a work in progress, being transformed and weakened in some aspects and strengthened in others, with its boundaries continually challenged by transnational communities and international law. The global north is evolving in ways similar to Africa, the Comaroffs suggest, and the 'postcolony' is a hyperextension of the contemporary world, linking postcolonies to former metropoles. It is in the margins that the massive shifts are first detected, and this is why the periphery is a crucial site for theory construction.

It takes intellectual courage to confront large issues like increasing global disorder, and the Comaroffs have done this with élan. Judging by the number of special symposia devoted to their work both in and beyond anthropology, it is obvious that their work has had a stimulating impact on academe and intellectuals as a whole.

Selected readings

Comaroff, J. (1985) *Body of Power, Spirit of Resistance. The Culture and History of a South African People*, Chicago: University of Chicago Press.
Comaroff, J. and Comaroff, J. L. (1991) *Of Revelation and Revolution: Volume One: Christianity, Colonialism and Consciousness*, Chicago: University of Chicago Press.
——(1992) *Ethnography and the Historical Imagination*, Boulder, CO: Westview.
——(1997) *Of Revelation and Revolution: Volume Two. The Dialectics of Modernity on a South African Frontier*, Chicago: University of Chicago Press.
——(2000) 'Millennial capitalism: first thoughts on a second coming,' *Public Culture* 12(2): 291–343.
——(2009) *Ethnicity Inc.*, Chicago: University of Chicago Press and Pietermaritzberg: University of Kwa-Zulu Natal Press.
Comaroff, J. L. and Comaroff, J. (eds.) (2006), *Law and Disorder in the Postcolony*, Chicago: University of Chicago Press.
Comaroff, J. L., Comaroff, J., and James, D. (eds.) (2008) *Picturing a Colonial Past: The African Photographs of Isaac Schapera*, Chicago: University of Chicago Press.
Comaroff, J. L. and Roberts, S. (1981) *Rules and Process: the Cultural Logic of Disputes in an African Context*, Chicago: University of Chicago Press.

ROBERT GORDON

DAME MARY DOUGLAS (1921–2007)

Mary Douglas, born Mary Tew in 1921, was a product of two powerful formative influences: the Catholic Church and the Oxford Institute of Social Anthropology. What emerged was an economic anthropologist with a strong belief that economic actions were taken for symbolic as well as survival reasons and that the maintenance of social order was a pre-eminent good. Politically Douglas was somewhat more conservative than most anthropologists of the second half of the twentieth century. She was a staunch supporter of the anthropology of Émile Durkheim, but, unlike Durkheim, she was devoutly religious, rather than a formerly religious agnostic who saw belief as a problem to be explained. Richard Fardon suggests that Douglas, orphaned at an early age, found the convent boarding school to which she was sent a place of refuge rather than a place of repression, and found its rules and order comforting after a life which had previously been characterized by upheavals (Fardon 1999: 6).

Douglas studied with **Edward Evans-Pritchard** at Oxford, and said in an interview late in her life that one of the most important lessons she learned during her time there shortly after the war was that African belief systems were not irrational, and that they needed to be understood in their entirety. Oxford, of course, was also where she was taught to revere the Durkheimian use of 'social solidarity' as an explanatory principle for many of the apparently strange things humans did, including the insight that economic facts were also social facts. In her own fieldwork among the Lele in the then Belgian Congo, she studied people's uses of animals, a point where the practical and symbolic were inextricably bound. She was particularly interested in the pangolin, a mammal which lacks teeth and has scales, and was the subject of many ritual practices. The interconnection of religion and economics figured both in her monograph on the Lele and in several articles she published about her research, including an influential one on the pangolin.

Her interpretation of the pangolin as an anomalous creature that disrupted the intellectual and social order formed part of the background to the work which gave Douglas an international reputation: *Purity and Danger* (Douglas 1966). In that work, named by *The Times Literary Supplement* in 1995 as one of the hundred most influential works of non-fiction since WWII, Douglas looked at taboos of many sorts in many societies, and at witchcraft, the demonization of certain categories of persons, and concluded that Lord Chesterfield's maxim

'Dirt is matter out of place' explained a lot of human activity which had hitherto received piecemeal, rather than systematic explanations. The part of the book which made her famous was her analysis of the Abominations of Leviticus, in which she suggested that ancient Hebrew taboos on pigs, shellfish, certain wild animals, homosexuality, menstruation, leprosy, yoking different species of animals to the same plough, and mixing different fibers in the same garment had congruent explanations. What they had in common, in her view, was the challenge they offered to a coherent system of mental categories, which were themselves mirrors of social categories. In *Purity and Danger*, Douglas asserted that the human body was a mirror of the social body, and that its internal and external boundaries needed to be guarded from improper intrusions, expulsions, and traversing, just as the integrity of the social group as a whole and its internal hierarchies needed protection. Ritual and taboo were what provided that protection. The Ancient Hebrews, Douglas suggested, had made their religious, gustatory, agricultural, and tailoring activities all of a piece, so that the underlying message was that confusion at any of these levels was a challenge to the borders of the Hebrew community as a whole or to the status system within it. Pigs, as animals which were anomalous when compared to the ungulates with which pastoralists were mainly concerned, shellfish, as sea animals without fins and scales, homosexual acts in which 'a man lies with a man as with a woman' and mixing of fibers and draft animals all constituted confusions of this kind, and thus had to be avoided.

Douglas's suggestion that one explanation could account for practices that had previously been either mysteries or the subject of limited, individual explanations (pigs might cause trichinosis; shellfish might be tainted with red tide; people might have an instinctive aversion to homosexuality) was a true paradigm-shifter. It was challenged by CULTURAL MATERIALISTS, such as **Marvin Harris**, but it was widely accepted by SYMBOLIC ANTHROPOLOGISTS and British STRUCTURALISTS.

Like **Rodney Needham** and **Edmund Leach**, Douglas was influenced by **Claude Lévi-Strauss**, as well as by the Durkheimians. Like them, she saw social and mental worlds as a system of categories, and also like them she was more interested in how these categories worked themselves out in social action than in their unconscious, formal properties. In the mid-1960s both Douglas and Leach undertook something which Lévi-Strauss had explicitly rejected, the application of structural analysis to the Judaeo-Christian tradition. As a devout Catholic, in Douglas's case, and someone socially secure enough to be a public atheist, in Leach's, they may have had less to fear from the establishment than the Jewish Lévi-Strauss.

In her subsequent book, *Natural Symbols* (Douglas 1970), Douglas attempted to provide a kind of universal grammar of the ways in which societies articulated the connections between the human body and the social body. In this book she employed the concepts of 'grid,' to stand for internal social borders, such as hierarchies, and 'group,' which stood for the external boundaries of society itself. Cultures could be weak or strong in either or both of these modes of boundary maintenance. A society with an elaborate hierarchy and an aversion to strangers, for example, would have 'high grid' and 'high group,' while an egalitarian society which welcomed outsiders would have 'low grid' and 'low group.' Societies in the latter category might be expected to be relatively free from taboos, while societies of the first kind might have many. Societies which were 'low grid' and 'high group' or the reverse might have taboos which reinforced the particular type of social boundaries they thought important.

Throughout her work Douglas was highly respectful of social boundaries, more concerned with preserving them than challenging them, which put her somewhat at odds with the emerging generation of graduate students and young faculty members who were active in espousing the opposite point of view. This perspective could lead to what some might consider misreading. Douglas wrote a highly complimentary review of **Pierre Bourdieu**'s *Distinction* (Douglas 1981), in which she praised Bourdieu extensively for discerning that taste, in everything from photographs to furniture, was part of an elaborate system of social hierarchy, but did not really engage with the critique Bourdieu offered of the system he described.

During the 1960s and 1970s Douglas applied her methodology to a diverse array of topics, most notably humor and tricksters. Her interpretation of these questions essentially reiterated opinions about humor which had appeared in various guises since the time of Plato, the notion that humor provided a harmless release for thoughts and actions that might otherwise pose a challenge to the social order. In the context of Douglas's other work, however, this notion received some added value, insofar as humor and taboo could be seen as inversions of each other, as part of a total system of boundary maintenance. The collection *Implicit Meanings* (Douglas 1975) brought some of this work, which appeared in numerous articles and book chapters, together. It also contained early essays on topics which were to occupy Douglas in the 1980s and beyond, such as risk taking and environmentalism. It was republished, with a new preface and a retrospective essay, in 2000 (Douglas 2000).

During the 1970s Douglas and her student Michael Nicod (Douglas and Nicod 1974) applied some of her earlier insights to British working class food habits. She argued that the structure of meals, and the use of specific food items, such as biscuits, served to signal and reinforce social integration as well as boundaries and hierarchies, so that the meanings of such food practices often made it difficult for working class people to accept the advice of scientific authorities who did not appreciate their social rituals (Fardon 1999: 130–32).

In the late 1970s Douglas moved to the US, after teaching at the University of London for more than 25 years. She held positions first at the Russell Sage Foundation and later at Northwestern University, before returning to England in retirement. During her years in the US, Douglas, sometimes in collaboration with other scholars, authored numerous books and articles, in which she applied her insights to Western economic and bureaucratic systems and aspects of public culture, notably the environmental movement. In this work she enjoined readers to take seriously the social and ritual bases of various forms of rhetoric and decision making, including consumer choices (Douglas and Isherwood 1978), environmental and other risk analyses (Douglas and Wildavsky 1982), and the decisions made by bureaucracies (Douglas 1986). According to her biographer, Richard Fardon, the analytical frameworks developed in *Purity and Danger* and *Natural Symbols* were deployed in all of these contexts to argue that notions of symbolic pollution and the dynamics of grid and group determined modern Americans' understanding of the world much as it did in rural Africa (Fardon 1999: 144–67).

After retiring from teaching and returning to Britain, Douglas returned to her work on the Old Testament, this time learning Hebrew in order to do a more systematic analysis. In *In the Wilderness: the Doctrine of Defilement in the Book of Numbers* (Douglas 1993), Douglas suggested that her original analysis had been too limited. This time she foregrounded the ancient Hebrews' relation to God, rather than merely to their society. She suggested that the whole process of taboo and atonement for its breach had served as a way to attain forgiveness, and thus closeness to God. This work represented something of a departure from her strong Durkheimian roots, insofar as closeness to God emerges as a human need in itself, apart from its social function. In this direction, Douglas mirrored the path taken by her close friend **Victor Turner**, another devout Catholic, who had begun by analyzing the social functions of ritual and progressed to seeing ritual as fulfilling inherent human needs.

In another work on Leviticus, *Leviticus as Literature* (Douglas 1999), Douglas analyzed Leviticus as a total symbolic system, in which such details as the arrangement of sacrifices on the altar were linked to grand cosmic and social themes. In an introduction to a 2002 edition of *Purity and Danger* Douglas argued that the eligibility of animals for sacrifice was the most important criterion for their permissibility as food, since sacrificial animals were the link between the Hebrews and their God. Many anthropologists, however, continued to prefer her earlier explanation. As in the case of Turner, a substantial number of anthropologists of religion are uncomfortable with explanations which do not deal with faith by relegating it to the status of an artifact in another discussion, for example the maintenance of social structure.

Douglas died in 2007, having been made a Dame Commander of the Order of the British Empire in 2006.

Selected readings

An extensive bibliography of Douglas's work may be found on the Internet at www.semioticon.com/people/Douglas.html, as well as in Fardon's biography.

Douglas, M. (1966) *Purity and Danger: An Analysis of Concepts of Pollution and Taboo*, London: Routledge and Kegan Paul.

——(1970) *Natural Symbols: Explorations in Cosmology*, London: Barrie and Rockliff: The Cresset Press.

——(1975) *Implicit Meanings: Selected Essays in Anthropology*, London: Routledge.

——(1981) 'High Culture and Low,' review of Pierre Bourdieu's *La Distinction*, *Times Literary Supplement*, February 13: 163–64.

——(1986) *How Institutions Think*, Syracuse, NY: Syracuse University Press.

——(1993) *In the Wilderness: The Doctrine of Defilement in the Book of Numbers*, Sheffield: Sheffield Academic Press.

——(1999) *Leviticus as Literature*, Oxford: Oxford University Press.

——(2000) *Implicit Meanings: Selected Essays in Anthropology*, 2nd edn, London: Routledge.

——(2002) *Purity and Danger: An Analysis of Concepts of Pollution and Taboo*, reissued with a specially commissioned introduction by the author, London: Routledge.

Douglas, M. and Isherwood, Baron (1978) *The World of Goods: Towards an Anthropology of Consumption*, New York: Basic Books.

Douglas, Mary and Nicod, M. (1974) 'Taking the Biscuit: the Structure of British Meals,' *New Society* (December) 19: 744–47.

Douglas, Mary and Wildavsky, A. (1982) *Risk and Culture*, Berkeley: University of California Press.
Fardon, R. (1999) *Mary Douglas: An Intellectual Biography*, London: Routledge.

HARRIET D. LYONS

ALAN DUNDES (1934–2005)

Born in New York City, Dundes grew up on a farmstead outside the city. His parents nurtured his love of books by paying him a dollar for every one hundred books that he read and his father inspired his love of words and jokes in particular. Another life-long love was music. He studied clarinet and attended the Manhattan New York School of Music. Graduating from Pawling High School in 1951 as class valedictorian, Dundes entered Yale College in 1952. Earning a BA in English in 1955, Dundes served in the Naval Reserve for two years as part of his ROTC obligation. In 1957, he returned to Yale to pursue an MAT in English. Here he met his wife Carolyn M. Browne, a graduate student at Yale Drama School. Together they spent a year in the French Alsace region where Dundes taught conversational English at a lycée before he began his doctoral studies in folklore. Dundes entered the folklore graduate program at Indiana University in 1958 where he studied with Richard Dorson, Felix Oinas, David Bidney, Warren Roberts, and Erminie Wheeler-Voegelin. Dundes's PhD dissertation, *The Morphology of North American Indian Folktales* (1962) formed a pivotal foundation for his life-long focus on theory and on the rigor required in defining folklore genres.

In 1962, Dundes took a position as an instructor of English at the University of Kansas. The next year brought a move to Berkeley as assistant professor of folklore and anthropology in the department of anthropology at the University of California. Dundes ascended through the academic ranks rapidly, becoming full professor in five years with over thirty articles, one single authored monograph, and two edited volumes. Dundes was also a gifted teacher, as all his students attest, and indeed became a legend in his own time. He spent the rest of his professional career at Berkeley, dying in March 2005 'with his boots on' – teaching a seminar on folklore theory and methods.

Trained as a folklorist, whose home base was in a department of anthropology, Dundes straddled the divide by bedevilling both folklorist and anthropologist with what each lacked, and with what each should learn from the other. In 1986, he criticized anthropologists for abandoning the comparative method and for dashing all hopes of arriving at 'general laws or principles of culture'; and he faulted folklorists for employing the comparative method pedantically, with 'their obsessive insistence' on compiling historic-geographic studies. Meting out criticism in equal measure, Dundes wrote: 'Just as the sum total of all the anthropologists' ethnographies don't add up to anything theoretical, so the sum total of all the folklorists' comparative studies don't add up to anything theoretical' (1986: 138). In his 2004 invited presidential plenary address to the American Folklore Society, Dundes returned to this theme. He derided folklorists – and particularly American folklorists – for not having developed a 'grand theory' of folklore (2005: 387). He called for a focus on underlying meaning, on symbolism, on analysis.

For Dundes, his subject matter was nothing if it was not international. His focus on the international and his comparative approach were coupled with his delight in feasting on bibliographic research. He seemed to live a good portion of his life in his beloved University of California, Berkeley library, always with his voluminous black leather briefcase bulging with papers and books. By his own admission a library researcher (he differentiated between library folklorists and fieldworkers), Dundes engaged in fieldwork only infrequently, and most notably in his fieldwork on the Palio of Siena conducted in conjunction with his then-graduate student from Siena, Alessandro Falassi. That project allowed for 'the fruitful collaboration of an insider and an outsider' (1975: xvi). The results yielded a stunningly detailed historical, social, symbolic, and psychoanalytic interpretation of the layered and deep meaning of this ritual horse race. In many ways, *La Terra in Piazza* is emblematic of the touchstones of Dundes's approaches to anthropology and folklore. There is the focus on genre, with attention to literal and free translation of the words and accompanying music. There is the focus on the surface or morphological structure of the ritual, the detailed, inter-locking order of the festival participants and events. There is the building crescendo to the analysis of worldview, with the interpretation of unconscious, psychoanalytic meaning.

'One of the goals of social science,' Dundes wrote, 'is, or ought to be, to make the unconscious conscious' (1987b: xiii). Through the study of folklore, Dundes stressed, the scholar was provided with the full palette of the unconscious cultural content. Riddle, narrative, jokes, ritual, superstition, and proverb, all of these provided a mirror to a people's culture, or 'the autobiographical ethnography of a people' (1969: 54). Dundes never ceased expressing his frustration with anthropologists who were either ignorant of the importance of folklore or actively dismissive of it as trivial. Coupled with this, which more than doubled his ire, were those anthropologists and folklorists who rejected out-of-hand any analysis arrived at through psychoanalytic interpretation. Dundes referred to this aversion to psychoanalysis as 'anthropological myopia.' He continued: 'One of the most infuriating, exasperating, and unfortunately all too common reactions of colleagues and students to my Freudian analyses of folklore consists of the comment that these Freudian analyses are "reductionistic"' (1987b: ix–x). Dundes wrote: 'No one criticizes Einstein for being reductionistic in having formulated the e $=$ mc^2 equation' (1987b: x).

Never one to be afraid of crossing disciplinary boundaries, playing on the similarity between 'Lore' and 'Law,' one of Dundes's more original contributions was the huge two volume work he jointly edited with his daughter on the study of unwritten indigenous law which was later republished in paperback.

Dundes's achievements were acknowledged abundantly and at all levels: University of California Berkeley Distinguished Teaching Award (1994); John Simon Guggenheim Fellow (1966–67); Sigillo d'Oro (Seal of Gold), which is the Pitrè Prize for lifetime achievement in folklore (1993); and elected member of the American Academy of Arts and Sciences (2001). In their obituary Laura Nader and Stanley Brandes remarked:

> Dundes's work, which was marked by thoroughness, originality, and intellectual provocativeness, gave us an entirely fresh look at familiar topics. One of his most ambitious articles (1993) was a cross-cultural consideration of the cockfight in the light of Clifford Geertz's work, which he critiqued by comparing variants of the cockfight through large parts of Asia and elsewhere, using bodies of linguistic, visual, and ethnographic data. In Two Tales of Crow and a Sparrow (1997), Dundes offered a new interpretation of caste and untouchability in India, differing completely from standard discussions of the topics.
>
> (Nader and Brandes 2006)

Dundes both studied popular culture and was part of popular culture. As he himself recounted in the Preface to Cracking Jokes, 'Someone responded to a newspaper story about my research by sending me a letter addressed simply to "The Joke Professor, University of

California, Berkeley." That was understandable; the writer had simply forgotten my name. What surprised me, however, was that the letter was delivered! I suppose the epithet wouldn't be a bad one really' (1987a: x).

Michael P. Carroll writes of Dundes's 'exuberance and helter-skelter style' that leads the reader further than the data might otherwise bear. Carroll continues:

> None of this, however, detracts from the incredible range of insights that he has offered over the past few decades, or from his ability to develop new and original interpretations of familiar materials, or from the conclusion that Alan Dundes is one of the most consistently creative minds at work in the field of either anthropology or folklore. ... And no matter how much his critics try to muddy the waters or thunder and rail, Alan Dundes will always come from behind and win the Grail.
>
> (1993: 20)

It says much for Dundes's stature and the intellectual love that he inspired that at least three Festschriften were published in his honour: *The Psychoanalytic Study of Society, Essays in Honor of Alan Dundes*, edited by L. Bryce Boyer, Ruth M. Boyer, and Stephen M. Sonnenberg (1993); *Proverbium, Festschrift for Alan Dundes on the Occasion of His Sixtieth Birthday*, edited by Wolfgang Mieder (1994); and with essays by his students, *Folklore Interpreted, Essays in Honor of Alan Dundes*, edited by Regina Bendix and Rosemary Lévy Zumwalt (1995). For a superb and thorough essay on the biographical, theoretical, and intellectual impact, see Simon Bronner's Introduction to his edited collection of Dundes's essays, 'The Analytics of Alan Dundes' (2007).

Selected readings

Bendix, R. (1995) 'Dundesiana: Teacher and Mentor in Campuslore, Anecdote, and Memorate,' in *Folklore Interpreted: Essays in Honor of Alan Dundes*, R. Bendix and R. L. Zumwalt (eds.), pp. 49–66, New York: Garland Publishing, Inc.

Boyer, L. B., Boyer, R. M., and Sonnenberg, S. M. (eds.) (1993) *Psychoanalytic Study of Society, Essays in Honor of Alan Dundes*, Vol. 18, Hillsdale, NJ: The Analytic Press.

Bronner, S. (ed.) (2007) *The Meaning of Folklore: The Analytical Essays of Alan Dundes*, Logan: Utah State University.

Carroll, M. P. (1993) 'Alan Dundes: An Introduction,' in *The Psychoanalytic Study of Society, Essays in Honor of Alan Dundes*, L. B. Boyer, R. M. Boyer, and S. M. Sonnenberg (eds.), Volume 18, pp. 1–22, Hillsdale, NJ: The Analytic Press.

Dundes, A. (1969) 'Thinking Ahead: A Folkloristic Reflection of the Future Orientation in American Worldview,' *Anthropological Quarterly* 42: 53–72.

——(1986) 'The Anthropologist and the Comparative Method in Folklore,' *Journal of Folklore Research* 23: 125–46.

——(1987a) *Cracking Jokes, Studies of Sick Humor Cycles and Stereotypes*, Berkeley, CA: Ten Speed Press.

——(1987b) *Parsing Through Customs: Essays by a Freudian Folklorist*, Madison: University of Wisconsin Press.

Dundes, A. (ed.) (1965) *The Study of Folklore*, Englewood Cliffs, NJ: Prentice-Hall.

——(1999) *International Folkloristics, Classic Contributions by the Founders of Folklore*, Lanham, MD: Rowman & Littlefield Publishers.

——(2004) *Folklore: Critical Concepts in Literary and Cultural Studies*, New York: Routledge Press.

——(2005) 'Folkloristics in the Twenty-First Century' (American Folklore Society Invited Presidential Plenary Address, 2004), *Journal of American Folklore* 118(470): 385–408.

Dundes, A. and Fallasi, A. (1975) *La Terra in Piazza, an Interpretation of the Palio of Siena*, Berkeley: University of California Press.

Dundes, A. and Renteln, A. D. (eds.) (1994) *Folk Law, Essays in the Theory and Practice of Lex Non Scripta*, two volumes, New York: Garland Publishing (University of Wisconsin Press paperback, 1995).

Mieder, W. (ed.) (1994) *Festschrift for Alan Dundes on the Occasion of His Sixtieth Birthday, Proverbium*, 11.

Nader, L. and Brandes, S. (2006) 'Obituaries, Alan Dundes, 1934–2005,' *American Anthropologist* 108: 268–71.

Zumwalt, R. L. (1995) 'Alan Dundes: Folklorist and Mentor,' in *Folklore Interpreted*, R. Bendix and R. L. Zumwalt (eds.), pp. 49–66, New York: Garland Publishing, Inc.

ROSEMARY LÉVY ZUMWALT

SIR E. E. EVANS-PRITCHARD (1902–73)

Edward Evan Evans-Pritchard became famous for his field studies of societies in eastern and northern Africa in the early to mid-twentieth century, and for the writing and teaching he did about them and others at Oxford University. Known mainly for his relativistic approach, for his serious attempt to write with empathy on the peoples he studied, and for his careful use of language and attention to problems of translation, he made important ethnographic and theoretical contributions to the study of religion, kinship, politics, religion, and other fields, building up a leading school of anthropological thought (initially FUNCTIONALIST and later more historical) and a tradition of eastern African studies.

Son of an Anglican vicar and his wife, Evans-Pritchard was born in Crowborough, Sussex. He went to Winchester College (1916–21), and took his first university degree in modern history at Exeter College, Oxford University (1921–24). The ecclesiastic element at home and in his schooling would influence his later work, not only by accustoming him to religious thinking but also by easing access to missionaries who would become some of his most important informants and cultural guides in Africa.

In a diffuse sense the ideas of Einsteinian relativity may have influenced Evans-Pritchard. He would do much to make anthropology a relativistic study of ecology, kinship, religion, and other topics: a field in which time and space made sense only in terms of each other, and in which human groups made sense only in terms of *other* groups, and ideas only in terms of other ideas.

Evans-Pritchard studied with and around some of Britain's best known anthropologists, beginning with R. R. Marett at Oxford. At the London School of Economics (LSE), he did his doctoral training under Charles G. Seligman and **Bronislaw Malinowski** (a former Seligman student himself), whose singular renown as an ethnographer he would later emulate. Malinowski's fieldwork-intensive, functionalist approach to anthropology deeply influenced Evans-Pritchard's thinking about the integral organization of culture. However, after he came under the influence of **A. R. Radcliffe-Brown** in the early 1930s, he distanced himself from Malinowski's shadow.

Seligman's brief researches on Nilotic peoples in the then Anglo-Egyptian Sudan, including the Shilluk, set an important precedent for him. Evans-Pritchard made three fieldwork trips totaling about 20 months between 1926 and 1930, visiting the agricultural Azande people near the borderlands of the southern Sudan and adjoining parts of what are now the Democratic Republic of Congo and the Central African Republic. Meanwhile, he was given a job as Lecturer in Anthropology back at the LSE (1928–31).

In several visits between 1930 and 1936 Evans-Pritchard lived in Nuer country in southern Sudan, in stays totalling about a year. He entered this upper Nilotic region at a time of local rebellion and government military retaliation. He also visited the Shilluk and Anuak peoples. Between 1932 and 1934 he taught as Professor of Sociology at Fouad I University (later the Egyptian University of Cairo), gaining much exposure to the Arabic language and Islam. Back at Oxford he took a Lectureship in African Sociology in 1935, which he held until entering the military in 1940 as an intelligence officer. In 1939, he married Ioma Gladys Heaton. The Second World War took him to Ethiopia (where he fought with the Anuak against the Italians), Sudan, and Syria, and last but not least to Libya. While serving in Libya he conducted historical-ethnographic research on the development of a century-old Islamic religious and political order which had formed the backbone of resistance to the Italians. That work resulted in his monograph, *The Sanusi of Cyrenaica* (1949).

In 1945 he spent a year as Reader in Social Anthropology at Cambridge before being offered the Professorship (chair) of Social Anthropology at Oxford University, succeeding Radcliffe-Brown. He retired in 1970, was knighted in 1971, and died on September 11, 1973.

Witchcraft, Oracles, and Magic among the Azande, published in 1937, cemented his fame as an ethnographer and an Africanist; this was in many ways the first intensive ethnographic field study on that continent by a professional social anthropologist. Evans-Pritchard's core question was why the Azande continued to believe that witchcraft and sorcery were the cause of much misfortune despite what we would regard as evidence to the contrary. The French philosopher Lucien Lévy-Bruhl had expressed the opinion that primitive people were raised from childhood with a pre-logical or mystical mode of thought that took for granted connections between physical events and non-natural agents that were in fact the creation of the collective imagination. Evans-Pritchard's findings revealed a more complicated picture. The Azande had a lot of practical knowledge which enabled them to plant, tend, and harvest crops, and to store them in granaries. Magical thought came in where everyday knowledge failed. A farmer might be skilled and diligent, and yet his crop might fail or his granary might fall down, while his lazy, careless neighbor met with every success. Such undeserved misfortune might or might not be attributed to witchcraft, but major illnesses and death were almost always deemed the result of unconscious witchcraft or conscious sorcery. To identify a witch one could consult a witchdoctor who would divine during a trance; alternatively one could utilize a number of oracles. The most important oracle was the poison oracle, operated by an individual who administered a potion to a chicken that might or might not consequently die. The oracles' answers to questions (e.g.

the chicken lives or dies) might result in the identification of a witch. Once confronted, the witch might or might not withdraw his or her witchcraft. Perhaps the patient would recover. If the patient did not recover, there were many explanations: this witchdoctor was a fraud; the oracle operator did not abstain from sex before the consultation; the patient was not a victim but rather a perpetrator of witchcraft who had been subjected to vengeance magic; someone had bewitched the oracle. In the end, there was no way to stand outside and question core beliefs.

There has been much discussion of the 'closed system of thought' (an expression probably derived from the work of Sir Karl Popper) over the last 70 years, and Evans-Pritchard's insights on Azande witchcraft have informed a number of political and philosophical discussions about Marxism, Freudianism, and many forms of religious thought.

The central problem of *The Nuer* (1940) was the maintenance of a political system in a stateless society that existed in a condition of 'ordered anarchy.' The Nuer, who moved from higher ground in the rains to slightly lower pastures in the dry season, had no central army, government, permanent chiefs, or police, but had other ways of fulfilling the same functions. Fluid geographical divisions were segmented into a pyramidal structure, and genealogy (patrifiliation) was the idiom in which ties were expressed. Thus 'the sons of O' (lineage O) might be the main (maximal) lineage of a tribe. If A had three sons, A, B, and C, 'the sons of O' might subdivide after quarrels or other pressures into three major lineages whose members would call themselves 'sons of A,' 'sons of B,' and 'sons of C.' Further subdivisions, further fissions might occur. However, there was always the potential for a temporary reuniting (or fusion of forces) in the face of a common enemy. In that event the sons of A, B, and C might once again refer to themselves as the 'sons of O.' This principle has been described by Louis Dumont as 'structural relativity.' In truth, the model of the segmentary lineage, which splits up like the branches of a tree, may better fit the social organization of the Luo in Kenya, whom Evans-Pritchard visited for six weeks in 1936, than it does the more sparsely settled Nuer in Sudan.

Other elements playing a role in Nuer political structure included a system of age grades (before and after initiation, for males; married and unmarried statuses for females) that obtained all over Nuerland, crossing over genealogical and territorial boundaries. There was also the position of 'leopard-skin chief,' which an individual from a structurally minor kin group assumed only when needed to resolve others' disputes. In times of distress, prophets emerged as charismatic religious-political leaders with their own followings.

So easily accessible was the stylized model of patriliny, and of pyramidal hierarchies of nested descent groups, that for many readers it overshadowed the serious attention Evans-Pritchard also gave to matrilateral and affinal kinship in *Kinship and Marriage among the Nuer* (1951). In this ethnography he also paid much more attention to the role of women in Nuer society. His discussions of woman-to-woman marriage, ghost marriage, and other culturally specific findings have much to contribute to the study of gender.

Among mobile herding peoples time and space made sense only in terms of seasonal movement. Social and political distance were reckoned in part by generational separation from common ancestors. And social distance also governed choice of weaponry. These were some of the relativities Evans-Pritchard found in Nuer thought.

Nuer boys and men identified closely with cattle (taking names and nicknames based on cattle, singing praise-songs linking them to specific animals, and so on). Evans-Pritchard found that cattle were used for marriage transfers, sacrifice, and homicide compensation; and that their milk, blood, dung, and body parts were used for countless other subsistence needs. Along with Daryll Forde but few others, Evans-Pritchard stood out in the British anthropological tradition for devoting such close attention to environment and ecology.

Nuer Religion (1956), a collection of essays, made a bold statement in its very title, since not all Evans-Pritchard's contemporaries supposed a people like the Nuer had religion at all. He showed skeptical readers that Nuer ways of understanding their world could be as devout, detailed, thoughtful, and imaginative as anyone's, and also as full of ritual and prescriptive and proscriptive rules. His account of the correspondence between Nuer social structure and some of the refractions or aspects of *kwoth* (God or Divinity) owe much to Durkheim and Radcliffe-Brown, and the account of Nuer sacrifice closely accords with the theoretical model of Henri Hubert and **Marcel Mauss**. However, Evans-Pritchard's Anglican upbringing and personal conversion to Catholicism (1944) led him to question the adequacy of the Durkheimian approach to the study of religion inasmuch as Durkheim purposefully neglected questions regarding truth and sentiment that resisted sociological explanation. Evans-Pritchard became convinced that religious anthropologists could gain a better understanding of 'primitive' religion than atheists and agnostics. His attempt to translate Nuer concepts for a Judeo-Christian readership led him to force some Nuer ideas into what some have deemed a procrustean bed of Judeo-Christian categories. God, priests, prophets, soul, sin, sacrifice, and similar English terms, hard to translate neatly into a Nilotic tongue, take over his book's main headings. He refers to Nuer religion as an interior state dependent on an awareness of God (*kwoth*). And yet the book's main lessons remain ones more relativistic, and more firmly rooted in local conditions and idioms, than those headings or categories would suggest.

Evans-Pritchard's methods involved scrupulous attention to language and interviewing in depth, with less attention to surveying, counting, or measuring. He also drew on the knowledge of missionaries, administrators, and jurists as well as hired assistants. All of these strategies helped establish British ethnography's place, suspended as a humanistic study between the life sciences and literary studies.

Evans-Pritchard turned increasingly toward historical modes of explanation in the later years of life. He thus lived down the reputation he had gained earlier in his career as a functionalist, and distinguished himself from both Radcliffe-Brown and Malinowski in the generation before, and from French STRUCTURALISTS across the channel.

His own students and close associates, some of whom taught with and after him at Oxford, included John Beattie, Thomas Beidelman, **Mary Douglas**, Wendy James, John Middleton, Godfrey Lienhardt, John G. Peristiany, Julian Pitt-Rivers, Brian Street, André Singer, and Talal Asad, among other well known scholars. Through his influence, Upper Nilotic studies became a focus of the Oxford Institute of Social Anthropology, and remained so until a decade or two after his death.

Not all of his contributions would remain unchallenged. Debate has continued about the nature of Nuer political allegiances to territory or descent. His portrait of Nuer egalitarianism has been called idealistic. POSTMODERNISTS would criticize what they deemed his presumptuousness in starting his book on Zande witchcraft with the phrase 'Azande believe that. ... ,' as though these people all fit one mold, and as if he, the ethnographer from outside, had full authority to represent them or to judge the veracity of their understandings. Other critics have chided functionalists like the early Evans-Pritchard for being too focused on stasis or repetition and not enough on change, and for under-representing the effects of church missions, long-distance trade, colonial government, and so on among peoples they portrayed as almost pristine.

Criticisms notwithstanding, when we read Evans-Pritchard's ethnographies, we are above all else reminded of the subtle sophistication of ways of life once deemed savage, the need for patience and empathy to comprehend and appreciate them, and the cyclical recurrence of some social processes and the historical contingency of others. These remain among the tenets of anthropological thought that have all survived serious challenges.

Selected readings

Beidelman, T. O. (ed.) (1974) *A Bibliography of the Writings of E.E. Evans-Pritchard*, London: Tavistock.
Douglas, M. (1980) *Edward Evans-Pritchard*, Harmondsworth: Penguin.
Evans-Pritchard, E. E. (1937) *Witchcraft, Oracles, and Magic among the Azande*, Oxford: Clarendon Press.
——(1940) *The Nuer: A Description of the Modes of Livelihood and Political Institutions of a Nilotic People*, Oxford: Clarendon Press.
——(1949) *The Sanusi of Cyrenaica*, New York: Oxford University Press.
——(1951) *Kinship and Marriage among the Nuer*, Oxford: Clarendon Press.
——(1956) *Nuer Religion*, Oxford: Clarendon Press.
——(1962) *Social Anthropology and Other Essays*, New York: Free Press.
Fortes, M., and. Evans-Pritchard, E. E. (eds.) (1940) *African Political Systems*, Oxford: Oxford University Press, for the International African Institute.

PARKER SHIPTON AND ANDREW P. LYONS

SIR RAYMOND FIRTH (1901–2002)

Raymond Firth was born in South Auckland, New Zealand, and as a schoolboy became interested in the Maori, the indigenous inhabitants, both as neighbors and from reading Frederick Manning's *Old New Zealand* (1863), the account of an English judge who became intimately connected with Maori. At the same time he discovered the *Journal of the Polynesian Society* and became a reader and later a contributor.

For his undergraduate degree at Auckland University College he studied economics. His Masters thesis was based on the economics of the local kauri gum industry. Finding no statistics on earnings in the industry, he went to the north of New Zealand and interviewed kauri gum miners about their lives, working conditions, and earnings. This was an unusual approach in economics but it was also, in effect, his first fieldwork and foreshadowed his later theoretical stance about the importance of multiple individual actions contributing to social organization.

In 1924 he went to London School of Economics to work towards a doctorate on the economics of the frozen meat industry in New Zealand. However, he came under the influence of the distinguished anthropologist **Bronislaw Malinowski**, and changed the direction of his work. His doctoral thesis, *Primitive Economics of the New Zealand Maori*, was published in 1929. In this thesis his sympathy for the Maori was evident: he showed that he was aware of the effect of colonization on them and the immorality of the expropriation of their land. He also showed how their loss of forest and land had limited their economic choices.

Firth was raised a Methodist but later experienced a crisis of faith and became a humanist. In a videotaped interview completed when he was in his nineties, he defined his humanistic rationalism as the recognition that human society exists and that humans must take account of others by whom they live, which leads to a morality in which the supernatural is not required (Husmann et al. 1993). He also described gods as defense mechanisms for argument and display. According to Sutti Ortiz, 'He considered religion as an artistic creation intended to bring coherence in a universe of social and physical relations, as well as coherence with individual impulses, desires and emotion' (Ortiz 2004). After his first anthropological fieldwork in Tikopia, a Polynesian outlier in the Solomon Islands, Firth regretted the attempts by Christian missionaries to convert the people of Tikopia, asking 'what justification can be found for this steady pressure to break down the customs of a people against whom the main charge is that their gods are different from ours?'(Firth 1936: 50); These elements – formal training in economics, recognition of the interrelation between individual and collective knowledge, and humanistic rationalism – provided a basis for his development as an anthropologist.

Anthropology in Britain in the first few decades of the twentieth century was moving away from the EVOLUTIONIST and diffusionist approaches of earlier decades. Under **Malinowski** the FUNCTIONALIST perspective became the dominant paradigm with its emphasis on extensive fieldwork. During the 1920s and 1930s many distinguished anthropologists were trained by Malinowski, Firth among them, and this period could be seen as one that defined *British* anthropology, as it was also developing in a different direction from American anthropology, something Firth would address later in his career.

In 1928–29 Firth carried out fieldwork on the isolated Polynesian island, Tikopia. Malinowski hoped that Firth would write a full and straightforward account of the Tikopian culture. It was important to Malinowski, as he wrote in a letter to Firth, 'to present the theoretical point of view which we now label "functional"'(Firth 1957: 10). Essentially that meant that customs exist for a purpose; they are the means by which people fulfil their needs. Firth's grasp of the Tikopian language (cognate with the Maori language of New Zealand with which he was familiar) was very good and he collected rich and detailed descriptions of the Tikopia. His first book about them, *We, the Tikopia* (1936), is Malinowskian in perspective, concentrating on family life through an economic functionalist lens. The word 'function' occurs often in this ethnography, as in statements such as 'In Tikopia the function of each of these elements [of marriage exchanges] can be clearly seen' (Firth 1936: 572–73). Firth believed that it was important to examine the fundamental beliefs behind the natives' economic behavior. However, Firth also looked at the 'calculating man.' His interest, based on the pre-Keynesian economics he had studied, was on individual choice-making, a perspective Malinowski would have contested, holding that individuals were mainly of interest as members of society, not as individuals per se.

By the late 1930s Firth, and many peers, explicitly recognized the weaknesses of the purely functionalist approach. He wrote, 'the basic problem raised by the functional theory of anthropology in its less sophisticated form – if everything is related to everything else, where does the description stop? – was much before the writers of the period' (Kuper 1997: 70). Moreover, the divergence between American and British anthropologists had become evident. The American anthropologist **G. P. Murdock** criticized the British school of anthropology for their concentration on kinship and British colonial dependencies. He suggested that they were not interested in the theoretical writings of their colleagues elsewhere or in history, culture change, or psychology, and that the British had become old-fashioned sociologists. Firth accepted Murdock's critique but said that the British had limited resources and therefore were concentrating on a limited set of issues with some success. In effect, the debate, and the divergence, was between British social anthropology and American cultural anthropology and its four-field approach (Kuper 1997: 129ff).

Firth, and other anthropologists, many of them not British, were developing alternative paradigms to that of their teacher, Malinowski.

While the Malinowskian emphasis on PARTICIPANT OBSERVATION in the field remained a hallmark of British anthropology, Firth had been moving away from the purely functionalist perspective for some time. He believed that to concentrate on structure alone obscured the role of the individual; that individual divergences and social change were more interesting than narrow descriptions of collective behavior and culture. His humanism, his warm understanding of the people of Tikopia and his obvious affection for some of them (Firth 1960) make his ethnography unusual at a time when much British anthropology aspired to generalized scientific detachment. It was said of Firth that he made his exotic informants both human and comprehensible and that five centuries of European colonial condescension were expunged in Firth's insistence on Polynesian rationality.

The importance he placed on individuals and social change was the reason for his interest in social organization rather than social structure. Social structure he saw as the major patterns of existing social relations that constrained the possibilities of future interactions. Social organization, by contrast, was the constant process of responses to fresh situations by adopting appropriate strategies. The study of social organization reveals how people make decisions or accept responsibility expected of them by virtue of their position in the social system. This emphasis on the patterns *of* observable human behavior rather than the underlying patterns *for* behavior was paradigmatically the difference between British social anthropology and American cultural anthropology and the basis of Murdock's charge of old-fashioned sociology (Firth 1954).

Firth's fieldwork in Tikopia in 1928–29 and subsequent visits in 1952 and 1966 produced a corpus of work that is probably unrivalled as an ethnographic record of a society. In addition to *We, the Tikopia*, his major works about the island include discussions of spiritual beliefs and practices in *The Work of the Gods in Tikopia* (1940, 1967), *Tikopia Ritual and Belief* (1967), and *Rank and Religion in Tikopia* (1970); change in *Social Change in Tikopia* (1959); language in *Taranga fakatikopia ma Taranga Fakainglisi: Tikopia-English Dictionary* (1985); and songs and stories in *History and Traditions of Tikopia* (1961) and *Tikopia Songs* (1991). He also wrote numerous articles about material culture, kinship, dreams, and authority structures as well as economic analyses of everyday life (notably in *Primitive Polynesian Economy*, 1939).

After his first period of fieldwork in Tikopia Firth became Acting Professor at Sydney University 1930–32 after which he returned to London School of Economics (LSE) where he became a lecturer

(1932–35), Reader in 1935 and Professor in 1944, inheriting Malinowski's position. He remained there with brief interruptions until his retirement in 1968. Social anthropology was not recognized as a separate discipline in the earlier part of the twentieth century, and Firth worked to change this perception as one of the founder members of the Association of Social Anthropologists, inaugurated in 1946. He was also associated with a distinguished group of anthropologists who trained at LSE in the years before and after World War II: **Sir Edward Evans-Pritchard**, **Meyer Fortes**, Audrey Richards as well as **Sir Edmund Leach**. Under Firth's aegis, important research projects were carried out in East Africa, South America, Oceania, southern Europe, Malaysia, and Japan. He also trained people from related disciplines, such as Ernest Gellner and Percy Cohen.

His own field research continued in 1939 and 1940 when Raymond and his wife, Rosemary, also an anthropologist, worked in what was then Malaya on the economy of a fishing village. This resulted in *Malay Fishermen: Their Peasant Economy* (1946) while Rosemary Firth published a book on Malay household economy. During the war years Firth served with the Naval Intelligence Division at the Admiralty, writing Pacific Island handbooks until 1944. In the following year he was involved in setting up the Colonial Social Science Research Council. Firth later went on to show the value of the anthropological approach in studying the kinship patterns of both the working and middle classes in London.

By the 1970s there was a crisis in anthropology, to use Adam Kuper's term – feminism and a postcolonial world required a new anthropology. Firth by this time was retired but he continued to write and contributed to seminars in many parts of the world. Staff and students remember his enthusiastic guidance. Maurice Bloch in his *Guardian* obituary (2002) remembers Sir Raymond at the age of ninety:

> talking animatedly with young graduate students about to go off on their first fieldwork. His eyes twinkled, his body danced with the stimulation of the conversation; he would listen, comment, criticise, advise and suggest further avenues of investigation and further reading.

Ortiz recalled that 'Firth rejected and continued to eschew sloppily constructed arguments, thoughtless use of terms and catch phrases, analogical thinking, and speculative generalizations that had no evidential underpinning' (2004: 130). The core of his practice and belief as an anthropologist – that the variation in individual knowledge is central to both social organization and to social change – obviously remained undiminished to the end and his pragmatic humanism suffused everything he did.

Sir Raymond Firth's influence on British social anthropology has been immense through both his writings and the effect he had on his many students. His contributions were recognized in a knighthood bestowed in 1973, and his appointment as a Companion of the New Zealand Order of Merit in 2001. In 2002 the British Academy announced that it was awarding him the first Leverhulme medal to be given to scholars of exceptional distinction in recognition of his 'outstanding and internationally acknowledged contributions to 20th century anthropology.' Raymond Firth died in 2002, a month before his 101st birthday.

Selected readings

Bloch, M. (2002) 'Obituary, Sir Raymond Firth,' the *Guardian*, February 26.

Firth, R. (1936) *We, the Tikopia*, London: George Allen and Unwin.

——(1954) 'Social organisation and social change,' *Man* 1(84): 1–20.

——(1957) 'Introduction: Malinowski as Scientist and as Man,' in *Man and Culture: An Evaluation of the Work of Malinowski*, R. Firth (ed.), pp. 1–14, London: Routledge and Kegan Paul.

——(1960) 'Pa Fenuatara, A Polynesian Aristocrat,' in *In The Company of Man: Twenty Portraits by Anthropologists*, J. B. Casagrande (ed.), pp. 1–40, New York: Harper.

Husmann, R., Loizos, P., and Sperschneider, W. (1993) *Firth on Firth: Reflections of an Anthropologist* (video), Gottingen: IWF.

Kuper, A. (1997 [1973]) *Anthropology and Anthropologists: The Modern British School*, London: Routledge.

Ortiz, S. (2004) *Sir Raymond Firth*, Proceedings of the American Philosophical Society, 148(1) (March): 130.

JUDITH MACDONALD

MEYER FORTES (1906–83)

Described by many as 'oracular,' but modestly referring to himself as a journeyman, Meyer Fortes was born in the rural Cape Colony, the son of impoverished East European Jewish immigrants. He was part of a remarkable generation of South African anthropologists, which included Isaac Schapera, **Max Gluckman**, Hilda Kuper, and

Monica Wilson. Along with Schapera he attended the University of Cape Town where he majored in English and was awarded a scholarship to pursue a doctorate in psychology at the London School of Economics, duly completed in 1930 under J. C. Flugel.

While doing post-doctoral research he was invited to **Bronislaw Malinowski**'s famous seminar. Malinowski's patronage resulted in Fortes obtaining one of the first International Institute for African Languages and Cultures fellowships in 1932 to undertake research in the more isolated north of the erstwhile Gold Coast (now Ghana) among the Tallensi from 1934 to 1938. Part of a five-year plan of research funded by the Rockefeller Foundation, his fieldwork focused on understanding 'the factors of cohesion in original African society, the ways in which these are affected by new influences, tendencies towards new groupings.' Fortes was accompanied by his first wife, Sonia Donen (deceased 1956) who jointly authored several papers on this fieldwork. His key mentors were **Raymond Firth**, whose ideas about kinship were to prove important, and Charles Gabriel Seligman. During this period he was also strongly influenced by **E. E. Evans–Pritchard** and **A. R. Radcliffe–Brown**, and soon fell out with Malinowski, who he felt was a biological reductionist, and whom he later regarded as simply practicing 'higher journalism.' Nevertheless, Fortes agreed with Malinowski that sustained fieldwork was essential for social anthropology.

Upon his return to Britain, Fortes taught briefly at the London School of Economics before taking up a Lectureship at Oxford. Here he co-edited *African Political Systems* (1940) with Evans-Pritchard, a book that became paradigm-shaping in political anthropology by emphasizing the Durkheimian principles of balanced opposition and segmentation. During the Second World War Fortes was involved in intelligence work in West Africa and from 1944–46 was head of the Sociology Department of the short-lived West African Institute in Ghana; during that time he carried out the Ashanti Survey. Fortes returned to work with Radcliffe-Brown, Evans-Pritchard, and Gluckman as a Reader in Sociology at Oxford from 1946 to 1950 in the new Institute of Social Anthropology, created in an effort to counteract the dominance of the London School of Economics. In 1950 he was called to the William Wise Chair of Social Anthropology at Cambridge where he remained until his retirement. Fortes traveled extensively, including a second spell of fieldwork among the Tallensi in 1963 with his second wife, Doris Mayer, and continued to lecture and write until his death in 1983.

With the presence of Fortes and colleagues such as **Edmund Leach**, with whom he had a difficult relationship, and his former student **Jack Goody**, Cambridge became a major center for social anthropology. Among his other students who became prominent anthropologists were **Marilyn Strathern**, Andrew Strathern, Adam Kuper, Peter Lawrence, Derek Freeman, and Alfred Gell. Not only did Fortes believe that kinship was important, he also practiced it in the way in which he created and adopted numerous classificatory kin, especially among his students. In addition, Fortes was very active in the profession and professionalization of anthropology, serving as President of the Royal Anthropological Institute and acting as one of the prime movers in the establishment of the Association for Social Anthropologists (ASA), the organization for anthropological professionals. While he served on the council of the International African Institute, Fortes never regarded himself as an Africanist.

Fluent in Talni, Fortes impressed with his thorough fieldwork that focused initially on 'family systems,' an interest derived from his psychology background. Kinship, he found, was the pervasive organizational principle, and Fortes became especially concerned about intergenerational conflict and co-option. The importance of kinship connections led to considerations of how they influenced and were embedded in marriage and residence patterns. At the same time, having commenced fieldwork during the 'dry season,' Fortes was acutely conscious of how precarious subsistence was and how stresses emerging from this were dealt with through magic and belief, which along with kinship, lineage, and politico-judicial relations were crucial for the regulation of Tallensi life.

Proud of what he called 'the monographic method,' Fortes argued that close empirical research that detailed close description of particular material could lead to insights of wider relevance. A self-described 'unreconstructed positivist empiricist' Fortes believed that 'social reality' existed independent of the fieldworker's awareness and could be verified by repeated field observations. Fieldwork, he felt, was the sine qua non for testing theory and making new discoveries. Fortes developed what became known as the structural approach and emphasized the distinction first made by Radcliffe-Brown between society (observable interactions) and culture (the realm of meaning that could only be inferred).

This approach was essential for the development of theory that emerged out of a process that combined ethnography with comparative analysis. His first book, *The Dynamics of Clanship among the Tallensi* (1945), is difficult to read because its close-knit arguments are not reducible to a few generalizations, as Fortes struggled to deal with the particularism of social life as social order was created. Through the sensitive use of language he tried to describe the complexities of the lives of real people in real places. Fortes always distinguished between the fieldworker's view and those of the natives – later labeled the etic versus emic distinction in anthropology. His sequel, *The Web of Kinship among the Tallensi* (1949), is seen by many as his finest ethnography and demonstrated, in addition to his linguistic fluency, his considerable statistical skills (developed by studying with Karl Pearson during his psychology days) as he demonstrated how statistically, and in terms of networks, kinship was life.

Though Fortes later also did fieldwork among the Ashanti, his Tallensi experience was pivotal and he continuously drew on his rich and nuanced understanding of this society to consider wider theoretical and comparative implications. Fortes's initial central concern was kinship and he spent much time developing theories about its role in a number of publications in later life, such as *Kinship and the Social Order* (1969) and *Rules and the Emergence of Society* (1983). In this latter publication his central concern was the social constraints on individual behavior. Human society, he argued, was only made possible by the emergence of the capacity to make, enforce, and break rules (1983: 6) in which 'prescriptive altruism,' generated in the mother–child bond, created the obligation of sharing and was fundamental to kinship which was again essential to social order. There was not, in fact, unanimity on the kinship front as relations were rife with contradictions derived largely from male and female roles and the contradictory principles of descent and filiation. While there were frequent splits or fissions, these did not destroy the overall unity, even though families frequently split over intergenerational rivalry about property and status. The distinction between descent and filiation later gave rise to two different modes of analysis – descent (as largely practiced by Fortes and his followers), and alliance theorists (personified by **Claude Lévi-Strauss** and **Rodney Needham**). The descent theorists argued that the study of kinship should focus on descent groups, constituted by their corporateness as a jural entity resulting from genealogical connections and bound together by consanguineals (people of the same blood). The alliance theorists saw relationships between groups constituted through exchanges, primarily of women as wives between groups of affines, as a vital element in kinship studies. Fortes noted that in some patrilineal societies in West Africa there was a secondary jural tie to an individual's mother and some of her patrikin. He viewed this tie, which he called 'complementary filiation,' as the product of notions of descent rather than the consequence of an in-law relationship between two kin groups.

Kinship, for Fortes, was 'a thing in itself.' Its inner logic derived from familial relationships developed under an 'axiom of amity,' but it cannot be inferred through ecological or economic reductionism because even 'self-interest' is based on conferred status. He believed that kinship terms combined to create categories of people and that these categories were generated by elemental relationships of parenthood, siblingship, and marriage. Kinship arose from the fact that women gave birth to children and, inasmuch as it had irreducible structural properties (verified by repeated observation), it was used to channel and promote altruism often in opposition to the realities of politics and economy that were also structurally specific. Social order emerged, in Fortes's view, as a balance between two analytically distinct orders: political and domestic or familial. In the latter rights and duties were maintained through personal trust and obligations derived from kinship. These were ego-centered in contrast to the former, which were often ancestor-oriented groups in which actual kinship ties were not necessarily demonstrated. This was the corporate lineage, an ideally perpetual juristic 'person' that had certain property and other religious and political rights residing in it. Other observers sometimes simplistically referred to this as 'communal property.' The politico-jural domain consisted of externally imposed rights and duties derived from the 'total society.' In practice though, he conceded, these two domains were virtually indistinguishable. Kinship was paramount and its impact was felt in all aspects of social life. What made this conceptualization unique was its ability to deal with change. It was a diachronic rather than a static view and owes its power largely to the use of 'the Development Cycle' to understand the transformations of domestic groups.

Fortes's classic *Oedipus and Job in West African Religion* (1959) is a model of detailed comparative method spanning a conjacent region. In this book belief is seen as primarily a mode of action or living within three contexts: situation, personal history, and social relationships. Distinguishing these contexts allowed him to emphasize the problems all humans face of biological growth and decline and the tensions which emerge in connection with these changes when they rub against social contingencies. He showed how such conflicts are dealt with in the region and how systems of belief and personhood have a built-in dialectic: they promote conflict while at the same time being capable of muting but never resolving it. Fortes examined interpretive decisions and how they were made during crisis moments. In this analysis he invoked psychoanalytic theory in understanding how biological processes of growth were managed.

Among the Tallensi this led to father–son conflicts that were dealt with by projecting them upon their ancestors.

Fortes's South African background, his personal experience of racial discrimination and economic hardship, profoundly shaped his approach. In his inaugural lecture at Cambridge he argued that anthropology was 'indispensable for coming to decisions about our own political and ethical values ... and for understanding the climate of our time.' It was an important tool in the fight:

> against obscurantism and the perversion of knowledge (like racism). ... there is not a shred of anthropological evidence to justify race discrimination. It is the duty of anthropology to proclaim this truth and to continue dispassionately to investigate the biological and social qualities of human groups without regard to race privilege.

Larger social entities such as colonial society were also subject to Fortes's critical eye. Taking a juridico/jural approach to norms and roles he extended the notion of 'plural societies,' an idea originally developed by his friend J. S. Furnivall. In these societies people mixed but did not combine. They were locked into a situation of economic interdependence (structure) brought about by the desire for private gain but balanced by social norms (culture). Fortes presciently concluded that the major problem was that of micro-nationalism and not even structural economic integration would abet this. What was needed was a habit of thinking about and categorizing people of different cultures as individual persons, not as representatives of designated groups (Fortes 1970).

Selected readings

Fortes, M. (1945) *The Dynamics of Clanship among the Tallensi*, London: Oxford University Press.

——(1949) *The Web of Kinship among the Tallensi*, London: Oxford University Press.

——(1953) *Social Anthropology at Cambridge since 1900: an Inaugural Lecture*, Cambridge: Cambridge University Press.

——(1959) *Oedipus and Job in West African Religions*, Cambridge: Cambridge University Press.

——(1969) *Kinship and the Social Order: the Legacy of Lewis Henry Morgan*, Chicago: Aldine.

——(1970) *The Plural Society in Africa*, The 1968 Alfred and Winifred Hoernlé Lecture, Johnnesburg: South African Institute of Race Relations.

——(1978) 'An Anthropologist's Apprenticeship,' *Annual Review of Anthropology* 7: 1–30.
——(1983) *Rules and the Emergence of Society*, London: Royal Anthropological Institute.
Fortes, M. and Evans-Pritchard, E. E. (eds.) (1940) *African Political Systems*, London: Oxford University Press.

ROBERT GORDON

CLIFFORD GEERTZ (1926–2006)

With the death of Clifford Geertz the academy lost one of its most prominent thinkers of the latter part of the twentieth century. For 50 years Geertz's writings had a vital impact on how the subject matter of culture, society, and meaning changed and developed through many disciplines.

Born in San Francisco, Geertz attended Antioch College in Ohio, graduating in philosophy in 1950. He finished his doctorate in Anthropology at Harvard's Department of Social Relations (1956), where he was immersed in Parsonian STRUCTURAL-FUNCTIONALISM. Geertz taught at the University of California/Berkeley (1958–60), at the University of Chicago (1960–70), and then joined the Institute for Advanced Study at Princeton as the first Professor of Social Science. He did fieldwork for various lengths of time in Indonesia, focusing on Java and Bali, and from 1963 to 1986 also worked at different intervals in Morocco.

Most of his writings situate theory or better, interpretation, within a dominant ethnographic context. *The Religion of Java* (1960) and *Agricultural Involution* (1963a) were his early key works and even today retain their relevance. His initial writings were heavily influenced by the Weberian side of the paradigm developed by the Harvard sociologist Talcott Parsons. Geertz's writings in the 1960s relied on Max Weber but subsequently they also increasingly differed in significant ways. The monolithic and essentializing aspect of the Weberian paradigm as in *The Religion of China* or *The Religion of India* did not play out for Islam, and Geertz realized this. Indeed, he apparently wanted the title of the religion volume to be *The Religions of Java*, while the publisher insisted on the singular to follow the titles of Weber's other works on religion in China, India, and Judaism. Geertz increasingly attempted to move away from Weber's writings, especially Weber's depiction of Islam as a consistent and unified entity. This distancing from Weber was due to Geertz's

72

increasing RELATIVISM and particularism. His analysis of Islam in Indonesia, especially Java, was pivotal for many years, but younger scholars, all supported by Geertz, eventually moved in various directions.

From the early 1970s, Geertz's position became more relativistic and particularistic. The relativism was filtered through German-Romantic thought primarily and was strongly influenced by Johann Wolfgang Goethe's ideas and writings on elective affinities, ideas which influenced Weber. Goethe described the processes by which social beings become associated with each other in an elaborate metaphor derived from the notion of 'affinities' in the chemistry of his time. Weber described the 'elective affinity' between the Protestant work ethic and the rise of capitalism, a relationship that is both unconscious and unintended, but nonetheless coherent.

For Geertz the particularist, terms and concepts with a capital, such as Economy and Kinship, were to be rejected or used with extreme caution. Something like Religion with a capital R embraced a number of features and meanings that might be highly variable and that variability is lost or minimized by the over-arching label or categorical designation. This position is also applicable to the concept of Culture. His interests were directed toward cultures in the plural.

After the 1950s, Geertz was one of the few writers on Islam who took the religion and its scriptural texts seriously in their own right, something that could not be converted into something else. Most social scientists then writing in the mode of development and modernity, especially in new nations and the 'Third World,' used titles like 'Education and Islam' and cast Islam as a dependent variable and thus it never enjoyed primary consideration or treatment; it was seen as an ancillary, dependent, and passive social force. Moreover, Geertz realized the shortcomings of his early work on Islamic Java and it was to his credit that a whole generation of younger scholars expanded on the textual and scriptural basis of Islam and how it co-varied with social differentiations in Javanese society.

From the early 1970s, Geertz's ethnographic analysis moves toward what I call 'cultural portraits.' The idea of Culture and cultures is similar to that in **Ruth Benedict's** work, minus her psychological characterizations. At the same time, Geertz jettisoned the formal model of society and culture implemented in the (Harvard-based) Parsonian model based on social needs and corresponding institutions, but maintained a vigorous interest in the 'informal processes of everyday life' that perpetually shape and reshape culture. Cultural portraits differed between Java and Bali and the differences might reflect culture and ideology or belief and action – but as with any portrait in art, literature, or music, the interpretation is made by the viewer or by the reader. In the writing of cultural portraits, Geertz was markedly dubious of generalized cultural theories that were universal or causal and he was always wary of entering a domain of theory that he found adverse. Reading his descriptions of Bali and Java, it is critical to note the virtual absence of any analysis of class either in the cultural description or the ideological portrait.

It is imperative to realize that Geertz always understands ideology as a cultural system, thus locating it squarely in the realm of culture. But at the same time, ideology is understood as a special variant of cultural trends. Balinese culture is described and set forth as a fundamental ethos, radiating both vertically and horizontally throughout all levels of Balinese society. However, the cultural portrait of Java is concerned primarily with ideology and Islam, and thus one must ask what it is about each local ethos that is Javanese and/or Islamic.

The distinction between ideology and culture comes in many forms. Bali is conceptualized as more culturally homogeneous in comparison to Java, which is portrayed as more diverse and heterogeneous. In the Balinese context, symbolic structures and ethos are interpreted as what I term ballast, in that they seldom are utilized as a sense of power and control over various segments of society. Cultural systems in Java are always expressions of the political and social dynamics and the kinds of stratifications that exist, and again the concept of ethos is differentiated according to social category. Geertz describes *abangan*, rural people who combine Islam with folk religion, *santri*, pious Muslims living mainly in the towns, and *priyayi*, bureaucratic elites. Thus in Java, we have a portrait that is far more 'post-traditional,' emphasizing the contestation among and between rival varieties of Javanese religion. In contrast, the model of Bali was far more conventional and unitary.

In his rejection of universal theories from Marxism to STRUCTURALISM, and in his treatment of the idea of culture in terms of its particularisms, Geertz contemplated the many ways in which humans differ from one another. In many of his early general essays, Geertz asks a critical question, namely why and how have humans invested so much in the particular? Overall, Geertz's approach is not a denial of the real existence of the world, but a means of getting at what is 'in' the world. Within this approach, culture, the self, and reflexive consciousness are crucial to the re-constitution of the world.

The task, then, is to explore cultural being. The aim is therefore the discovery and understanding of the features or principles that order and define the world for Balinese.

Apart from *Agricultural Involution* Geertz's writings moved in essentially humanistic directions. Thus the interest in explanation became almost mute. Within this tradition, description and explanation are essentially compounded. Thus explanation was not an issue; it was solely based on the depth and detail of the description. Description that was detailed, heavily documented, and ethnographically rigorous stood as the explanation. In short, culture is there and it describes and explains itself.

Some argue that Geertz gave up on social science explanations for cultural explanations or cultural portraits. But for Geertz, the real difference was that, unlike mainstream social science, he recognized the cultural contingency of his own position although he might not have quite resolved the relationship between explanation and interpretation. He saw them not as opposed, but as premised on different criteria of critical self-awareness.

The Benedictian cultural position solidified in *Islam Observed* (1968) and in 2005 he noted that his work on Islam needed to be coupled with textually oriented studies of Qur'anic, Hadith, and Shari'a traditions if one were to grasp the role of 'scripturalism' in nationalist politics. Bali posed a different challenge. Here the Dutch tradition had utilized structural models for understanding the complexity of Bali. The internal complexity of Bali was pivotal to both Dutch scholarship and the writings of Geertz and his first wife, Hildred Geertz. Themes such as stasis appear in virtually all of their descriptions. Stasis is not stationary, it works back on itself and in Bali stasis pervades most of the cultural, aesthetic, and philosophical life and cannot be reduced to any single factor. The best example of stasis and involution is Balinese *teknonymy* which is pervasive throughout the Balinese culture. The term refers to a complexity of relationships and to a form of naming which interconnects all relatives in a combination of ways – a married adult might be referred to as 'father of X,' his first child. Teknonymy is interpreted as a cultural paradigm creating and enhancing ongoing complexities and establishing new cultural connections that bear its stamp.

In *Negara* (1980) Geertz argues that concepts like power need to be re-thought from the top to the bottom using a center/periphery model. State power was also partly and possibly primarily symbolic and must be interpreted within the context of Balinese symbolism.

One of the lasting influences of Geertz's scholarship relates to the humanities in general and history in particular. By the 1970s, many fields in the humanities turned to anthropology and the idea of culture. Philosophers and linguists were especially interested in the culture concept and how systems of meaning were part of various discourses. At the same time, some social scientists found theoretical connections with the biological sciences and models of rational choice theory. As Geertz noted it was a time of 'blurred genres,' but Geertz's own interest was in a history that he perceived as essentially relativistic. Furthermore, history as he saw it in its various forms of significance and interpretation was based on empiricism, not embedded or based on abstractions or on theories which he labeled 'bootless.' Moreover, 'Anthropology gets the tableau, History gets the drama; Anthropology the forms, History the causes' (Geertz 2000: 124).

According to Geertz, textual tactics allow scholars to move from the local and marginal to broad issues, such as how the power of meaning is created through the panorama of political theology. Here the role of symbolic forms and forces are critical to understanding Bali as a cultural portrait, and the parallels with medieval European divine kingship and funerary cremation may be revealed by tacking back and forth. Anthropologists seek to find out how things fit together, historians venture into how things are brought forth.

Geertz's adherence to history had much to do with history's relativistic foundations and provided him with a means of not having to address any theory in social anthropology. The only larger 'ism' that Geertz would accept was that of relativism, but even relativism became problematic since it was compounded into various versions of POSTMODERNISM. That is why Geertz is better described as particularist than relativist and 'labeled' himself an anti-anti-relativist. Interestingly, historians generally read Geertz as a highly theoretical thinker. His move to history starts early and, by the late 1960s, anthropological theory hardly comes into his work. 'Thick description' and 'webs of meaning,' his most famous coinages, are hardly theory. He rejected global theories like structuralism, Marxism, and cultural Marxism.

Geertz wrote with conviction that explanation and interpretation were the same; thus the move to history was a safe departure. Yet relativism and particularism were always the critical foundations to his thinking, thus explaining the gradual and emerging departure from Weber and Parsons. And postmodernism was only a by-product of these positions and not of his making. These issues are further explored in Yengoyan (2009).

Selected readings

Geertz, C. (1960) *The Religion of Java*, Glencoe, IL: The Free Press.

——(1963a) *Agricultural Involution, The Processes of Ecological Change in Indonesia*, Berkeley: University of California Press.

——(1963b) *Peddlers and Princes*, Chicago: University of Chicago Press.

——(1968) *Islam Observed: Religious Development in Morocco and Indonesia*, New Haven, CT: Yale University Press.

——(1973) *The Interpretation of Cultures: Selected Essays*, New York: Basic Books.

——(1980) *Negara: The Theatre State in Nineteenth Century Bali*, Princeton, NJ: Princeton University Press.

——(1983) *Local Knowledge: Further Essays in Interpretive Anthropology*, New York. Basic Books.

——(1988) *Works and Lives: The Anthropologist as Author*, Stanford, CA: Stanford University Press.

——(1995) *After the Fact: Two Countries, Four Decades, One Anthropologist*, Cambridge, MA: Harvard University Press.

——(2000) *Available Light: Anthropological Reflections on Philosophical Topics*, Princeton, NJ: Princeton University Press.

Ortner, S. B. (ed.) (1999) *The Fate of 'Culture': Geertz and Beyond*, Berkeley: University of California Press.

Shweder, R., and. Good, B. (eds.) (2005) *Clifford Geertz by His Colleagues*, Chicago: University of Chicago Press.

Yengoyan, A. (2009) 'Clifford Geertz, Cultural Portraits and Southeast Asia,' *Journal of Asian Studies*, 68(4): 1215–30.

ARAM YENGOYAN

MAX GLUCKMAN (1911–75)

Gluckman made significant and lasting contributions to social, legal, and political anthropology. As a researcher in South Africa and British Central Africa in the late 1930s and 1940s he, along with his colleagues, initiated the critical study of colonialism, racial segregation, urbanization, industrialization, wage labor, and comparative law, and sought to push anthropology beyond STRUCTURAL-FUNCTIONALISM, at that time a dominant anthropological approach. As director of the Rhodes-Livingstone Institute (RLI) in Northern Rhodesia (present-day Zambia) in the 1940s and later as the founder of the Department of Social Anthropology at Manchester University, Gluckman trained and promoted a generation of talented, influential anthropologists whose work continues to inform anthropological practice today.

Born in Johannesburg, South Africa, Gluckman entered the University of the Witswatersrand in 1927 at a time when the segregationist government had recently enacted legislation to protect 'white civilization' and white employment advantages. Gluckman started out in law but shifted to anthropology after he came into contact with Isaac Schapera and especially Winifred Hoernlé.

After graduation, Gluckman went to Oxford as a Rhodes Scholar. He studied under Robert Marett but was more influenced by **Radcliffe-Brown** and **Evans-Pritchard**. Upon completing his doctorate in 1936, he undertook 14 months research on the Zulu of Natal. At that time, British anthropology was dominated by structural-functionalist studies that depicted African societies as though they were rooted in a timeless pre-colonial present. Gluckman, however, began to assess the impact of colonization and white settlement.

In his influential paper (later published as a book), 'Analysis of a Social Situation in Modern Zululand,' (1958 [1940]), Gluckman introduced an important analytical and methodological approach, later called 'situational analysis,' by which anthropologists described and analyzed specific social events and processes to get at social relations, structures, institutions, alliances, and contradictions in a particular society. Gluckman used the detailed examination of a bridge-opening ceremony to explore structural relations and divisions between South African whites and blacks, underlining that the 'economic integration of Zululand into the South Africa industrial and agricultural system dominates the social structure' (1958: 14–15). Indeed, not only were blacks and whites part of a single social system but despite different beliefs, customs, and modes of life, they had to cooperate and thus adapt to each other in specific, socially determined ways. Economic differentiation also contributed to integration. Themes of conflict and cohesion would characterize his approach to anthropology for the rest of his career.

In 1939, Gluckman had joined the staff of the Rhodes-Livingstone Institute where he began a long-term study of the Lozi of Barotseland, especially of judicial and government institutions and processes. Two years later, he succeeded Godfrey Wilson as director. Both at RLI, and later at Manchester, Gluckman mobilized a group of scholars committed to the elaboration of a new anthropology. Gluckman and his colleagues pursued an ambitious research agenda that sought to investigate the region as a total social system that included whites and Indians, rural and urban areas, peasants and workers. In 1943, he drafted an ambitious seven-year research plan that sought to place ethnographic fieldworkers at strategic locations. A key goal of the plan was to study the impact of labor migration upon different ethnic groups with varying migration rates and the ways in which migration transformed family and kinship, economic life, politics, and religion and magic. RLI researchers studied contemporary problems, conflict and conflict resolution, and the impact of external forces.

Gluckman's Barotse studies sought to explain how dual spheres – one rural and tribal, the other urban and industrial – formed a total social field and how under colonial rule, labor migration and urbanization paradoxically strengthened rather than weakened rural political and kinship systems.

In 1947, Gluckman took up a lectureship at Oxford but left two years later to found the department of social anthropology at Manchester University, which he chaired until 1965. At Manchester, Gluckman trained and worked with a number of prominent anthropologists, many linked to the RLI, including J. A. Barnes, Elizabeth Colson, A. L. Epstein, J. Clyde Mitchell, **Fredrik Barth**, Max Marwick, W. Watson, J. Van Velsen, **F. G. Bailey**, and **Victor Turner**. Later students included Richard Werbner, Bruce Kapferer, Ronald Frankenberg, and Peter Worsley. Many of Gluckman's early students were leftists, like Gluckman, and critical of colonialism. This group's closely connected methodological and theoretical preoccupations, constant exchange of research and ideas in lively weekly seminars, continual cross-citation, and compulsory attendance at Manchester United football games served to forge a distinctive Manchester approach to anthropology. Convinced of the universal applicability of anthropology and the importance of the comparative method, Gluckman insisted that his Africanist fieldworkers study the British equivalent of what they had studied in Africa.

Manchester School members developed structural models of cohesion and contradiction which they explained in relation to social institutions, processes, and events. They explored the relation between village organization and the colonial state, traced connections between peasant villages and industrial towns, and, in towns, between worker organizations and the broader social systems. Methodological and conceptual innovations included the social field, above-mentioned situational analysis, intercalary roles, cross-cutting ties, the dominant cleavage, redressive ritual, and processual change.

Most of the monographs on central African societies produced by Gluckman and his students focused on village structures, conflicts that arose from structural contradictions, and processes of conflict resolution. Most famously, perhaps, they developed the 'extended case method' which entailed following and analyzing a single case through time and space.

Gluckman developed the concepts of intercalary and interhierarchical roles to explore tensions between kinship and political systems. RLI researchers investigated interhierarchical roles of chiefs and district commissioners who faced conflicting pressures as they sought to mediate between sub-hierarchies with competing values and interests. Gluckman also introduced the concept of social fields in order to get at social processes, dynamics, and transformations that were not confined to well defined, bounded, social systems.

Gluckman's students and colleagues produced many important monographs and insights. **Victor Turner** used the concept of social dramas to explore how conflicts brought out underlying stresses within village social structure and later developed new approaches to Ndembu rituals as richly ambiguous ways of communicating statements about social relationships.

Protégés A. L. Epstein and J. Clyde Mitchell wrote pioneering urban ethnographies on labor migration and the structural oppositions of blacks and whites in Central African Copperbelt towns. Mitchell, for example, analyzed the composition of urban dance groups, song lyrics, and daily events to underline the distinct and uneven character of urban ethnicity, while Epstein examined the urban social system composed of multiple sets of social relations and different types of social interactions. For Gluckman and his students, urban ethnicity was not the result of ethnic primordialism or 'traditionalism' but was rather a product of urban individualism, identity construction, and elite politics that arose in the context of colonial capitalism and industrial labor relations.

At Manchester, Gluckman continued to publish actively on both anthropological theory and Barotse jurisprudence. *The Judicial Process among the Barotse* (1967 [1955]) presented detailed accounts, based on fieldwork, of how Barotse judges treated legal cases and disputes. Gluckman then drew out the underlying reasoning and legal principles employed by the judges. Later Gluckman addressed problems of using English terminology and concepts in the analysis of African judicial systems, the possibility of comparing Lozi and Western law, the hotly contested concept of 'the reasonable man,' Lozi use of judicial precedents, and the values held by different judges.

In *Custom and Conflict in Africa*, based on a series of BBC radio lectures, Gluckman drew on both Marxist approaches to conflict and Durkheimian concepts of social solidarity to explore how social tensions, feuds, rebellions, family strife, and ritualized expressions of hostility paradoxically promoted social stability. The central theme was 'how men quarrel in terms of certain of their customary allegiances but are restrained from violence through other conflicting allegiances which are also enjoined on them by custom. ... [and] lead to the reestablishment of social cohesion' (Gluckman 1955: 2). He used the famous example of the Nuer to show how loyalty to agnatic descent groups (who waged feuds against other similar groups) should have led to endless strife. Cross-cutting ties to affines, local communities, and maternal kin, however, facilitated peaceful relations between structurally opposed agnatic groups. Gluckman argued that the political structure of African kingdoms frequently consisted of conflicting groups and rival princes vying for power and influence around the king. Kings were vulnerable because they faced the impossible task of balancing the competing interests of these opposed factions as well as the contradictions between kingly virtues and their own human shortcomings. Ultimately popular princes became despised kings, but when rebellion occurred and a new king took power, faith in the political system and the kingship was renewed. Gluckman also argued that in order to study social change, one had to analyze equilibrium at different times and to show how different moments of equilibrium were related to each other.

Order and Rebellion in Tribal Africa (1963) includes essays written since the mid-1940s in which Gluckman retraced his approaches to the study of social and political equilibrium; process, conflict, and change; how opposing forces operated to maintain social equilibrium; and how competing royal branches struggled for power in ways that often led to the overthrow of kings while nonetheless reaffirming the kingship itself. Importantly he abandoned the organic metaphor of social systems championed by Radcliffe-Brown, who saw social systems as akin to complex living organisms. Instead, Gluckman espoused a more processual approach that emphasized unfolding processes of social tension, conflict, and cohesion. This volume includes essays that explore intercalary and interhierarchical roles to illuminate tensions between kinship and political systems and concludes with a critical assessment of **Malinowski**.

In *The Ideas of Barotse Jurisprudence* (1965), Gluckman expands on his earlier study of Barotse case law and adds considerable comparative material. He provides comparative and conceptual discussions of land tenure; crimes against the state; judicial ideas of contract, injury, responsibility, and debt; and the relation between law and social structure while assessing the strengths and limits of the comparative method itself. In response to critics, he also defends and clarifies his use of the concept of 'reasonable man.'

Gluckman's final book, *Politics, Law, and Ritual in Tribal Society* (1965), written primarily as an undergraduate textbook, provides a systematic introduction to the political systems of 'tribal societies,' by which he meant societies that produced little economic surplus, wealth differentiation, or capital accumulation and where kinship status and multiplex social relationships were predominant. He laid out some of the main contributions of twentieth-century British social anthropology and used African and other ethnographic examples to illustrate property rights and economic activity: political systems, power relations, and strife in African societies; tribal law; ritual, magic, and witchcraft; and stability and change.

In the late 1950s, Gluckman obtained grants that allowed him to develop an ambitious research program in Israel which profoundly shaped Israeli anthropology. He trained anthropologists such as Don Handelman, Emanuel Marx, Shlomo Deshen, and Moshe Shokeid. He died on April 13, 1975 while serving as a visiting professor at Hebrew University in Jerusalem.

The accomplished Australian anthropologist and Gluckman student, Bruce Kapferer (2005: 113), aptly summarizes the ongoing impact of Gluckman's career as a teacher, researcher, mentor, and anthropologist:

> Gluckman is still an inspiration to the many of us who were influenced by his energy and thought. His generosity, humour, and warmth were not only the defining character of the man but a critical dimension of his intelligence, whereby he easily acknowledged the contributions of others and tried to develop his own thought around them. Perhaps of greatest importance was his commitment to the discipline of anthropology and his drive to make it thoroughly critical and alive to the problematics of the contemporary world.

Selected readings

Evens, T. M. S., and Handelman, D. (eds.) (2006) *The Manchester School*, New York: Berghahn.

Gluckman, M. (1940) 'The Kingdom of the Zulu of South Africa,' in *African Political Systems*, M. Fortes and E. E. Evans-Pritchard (eds.), pp. 25–55, Oxford: Oxford University Press.

——(1955) *Custom and Conflict in Africa*, Glencoe, IL: Free Press.

——(1958 [1940]) *Analysis of a Social Situation in Modern Zululand*, Manchester: Manchester University Press.

——(1963) *Order and Rebellion in Tribal Africa*, Glencoe, IL: Free Press.

——(1965) *The Ideas of Barotse Jurisprudence*, New Haven, CT: Yale University Press.

——(1965) *Politics, Law, and Ritual in Tribal Society*, Oxford: Blackwell.

——(1967 [1955]) *The Judicial Process among the Barotse of Northern Rhodesia*, Manchester: Manchester University Press.

Kapferer, B. (2005) 'Situations, Crisis, and the Anthropology of the Concrete: The Contribution of Max Gluckman,' *Social Analysis* 49(3): 85–122.

Werbner, R. (1984) 'The Manchester School in South-Central Africa,' *Annual Review of Anthropology* 13: 157–85.

JOHN M. CINNAMON

SIR JACK GOODY (1919–)

Widely acknowledged as one of the most versatile intellectuals of the late twentieth century, John Rankine (Jack) Goody is the author of work marked by its breathtaking curiosity, encyclopedic range, and erudition that has had an impact way beyond the confines of anthropology. Born in 1919 into a lower–middle-class family, Jack Goody went to St John's College, Cambridge in 1938 to study English Literature. Here he associated with leading left-wing intellectuals such as E. P. Thompson, Eric Hobsbawm, and Raymond Williams. The Second World War saw him captured in North Africa and spending three years in prisoner-of-war camps. While in a prisoner-of-war camp, Goody claims, he discovered two books that inspired him to become an anthropologist: Sir James Frazer's *Golden Bough* and Gordon Childe's *What Happened in History*. Resuming university study in 1946, Goody graduated and transferred to Anthropology and Archaeology where he took the post-graduate diploma and was then briefly involved in Adult Education before returning to study for his doctorate with **Meyer Fortes**. His initial interest was sociology but there was no post-graduate program in it at that time.

Africa was chosen as a field site simply because it was an exciting place to be politically and intellectually, thanks to the work of **Edward Evans-Pritchard**, Fortes, and **Max Gluckman**. In addition, research funding was available from the Colonial Social Science Research Council. Fieldwork was done in northern Ghana, initially in Gonja but later in other areas close by in order to examine comparative differences. Overall Goody spent about four years doing fieldwork in Ghana with his then wife, anthropologist Esther Goody. He strongly believed in linguistic competence and spoke several of the local languages. PARTICIPANT OBSERVATION meant more than local participation; Goody was an active member of Nkrumah's party campaigning for independence. Because his coming of intellectual age occurred as the impact of FUNCTIONALISM was fading and a renewed interest in history was emerging, Goody managed to bridge these two styles and increasingly made his mark in broad-ranging comparative studies involving Asia, Europe, and Africa.

He returned to St John's College, Cambridge and taught there from 1954 to 1984, and to date still remains active, publishing books and articles on a wide array of topics from flowers to how the West stole the history of others. He has received numerous academic honors including election to the British Academy, and recently capped his career with a knighthood. Cambridge in the 1960s and 1970s, with colleagues like Fortes and **Edmund Leach**, was perhaps the foremost center for social anthropology in Great Britain, certainly for those specializing in Africa, and produced a prominent array of alumni including **Marilyn Strathern**, Andrew Strathern, Keith Hart, Caroline Humphrey, Chris Hann, Steve Gudeman, and Jonathan Parry. Changes in the structure of the universities which began in the 1960s eroded the power of the professoriate, and the closing off of fieldwork opportunities profoundly changed the practice of anthropology. Goody's work reflected these changes in the discipline.

Goody's original interests in the field centered, not surprisingly given the importance of **Radcliffe-Brown** and Fortes, on kinship and how this was used, especially in the transmission of inter-generational property rights. His masterpiece, *Death, Property and the Ancestors* (1962), demonstrated impressive knowledge of a wide array of ethnography and literature. Goody utilized all this knowledge in a comparative study of the domestic relations through which people managed their own production and participation in wider society. Because of his materialist bent, he saw that the transmission of property was crucial in such relations. This extended fieldwork formed the point of departure for a number of projects. With

Cambridge colleagues he edited a volume on the development cycle of domestic groups that shifted the focus from functionalism to how institutions change, and the role of ritual and kinship in these processes. He may be said to have pioneered the anthropology of inheritance, and this interest later evolved into two directions. First it led him to explore the comparative history of the family and marriage beyond Africa, in Europe and Asia. Perhaps his most controversial argument here was to show how by changing the rules of inheritance the Roman Catholic Church became the wealthy powerhouse it is today. Secondly, Goody focused on the means of *Production and Reproduction* (1976) and how kinship and productive factors might have contributed to divergent paths of development. He extended his argument using **George Peter Murdock**'s Human Relations Area File and Ethnographic Atlas to see the phenomenon in world historical terms. He tried to show that from the standpoint of family, marriage, and indeed inheritance, which are closely linked, there are fewer differences between the East and West than conventional theories allow and that the advanced societies in both continents displayed what he termed, 'the woman's property complex,' essentially dowry, in contradistinction to African societies which provided bride-wealth. This difference, he argued, resulted from the difference between the advanced plough and irrigation systems of much of Eurasia and the hoe farming in Africa (Goody 1976). This difference would affect the speed of the demographic transition, since the stratification and transmission systems of the former would require some greater calculation of the relation of people to limited resources, whereas in the traditional societies of Africa land was almost a 'free good.'

Goody's thorough fieldwork and language skills enabled him to launch a weighty critique on STRUCTURALISM especially **Lévi-Strauss**'s theory that society is based on marriage conceptualized as an exchange of women. In some societies women held a greater degree of rights than in others.

In seeking to expose the 'structures of the mind,' Lévi-Strauss and the Structuralists projected literate cultures' tendency toward elaborate classification onto simpler societies. In analyzing oral cultures, a more flexible approach had to be employed to take in the inconsistencies in myth making, something made apparent by modern recording technology in the 1960s. Lévi-Strauss's analysis of myth was flawed because it was by design acontextual and atemporal. Myths come in many different versions and change all the time depending on the telling, and the introduction of literacy has profoundly influenced their style and mode of presentation. Literacy abstracts from the flow of speech and renders matters static. It is erroneous to project these characteristics back into oral cultures where things are much freer, a fact which makes elaborate, binary combinations less likely. Lévi-Strauss confused oral and written communication technologies with mentalities constructed according to the imperial binary of primitive and civilized.

The distinction then that Goody makes is between literate and non-literate societies rather than between 'civilized' and 'savage' and this is important for a number of reasons. It provides a focus on a process which is not only comparative but chronological, applicable to the same place at different times. By setting a single process of change as an independent variable, rather than examining multiple changes in a more or less random fashion, one can find correlations that may have powerful comparative utility. This is based on Goody's first hand experience of the effects of schooling in Ghana where he was intrigued by the unintended consequences, such as obsessive discipline and hygiene and a consequential impact on fertility.

Goody has written on a wide array of seemingly diverse topics including food and cooking, flowers, and styles of representation. Whatever the topic, his method has always been one of comparative sociology. He prefers to break down abstract cultural concepts into analytical frameworks that permit empirical investigation across a wide historical range of societies. His concern is with structural similarities referring to the widespread adoption of specific practices. Similar problems generally require similar solutions that are not reached by borrowing or diffusion but generated locally. His vision is one of durable continuities rather than of decisive breaks, at least since the 'urban revolution.'

Generally Goody emphasizes three factors in explaining social structure and socio-cultural change. The first is the development of intensive forms of agriculture that allowed for the accumulation of surplus. The surplus, he felt, explained many aspects of cultural practice from marriage to funerals as well as the great divide between African and Eurasian societies. Second, Goody explained social change in terms of urbanization and growth of bureaucratic institutions that modified or overrode traditional forms of social organization, such as family or tribe, identifying civilization as 'the culture of cities.' Third, Goody attached great weight to the technologies of communication as instruments of psychological and social change. His adult educational experience that led to a lifetime interest in literacy and its role in society is said to have been influential here.

Goody associated the beginnings of writing with the task of managing the surplus (Goody and Watt 1963, reprinted 1968) and argued that the rise of science and philosophy in classical Greece depended importantly on their invention of an efficient writing system. Because these factors could be applied either to any contemporary social system or to systematic changes over time, his work is equally relevant to many disciplines.

What modernity is and its origins, is another question Goody has examined largely by comparing Africa to Euro-Asia. In a number of publications he has challenged the view of the East as 'static' because its institutions prevented modernization, as believed by both Marx and Weber, in accounting for the rise of Western capitalism. Goody challenged the notion of a special Western rationality that enabled 'us' not 'them' to modernize. He focused on 'rational' bookkeeping, which several social and economic historians have seen as intrinsic to capitalism, arguing that there was little difference between East and West in terms of mercantile activity. Other factors alleged to inhibit the East's development, such as the role of the family and forms of labor, have also been greatly exaggerated. This Eurocentrism both fails to explain the current achievements of the East and misunderstands Western history.

Goody emphasizes knowledge systems (like printing and encyclopaedias) that preserve rather than stimulate innovation and technological change. His materialist comparative perspective emphasizes differences rooted in the conditions of production, thus he finds one of the most striking aspects of the contemporary world, globalization, to be the remarkable convergence of aspects of familial relations, especially in the small domestic group. Goody has long resisted the export of Western concepts like 'feudalism' and the attendant suggestion that it provided a unique launching pad for Capitalism. Capitalism – a term which should not be restricted to advanced industrialism – was far more widespread, and was first a product of sowing cotton and the exploitation of silk in China and India. The past, Goody argues, has been conceptualized largely within the framework of western Europe and then imposed on the rest of the world. One consequence of the West's global hegemony has been to impose a universal system of time-space on the rest of the world. Above all, and especially in his most recent work, he has tried to deconstruct the ideology of inevitable and eternal Western hegemony over the peoples of the world. Only **Eric Wolf** in his *Europe and the Peoples Without History* (1982) has attempted world history on a similar scale.

Selected readings

Goody, J. R. (1962) *Death, Property and the Ancestors: A Study of the Mortuary Customs of the LoDagaa of West Africa*, Stanford, CA: Stanford University Press.

——(1972) *The Myth of the Bagre*, Oxford: Oxford University Press.

——(1976) *Production and Reproduction*, Cambridge: Cambridge University Press.

——(1977) *The Domestication of the Savage Mind*, Cambridge: Cambridge University Press.

——(1982) *Cooking, Cuisine and Class: A Study in Comparative Sociology*, Cambridge: Cambridge University Press.

——(1983) *The Development of the Family and Marriage in Europe*, Cambridge: Cambridge University Press.

——(1986) *The Logic of Writing and the Organization of Society*, Cambridge: Cambridge University Press.

——(1993) *The Culture of Flowers*, Cambridge: Cambridge University Press.

——(1996) *The East in the West*, Cambridge: Cambridge University Press.

——(1997) *Representations and Contradictions*, Oxford: Blackwell.

——(2000) *The European Family: A Historico-anthropological Essay*, Oxford: Blackwell.

——(2004) *Islam in Europe*, Cambridge: Polity Press.

——(2007) *The Theft of History*, Cambridge: Cambridge University Press.

Goody, J. (ed) (1968) *Literacy in Traditional Societies*, Cambridge: Cambridge University Press.

Olson, D. R. (ed.) (2006) *Technology, Literacy and the Evolution of Society: Implications of the Work of Jack Goody*, Mahwah, NJ: Lawrence Erlbaum Associates.

ROBERT GORDON

ULF HANNERZ (1942–)

Urban anthropologist. Creolizing pioneer. Transnational cosmopolitan. Fieldworking flaneur. Each of these epithets can be applied to Swedish socio-cultural anthropologist Ulf Hannerz, yet like his work on cities, globalization, and cultural theory more generally, the significance of his contributions to anthropology is to be found in the connective density *between* such descriptions as well as the ideas upon which they are based.

Born in Malmö, Sweden, Hannerz is currently Professor Emeritus in the Department of Social Anthropology at the University of Stockholm. Originally intending to study zoology he serendipitously took a course in Comparative and General Ethnography at the University of Stockholm and was 'hooked.' After earning a BA (1963) and an MA degree in Anthropology at Indiana University in 1966, he continued his studies in the Department of Comparative and General Ethnography at the University of Stockholm, earning his PhD in 1969 with a dissertation based on two years of fieldwork in an African-American community in Washington, DC.

Hannerz has taught at universities around the world as a visiting professor or research fellow including Berkeley, City University of New York, Stanford, Manchester, Oxford, London School of Economics, Tel Aviv, and Tokyo, but his professional home has always been Stockholm, which he joined after earning his doctorate. A leader both as a teacher and scholar, Hannerz is credited with turning a traditional diffusionist, museum-oriented department into a prominent center of social anthropology.

Some of his honors include: memberships in the Royal Swedish Academy of Sciences and the American Academy of Arts and Sciences; honorary fellowships in the Royal Anthropological Institute and in the European Association of Social Anthropologists; the 2000 Lewis Henry Morgan Lectures at the University of Rochester; and an honorary doctorate from Oslo (2005).

In terms of scholarly substance Hannerz has made pioneering contributions in urban anthropology and transnational studies. The significance of Hannerz's work stems from his efforts to combine rigorous anthropological research with creative and critical thought, and eloquently yet persistently questioning the orthodoxies of anthropological methodology and theory. From the very outset, Hannerz's work is also defined by his meticulous efforts to integrate theoretical perspectives within anthropology as well as across the social sciences, an intellectual version of what he would later come to call a 'creolist point of view' (Hannerz 1987) on cultures more generally.

All of these elements were present in his first major work, *Soulside: Inquiries into Ghetto Culture and Community* (2004, first published 1969). Based on his PhD dissertation, *Soulside* was a groundbreaking work in which Hannerz combined his fluency in British social anthropology, particularly an emphasis on the structures of social relationships, with a Chicago School of sociology commitment to urban ethnography to produce a vivid, humane, and powerful account of inner-city, African-American cultures in Washington, DC. In addition to his groundbreaking work as an anthropologist of urban contexts, Hannerz also challenged then-prevailing theories of the 'culture of poverty' as developed, *inter alia*, by **Oscar Lewis**, by offering nuanced ethnographic observations of the cultural diversity and complexity among his informants.

Still committed to ethnographic fieldwork but now with an eye towards 'grasping the totality of clusters of relationships' (Hannerz 1983 [1980]: 15) within an entire urban community, Hannerz turned his attention to Kafanchan in northern Nigeria. However, this shift in field site was largely overshadowed by his analytic and conceptual moves away from ethnographic particulars and towards more meta-theoretical analyses concerned with defining urban anthropology and transnational dynamics more generally. This turn to explicit questions about the broader goals and methods of anthropology culminated in the 1980 publication of *Exploring the City*. In some ways picking up where he left off in *Soulside*, Hannerz was determined to redefine the concerns of anthropology. Pushing against the non-Western, small-scale, largely rural focus in classical anthropology, Hannerz sought to place cities and urban experiences precisely at the center of anthropological research agendas, noting that 'as we think about culture, cities can also be good to think with – at least as good as villages' (Hannerz 1992: 214).

A cornerstone in urban anthropology, *Exploring the City* saw Hannerz not only revisit the city as a field site but also refine his theoretical roots as he masterfully surveyed key contributions from the Chicago School, particularly those of Robert E. Park and Louis Wirth, as well as the efforts of the Manchester School of anthropology in Central Africa. Hannerz also innovated in *Exploring the City* by including the dramaturgically influenced sociology of Erving Goffman, reasoning that the unconventional anthropological topic of cities invited if not required unconventional thinking and perspectives. Deftly wielding this new theoretical amalgam, Hannerz tacked between the structural and organizational concerns of urban sociology and the immediacy and intimacy of anthropological fieldwork imperatives, ultimately identifying what would become a core feature of much of his theoretical writing: the movement of meaning. Rather than calling for urban anthropologists to focus on institutions *or* individuals, networks *or* the roles people inhabit within them, whole cities *or* domains within them, Hannerz insisted that urban anthropology seek to locate and analyze the relationships and movements *between* all of these various spheres.

Kafanchan continued to inspire Hannerz after *Exploring the City*, for as he presciently observed in that book, the urban 'mosaic turns into a kaleidoscope, where the multitude of parts again and again take on new configurations' (Hannerz 1983 [1980]: 15), and it was precisely this view on ceaseless cultural creativity that defined his work throughout the mid 1980s, remaining the vibrant core of his work to this day. Against a backdrop of growing transnational connections mixed with an general anthropological wariness of the threats of cultural imperialism, Hannerz went to 'Nigeria and saw that there was all this wonderful new stuff being born out of global interconnectedness, very appealing new popular music, new folklore in a sense, new stories, new literature, new art forms' (Rantanen 2007: 16). Noting these changes but refusing to see them as decline, decay, or otherwise purely destructive of local cultures, Hannerz insisted that anthropologists need to use their privileged perspectives afforded by PARTICIPANT OBSERVATION *in* as well as *of* these novel cultural processes and formations to analyze what he very early on termed the 'intercontinental traffic in meaning' (Hannerz 1987: 547).

While not the originator of globalization as a social scientific concern, Hannerz is responsible for helping to make globalization a topic of specifically anthropological concern. Perhaps optimistic but certainly not naïve, Hannerz's approach acknowledged the role of corporations and capital but was critical of then-prevailing world-systems approaches to global dynamics because they downplayed or ignored culture in their generally materialist orientations. Further, Hannerz disagreed with the world-systems emphasis on centers and peripheries based on his ethnographically driven vision that 'the world has become one network of social relationships, and between its different regions there is a flow of meanings as well as of people and goods' (Hannerz 1990: 237). Building on his work in Kafanchan, Hannerz, along with others such as **Arjun Appadurai**, helped to define new concepts such as cultural flows and urban swirls for approaching culture as irreducibly and transnationally mobile and in the process, Hannerz recast the central problem for anthropologists: getting a 'grasp of the flux' (Hannerz 1992: 267) that now defined global cultural processes and meanings.

Emerging at a critical time in world history marked by the end of the Cold War and against a backdrop of critical scholarship about New World Orders, Hannerz's work, in particular *Cultural Complexity* (1992), quickly became required reading for scholars of globalization. Filling an important void in the emerging study of global dynamics, Hannerz navigated the terrain between exclusively economic, political, and even cynical readings of globalization. Rather than the pessimism that pervaded the Huntingtonian 'clash of civilizations,' it was Hannerz's refusal to give in to what he termed 'cultural fundamentalism' (Hannerz 1999: 395) (e.g., 'us-vs.-them,' 'the West-vs.-the Rest,' etc.) that encouraged people to understand not only how such stark contrasts are less empirically valid but also how they can be politically dangerous.

So, rather than a civilizational war of all against all or the universal embrace of liberal democracy and free markets, Hannerz offered a vision of global unity and complexity at the same time. Hannerz felt that cultural homogenization, or more pointedly, the 'Westernization' or 'McDonaldization' of the world, gave too much credit to the West and not enough to the rest, as cultural creativity, even under conditions of late capitalism, has never been the exclusive provenance of cultural elites. As an alternative, Hannerz proposed and promoted the importance of ideas such as 'cosmopolitanism' and 'creolization,' the latter becoming one of his most referenced concepts in which the fundamental mixing of local and foreign becomes a paradigm for understanding globalization, with the distinct advantage being:

> [t]he outcome is not predicted. Creolization thought is open-ended; the tendencies toward maturation and saturation are understood as quite possibly going on side-by-side, or interweaving. There may come a time of decreolization, the metropolitan Standard eventually becoming dominant, but a creole culture could also stabilize, or the interplay of center and periphery could go on and on, never settling into a fixed form precisely because of the openness of the global whole ... As the world turns, today's periphery may be tomorrow's center.
>
> (Hannerz 1992: 266)

For all that he has contributed to urban and transnational anthropology Hannerz is not without his critics. As Kapferer (1994) notes, many of these formulations such as flows, flux, and 'a network of perspectives' often remain evocative while lacking empirical grounding. Likewise, Hannerz's formulation of creolization has been queried for extending this dynamic beyond the particular histories and cultures of the Caribbean basin where creolization first emerged (see Mintz 1996). Finally, Hannerz's articulation of cosmopolitanism has been criticized because his cultural rather than political emphases can be seen to elide real relations of power in global flows of not only ideas but also people (see Werbner 2006).

Hannerz's more recent work indicates an awareness of these issues. In *Foreign News* (2004), he returns to his ethnographic roots, but, true to form, he does so with a dynamically multi-sited approach, suggesting that the best way to study cosmopolitanism is to be cosmopolitan. And, in his most recent articles, Hannerz, while refusing to cede the importance of the cultural study of transnational and global processes, increasingly engages political questions of globalization such as the relationship between political-economic privilege and cosmopolitanism as well as the differences between so-called hard and soft power in shaping contemporary transnationalism.

These recent shifts demonstrate Hannerz's basic commitments to openness, not only to a world that keeps unfolding before him but to the ways and means people continuously create and deploy for making sense of this unfolding. Thus, Hannerz's approaches to both globalization and anthropology may be understood to resist most fundamentally any sense or form of closure, with the point being always 'to leave us with more open minds' (Hannerz 1983 [1980]: 245).

Selected readings

Hannerz, U. (1983 [1980]) *Exploring the City: Inquiries toward an Urban Anthropology*, New York: Columbia University Press.
——(1987) 'The World in Creolisation,' *Africa* 5(4): 546–59.
——(1989) 'Notes on the Global Ecumene,' *Public Culture* 1(2): 66–75.
——(1990) 'Cosmopolitans and Locals in World Culture,' *Theory, Culture & Society* 7: 237–51.
——(1992) *Cultural Complexity: Studies in the Social Organization of Meaning*, New York: Columbia University Press.
——(1996) *Transnational Connections: Culture, People, Places*, London: Routledge.
——(1999) 'Reflections on varieties of culturespeak,' *European Journal of Cultural Studies* 2(3): 393–407.
——(2004) *Foreign News: Exploring the World of Foreign Correspondents*, Chicago: University of Chicago Press.
——(2004 [1969]) *Soulside: Inquiries into Ghetto Culture and Community*, Chicago: University of Chicago Press.
——(2008) 'Geocultural Scenarios,' in *Frontiers of Sociology*, P. Hedström and B. Wittrock (eds.), pp. 257–90, Leiden: Brill.
Kapferer, B. (1994) 'Review of *Cultural Complexity*,' *American Anthropologist* 96(2): 460–62.
Mintz, S. (1996) 'Enduring Substances, Trying Theories,' *The Journal of the Royal Anthropological Institute* 2(2) (June): 289–311.

Rantanen, T. (2007) 'A transnational cosmopolitan: an interview with Ulf Hannerz,' *Global Media and Communication* 3(1): 11–27.
Werbner, P. (2006) 'Transnational cosmopolitanism,' *Theory, Culture & Society* 23(2–3): 496–98.

BENJAMIN EASTMAN

MARVIN HARRIS (1927–2001)

Marvin Harris was deservedly one of the most prominent and influential anthropologists of his time. In his elegant, disarmingly straightforward, no nonsense approach to anthropology, he wrote about race, the concept of culture, colonialism, religious rituals, cannibalism, witchcraft, cultural ecology, cultural and biological evolution, and anthropological theory and methods. He tried to explain the sacred cow of India, racial identity in Brazil, war and aggression, food taboos, why the Soviet empire fell apart, the rise of the women's movement, and why things did not work in America. Throughout his distinguished career, in print and in person, Harris was consistently provocative, critical, witty, entertaining, and ready to engage his critics head on in debate. Revered and reviled in anthropological circles, Harris's influence could be discerned in academic journals, defenses and critiques of his work, scholarly meetings, and references cited. His much cited classic, *The Rise of Anthropological Theory* (RAT) has been read by most anthropology graduate students in North America for the past 40 years.

Marvin Harris, born and raised in Brooklyn, New York, did his undergraduate and graduate work at Columbia University, obtaining his PhD in 1953. He spent the next 28 years of his career as a professor of anthropology at Columbia. In 1980 he left Columbia for the University of Florida, where he joined his former teacher and colleague Charles Wagley, serving as a distinguished research professor until his retirement in 2000. Harris had participated in student and faculty protests during the tumultuous Viet Nam War era; he maintained that despite his long service to Columbia, his criticisms and conflicts with the university's administration were never forgotten or forgiven.

Harris conducted fieldwork in Brazil, Ecuador, Mozambique, India, and the United States. In addition to seventeen books, numerous journal articles, talks at most major colleges and universities, distinguished lectures, and his pioneering work using video in ethnographic studies, Harris also wrote for *Natural History*

Magazine, Psychology Today, and the *Sunday New York Times.* He made nationwide appearances debating Edward O. Wilson and appeared on PBS stations to counter Wilson's sociobiology with an approach emphasizing the central nature and importance of culture in human affairs.

Harris considered himself to be a missionary whose goal was to establish his intellectual approach to the field, CULTURAL MATERIALISM, as the predominant method and theory of anthropology. Harris often said that he would speak anywhere he thought he might make converts. Harris could be engaging and invigorating, or abrasive and intimidating, sometimes simultaneously. His intellectual fervor was never dull or pedantic, and his missionary zeal was always evident.

If, as Harris and many others have maintained, the history of anthropological theory is a debate about the meaning and nature of culture, then it cannot be surprising that at the heart of Harris's theoretical approach or strategy of cultural materialism is a core definition of 'culture.' Throughout his extensive writings – with nuanced shifts, amendments, clarifications, and even occasional concessions – Harris's definitions of culture always included two essential elements: ideas and behaviors, with both the product of material processes.

In contrast to what Harris called 'ideational' approaches to culture – including cognitive anthropology, SYMBOLIC ANTHROPOLOGY, STRUCTURALISM, componential analysis, INTERPRETIVE ANTHROPOLOGY, and much if not all of POSTMODERNIST approaches – the strategy of cultural materialism is concerned with both the thought processes of humans and the full range of the behavior engaged in by them.

The strategy of cultural materialism Harris championed is erected on a foundation of the materialism of Marx and Engels, Julian Steward's cultural ecology, and (to a lesser extent) **Leslie White**'s evolutionism. Cultural materialism is a scientific approach to anthropological research that emphasizes sociocultural causality and more specifically, infrastructural causality.

In other words the economy and the environment affect other facets of culture such as religious and political actions and beliefs in predictable ways. Harris treats cultural evolutionism and cultural ecology as 'subcases' of cultural materialism (see 1968: 658). According to Harris, 'The essence of cultural materialism is that it directs attention to the interaction between behavior and environment as mediated by the human organism and its cultural apparatus'

(1968: 659). In laying out the parameters of cultural materialism Harris explains his position on Marx and the dialectic:

> I shall recognize in the writings of Marx and Engels achievements of unparalleled importance for a science of man; but I shall also insist on the error of Marx and Engels's attempt to shackle cultural materialism to the spooks of Hegel's dialectic.
>
> (1968: 5)

Cultural materialism builds on what Harris called a neglected legacy of 'techno-economic and techno-environmental determinism,' which he argues 'has never been consistently applied across the range of phenomena with which anthropologists are familiar' (1968: 5). Less remembered are Harris's claims that the cultural-materialist approach was strengthened in early American anthropology by the broad range of studies carried out in diverse communities, many of them unfamiliar to those schooled in the European tradition, making broadly based comparisons possible and leading to the possibility of formulating causal laws in human history. He cites **Julian Steward**'s article 'Cultural Causality and Law' (1949) as illustrative of this development. Harris suggested that American anthropologists had helped establish a basis for cultural materialism through cultural-ecological interpretations of the findings of New World archaeologists. It is notable that the influence of cultural materialism is strongest today in the subdiscipline of archaeology.

The importance of the methodologies of science to Harris's approach cannot be overemphasized. He railed against 'eclecticism' and other approaches that offered answers to understanding cultural lifestyles such as 'Only God knows,' 'We have always done it that way' (i.e., tradition), or 'Lifestyles are inscrutable.' Harris urged anthropologists to study broad patterns of belief and behavior, not 'random' individual acts. His underlying assumption was that most broad patterns of thought and behavior had rational and practical explanations, and in his major works (1966, 1974, 1977, 1981, 1985, 1987, 1989) he offered explanations for the inscrutable thoughts and behaviors he called 'riddles of culture.' His answers were grounded in the 'practical circumstances' of the human condition, and were to be 'based on ordinary, banal, one might say "vulgar" conditions, needs, and activities ... built up out of guts, sex, energy, wind, rain, and other palpable and ordinary phenomena' (1974: 5). One such riddle was the Hindu sacred cow complex in India. Harris claimed that the Hindu prohibition on cattle slaughter, regardless of indigenous explanations, was best explained by the utility of living cattle as plough animals and suppliers of fuel (dung), and milk, making it essential to preserve them, even during famines.

Additionally, Harris argues that culture often creates in people a kind of 'false consciousness':

> Ignorance, fear, and conflict are the basic elements of everyday consciousness. From these elements, art and politics fashion that collective dreamwork whose function it is to prevent people from understanding what their social life is all about. Everyday consciousness, therefore, cannot explain itself.
>
> (1974: 6)

False consciousness, and the use of ideologies to maintain elite privilege and provide social control, was a major theme throughout Harris's writings, especially as it applied in complex societies such as his own.

Harris made the *emic/etic* distinction – developed by the linguist Kenneth Pike – a major component of his methodology. Extensive debates, literature, and discussions have ensued surrounding these terms, and Harris wrote extensively to clarify, amend, and defend the importance of this distinction. Emics and etics refer to the perspective from which cultural phenomena are interpreted. In the simplest terms, with *emics* the orientation is from the perspective of the participants in cultural events; while with *etics* the orientation is from the perspective of the observers. Etic interpretation is emphasized in cultural materialism because it produces results dependent on the methods of science.

Equally important, controversial, and challenging is Harris's use of the concept of the 'universal pattern' of culture for facilitating cultural comparisons. According to Harris: 'The universal pattern is a set of categories that is comprehensive enough to afford logical and classificatory organization for a range of traits and institutions that can be observed in all cultural systems' (2003: 20, with O. Johnson). This pattern consists of *infrastructure*, *structure*, and *superstructure*, terms that originate with Marx and Engels, and whose meanings remain hotly contested. For Harris, infrastructure consists of 'modes of production' (including technology of subsistence, techno-environmental relationships, ecosystems, work patterns) and 'modes of reproduction' (fertility, natality, mortality, nurturance of infants, demographics, contraception, etc.). Structure consists of 'domestic economy' (family structure, *domestic* division of labor, socialization, enculturation, education, age and gender roles, discipline, hierarchies and sanctions) and 'political economy' (political organizations, division of labor, taxation, political socialization, law and order, class, societal discipline, police, military, war, etc.). Finally, superstructure consists of art, music, dance, literature, advertising, values, meaning, symbols, religious rituals, myths, beliefs, sports, games, hobbies, and science (2003: 21). What is essential to the research strategy of cultural materialism is that it aims 'to explain the probable causes of sociocultural differences and similarities by *giving theoretical priority to infrastructure*' (2003: 23, emphasis added).

Harris's confidence in the scientific method and his belief that cultural materialist explanations (whether or not they accorded with explanations offered by culture bearers) offered the best approach to even the strangest seeming customs, together resulted in his rejection of many other theoretical approaches, including **Boas**ian 'historical particularism,' strong CULTURAL RELATIVISM, cognitive anthropology, STRUCTURAL-FUNCTIONALISM, French and British structuralism, and postmodernism. For Harris these approaches suffered from one or more of the following defects: they rejected infrastructural determinism, advocated emic (ideological) research strategies, were ahistorical, or unscientific. He strongly disapproved of postmodernism and interpretive anthropology (1999).

Marvin Harris's role as a provocateur of controversy knew few bounds. He set off or took part in a number of anthropology's most significant debates. For example, in 1971 his student Jane Ross wrote a seminar (and seminal) paper on the Yanomamo of Venezuela and Brazil in which she suggested that Yanomamo warfare and aggression might result from scarcities, particularly protein scarcities. Thus began the 'great protein debate,' setting Harris and his students against Napoleon Chagnon and his students. In 1977 Michael J. Harner published two articles (based on research previously presented in 1975 to the American Anthropological Association) arguing that human sacrifice among the Aztec was the result of protein shortages, a departure from previous theories of these practices. Harris summarized Harner's findings in *Cannibals and Kings* (1977). Though he was not the originator of the ideas behind these controversies, Harris's publications fanned the flames of the academic firestorms that ensued. Ironically, in both cases, Harris's name became synonymous with the positions that underscored these debates. Not ironically, his name is justly synonymous with cultural materialism, the sweeping theory and research strategy that he did not invent, but worked tirelessly to promote and defend throughout his most illustrious anthropological career.

Selected readings

Harner, M. J. (1975) 'The Material Basis of Aztec Sacrifice,' Paper read at the Annual Meeting of the American Anthropological Association, San Francisco.

——(1977a) 'The Ecological Basis for Aztec Sacrifice,' *American Ethnologist* 4: 117–35.

——(1977b) 'The Enigma of Aztec Sacrifice,' Natural History 86(4): 46–51.

Harris, M. (1966) 'The Cultural Ecology of India's Sacred Cattle,' *Current Anthropology* 7: 51–66.

——(1968) *The Rise of Anthropological Theory*, New York: T. Y. Crowell.

——(1974) *Cows, Pigs, Wars and Witches: The Riddles of Culture*, New York: Random House.

——(1977) *Cannibals and Kings: The Origins of Cultures*, New York: Random House.

——(1979) *Cultural Materialism: The Struggle for a Science of Culture*, New York: Random House.

——(1981) *America Now: The Anthropology of a Changing Culture*, New York: Simon & Schuster. An updated edition was published in 1987 by the same publisher as *Why Nothing Works: The Anthropology of Daily Life.*

——(1985) *Good to Eat: Riddles of Food and Culture*, New York: Simon and Schuster. [Also published as *The Sacred Cow and the Abominable Pig: Riddles of Food and Culture.*]

——(1989) *Our Kind: Who We Are Where We Came from Where We Are Going*, New York: Harper & Row.

——(1999) *Theories of Culture in Postmodern Times*, Walnut Creek, CA: Altamira Press.

Harris, M., with Johnson, Orna (2003) *Cultural Anthropology*, 5th edition, Boston, MA: Allyn and Bacon.

Ross, J. (1971) 'Aggression as Adaptation: The Yanomamo Case,' Mimeographed manuscript, Columbia University.

JEFFREY DAVID EHRENREICH

MELVILLE JEAN HERSKOVITS (1895–1963)

Possessed of a quick grasp of the essentials, an exceptional work ethic, and an appreciation of new ideas, Herskovits was to become a most productive anthropologist, pioneering and making original contributions in several fields in his almost 500 publications that included several major books and textbooks.

Herskovits was born in Ohio. After a brief period in a rabbinical seminary he dropped out to serve in the Great War and then obtained his first degree at the University of Chicago, majoring in history and biology, in 1920. He then briefly worked with Alexander

Goldenweiser before moving to Columbia University to work with **Franz Boas**, obtaining his doctorate there in 1923. Throughout his life he was to claim Boas and the renegade economist, Thorstein Veblen, as major influences on his approaches to anthropology. His library-based dissertation was an attempt to identify Boasian-inspired cultural areas in Africa in which geographical contiguity implied relationships and thus trait diffusion. He identified the so-called 'cattle-complex' areas in East Africa which were characterized by a strong cultural emphasis on bovines as property, food, sources of fuel, objects of exchange, and sacrificial victims. Fifty years later that identification still stands.

Funding sources largely determined his early research priorities. After failing to obtain funding to do fieldwork in Africa he undertook a large biological anthropological study on 'variability under racial crossing,' courtesy of the National Research Council, from 1923–27 which examined Mendelian genetics and 'race crossing' among US Blacks. In this study he realized the importance of social selection and this led to a lifelong interest in the social problems of race and the supposed issues of inheritance of temperament. Apart from teaching at Howard University in 1925 – where he was profoundly influenced by Black intellectuals like Alain Locke and recruited **Zora Neale Hurston**, then a student at Columbia, as a research assistant – he spent his academic career from 1928 at Northwestern University, despite initially feeling isolated there as both a Jew and an anthropologist. Until the end of the Second World War, frequently assisted by his wife, Frances, he focused on New World Blacks, undertaking fieldwork among the 'Bush Negroes' of Surinam (funded privately by Elsie Clews Parsons), Haiti, and Brazil. He also undertook an expedition to West Africa in 1931, concentrating on Dahomey where he spent five months. Given some problems in securing fieldwork funding, Herskovits developed a magpie style of research and collection, ranging from recording music to filming to purchasing artifacts as well as taking copious notes on a wide array of topics. This generalist mode suited him and he became critical of the narrowness of British social anthropology that then dominated Africa. He later referred to himself as a 'dogmatic anti-FUNCTIONALIST.'

This short but intense fieldwork experience allowed Herskovits to appreciate issues concerning comparativism, syncretism, change, and stability as well as ethnohistory, enabling him to argue in his landmark *The Myth of the Negro Past* (1941) that New World Black cultures had strong African roots and that indigenous culture had not been wiped out under the trauma of slavery. Rather there was a cultural continuity, despite the many changes that occurred during and after the period of slavery. Many, including prominent pre-civil rights Afro-American intellectuals, initially remained skeptical of this argument as did Gunnar Myrdal who was supervising the well-funded Carnegie Foundation study of American race relations which resulted in the definitive *American Dilemma*. Myrdal, who was an assimilationist, dismissed Herskovits's work as 'Negro History propaganda' and managed to avoid bringing Herskovits into his project by commissioning *The Myth* as a special publication. It is now accepted that Herskovits legitimized the field of Afro-American anthropology. His diffusionist interest in tracing African-American traditions across the Atlantic was an influential forerunner of contemporary studies of the Black Atlantic.

After the Second World War Herskovits turned his interests increasingly back to Africa: he was responsible for the creation of the first African Studies center in the US and became the first President of the African Studies Association in 1958. In 1961 he was named to the first Chair of African Studies. The role of Area Studies and its major sources of funding – foundation funded and possibly CIA inspired – is seen by some as a precursor to the globalization of anthropology. In the debate about policy in Africa he argued that Africa should follow its own course and not cleave to European models so as to maintain cultural stability while dealing with change. His publications increasingly became problem centered, dealing with broader issues such as education, land tenure, and change. He strove to focus on people and their reactions to the situations they found themselves in.

In terms of anthropological theory Herskovits made notable contributions on several fronts. He popularized the concept of culture, introduced the notions of 'cultural focus' and *enculturation* (the process by which people learn the customs and values of the community in which they are raised), and subtly pointed out the problems of learning with his idea of 'socialized ambivalence.'

His fieldwork brought to the fore questions of culture change, and he worked with Robert Redfield and Ralph Linton on how to operationalize the study of *acculturation*, loosely defined as the modification of the culture of a group or individual as a result of contact with a different culture. In 1938 he published the definitive *Acculturation*, which sought to define the concept and suggest directions for future research, two years after the American Anthropological Association had formally declared that acculturation was not a 'proper' concern for the discipline. Their memorandum on the subject was widely circulated in premier anthropology, sociology, African, and Oceanic journals. His theoretical and intellectual perspective on the discipline are well represented in *Man and his Works* (1948), a 678 page tome later abbreviated as *Cultural Anthropology*, a leading textbook during the 1950s.

Herskovits so much appreciated the worth of each culture he studied that he became a major, if not the leading, proponent of CULTURAL RELATIVISM, the doctrine that cultural practices should be interpreted in terms of the internal logic of the cultures in which they occurred, and was one of the major figures to argue against the American Anthropological Association ratifying the Universal Declaration of Human Rights. After his death, his wife and long-time collaborator, Frances edited a volume that features his views on this topic. This was a position that evolved over time from an earlier universalism to a later particularism and was resolved by the concept of socialized ambivalence.

Consistent with this position, he had little time for applied anthropology, indeed he was uncompromisingly opposed to it. He famously took on **Malinowski**'s plea for practical anthropology by showing how, by enacting Malinowski's recommendations, the anthropologist would serve administrative rather than indigenous purposes. From a long-term perspective he rejected applied anthropology for two main reasons: first, anthropologists would not be able to significantly help indigenes because of the power of the colonial superstructure and, secondly, expediency would lead to a decline in scientific rigor. Anthropologists would be co-opted. At the same time he felt that by being scientifically rigorous anthropology would be of greater value all round and anthropologists would be trusted by all persons concerned. Herskovits argued that problems should be seen from the local point of view and the initiative should come from insiders rather than outsiders. Nevertheless he was willing to discuss 'development,' if only to present a relativistic perspective. This however had the consequence that he consistently overlooked the policy implications of the positions he took. Nevertheless Herskovits was heavily involved in government work during the Second World War, serving as chief consultant for African affairs for the Board of Economic Warfare and in 1960 prepared a major study for the US Senate on African Affairs. At the same time he was also rather politically naïve, visiting South Africa and lecturing at a number of local universities in the 1950s and ignoring the emerging problem of apartheid.

Herskovits maintained a long-time interest in economics, partially inspired by Veblen, and wrote one of the earliest texts on this subject, *The Economic Life of Primitive Peoples* (1940). This book was intended as a bridge between economics and anthropology and worked with universals: fundamental categories all economic systems have in common and the differences in how they are classified. It assumed that maximization (endeavoring to the maximum reward or profit out of one's resources) was a universal principle. Later both sides in the **FORMALIST/SUBSTANTIVIST** debate in economic anthropology were to claim him as theirs. His work on Dahomey markets was to inspire the famous economic historian Karl Polanyi. He also addressed problems of *Economic Transition in Africa* (1964).

So broadly did Herskovits construe culture as 'the man-made part of the human environment' that he was able to develop catholic interests ranging beyond the purview of what cultural anthropologists normally do. So, for example, he collaborated with psychologists to investigate the interplay of psychology and culture, examining *inter alia* Freudian mechanisms in Africa and the New World, and cross-cultural perception of color and form. Enculturation was key for Herskovits: 'it is the instrument whereby the individual adjusts to his [sic] total setting and gains the means for creative expression' (1948: 17). He distinguished *enculturation* – which was the actual process of learning by an individual – from socialization – the abstract statements about learning as a universal process. This emphasis on enculturation led to an interest in education and how learning contributed to stability and change at the same time.

This all-encompassing definition of culture also meant that Herskovits was able to contribute to the appreciation of the aesthetics of art and music to such a degree that he was elected President of the American Folklore Society and his obituary was published in *Ethnomusicology*.

Herskovits was not afraid to take on unpopular causes, and he was one of the first to attack Nazi racial science when in 1928 he dismissed Hans K. Gunther's work as absurd. He wrote extensively in popular journals such as *The Nation* challenging the hegemony of the eugenics viewpoint, and authored several of the key entries in the *International Encyclopedia of the Social Sciences* and the *Encyclopedia Britannica*. At various times he publicly argued for desegregation, supported civil rights and praised the inter-racial unionism of the CIO and Southern Tenant Farmers Union (Gershenkron 2004).

From being a token anthropologist in a sociology department Herskovits went on to build up one of the most prominent anthropology departments, which he founded in 1938. He also served the

American Anthropological Association in a number of positions and edited the *American Anthropologist*. In 1948 he created the first African Studies Program in the US at Northwestern University and in 1957 he helped found, and later became the first President of, the African Studies Association. He also organized the first International Congress of Africanists in 1962. Indeed the most prestigious academic prize in African Studies is named after him. Herskovits was renowned for his loyalty towards his students and his ability to secure them research grants. Northwestern was especially celebrated for Africanist anthropology and includes many prominent alumni such as William Bascom, Jim Fernandez, Igor Kopytoff (who married Herskovits's daughter), Joseph Greenberg, Alan Merriam, Richard Dorson, and Erika Bourguignon. Such was his stature that the journal *Current Anthropology* commissioned a series of impressive papers to honor him and he has been the subject of at least two biographies.

Selected readings

Gershenkron, J. (2004) *Melville J. Herskovits and the Racial Politics of Knowledge*, Lincoln: University of Nebraska Press.
Herskovits, F. S. H. (ed.) with introduction by Campbell, D. T. (1972) *Cultural Relativism: Perspectives in Cultural Pluralism*, New York: Vintage.
Herskovits, M. J. (1928) *The American Negro: A Study in Racial Crossing*, New York: Knopf.
——(1934) *Rebel Destiny, Among the Bush Negroes of Dutch Guiana* (with Frances Herskovits), New York: Whittlesey House.
——(1937) *Life in a Haitian Valley*, New York: Knopf.
——(1937) *Dahomey: an Ancient West African Kingdom*, 2 volumes, New York: J. J. Augustin.
——(1938) *Acculturation*, New York: J.J.Augustin.
——(1940) *The Economic Life of Primitive Peoples*, New York: Knopf.
——(1941) *The Myth of the Negro Past*, New York: Harper.
——(1946) *Trinidad Village* (with Frances Herskovits), New York: Knopf.
——(1948) *Man and his Works*, New York: Knopf.
——(1953) *Franz Boas, the Science of Man in the Making*, New York: Scribners.
——(1962) *The Human Factor in Changing Africa*, New York: Knopf.
Herskovits, M. J. and Bascom, W. (eds.) (1959) *Continuity and Change in African Cultures*, Chicago: University of Chicago Press.
Herskovits, M. J. and Harwitz, M. (eds.) (1964) *Economic Transition in Africa*, Evanston, IL: Northwestern University Press.
Simpson, G. (1973) *Melville Herskovits*, New York: Columbia University Press.

ROBERT GORDON

ZORA NEALE HURSTON (1891–1960)

A pioneer on many fronts in anthropology, Zora Hurston did not achieve due recognition until some years after her death. Some analytical and professional practices which are now standard in the discipline might have been introduced sooner had her contributions been better appreciated. Although her direct 'influence' was limited by non-recognition, her achievements deserve to be celebrated and the effects of their rediscovery documented. Moreover, there are still new things to be learned from following her example, as well as great pleasure to be gained from reading and re-reading her work. In addition to being a female African-American anthropologist at a time when this was a very difficult position to sustain, Hurston experimented with modes of writing which put the anthropologist squarely in the midst of the data. Rosemary Hathaway (Hathaway 2004: 172) says of Hurston that she 'seemed to recognize the fictiveness of ethnography and the ethnographic possibilities of fiction decades before the likes of Bruner, **Clifford Geertz**, and James Clifford.'

Hurston was born in Notasulga, Alabama in 1891, though she frequently altered these facts in accounts of her life. She routinely deducted at least 10 years from her age and implied that she had been born in Eatonville, Florida, where her parents, John and Lucy Hurston, moved shortly after her birth. These and many other details of Hurston's life can be found in the excellent biography *Wrapped in Rainbows: The Life of Zora Neale Hurston* (Boyd 2003). Eatonville was an all-black town in Florida, where schools, churches, stores, and the municipal government were run by African-Americans. Eatonville was the location of Hurston's most famous work, including the opening section of *Mules and Men*, Hurston's innovative collection of Negro folklore from Florida and hoodoo in New Orleans, and her novel, *Their Eyes Were Watching God* (1937), her most famous and acclaimed literary contribution. John Hurston was a carpenter and a preacher, and, so long as her mother was alive, Hurston enjoyed a relatively free and secure childhood, compared to other African-American children of the period. She also was exposed to many genres of folklore: traditional healing, magic and superstition, work songs and spirituals, dances and games, and, most famously, the legends, riddles, and folktales (or 'lies') that were told on porches and verandas. It was these tales Hurston made famous.

Hurston's mother died when Zora was 13, leaving eight children. Zora, the second of two girls, was her father's least favored child, and

105

her position in the household became worse when her father remarried. She was sent to boarding school but had to leave when her family ceased to pay her fees. She began a long period of wandering, spending time as a domestic help to her eldest brother as he began his medical career, dropping out of public sight for some years, traveling as a wardrobe assistant with a Gilbert and Sullivan theater troupe, and finally enrolling at Morgan Academy (a school mostly attended by students from well-off Negro families) in Baltimore in 1917, subtracting 10 years from her age to be eligible for free high school education. After a successful year at Morgan Academy, Hurston moved to Howard University in Washington DC. She supported herself as a waitress at a white men's club and as a manicurist in a black-owned business serving white clients. After her first published story attracted the notice of a leading mentoring figure among black intellectuals, Hurston moved to New York and became part of the 'Harlem Renaissance' of the 1920s, although most of her work did not appear until after the Renaissance ended with the onset of the Depression. Recognized as an emerging writer she made many important contacts, one of whom, Annie Nathan Meyer, helped Hurston enter Barnard College in 1925 on a partial scholarship and become its first black graduate.

Barnard was not easy – Hurston had to juggle her education with paid work to survive. The novelist Fannie Hurst briefly employed Hurston and offered a connection which made Zora socially acceptable to Barnard classmates. Though she had come to Barnard to study literature, Hurston fell under the influence of **Franz Boas** and **Ruth Benedict**. Anthropology provided Hurston with a framework for approaching the 'Negro culture' of the South while stepping at least partially outside to get a better view. For the rest of her life Hurston would alternate and combine the collection and documentation of folklore with the writing of fiction. She sought to record the thriving culture of those referred to as 'the Negro furthest down' at a time when lower-class blacks were widely thought of in terms of culture loss and social problems, even by those who blamed those problems on white oppression. Like **Melville Herskovits**, Hurston affirmed the existence of African survivals in the Western Hemisphere, but also affirmed and recorded vibrant, independent (if hybrid) black cultures in the US South and the Caribbean.

In 1927, Boas secured funding for Hurston to travel south to collect folklore. She traveled through Florida and parts of Alabama and Georgia (accompanied some of the time by Langston Hughes), but found people were often unwilling to provide material, to her and

Boas's disappointment. She did learn valuable lessons on this trip: she developed the nuances of style which would serve her well as a creative writer and she discovered that the cultivated speech which she had acquired at Barnard was a bar to attracting the confidence of rural African-Americans. From that point on, her speech and self-presentation were always 'unabashedly black and unapologetically southern' (Boyd 2003: 142).

Language was an important focus of Hurston's work, whether she was writing fiction or ethnography. In her novels and folklore collections Hurston juxtaposed southern black dialect with the 'educated' English of her authorial voice, and in *Moses Man of the Mountain* (1939), she told the entire story of Exodus in what would today be called Ebonics, transforming Moses into a figure akin to culture heroes like 'High John de Conquer' whose exploits in turning the tables on slave owners figured prominently in Hurston's other work, notably *Mules and Men* (1935).

Returning to New York, Hurston was introduced to Charlotte Osgood Mason, a wealthy widow and amateur anthropologist who funded a number of black cultural endeavors. Mason believed that American Indians and Negroes retained a 'primitiveness' that was more spiritual and more in tune with nature than white culture. She helped fund Hurston's field trips and living expenses until 1932, though she demanded considerable obsequiousness. Hurston has been criticized by some African-American writers for adopting a deferential attitude towards her sponsors like Mason and Boas. It has been suggested, however, that in *Mules and Men*, Hurston uses the veiled language of African-American 'signifying' to settle some scores with her benefactors. *Mules and Men* certainly offers strong commentary within the framework of a well-told, personalized story.

Mules and Men presents data collected in three locations: Eatonville, a Polk County, Florida logging camp, and among Hoodoo practitioners in New Orleans. The circumstances of collecting this data form an important part of the book. Stories are sometimes presented in a call and response pattern in which men and women use tales as a vehicle for verbal dueling about gender superiority. Harsh conditions in the logging camp are documented, though without foregrounding this risky political message. Hurston's own maneuvers as a native ethnographer are described. We learn that at the lumber company she claimed to be a gangster's runaway mistress in order to explain her car and middle-priced dress and left suddenly to avoid violent retaliation by a woman who thought Zora was after her man. In Eatonville

Hurston had to convince her old friends that she was still one of them, offering rides and other favors in exchange for folklore. The parties Hurston attended and the attitudes of her informants in both locales become part of the folklore itself. In New Orleans, Hurston went through a grueling initiation as a Hoodoo priestess.

Hurston's sensitivity to gender issues and respect for New World manifestations of African magic and healing continue to be evident in *Tell My Horse* (1938), an account of Hurston's Guggenheim-funded research in Jamaica and Haiti. In Jamaica, Hurston described funeral rituals and magic among Maroons in Accompong, while in Haiti she studied with several Voodoo practitioners and claimed to have seen and photographed a zombie, though she explained that phenomenon in naturalistic terms. In describing Jamaica, Hurston was incensed about the class system based on skin-color and the subservient attitude women were expected to display. These themes are also present in the novel *Their Eyes Were Watching God*, written during her fieldwork in the Caribbean.

Their Eyes Were Watching God conveys much ethnographic information. Through the voices of Janie, the heroine, and her grandmother, husbands, and friends, we learn how southern African-American men and women coped during the half century after the abolition of slavery. Though the backdrop of racism is present, white people are virtually absent from the book. This is a book about black men and women and their culture; whites are an environmental challenge with which they must deal.

Janie's life is divided between the restrictions associated with marriage to relatively successful black men (including the mayor of Eatonville) and the joy and freedom associated with elopement with a handsome laborer, picking vegetables in the Everglades. Janie ultimately gains her independence as a widow with a substantial inheritance, after she shoots her beloved Tea Cake in self-defense. Tea Cake had attacked Janie while suffering from rabies. Having been bitten by a rabid dog while protecting Janie during the aftermath of a hurricane, Tea Cake was not vaccinated because of the inadequate medical care available to blacks in the South. In her personal life, Hurston tried both marriage and romantic entanglement, and ultimately rejected them in favor of work and freedom.

Hurston wrote a great deal more than can be described here. The works discussed above are the ones most likely to be of interest to anthropologists, especially those who are not regional specialists. Hurston wrote plays, short stories, and other novels, as well as journalistic pieces, articles on folklore, a posthumously published study of a black church, *The Sanctified Church* (1981), and an autobiography, *Dust Tracks on a Road* (1942). During the 1930s she collected folklore for the Works Progress Administration (WPA), working with, among others, the great collector of folklore, Alan Lomax. She held some controversial political opinions, notably her disagreement with *Brown vs. Board of Education*'s mandate of school integration. She argued that African-Americans didn't need to go to school with whites to be smart.

By the end of Hurston's life her health was bad, sources of funding had dried up, her books were out of print, and she was too proud to accept offers of help from her relatives, many of whom were successful professionals. She died in 1960 in Fort Pierce, Florida, where she had lived in a segregated county nursing home, and was buried by public subscription. Her funeral was well attended by the local black community, and tributes were written by Fannie Hurst and others who had known her during her years of literary accomplishment. In 1973 the novelist Alice Walker found Hurston's grave and put a headstone on it, and began the process by which Hurston became known and loved by a new generation.

Selected readings

Boyd, V. (2003) *Wrapped in Rainbows: The Life of Zora Neale Hurston*, New York: Scribner.

Hathaway, R. V. (2004) 'The Unbearable Weight of Authenticity: Zora Neale Hurston's *Their Eyes Were Watching God* and a Theory of "Touristic Reading",' *Journal of American Folklore* 117(464): 168–90.

Hurston, Z. N. (1937) *Their Eyes Were Watching God*, Philadelphia: J. Lippincott.

——(1938) *Tell My Horse*, Philadelphia: J. Lippincott.

——(1939) *Moses Man of the Mountain*, Philadelphia: J. Lippincott.

——(1942) *Dust Tracks on a Road*, Philadelphia: J. Lippincott.

——(1963 [1935]) *Mules and Men*, Bloomington: Indiana University Press.

——(1981) *The Sanctified Church*, Berkeley: Turtle Island Foundation.

HARRIET D. LYONS

ALFRED L. KROEBER (1876–1960)

Kroeber wrote and published on a wide variety of subjects and, from 1896 to 1961, produced over 500 publications. Moreover, he seldom wrote autobiographical pieces, leaving one with only a small smattering of the person and mind, usually obtained through his students, colleagues, and other contemporaries.

Born in Hoboken, New Jersey, to an upper-middle class German family, Kroeber was primarily raised in New York City, and attended Columbia College. A few years later, based on three months of fieldwork among the Arapaho, Kroeber was awarded a PhD in Anthropology in 1901 under **Franz Boas**, and in the same year began his professional career by starting the Anthropology Department at the University of California, Berkeley, where he taught and wrote until his death in 1960. **Julian Steward** (1973) provides an excellent overview of his personal life and his major publications.

Given the diversity of Kroeber's interests and publications, some points need clarification. Kroeber, in building the Berkeley anthropology department, played a vital role in getting scholars to work with him on the native populations of California, the Great Basin, and other parts of the West. Over a 60-year period, the presence of **Robert H. Lowie** as a colleague, and occasionally that of **Edward Sapir**, Thomas Waterman, Walter Gifford, and Steward helped to establish Kroeber's ethnographic writings on native California societies and culminated in his critically acclaimed 1925 *Handbook of the Indians of California*.

Kroeber also published on Hawaii, Mexico, Peruvian cultures, and other populations. However, in the pre-1930s period, his most significant non-California ethnographic writings were on the Philippines, especially his *Peoples of the Philippines* (1919), which is still a superb source, although he probably never visited there.

While his writings cover a vast range of native societies in California, Kroeber was not dedicated to long-term fieldwork in any one area. With a few groups, however, he appears to have spent more time and was able to encourage a younger generation of fieldworkers. Thus as early as 1905 to 1910, he worked on Maidu languages with Roland Dixon. Another group with whom both Kroeber and Sapir did extensive work was the Yurok of the northwest California coast. What seems to have attracted Kroeber to the central and southern California valleys was the dominance of acorn production among many of the groups, notably the Yokuts. Recent work on the Yokuts demonstrates how Kroeber's early dedication to understanding local developments is still of overriding importance.

At various times Kroeber's research took him to Peru, back to the central Plains, Oregon, and the northwest coast. All of these field trips were short term, nothing in comparison to the time spent by his students and far less than **Bronislaw Malinowski**.

Within the tradition of American anthropology going back to Boas, anthropology consisted of four subfields: ethnology/social anthropology, linguistics, physical/biological anthropology, and archaeology. Kroeber wrote in all of its four fields, but exhibited little sustained interest in either archaeology or biological/physical anthropology. Yet, even if Kroeber was not interested in archaeology, he had a total commitment to history, especially what we now call global history. Within this broad anthropological framework, certain themes stand out. Kroeber basically envisioned anthropology as a humanistic discipline, and thus most of his general interpretations and writings dealt with issues of natural and cultural history. Accompanying this was a total dedication to understanding Culture and cultures, and interpreting these categories through their aesthetics and striving to conceptualize the idea of the whole. Thus Kroeber's anthropology and how it emerged over time must be understood as both what it was and what it was not.

Kroeber's theoretical and historical statements firmly opposed viewing anthropology as a social science, or as a comparative science and a predictive enterprise, or indeed as any kind of science. Thus while social science forged ahead from the 1910s to the 1960s in Europe and the United States, developing as a highly empirical and predictive endeavor, Kroeber had no part in this movement. This stance also meant that most of his interpretations are anti-causal; Kroeber was committed to the idea that cause was inherent in the nature of the phenomenon itself, and not to be imposed by the social scientist.

Virtually all his major works were challenged within cultural/social anthropology. His 1909 article 'Classificatory Systems of Relationship,' argued that kinship terms should not be regarded as reflections of the social system, especially in marriage systems where different relatives were classified under the same term; in its inferences and connotations, he noted, this leads to the best interpretation of kinship terms as primarily linguistic rather than sociological. This position is also basic to his 'Zuni Kin and Clan' (1917b). Throughout the following decades, Kroeber's linguistic position was challenged by virtually every British social anthropologist, especially **A. R. Radcliffe-Brown**. These two major combatants never settled the matter, which might have been one reason why Radcliffe-Brown was not hired at Berkeley in 1931 and chose to teach at the University of Chicago.

Several issues characterize the totality of Kroeber's writing. Following Boas, Kroeber was concerned with total systems, ones that combined a sense of holism and CULTURAL RELATIVISM. Within this framework, the concern was to understand total systems of human behavior, be they cultures in the plural or the concept of Culture. This type of holism was central to whatever he approached. And thus the natural history of culture must be approached as a totality and not simply as a matter of STRUCTURE and FUNCTION, the central concepts in British social anthropology.

Probably the most pivotal of Kroeber's writings was his article on 'The Superorganic' (1917a), which had a lasting impact on cultural anthropology. Proposing a three-tier level of psychological and cultural understanding, Kroeber developed a hierarchy of fields of inquiry called inorganic, organic, and superorganic. The basic fields dealing with subject matter of non-living forms such as chemistry and physics were labeled inorganic. Second, the organic were fields dealing with psychological and biological life. And the third in the hierarchy were what Kroeber called the superorganic: fields, which dealt with collective (as opposed to individual) phenomena, such as anthropology and sociology. Furthermore, Kroeber insisted that each of the three levels had its own modes of inquiry and explanations that stem from and pertain to only its own level of the hierarchy. Here, he used the term 'reductionism' when cultural phenomena and cultures themselves were reduced to biological and psychological factors and explanations – anathema to Kroeber, and emphatically rejected in all his writings.

The historical and philosophical basis of Kroeber's hierarchical framework has multiple roots. Within a sociological context, this type of inquiry is a key element in the writings of David Hume and Adam Ferguson and later Herbert Spencer. At the time when Kroeber was writing, Toynbee and Spengler were also expressing similar views. Interestingly, Kroeber apparently overlooked Émile Durkheim's writings on the subject. What Durkheim meant by drawing the contrast between psychological and social facts is to be understood and explained within the concept of society, thus society is the source of all actions which are collective. A social fact is general to the community and exercises external constraints on the individual, while psychological facts are the products of individual minds. In making the contrast between psychological and social facts, Durkheim emphatically states that when a social fact has been explained by a psychological fact, we know the explanation to be false – a conclusion that Kroeber would fully support.

In more recent times, this contrast also appears in the writings of Thomas Kuhn, who deals with the subject of levels of inquiry in a different way, by stressing that the superorganic is a paradigmatic change. For Kuhn, it is partly that the former paradigm is no longer explanatory, and also that it cannot deal with certain shifts. Within the history of American anthropology, Kroeber's superorganic paper was a key element in eventually establishing the psychological side of the Boasian enterprise. Boas himself had recognized the role of, and the need to account for, the individual in cultural studies, and his basic insistence was that the individual was not simply a passive partner in the cultural process. But only in the late 1910s and 1920s (and after the Kroeber essay) did Sapir, **Ruth Benedict**, and **Margaret Mead** move ahead with psychological accounts in what eventually became identified as the CULTURE AND PERSONALITY school in American anthropology.

The issues of cultural creativity recurred in particular over the last 30 years of Kroeber's life. He was concerned with exploring where, how, and why the numerous loci of cultural creativity formed. And while the more general nature of cultural aesthetics is what Kroeber sought to comprehend, he simultaneously recognized the specific nature of this creativity for particular cultures, and its importance for understanding cultures in a comparative way. Kroeber also focused on the idea of creative genius, being dubious of how and why this concept is utilized in trying to explain the creativity of a culture. Thus, throughout *Configurations of Culture Growth* (1944), Kroeber makes it clear that a sense of history always plays a supreme role, and that, historically, great cultural products were always associated with great individuals. To those who chronicle it, the flowering of High Culture is synonymous with the name of Shakespeare.

Developing the configurations of Culture was a constant theme. As part of this, Kroeber expands the Greek concept of Higher Civilizations, *Oikoumene*. Among the ancients, this stood for the Greek idea of the 'inhabited world' and even more importantly, the 'Civilized World.' What Kroeber added was the idea that higher civilizations existed not only in various parts of the Old World but also in the New World. And it was the *Oikoumene* that gave rise to the philosophies and historical supremacy that would later be attributed to individuals.

Kroeber's 'Basic and secondary patterns of social structure' (1938) sets out how cultures could be compared. It established a distinction between basic patterns, such as economy, technology, and modes of subsistence, and secondary patterns, such as aesthetics, myth, and philosophies. Cross-cultural regularities would be found in the primary structures, such as hunting and gathering societies, while secondary structures were more particular and were expressions of cultural creativity and the aesthetic domain. A good example is ritual and myth. Traditionally they have been coupled in that a change in one brings forth a change in the other. But once they were understood as partly separate, it became clear that, while ritual was social action, myth dealt with a range of cultural creativity that brought forth aesthetic features and philosophical questions which characterize particular cultures. These metaphysical properties dealt with a sense of mystery that could only be understood and emblemized within each culture. All of these secondary structures are aesthetic subjects, they cannot be reduced to primary structures, and these features bring forth the particularism and uniqueness of all cultures in the plural.

The implications of this article are critical to all of Kroeber's writings from the 1940s onwards. Over the next decades, Kroeber developed the contrast between reality culture and value culture. Reality culture referred to those properties of society which were adaptive and based on economic/ecological features. Value culture referred to those aspects of culture which were non-adaptive, particular to a society, and primarily to the metaphysical basis of each society. Thus, reality culture was causal while value culture was primarily non-causal and could not be reduced to adaptive and functional features. Furthermore, in the natural history of culture, cultures must be understood as holisms, and configurations such as the superorganic were subsumed, and the individual and the idea of genius basically were ruled out. In the cultural process, each culture sees itself as unique and distinct from its neighbors; thus inversion and proximity occur, and differences are maintained. This became a critical hallmark of Benedictian anthropology. The overall perspective is brilliantly summarized in Kroeber and Kluckhohn (1963 [1952]) – a volume that still bears a close reading.

Reading Kroeber's writing is a pleasure, especially for his insistent anti-eclecticism. Today, many contemporary anthropological theories or interpretations appear dominated by a concern to cover all bets – eclecticism in its basic form. Such a posture was anathema to Kroeber, who always allowed his readers to make their own decisions, and similarly, never strove to be a public intellectual. His legacy lives on in unexpected places including science fiction, as his daughter, famed novelist Ursula LeGuin, clearly was inspired and influenced by him.

Selected readings

Kroeber, A. L. (1909) 'Classificatory systems of relationship,' *Man* 39: 77–84.

——(1917a) 'The Superorganic,' *American Anthropologist* 19: 163–213.

——(1917b) 'Zuni kin and clan,' New York: Anthropological Papers of the American Museum of Natural History, 18.

——(1919) *Peoples of the Philippines*, New York: American Museum of Natural History.

——(1925) *Handbook of the Indians of California*, Washington, DC: Bureau of American Ethnology.

——(1938) 'Basic and secondary patterns of social structure,' *Man* 68: 299–309.

——(1944) *Configurations of Cultural Growth*, Berkeley: University of California Press.

Kroeber, A. L. and Kluckhohn, C. (1963 [1952]) *Culture: A Critical Review of Concepts and Definitions*, New York: Vintage.

Steward, J. H. (1973) *Alfred Kroeber*, New York: Columbia University Press.

ARAM YENGOYAN

SIR EDMUND LEACH (1910–89)

How did a man who conducted only a modest amount of original (and successful) field work, who rebeled against the conventional approaches to his discipline and trashed the writings of his colleagues, who was 37 years old by the time he obtained his PhD and 44 before his first major book was published, end up being regarded as perhaps the most outstanding British social anthropologist since the Second World War, as well as a fully accepted establishment figure, ritualized by the award of a knighthood? The quick answer is not simply the dazzling productivity – eight self-authored books, several edited works, numerous journal articles, and dozens of contributions to magazines and the popular press. Rather it is the consistently original quality of the work and the enormous range of topics addressed.

Edmund Ronald Leach was born into an upper-middle-class family in Sidmouth, Devon, England in 1910 and died in 1989. The family fortune came from textiles and later from interests in a sugar plantation in Argentina. His path to anthropology was circuitous. In 1929 he entered Clare College at Cambridge University. After one year of studying mathematics, he switched to engineering and graduated with first-class honors in 1932. Undecided about his future, he signed on with Butterfield and Swire, a leading British trading company operating in the Orient. Over a period of three and a half years he was posted to various locations in China. That experience taught him

115

that he was not cut out for the commercial world. While in Peking in 1936 he met an adventurous American who invited him to travel to Botel, Tobago, a small island south-west of Taiwan inhabited by the Yami, whom Leach referred to as his first 'real primitives' (Kuper 1986). Two months later Leach headed back to England, taking with him various notes and sketches that he had made about the Yami and their material culture.

By coincidence, a childhood friend had married **Raymond Firth** (later Sir Raymond), who taught anthropology at LSE (London School of Economics). Leach asked her to introduce him to Firth, who in turn took him to meet **Bronislaw Malinowski**. When Malinowski persuaded Leach that anthropology was his destiny, it appeared that the path to eventual professional status would be smooth sailing. That did not prove to be the case. Leach's first effort at field work was in Iraqi Kurdistan, his choice of site apparently related to a love affair with an archaeologist. Five weeks later he aborted the project. Whether that was due to a cooling off of the romance or to signs of war emanating from Germany is not clear.

In 1939 Leach headed off to Burma (now Myanmar) to conduct field work among the Kachin. Less than a week after he arrived, the Second World War broke out. By 1940 Leach had joined the Burmese Army. After the Japanese occupied the country in 1941, Leach, by then fluent in the Kachin language, was assigned to a cloak and dagger unit of the Army, and spent the next years roaming throughout Kachin territory.

In 1946 Leach was demobilized. He was still enrolled as PhD candidate at LSE. Tragically, however, his field notes and a rough draft of his thesis had been lost during the War. Leach decided to produce a thesis based on a thorough reading of all the available historical records on the Kachin. In 1947, 15 years after he had graduated from Cambridge, he finally received his PhD. At the same time he accepted a position as Lecturer at LSE. He later resigned the position for a year in order to convert his thesis into a book. Before the book was published in 1954, Leach joined the Department of Anthropology at Cambridge, then headed by **Meyer Fortes**. The book, *Political Systems of Highland Burma*, was destined to become one of the most influential monographs in post-Second World War anthropology.

Highland Burma was a complex mixture of cultural, linguistic, and political units which were constantly changing. Leach realized that it made no sense to talk about distinctive tribes because the borders were porous and blurred. For similar reasons, he found little value in the concept of culture. Influenced by Malinowski, he stressed the inconsistent, contradictory nature of human interaction and the choice-making, manipulative capacity of individuals. Added to this perspective, Leach argued, must be the assumption that people are mainly motivated by a desire for power.

In order to make sense of Highland Burma, Leach took the position that the region had to be treated as a totality and examined over a long stretch of history. To cope with such a complex project, he turned his attention to model-building. His starting point was to draw a distinction between actual behavior and the models erected to explain it. Everyday behavior is dynamic and messy; it is never in equilibrium. Anthropological models, in contrast, are always equilibrium models. The best the anthropologist can do is to erect 'as if' fictional models – fictional because they constitute verbal cate-gories not behavior on the ground. One of the novel features of this study is the assertion that in their everyday lives people do the same thing. They too erect 'as if' equilibrium models, often represented in ritual, which are idealized representations that provide a sense of orderliness in an otherwise chaotic universe. If the anthropologist has done her or his job well, the only difference between the observer's and actor's model is the greater precision of the former.

It was this framework that Leach employed to understand Highland Burma. He identified three models of society in the region: an egalitarian, democratic model among the Kachin called *gumlao*; a hierarchical, autocratic model among the neighboring Shan people; and an intermediate model among the Kachin called *gumsa*. Over long stretches of history, the Kachin switched back and forth between *gumsa* and *gumlao*, reflecting the choices made by individuals and their attempts to maximize power.

One of the persistent criticisms of *Political Systems of Highland Burma* was that it lacked solid data. In view of the impact of the War on Leach's research, this would appear to be a low blow. Nevertheless, he was determined that his next project would be data-saturated. His choice was a study of irrigation systems in Ceylon (now Sri Lanka). Curiously, he only spent six months in the field in 1954, although he returned briefly in 1956. Yet the rich archives allowed him to accu-mulate a mass of data on which to base his argument. That argument was surprising. Whereas *Political Systems* is often referred to as idealist (concerned with mentalist data), *Pul Eliya*, the Ceylon study (1961a) was materialist in orientation. Leach's thesis was that economic and ecological factors embedded in the irrigation system shaped every-thing else in the village. Meyer Fortes and **Jack Goody**, Leach's senior colleagues at Cambridge, assumed that kinship was a thing in itself, irreducible to any other feature of society. Leach, in contrast, portrayed kinship in *Pul Eliya* as an idealist structure generated by the ecological and geographical properties of the irrigation system. The upshot was the deepening of a long and bitter feud in the Cambridge Anthropology Department which became notorious throughout the anthropological community.

The Ceylon study turned out to be the last original field work conducted by Leach. By then he had discovered **Claude Lévi-Strauss** and STRUCTURALISM, and soon became known as the French scholar's English prophet. In a number of clear and authoritative publications (for example, 1970 and 1973), he set out to explain structuralism and to persuade his colleagues and their students that something novel and exciting was happening in France.

By the time Lévi-Strauss had become a leading figure in the anthropological world, Leach characteristically switched gears and began to criticize him. Leach rejected Lévi-Strauss's distinction between hot and cold societies, arguing that no society is static or 'outside history.' He also criticized the tendency of structuralism to prioritize reified social structure over the agency of individuals. Lévi-Strauss's cavalier approach to data also brought a rebuke. Leach's position was that structuralist interpretations must be related to poli-tical and economic factors in the empirical world, something that Lévi-Strauss failed to do. Leach selected the Bible as the basis of some of his own structuralist articles (1961b, 1962, 1966) partly because the source material was readily accessible to readers, unlike the exotic examples of myths usually supplied by Lévi-Strauss.

As Hugh-Jones and Laidlaw have indicated (2000, vol. 1) there has been a tendency in the discipline to regard Leach's early (modified FUNCTIONALIST) and later (structuralist) writings as separate programs (see Kuper 1975). Leach strongly disagreed. His interest in structural-ism began when he read the analysis of the Kachin in Lévi-Strauss's *Elementary Structures of Kinship* (1949). While Leach thought that the French scholar had got some of the data wrong, he nevertheless appreciated the novelty and significance of the latter's interpretation of Kachin society. Indeed, after reading Lévi-Strauss's work, Leach modified the arguments of his PhD thesis, thereby sharpening the theoretical edifice of *Political Systems of Highland Burma*.

Even earlier, Leach's analysis in 'Jinghpaw Kinship Terminology' (1945, reprinted in Leach 1961c) contained clear structuralist principles. And the structuralist themes of ritual and myth so central to Lévi-Strauss's work were prominent features of *Political Systems*, not least because of the author's novel argument that myth and ritual are one and the same thing, both of them saying something about power and status.

Leach's work has been characterized as 'petulant inconsistency' (for a rebuttal see Fuller and Parry 1989). The petulance presumably refers to Leach's penchant for attacking virtually every conventional idea in the discipline, as well as the scholars who promote them. In his inaugural Malinowski Memorial Lecture in 1959 Leach criticized not only Malinowski but also Fortes, Goody, and Richards – all of them his senior colleagues at Cambridge. At one point in *Political Systems* (p. 227), he boldly announced that the 'facts' in his colleagues' books bored him.

Leach's deepest scorn was reserved for **A. R. Radcliffe-Brown**. On the occasion of delivering the 1976 Radcliffe-Brown Memorial Lecture, Leach came close to labeling his famous predecessor an intellectual fraud (Hugh-Jones and Laidlaw, vol. 1, 2000: 19). In Leach's judgment, Radcliffe-Brown's natural science of society program had run out of steam. The reason, thought Leach, was that anthropology is not a science. Indeed, he argued not only that the personality of the field worker inevitably shapes the collection and interpretation of data, but so do the investigator's national and social class origins (see Leach 1984 and Tambiah 2002, ch. 19). It was because he thought (or hoped) that structuralism might represent a scientific approach more suitable for the social sciences that he originally was so enthusiastic about it.

As for the charge of inconsistency, certainly the evidence is plentiful: notably the alleged gap between his functionalist (or empiricist) and structuralist periods, and the idealism of the Burma study in contrast to the materialism of the Ceylon study. Yet these shifts in intellectual position could equally be applauded for their flexibility and scope.

Leach was a public anthropologist well before that term ever caught on in the discipline. In 1967 he became the first anthropologist to deliver the Reith Lectures (on radio) in Britain, then an annual intellectual event. Moreover, he lectured to a wide range of non-academic audiences, and contributed numerous pieces to the popular press.

Long before Leach retired in 1979, he had become transformed into an establishment figure. He was Provost at King's College, Cambridge from 1966 to 1979. He was invited to deliver many of the most prestigious lectures in Britain and the USA, and awarded some of the most prestigious prizes. He occupied positions of leadership in various professional associations, including serving as president of the Royal Anthropological Institute from 1971 to 1975. To cap it all off, he was knighted in 1975.

It could be argued that Leach never was an anti-establishment figure. He simply possessed an exceptionally critical mind, and took it upon himself, as he remarked in the Preface to *Rethinking Anthropology*, to provoke his colleagues into questioning their orthodoxies. Certainly Leach expressed little interest in changing the world, whether through Marxism or applied anthropology. Yet by rendering the familiar strange and the exotic familiar, he promoted the universality of humankind, and viewed the discipline's broader mission as encouraging people to appreciate that their way of life was not the only one.

Leach reputedly was a superb teacher – challenging, inspiring, and supportive. Nonetheless, he did not create a school, possibly because he was not a systematic thinker in the style of Radcliffe-Brown or Lévi-Strauss. Yet he certainly was an original thinker, and it would be difficult to name another anthropologist of his era, or since then, who can match the range of his ideas and interests. As for his legacy, his contribution to structuralism may have suffered under the weight of Lévi-Strauss's fallen star. Yet there still is *Political Systems of Highland Burma*. If the day ever arrives when this powerful study is ignored, anthropology will have lost its way.

Selected readings

Fuller, C. and Parry, J. (1989) 'Petulant Inconsistency?' *Anthropology Today* 5(3): 11–14.

Hugh-Jones, S. and Laidlaw, J. (eds.) (2000) *The Essential Edmund Leach*, Volumes 1 and 2, New Haven, CT: Yale University Press.

Kuper, A. (1975 [1973]) *Anthropologists and Anthropology*, London: Peregrine Books.

——(1986) 'An Interview with Edmund Leach,' *Current Anthropology* 27(4): 375–81.

Leach, E. (1945) 'Jinghpaw Kinship Terminology,' *Journal of the Royal Anthropological Institute* 75: 59–72; reprinted in Leach 1961c.

——(1954) *Political Systems of Highland Burma*, London: Athlone Press.

——(1961a) *Pul Eliya: a Village in Ceylon*, Cambridge: Cambridge University Press.

——(1961b) 'Lévi-Strauss in the Garden of Eden,' *Transactions of the New York Academy of Sciences* Series 2: 386–96.

——(1961c) *Rethinking Anthropology*, London: Athlone Press.

——(1962) 'Genesis as Myth,' *Discovery* May: 30–35.
——(1966) 'The Legitimacy of Solomon: Some Structural Aspects of Old Testament History,' *European Journal of Sociology* 7: 58–101.
——(1970) *Lévi-Strauss*, London: Fontana.
——(1973) 'Structuralism in Social Anthropology,' in *Structuralism: An Introduction*, D. Robey (ed.), pp. 313–31, Oxford: Clarendon Press.
——(1984) 'Glimpses of the Unmentionable in the History of British Social Anthropology,' *Annual Review of Anthropology* 13: 1–23.
Tambiah, S. J. (2002) *Edmund Leach: An Anthropological Life*, Cambridge: Cambridge University Press.

STANLEY R. BARRETT

ELEANOR BURKE LEACOCK (1922–87)

Renowned as a pioneer feminist theorist, Marxist scholar, ethnographer, and ethnohistorian, Eleanor Leacock – friends and colleagues called her by her childhood nickname 'Happy' – was known for her successful combination of scholarship and social activism. While her ethnohistory of the North American fur trade and her ethnography of the hunting and gathering Naskapi Indians remain classics, she also conducted research in Africa, Europe, the Pacific, and urban America. Her research spanned such diverse topics as schooling in New York City and Zambia, critiques of Culture of Poverty studies, and critiques of biological determinism. Leacock made major contributions not only to feminist and Marxist theory, but also theories relating to foraging societies. She was a major authority on the ethnography and underlying dynamics of egalitarian societies and on the origin and evolution of social and gender inequality.

The daughter of literary critic Kenneth Burke and Lily (Batterham) Burke, she grew up in a 'Bohemian' household in New York's Greenwich Village, and spent summers on family forestland in northern New Jersey, a tract of 150 acres that remains in the family's hands today.

Educated at Radcliffe and Barnard Colleges, in 1941 she married Richard Leacock, a documentary filmmaker and cinematographer. ('Rickie' Leacock was the cameraman on Robert Flaherty's *Louisiana Story*.) The Leacocks had four children – Elspeth, Robert, David, and Claudia. Her second husband, James Haughton, married in 1966, was a Harlem-based community activist and director of the labor rights organization *Harlem Fight-Back*.

At Columbia University for her PhD, combining social history and social evolution, she was most influenced by Gene Weltfish and

William Duncan Strong. At Radcliffe Carleton Coon had introduced her to the work in ecological and evolutionary anthropology represented by V. Gordon Childe and Daryll Forde. Duncan Strong directed her attention to the boreal forests of northern Quebec and Labrador where she conducted fieldwork with the Montagnais-Naskapi (Innu) in 1950–51.

A landmark theoretical work, *The Montagnais Hunting Territory and the Fur Trade* (1954), resulted, based on her 1952 doctoral dissertation. The research addressed an important issue in social evolution: the question of the antiquity of the concept of private property. Earlier ethnographers, such as Frank Speck, had used the supposed existence of the Family Hunting Territory (FHT) among the Montagnais-Naskapi as evidence *against* the theory of primitive communalism developed by **Lewis Henry Morgan** and elaborated by Marx and Engels.

Before the very word 'communism' had become anathema to twentieth century Western bourgeoisie, Morgan had rigorously documented the practices of 'communism-in-living' among Native North Americans (1884). Leacock's evidence strongly supported Morgan. She demonstrated convincingly that the Family Hunting Territory was an historical artifact, a form of land tenure generated by the European Fur Trade, and therefore *not* an indication of the primordiality of private property.

Leacock's espousal of the theory of communism, even of the 'primitive' variety, did not endear her to the arbiters of accepted Anthropological views in Cold War America, and her academic career did not follow a conventional path. In later years she often spoke of the discrimination against female anthropologists of her generation. As a woman and a committed political radical in the 1950s, she experienced a double-marginalization. She spent the decade engaged in inner-city research projects on mental health, inter-racial housing, and schooling. Only in 1963 did she take up her first regular appointment: at the Brooklyn Polytechnic Institute. In 1972 she became chair of the Department of Anthropology at the City College of New York, and a member of CUNY's Graduate Faculty, a position held until her death. With her close colleague June Nash, Leacock turned the CCNY department into a formidable center for politically engaged, Marxist-feminist research.

Her research followed several pathways, always anchored in her political paradigm. Her studies of the schools of New York (1958–65) took her into the city's classrooms and homes to address the ways in which poverty, race, and mental health combined to stratify students into streams and limit life chances (1969). She also later adapted this methodology to examine schooling for rapidly urbanizing Africans in Zambia. She then deployed many of the insights gained in a thoroughgoing critique of then popular theories of the *Culture of Poverty* (1971).

Another area of Leacock's interest was in general social theory. She co-edited with colleagues at the Brooklyn Polytechnic a major set of collected readings: 'Social Science Theory and Method: An Integrated Historical Introduction' (1967–68). And in the 1960s and 1970s Leacock reissued two nineteenth century anthropological works, Lewis Henry Morgan's 1877 classic, *Ancient Society* (Leacock 1963), and Engels' 1884 *Origin of the Family Private Property and the State* (Leacock 1972). Leacock's edition of Engels has come to be accepted as the primary modern source on this still influential work. Her critical reassessments helped to spark renewed interest among scholars in these classics.

The ethnography of native North America had long suffered a lack of understanding of the complex historical pathways of the continent's societies. With Nancy Lurie she edited *North American Indians in Historical Perspective* (1971), a groundbreaking volume on American Indian ethnohistory that traced the trajectories of key case studies from aboriginality to modern times. Contributors to that volume included Gene Weltfish on the Plains Indians, Darcy McNickle on the Pueblos, and William Sturtevant on the Indians of the southeastern states. The effect of this volume was to accelerate the trend in anthropology away from the outmoded strictures of acculturation theory (see **Melville Herskovits**) that treated indigenous societies ahistorically.

Ethnohistorical research also informed her edited volume with Mona Étienne on *Women and Colonization* (1980). They argued that, case-by-case, women's status before colonialism was generally *higher* than it was under European-imposed rule. This thesis challenged the view of the universal subordination of women and offered instead a more historically nuanced view of the contingencies determining women's status.

Leacock critiqued theories of development that failed to take gender into account. This led to another widely cited volume, her collaboration with Helen Safa on *Women's Work: Development and the Division of Labor by Gender* (1986). This volume anticipated the major interest of the social sciences on the changing roles of Third World women under the impact of globalization.

In a similar theoretical vein is her co-edited volume with Richard Lee, *Politics and History in Band Societies* (1982). Here the authors were charged with reshaping and redirecting the study of hunting and gathering societies away from a strictly ethnographic enterprise towards one that included detailed consideration of history, political economy, and contemporary struggles for justice and human rights. Her collected essays appeared in *Myths of Male Dominance* (1981). Of the many major issues she tackled in the papers in this volume, three need to be highlighted: the historical and contingent nature of the subordination of women, the critique of biological determinism, and the origins and evolution of social inequality. Leacock was an unapologetic advocate of social evolutionary theory. But in carrying this forward she had to address criticisms on two fronts. There were postmodern anti-evolutionists, including many feminists, who argued for the universality of patriarchy and the universal subordination of women. And there were the socio-biologists, pro-evolutionists who argued that any attempt at evolutionary theory had to be grounded in the biology of natural selection and reproductive success. Leacock rejected both these viewpoints, the first as ahistorical and the second as biologically reductionist. Neither view took into account the political economy of pre-class and class-based societies, the forces transforming one into the other, and the contingent but determinable material conditions of life out of which various forms of consciousness emerged.

A prime example of the biological reductionist position was the critique by Derek Freeman of **Margaret Mead**'s famous 1920s Samoan fieldwork and his attack on American cultural anthropology more generally. Freeman argued that Mead had a serious blind-spot. Under the influence of **Franz Boas**'s cultural determinism, she portrayed Samoan youth culture as idyllic and relatively conflict-free. Freeman's own work on Samoan youth, decades later, found conflict, delinquency, suicide, and dysfunction, which he attributed to Samoan core culture and ultimately to underlying biological aggressiveness. He used these observed differences as a launching pad for an ad hominem attack on Mead and a general attack on cultural anthropology's failure to acknowledge the centrality of biology in human affairs.

Disturbed by Freeman's attack, Leacock traveled to Samoa in 1985 to undertake research among urban youth. While not uncritical of Mead's original work, Leacock's research indicated serious flaws in Freeman's assertions and vindicated much of Mead's original findings. Leacock pointed out that Mead had worked on an outer island relatively unaffected by the forces of colonialism, whereas Freeman had chosen to work in an urban slum where drugs, chronic unemployment, and gang violence were common. The differences were well accounted for by historical circumstances, and not to be attributed to Margaret Mead's alleged 'blind-spot.' Freeman's misreading of the ethnographic evidence rendered his assertions of biological determinism invalid. Leacock wrote a short piece summarizing her findings, as a postscript in a book on Samoa by Lowell Holmes (1987). This Samoan work was tragically cut short in the early months of 1987. Leacock became seriously ill during fieldwork. Diagnosed with pneumonia she was medically evacuated to Hawaii but efforts to save her life failed and she died in a Honolulu hospital on April 2, 1987. The critique of Derek Freeman, so representative of her mode of argument and the issues she fought for, was to be among the very last pieces Leacock wrote.

Within the discipline of anthropology, Eleanor Leacock championed a strand of humanistic Marxism that differed from the more political-economic Marxism of some of her New York contemporaries, as well as from the structural Marxism espoused by colleagues in France and England. But merely listing her publications, however influential, does not do justice to Leacock as a person. She was a stalwart in political campaigns across a wide spectrum of issues: women's rights, gay rights, indigenous people's rights, anti-war, anti-imperialist, and disarmament struggles were all part of her persona. As well she was a mentor for two generations of radical scholars and activists. To take just one example, in 1972 she co-founded Anthropologists for Radical Political Action (ARPA) a major force on the anthropological left in the 1970s.

Her legacy to anthropology therefore is a dual one: as a scholar for her advances in feminist theory and historical materialism, and as an activist for providing a role-model for the politically engaged anthropologist. A memorial volume of essays on her multifaceted oeuvre was published soon after her death (Sutton 1988), and The Eleanor Leacock Award was instituted by the Association for Feminist Anthropology to honor her memory.

Selected readings

Étienne, M. and Leacock, E. (eds.) (1980) *Women and Colonization*, New York: Bergin and Garvey/Praeger.

Gettleman, M., Gruber, H., Leacock, E., Menashe, L., and Millman, S. (eds.) (1967–68) *Social Science Theory and Method: An Integrated Historical Introduction*, Brooklyn, NY: Department of Social Sciences, Brooklyn Polytechnic Institute.

Leacock, E. B. (1954) *The Montagnais Hunting Territory and the Fur Trade*, Washington: American Anthropological Assn. Memoir 78.

——(1969) *Teaching and Learning in City Schools*, New York: Basic Books.

———(1971) *Culture of Poverty: A Critique*, New York: Simon and Schuster.

———(1981) *Myths of Male Dominance*, New York: Monthly Review Press.

———(1987) 'Postscript: The problems of youth in contemporary Samoa,' in *Quest for the Real Samoa: The Mead/Freeman Controversy and Beyond*. L. D. Holmes (ed.), pp. 177–93, South Hadley, MA: Bergin and Garvey.

Leacock, E. B. (ed.) (1963) *Lewis Henry Morgan's Ancient Society*, New York: Meridian Books.

———(1972) *Engels' Origin of the Family, Private Property and the State*, New York: International Publishers.

Leacock, E. B. and Lee, R. B. (eds.) (1982) *Politics and History in Band Societies*, New York: Cambridge University Press.

Leacock, E. B. and Lurie, N. (eds.) (1971) *North American Indians in Historical Perspective*, New York: Random House.

Leacock, E. B. and Safa, H. (eds.) (1986) *Women's Work: Development and the Division of Labor by Gender*, South Hadley, MA: Bergin and Garvey.

Sutton, C. R. (ed.) (1988) *From Labrador to Samoa: The Theory and Practice of Eleanor Burke Leacock*, Washington, DC: Association for Feminist Anthropology/American Anthropological Association.

RICHARD BORSHAY LEE

CLAUDE LÉVI-STRAUSS (1908–2009)

Lévi-Strauss was born in Brussels and raised in France by a family with an Alsatian Jewish background. He took a degree in law and philosophy at the Sorbonne.

After a few years as a teacher in a lycée he obtained a job as part of a French cultural mission to Brazil from 1935 to 1939, lecturing in philosophy at the University of Sao Paulo. A growing interest in anthropology led him to visit the Bororo, Caduveo, Nambikwara, and Tupi-Kawahib peoples. This was survey fieldwork rather than fieldwork based on PARTICIPANT-OBSERVATION. His return to France was short in duration, because he was no longer safe after the Nazi invasion. From 1941 to 1948 he was based in New York. During the war, he was affiliated with the New School for Social Research in New York City and also taught at Barnard College. In 1959, he became Professor at the Collège de France, holding this position until retirement.

For 60 years Lévi-Strauss was associated with a body of theory and a kind of practice known as (French) STRUCTURALISM that exercised a powerful influence in France, Britain, and the United States, particularly between 1955 and 1975. Outside anthropology, Louis Althusser, Michel Foucault, Georges Dumézil, Jacques Derrida, Roland Barthes, and Jean Piaget were all described rightly or wrongly as structuralists. In French anthropology, Pierre Smith, Françoise Héritier, and Philippe Descola were heirs to the tradition and Dan Sperber emerged from within as a critic; in Britain, **Edmund Leach** and **Rodney Needham** developed an empirical, grounded version of structuralism; in the United States in the 1970s **Marshall Sahlins**, formerly a NEO-EVOLUTIONIST, became a fervent defender of structuralism, whereas **Marvin Harris** became an equally fervent opponent of it.

It would be a good application of structuralist method, were we partially to define structuralism by its differences from other theories. Lévi-Strauss claimed that he avoided evolutionist assumptions about human reason. 'Primitives' might not think the same thoughts that we did but they had the same mental equipment. While he was interested in kinship, myth, and cosmology as human institutions, he possessed little interest in individual actors, specific marriages, particular storytelling events, or day-to-day politics in other cultures. He was particularly skeptical of bodies of theory, such as the FUNCTIONALISM of **Bronislaw Malinowski**, which explained the existence of institutions by their utility to individuals and societies. Unlike many American members of the CULTURE AND PERSONALITY school and linguistic anthropologists, Lévi-Strauss wished to demonstrate cultural universals rather than cultural differences. However, these universals existed at the level of structure rather than specific content or behavior.

Lévi-Strauss inherited from Émile Durkheim and **Marcel Mauss** a preoccupation with exchange/reciprocity and symbolic classification as cultural universals. From Ferdinand de Saussure, the Swiss founder of structural linguistics, and from his friend, the Russian phonologist Roman Jakobson, he derived his ideas of relational structures based on rules of contrast/differentiation and combination. All these themes first became evident in his first major work, *The Elementary Structures of Kinship* (1949).

Mauss had described ceremonial exchanges such as KULA in Melanesia and the POTLATCH of the North American northwest coast in *The Gift*, and had further indicated that in archaic societies everything was subject to the rules of reciprocity. Reciprocity was an expression of the social bond that did more than stave off hunger. It was concerned with more than the most practical utility. Reciprocity as a universal imperative is invoked by Lévi-Strauss as an explanation of the incest taboo which he equates with exogamy. The traffic in women for sex and marriage is merely one more important form of ceremonial exchange; indeed it is a hub of exchange activity. Other theories explaining the taboo, including the genetic risk of inbreeding, avoidance resulting from excessive familiarity, and Freudian repression of Oedipal drives, are all weighed in the balance and found wanting.

In very small scale societies which have 'elementary structures' there are rules which not only prescribe exogamy but restrict the choice of the male and his group to a specified category of women belonging to an appropriate group. The simplest form of this is *direct exchange* involving bilateral cross-cousin marriage (in an ideal case a male marries someone who is simultaneously his mother's brother's daughter and father's sister's daughter). This is sometimes combined with *dual organization*. The group is divided into opposed halves (a division which may be represented in the organization of village space) which exchange services, goods, rituals, and wives. The two moieties may be opposed with respect to certain symbolic properties (one may represent the moon whereas the other represents the sun; one may represent nature and the wild, whereas the other represents culture and domestication). *Indirect exchange* involving matrilateral cross-cousin marriage (a male marries a real or classificatory mother's brother's daughter) is consistent with a more delayed reciprocity. In the simplest form of indirect exchange, Group A gives women to Group B which gives women to Group C which gives women to A (note that these groups may be subdivided). There is a potential for inequality in such a system inasmuch as wife-givers are often deemed superior to wife-takers; the potential conundrum that A might end up superior to itself is avoided by the subdivision of the group. The giver/taker distinction is often reflected in forms of binary symbolic classification. In some lineage-based, small groups, and in modern societies, there are more 'complex' structures, inasmuch as one cannot marry within one's group but there is no specific category of partner specified.

Elementary Structures gave rise to many controversies. **Eleanor Leacock** disputed Lévi-Strauss's depiction of women in 'primitive' societies as the objects of exchange. **Gayle Rubin** was less inclined to doubt the conditions that he portrayed but was dismayed by his failure to ask why women were treated in this way.

In 1955, *Tristes tropiques*, an account of his fieldwork experiences in Brazil which was directed toward a general, albeit intellectual readership, made Lévi-Strauss into a celebrity. The book is full of memorable stories: the Caduveo paint their bodies in dualistic designs like our colored playing cards; Bororo dual organization faces collapse when the missionaries insist on altering the plan of the village; the egalitarian Nambikwara do not need bloody revolutions – when their leader fails, they simply leave him.

Totemism (1962) begins with a description of the late nineteenth century theory which amalgamated a number of practices, actual or hypothetical, into a putative primordial form of religion and social organization: totemism. These included clan exogamy, matrilineal descent, and the worship by the clan of a species of plants or animals from which it supposedly descended – they might be ceremonially avoided most of the year, but eaten just once a year after sacrifice.

In fact, individuals, families, and territorial groups might claim special relations with animals or plants. They might or might not be avoided. Exogamy might not be involved. Animals might be individual guardian spirits and whole species might not be involved. Nonetheless, 'totemism' persisted. Durkheim and Radcliffe-Brown stressed its function in maintaining group solidarity. Malinowski noted that totems tended to be useful and edible. Others such as **Meyer Fortes** tried to examine symbolic resemblances between clans and their totems.

Elaborating an argument made by Radcliffe-Brown, Lévi-Strauss reconstituted the totemic phenomenon. Some aboriginal groups in West Australia are divided into two moieties, which intermarry and exchange services. They have totemic names such as Eaglehawk and Crow. If one asks why Group A is like an eaglehawk, and what constitutes the 'crowness' of Group B, one has no answer. However, there is a folktale which says that Eaglehawk is Crow's mother's brother, and expects to receive respect and presents from his sister's son who is also his prospective son-in-law. Crow as a scavenger removes the game which hunters like Eaglehawk kill. In the folktale, Crow eats a wallaby he is supposed to bring to Eaglehawk, and pretends that the hunt failed. Eaglehawk tickles Crow's belly so that he vomits the wallaby's remains and then throws him in the fire till his eyes are red and his plumage is blackened. This is a just-so story about the complementary opposition between hunters and scavengers, senior and junior kin/affines, black and colored/non-black. One might say that the differences between Eaglehawk and Crow conceptually mirror the social differentiation between the two exogamous moieties. Members of A and B eat and utilize neither eaglehawks nor crows (which follow them during the hunt) but they find them *good to think with* if they wish to contemplate their social relationships.

In *The Savage Mind* (1962) Lévi-Strauss explored many relationships of this type. An example might be the astrologer's zodiac which relates differences in the heavenly bodies to different months of the year and ultimately to differences in human temperament. Lévi-Strauss's mode of analysis was rooted in structural linguistics. The slight difference between a voiced 'b' sound and an unvoiced 'p' sound becomes important only when it's given social recognition and used to distinguish the meaning of lexemes for example '*big*' and '*pig*,' that can then be combined into meaningful utterances, for example 'The boat is big,' or 'The pig ate its supper.'

The same mode of analysis was applied to myth in a number of early analyses, including the Oedipus cycle, Winnebago myths, and the Asdiwal myths of British Columbia and Alaska. In a tetralogy that began with *The Raw and the Cooked* in 1964 and ended with *The Naked Man* in 1971 Lévi-Strauss examines and compares a few hundred myths from all over the Americas that are more or less related to a myth (M1) about the creation of fire. Myths are broken down into episodes (mythemes). When they are compared, similarities, inversions, additions, and absences can be noted as one myth transforms temporally or spatially into another. One version of the Asdiwal myth tells of a Tsimshian culture hero who is born from a union between a widow and a sacred bird, lives on the land where people forage for berries, and has a liaison with she-bear (the Evening Star) whom he pursues up a ladder to Heaven. After the union with She-Bear fails he has two more marriages on earth, the latter of which produces a son. In both cases there are quarrels following boasts by him about his hunting prowess, first as a killer of mountain game, latterly as a killer of sea lions. Abandoned at sea by angry in-laws from his third marriage, Asdiwal is rescued by Mouse Woman and saved by the very sea lions he hunted. He returns to land after killing his former in-laws, and dies after he goes on a mountain without snow-shoes. The myth and its variants are analyzed in terms of oppositions such as foraging/fishing, land game and sea mammals, upstream/downstream, patrilocal residence (the widows at the beginning) and matrilocal residence, male/female and endogamy/exogamy. Inasmuch as Asdiwal dies on a mountain he is seen as attempting to mediate these oppositions. This is not an explanation of what the myth 'means' to the average Tsimshian (it's a story about a hero's life) so much as an exposition of the formal relation between its contents. Indeed, the average Tsimshian might well be as unaware of these structural oppositions as most people are about the rules of sound systems in languages. This is one reason why Lévi-Strauss talked of the 'unconscious' in culture. It must be noted that he had no interest in supposed universals of 'unconscious' content such as the Jungian

archetypes, because his real subject was the human mind which created structures and their permutations. He compared the episodes/
content or events of mythic thought to granules continually
re-arranged into new patterns in a child's kaleidoscope.

To conduct such analyses one must first understand local ethno-
botany, ethnozoology, diet, habitat, and social organization. In *The
Savage Mind* (1962) Lévi-Strauss demonstrates that the folklore and
cosmology of indigenous peoples are the products of elaborate
knowledge systems which in many ways compare favorably with
modern science. The modern scientist does have an advantage
because scientific thought is self-reflexive and progressive and scientific method is always specialized to the task at hand. The 'savage
mind' at work may be compared to the jack-of-all-trades or *bricoleur*,
who has to use a non-specialized toolkit. Pieces that are adapted from
one purpose for another (e.g. a bathroom stopper used to prevent oil
from leaking out of a car during a wartime parts shortage!) carry historical baggage. The reflexivity of scientific thought involves a power
of self-criticism – thought can think about itself. Human thought of
all kinds conceals and reveals things and ideas, creates difference and
mediates it. Parallel cousins and cross-cousins are 'different' only
because culture says they are – a fact that must be hidden for the
system to work. On the other hand, having convinced ourselves of
the reality of difference, our social and intellectual systems are largely
concerned with building bridges across the distinctions we ourselves
have created. This paradox is at the core of all of Lévi-Strauss's work,
and, if he is to be believed, at the core of human experience.

Selected readings

Hénaff, M. (1998) *Claude Lévi-Strauss and the Making of Structural Anthropology*,
trans. Mary Baker, Minneapolis: University of Minnesota Press.
Leach, E. (1974) *Lévi-Strauss*, Glasgow: Fontana/Collins.
Lévi-Strauss, Claude (1969 [1949]) *The Elementary Structures of Kinship*,
translated from the French edition by J. H. Bell, J. R. von Sturmer, and
R. Needham, London: Eyre and Spottiswoode.
——(1973 [1955]) *Tristes tropiques*, trans. J. and D. Weightman, London:
Cape.
——(1983 [1958]) 'The Story of Asdiwal,' trans. N. Mann (1967) with some
revisions translated by M. Layton, in his *Structural Anthropology, Volume
Two*, pp. 146–97, Chicago: University of Chicago Press.
——(1964 [1962]) *Totemism*, trans. R. Needham, London: Merlin Press.
——(1966 [1962]) *The Savage Mind (La pensée sauvage)*, London: Weidenfeld
and Nicolson; reprinted by Oxford University Press (1996).

——(1969 [1964]) *The Raw and the Cooked*, trans. J. and D. Weightman, London: Cape.

——(1973 [1966]) *From Honey to Ashes*, trans. J. and D. Weightman, London: Cape.

——(1978 [1968]) *The Origin of Table Manners*, trans. J. and D. Weightman, London: Cape.

——(1981 [1971]) *The Naked Man*, trans. J. and D. Weightman, London: Cape.

ANDREW P. LYONS

OSCAR LEWIS (1914–70)

It says much that Oscar Lewis could write ethnography so exceptional that a feature film was made of it. *Children of Sanchez* (1978), starring Anthony Quinn with Grammy-winning music by Chuck Mangione, is unique in the annals of anthropology. It also says something about Lewis's *oeuvre*: His popularized, novelistic autobiographies of individuals and their families continue to fascinate not just scholars but popular audiences as well. They represented a major break from standard ethnographic monographs. In addition, Lewis pioneered the notion of restudying communities and perhaps most controversially proposed the 'Culture of Poverty.'

Oscar Lewis grew up in upstate New York in poverty, and then went to New York City where he majored in history at City College NY (1936). At one stage he considered becoming an opera singer and his fine ear for sound was to show in the ethnographies he was to write. While an undergraduate he met and married Ruth Maslow (1916–2008), the sister of psychologist Abraham Maslow. She was to be his life-long co-researcher and collaborator, and indeed it is difficult to say where her influence ended, especially in view of the fact that she continued to edit and publish his work after his untimely death of a heart attack at the age of 56. While in New York City Lewis became involved in radical and Marxist politics and enrolled in a PhD in History at Columbia, but then at Maslow's suggestion spoke to **Ruth Benedict** and switched to Anthropology instead, working with Benedict, Ralph Linton, and **Margaret Mead**. Lack of funding meant that he completed a library dissertation for his 1940 doctorate on 'The Effects of White Contact upon Blackfoot Culture, with Special Reference to the Fur Trade.' His early interest was clearly in 'CULTURE AND PERSONALITY,' although his immersion in New York radical politics led him to emphasize the role of economics and heterogeneity in that field. After peripatetic employment at the Human Relations Area Files and the US Department of Justice, Lewis was appointed US Representative to the Inter-American Indian Institute in Mexico. Here he worked with the Mexican anthropologist, Manuel Gamio on issues of rural development. While there he undertook a restudy of Tepotzlan, a village first studied by Robert Redfield in 1926. Further short-term jobs followed at the US Department of Agriculture, Brooklyn College, and Washington University before he was hired at the University of Illinois in 1948, where he was to remain until his untimely death. Lewis now proved to be remarkably adept at obtaining funding for large-scale and long-term projects, which enabled him to do fieldwork in India, Spain, Puerto Rico, Mexico, Cuba, and New York City. He also established an enviable publishing record, producing more than eleven books and numerous articles. An indication of his productivity is provided by the year he spent in India. Despite spending much time as a Ford Foundation administrator, he produced a highly regarded monograph, *Village Life in Northern India*, incorporating the work of his students, plus at least seven articles.

Perhaps Lewis's first significant contribution to anthropology was the idea of restudying communities that had already been described by ethnographers. His Tepotzlan study was done with Redfield's encouragement and provoked considerable controversy, given their radically different interpretations of village life. This was attributed largely to their respective framing questions: Redfield, using a consensus paradigm, implying shared values, asked: 'What do these people enjoy?' while Lewis, who was applying conflict theory, was concerned with 'What do these people suffer from?' Lewis's monograph remains a classic, combining as it did FUNCTIONALISM with history in a narrative that showed how the village was embedded in a wider social world. Lewis's explicit purpose in undertaking this study was not to discover who was right or wrong, but rather to develop a theory of 'error observation' that would allow anthropologists to be aware of how their assumptions and values, often implicit, shape the material they produce. This was also an issue in British social anthropology, and a few years later Siegfried Nadel went so far as to suggest that ethnographers should attach a psychoanalysis of themselves as an appendix to their monographs. A positivist to the end of his life, Lewis believed that his method of studying families by using multiple autobiographies that discuss the same events would reduce the element of investigator bias. Different narratives of the same events also served to inform the reader of each family member's interests and character. These multiple autobiographies, representing a genre that Lewis was to perfect in mid-career, allowed family members to tell their stories in their own words, thereby creating an air of authenticity and enhanced readability. So rich were the stories that many reviewers asked for more analysis. We do not know if Lewis was going to provide this in later work given that he died in the prime of his career. In short, Lewis anticipated an important strand of reflexive anthropology, and raised concerns about the relationship between the fieldworker and subjects, theory and methods.

While he retained a long-term interest in peasants, Lewis followed his villagers to cities where he found that they nestled in small almost self-contained groups in the slums, and that, contrary to conventional wisdom, they were not disorganized. In this he challenged Redfield's famous Folk–Urban continuum that saw rural life as 'good,' happy, and well integrated while the urban end was supposedly atomistic, disorganized, and bad. In particular he critiqued Redfield's continuum as simplistic, overly romantic, atemporal, and static, and tried to develop a more complex approach involving multilinear and heterogeneous change (along with his Illinois colleague **Julian Steward**).

While Ellen Hellman had done the first anthropological study of a slum, *Rooiyard*, in South Africa in the 1930s, Lewis brought the study of urban areas and slums forcefully into the anthropological sphere. In trying to understand the social organization of the slums he found remarkable similarities in a variety of cities and thus developed the notion of a 'Culture of Poverty,' which he believed would be useful in 'formulating cross cultural regularities.' In many ways this is similar to **Gluckman**'s famous formulation that 'An African Miner is a Miner' (and should be analyzed as a miner rather than as an African). This is not surprising given that both Lewis and Gluckman were imbued with Marxism. Essentially, Lewis added a cultural dimension, arguing that poverty had profound and distinctive psychological and social consequences and that this culture stretched across the rural–urban divide as well as national boundaries. It was not found in isolated groups or among 'primitives' but rather it was evident among people incorporated or being incorporated into the global capitalist system. Lewis blamed both structural and cultural factors for the persistence of poverty, but stressed cultural factors like unstable families, distrust of public institutions, and failure to defer gratification. In 1959 he illustrated the concept with finely drawn portraits of families in a variety of parts of Mexico in *Five Families*. Other well-received studies came out in rapid succession including *La Vida* (winner of the National Book Award for non-fiction in 1967). Lewis rather naively believed that the culture of poverty would disappear under socialism, and so impressed was Fidel Castro that he invited Lewis to test this hypothesis in Cuba. However this project was shut down after several key informants were arrested and members of the Lewis team were accused of espionage. It is said that the stress caused by these events contributed to Lewis's fatal heart attack.

While fashionable, the Culture of Poverty concept evoked a spate of criticism largely because it had direct policy impacts and was presented in accessible, non-technical language. The criticisms included the accusation that it simply blamed the victim for poverty and provided a convenient middle-class rationale for the status quo, since all that was required was for the poor to change their values. There was also concern about how Lewis's failure to properly contextualize his material could result in its misuse by policy-makers, a misfortune the researcher would be unable to remedy. This is perhaps unfair as, given his Marxist approaches, ethical commitments, and own first-hand experience, he was clearly committed to measures aimed at the eradication of poverty, although he believed that the culture of poverty might prove resistant to such steps. Lewis, who styled himself as an 'eclectic materialist,' did not regard the culture of poverty as an important theoretical concept and indeed did not see himself as a theoretician, but rather as an empirically grounded fieldworker.

Given Lewis's background in 'culture and personality' studies it is not surprising that he felt that the family, or as he defined it, the grouping of 'primary relatives,' should be his main focus. The family was a natural social unit and could be studied holistically even if its members did not necessarily live together. It bridged the divide between culture and the individual. Rather than see culture in traditional terms, he saw it from the individual standpoint and emphasized the role of the family in socialization. He was very much a comparativist, and for this study he insisted on 'base-line' data that combined qualitative and quantitative approaches. His goal was to convey how peasants and the poor feel, think, and express themselves. While he also undertook projective psychological tests, Lewis is perhaps best remembered for his innovative and extensive use of tape-recorders in collecting material. He then wrote up his accounts, using the words of his informants (as he termed them) to telling effect. The poor, he insisted, should speak for themselves. His sensitivity and ability to sympathize with the poor was such that they opened up to him in ways truly remarkable, and Lewis continued to concern himself with their wellbeing long after fieldwork. As he put it in *Children of Sanchez*, he wanted to give the reader 'an inside view of family life and what it means to grow up in a one-room home in a slum tenement' (1961: xi). Indeed so raw were the words sometimes that when the Spanish edition of *Children of Sanchez* was published he was unsuccessfully sued for obscenity and slander 'against the Mexican nation.'

Above all, Lewis wanted everyone from the general reader to the political leaders to understand what poverty was like and how it was perpetuated. The purpose of anthropology was to document how the great mass of people, the poor – peasants and urban dwellers – survived. While Lewis's deeply humanistic ethnographic portrayals were well received in both the literary and scientific world and garnered several prestigious prizes, and while he claimed only to deal with a small segment of the slum population, questions were raised about how typical the families were. There is also the question of agency, especially that of the anthropologist. What were the guiding questions and how did the fieldworker help shape the story through editing? Nevertheless his material is so rich that it has been mined for ideas and notions about topics Lewis did not consider, such as those dealing with gender dynamics. Oscar Lewis represents a multifaceted blend of political conviction, scientific data collection, and humanistic presentation of life. He was indeed a complex person who stubbornly refused to abandon his concept of the 'culture of poverty,' and, although he was an empathetic and humanistic ethnographer, students found it difficult to work with him. In consequence he trained relatively few anthropologists. The most prominent of them was his protégé, Douglas Butterworth.

Selected readings

Lewis, O. (1951) *Life in a Mexican village: Tepotzlan Restudied*, Urbana: University of Illinois Press.

——(1958) *Village life in Northern India*, Urbana: University of Illinois Press.

——(1959) *Five Families, Mexican Case Studies in the Culture of Poverty*, New York: Basic Books.

——(1961) *The Children of Sanchez, Autobiography of a Mexican Family*, New York: Random House.

——(1964) *Pedro Martinez, A Mexican Peasant and his Family*, New York: Random House.

——(1966) *La Vida, A Puerto Rican Family in the Culture of Poverty*, New York: Random House.

——(1969) *A Death in the Sanchez Family*, New York: Random House.
——(1970) *Anthropological essays*, New York: Random House.
Lewis, O., Lewis, R., and Rigdon, S. (1977) *Four Men*, Urbana: University of Illinois Press.
——(1977) *Four Women*, Urbana: University of Illinois Press.
——(1978) *Neighbors*, Urbana: University of Illinois Press.

ROBERT GORDON

ROBERT H. LOWIE (1883–1957)

Robert Lowie is perhaps most often remembered for the closing thoughts in his most important book, *Primitive Society*, first published in 1920. He spoke of Civilization as a 'planless hodgepodge, that thing of shreds and patches' (Lowie 1961: 441). Generations of anthropologists have used this phrase to characterize the perspective of a whole generation of anthropologists, referred to collectively as 'Boasians,' or 'diffusionists.' Their work dominated American anthropology for much of the first half of the twentieth century.

These men and women were highly critical of what they saw as the speculative, 'arm-chair' anthropology of nineteenth century anthropologists such as **Lewis H. Morgan** and **E. B. Tylor**. They stressed fieldwork, collecting information directly among the groups they were interested in. Anthropology was a science, and their view of science was strongly empirical. One gathered facts and any inferences one drew were to be based strictly on this data. They were impressed by the transmission of social and cultural practices between groups – *cultural diffusion* – and saw this as the principal determinant of any given culture. This led to an intense interest in mapping the geographical distribution of culture traits and in the delineation of *culture areas*. It also led to speculation about possible past interaction between cultures with similar traits. Most American diffusionists, including Lowie, were students of **Franz Boas**, a German geographer turned anthropologist who taught at Columbia University in New York City.

Lowie stuck to his commitment to diffusionism throughout his career. However, his own fieldwork and his comparison of data from different cultures often led him to innovative conclusions. He often commented on the social function of cultural traits, and made the important observation that these same links sometimes recurred in different cultures, even when these cultures clearly had no history of contact with one another. This work has led careful students of

Lowie to agree that in this he anticipated many of the ideas later articulated by **A. R. Radcliffe-Brown** and the British STRUCTURAL-FUNCTIONALISTS. This progressive aspect in Lowie's work has earned him a place in the history of anthropological theory, although he is best known for his contributions to the study of Plains Indian cultures, especially the Crow.

Lowie was born in Austria, in Vienna, but came to New York with his family when he was ten years old. Although educated in New York, he grew up in a Germanic and German Jewish social world among people who spoke German and celebrated Germanic cultural traditions. He continued to draw inspiration from German scientific and philosophical traditions throughout his life. Early on he was influenced by Haeckel and Mach, and later in his career he professed to enjoy reading in the philosophy of science. His devotion to a strict empiricism and inferences tied closely to observation was a product of this. He also published in German from time to time as well as in English and was responsible for bringing work by German ethnologists, especially Heinrich Schurtz, to the attention of American colleagues. Moreover, he expected professional colleagues to command German. His writings are peppered with quotations in German, which he never bothered to translate. Late in his career, in 1950, not long after the end of World War II, he traveled to Germany and published a book based on six months of research among the Germans.

Lowie received his PhD at Columbia in 1908 under Boas' direction. However, two years before he had already begun work as an assistant to Clark Wissler, a major proponent of 'Culture Areas,' at the American Museum of Natural History in New York City. He was to remain at the Museum until the early 1920s, when he moved to Berkeley. Under Wissler's direction, he conducted research among many Indian groups in the American West including the Blackfoot, Cree, Assiniboin, Chippewa, Hidatsa, Hopi, and Shoshone. These research trips were of relatively short duration, ranging from a week or so to several months, and most of his information was gathered with the help of an interpreter. However, while he visited many groups in the Plains, the Southwest, and even in the Canadian wilds, Lowie is primarily known for his ethnological research among the Crow.

He was enamored of the Crow from the time of his first visit in 1907. He returned to them in 1910 and continued to visit them every summer until 1916. This was the most intensive field research by any anthropologist until **Bronislaw Malinowski** set a whole new standard in his 1915–18 stays in the Trobriand Islands of Melanesia. Over the years Lowie wrote extensively about kinship, marriage, and the family. He advanced the understanding of kinship terminologies and their social significance at a time when the prevailing view was that kinship had little but linguistic or psychological significance.

He did this by showing how differences in kinship terms were related to differences in social behaviors, such as who one could marry, who one cooperated with, and who one avoided. But he also demonstrated that kinship was not the only determinant of social behavior. His work on Plains military societies is still one of our best examples of the workings of *sodalities*, organizations that rely on recruitment rather than kinship. He also made clear the presence of age grades as important social elements in many cultures.

Thus did Lowie's careful recording of cultural facts and comparison between cultures greatly expand and improve anthropological understanding. It is not farfetched to say that he set the agenda for ethnology in America for decades to come.

Lowie's field research was mainly confined to the period when he was employed at the Museum of Natural History. After his move to California he rarely went into the field, although he did visit the Crow one more time, in 1931. With his employment in the Berkeley Department of Anthropology he devoted most of his time to his academic duties. Together with **A. L. Kroeber**, Lowie helped make Berkeley one of the leading anthropology departments in the United States. Students from this department include many of the most important anthropologists of the next generation, including, Ralph Beals, Cora Du Bois, Harold Driver, George Foster, Robert Heizer, Theodore McCown, Dmitri Shimkin, Robert Spencer, **Julian H. Steward**, and Carl Voegelin. All of these individuals have acknowledged the important role that Lowie played in their education.

Lowie did continue to write, however. While he still had much to contribute to Crow ethnography and comparative ethnology, his writings become more often theoretical or philosophical, or had a pedagogical intent. His *Introduction to Cultural Anthropology* (1934) was a textbook. His 1948 revision of *Primitive Religion* reflected one of his special interests, but was not well received by his colleagues. *Social Organization* (1948b) was written to replace his earlier *Primitive Society* and contained much new ethnographic material. However, none of these later works had the innovative edge of *Primitive Society* (1961 [1920]).

Following his retirement in 1950, Lowie carried out six months of field research in Germany accompanied by his wife. Clearly, this was a striking departure from research among reservation Indians. He carried out observations in a wide variety of settings and interviewed people from many different backgrounds. He stuck to his commitment to scientific objectivity, and produced a book that took a dispassionate view of Germans and their behavior during the Nazi era. For this, he received a good deal of criticism, some critics even concluding he was a Nazi sympathizer. He took strong exception to this charge, pointing out that it was hardly likely that he would approve of a regime responsible for gassing many of his European relatives.

As his career drew to a close, Lowie received many awards and accolades. In 1948 he received both the Viking Fund Medal in Anthropology and the Huxley Memorial Medal in England. While in Germany his research was frequently interrupted by requests to give a lecture or to receive an award. After his return, he was invited to teach at several of America's leading universities, including Columbia, Harvard, and the University of Washington. He also taught for a time at the University of Hamburg in Germany. In 1960, three years after his death, the museum at Berkeley was named in his honor only to be renamed later as the Hearst in honor of a wealthy sponsor.

Anthropology's mission until well into the 1950s was to reconstruct the culture of non-Western societies as it had been practiced before the colonial era, before the arrival of Europeans. Ethnographers employed a mental filter to what they observed, eliminating every perceived Western influence. They depended heavily on the memories of older individuals in their attempts to conjure up pristine life ways. So, the study of American Indians, which tried to conjure up cultures that no longer existed, came to be known as 'salvage anthropology.' Lowie shared this mission. In writing about the Indians of the Canadian woodlands, for example, he accepted their exclusive hunting territories as aboriginal and proof that private property was common in aboriginal America. More recent research has demonstrated that these territories were a product of the post-contact *fur trade* and that multifamily bands controlled aboriginal hunting territories. Moreover, Lowie and his colleagues presumed that the Plains life ways were aboriginal. However, we have since come to understand that they were in part a by-product of the displacement of peoples brought about by European settlement, by the fur trade, and by the introduction and assimilation to native use of much that had been brought to America by Europeans, notably the horse and the gun.

Nevertheless, the corpus of information and insights about the Crow and other Native American cultures studied by Lowie constitute a lasting legacy to American Anthropology. We can also appreciate the historical significance of the leads he provided to ethnological method and we can admire his dedication to rigor and caution in the construction of ethnological theory.

Selected readings

Du Bois, C. (ed.) (1960) *Lowie's Selected Papers in Anthropology*, Berkeley: University of California Press.

Lowie, R. H. (1927) *The Origin of the State*, New York: Harcourt Brace & Co.

——(1934) *An Introduction to Cultural Anthropology*, New York: Farrar & Rinehart.

——(1937) *The History of Ethnological Theory*, New York: Holt Rinehart & Winston.

——(1948a) *Primitive Religion* (Revised Edition of 1924), New York: Liveright.

——(1948b) *Social Organization*, New York: Rinehart & Co.

——(1954) *Toward Understanding Germany*, Chicago: University of Chicago Press.

——(1956 [1935]) *The Crow Indians*, New York: Rinehart.

——(1959) *Robert H. Lowie, Ethnologist: A Personal Record*, Los Angeles: University of California Press.

——(1961 [1920]) *Primitive Society*, with an introduction by Fred Eggan, New York: Harper Torchbook.

Murphy, R. F. (1972) *Robert H. Lowie*, New York: Columbia University Press.

JOHN W. COLE

BRONISLAW MALINOWSKI (1884–1942)

Bronislaw Kasper Malinowski was the first anthropologist to promote PARTICIPANT OBSERVATION as the primary fieldwork technique, and was also the self-described 'high priest' of FUNCTIONALISM. He was born in Cracow, which was in the Austrian controlled portion of Poland. Here his father, a professor, conducted some research into the folklore of Polish peasants. Malinowski studied physics, chemistry, and philosophy at Cracow in preparation for his first (1908) doctorate. After a period in Leipzig, he came to London to study anthropology with Edward Westermarck and C. G. Seligman. It is said that he decided to become an anthropologist after reading Sir James Frazer's

The Golden Bough. His London doctoral thesis, inspired by Westermarck and showing Durkheimian influences, was published as *The Family among the Australian Aborigines* (1913). Malinowski claimed that something recognizable as the family did indeed exist in a continent then regarded as the living kindergarten of the human race. He convincingly contradicted evolutionist theories, which assumed that promiscuity and wife abuse were normal in such societies, and showed how evidence of occasional ceremonial licence had been misinterpreted.

Malinowski went to Australia in 1914 to attend the meetings of the British Association. He stayed on for five years to conduct fieldwork in Papua and write up some of the results. Although funded by both Australian and British sources, he had to report regularly to the authorities during the years of the First World War because he was an enemy alien. His first trip to the southern coast of Papua took place between September 1914 and March 1915, and involved ethnographic surveys of the Motu, Mailu, Suau, and Sinogolo peoples. The Mailu work was published as a journal monograph (1915). Malinowski's two visits to Kiriwina in the Trobriand Islands (June 1915 to February 1916, October 1917 to October 1918), established his reputation as a pioneer fieldworker. In his first great ethnography, *Argonauts of the Western Pacific*, he claimed to have pitched his tent in the middle of the native village (although he actually worked in a few villages) in order to immerse himself in a strange culture virtually cut off from missionaries, whom he disliked, traders, and government officials. This was an exaggeration, because Malinowski spent up to a quarter of his time with trader friends, and there were a few missionaries whom he admired (for more details see Young 2004). He was not the only pioneer of participant observation – his fellow Pole Maria Czaplicka, the Finns Gunnar Landtman and Rafael Karsten (all fellow students of Westermarck), the New Zealander Diamond Jenness, and, in a prior generation, the American Frank Cushing may also have played such a role. What set Malinowski apart was his remarkable linguistic talent, his writing skills, and that he utilized his many gifts explicitly to claim his status as pioneer of fieldwork in the opening pages of *Argonauts.*

There was surprise and some consternation when Malinowski's field diaries from his first (Mailu) and third (Trobriand) field trips were published in 1967. Malinowski took arsenic, aspirin, various tonics, and quinine, wore a truss, suffered sexual frustration, made records of his erotic dreams, observed taboos about interracial sex but occasionally pawed native women. He jilted Nina Stirling, the daughter of a prominent physical anthropologist in favor of Elsie Masson, thereby incurring the wrath of a patron, the anthropologist Baldwin Spencer. While contemptuous of missionary prescriptions for the improvement of native culture, he absorbed some of the ethnocentrism of the traders whose company he enjoyed and referred to Melanesians as 'niggs' or 'niggers.' Nonetheless, the volume of ethnographic detail he obtained, as well as stories which are still told about his stay in Kiriwina, indicate that he enjoyed considerable rapport with his informants.

Malinowski married Elsie Masson in March 1919, and sailed to England in 1920. He had already published a major paper on the Trobriands in 1916, on 'Baloma: The Spirits of the Dead.' He worked for a while on a huge, comprehensive monograph on Kiriwina, but decided instead to write a shorter monograph on the KULA trade among the Trobrianders and inhabitants of other islands in the Massim archipelago. *Argonauts of the Western Pacific* was published in 1922 just after he had begun to teach at the London School of Economics. No haggling or bragging was allowed in kula. However, magic – to ensure safe passage and to cause one's partner to surrender his best valuable – surrounded all stages in the ceremony. Elaborate folklore and myth surround the kula and some of the valuables that were exchanged. Malinowski distinguished kula and other formal exchanges from practical trade and barter that also occurred. He compared kula valuables to the British Crown Jewels but could not initially think of equivalents in the ethnographic record. Inasmuch as etiquette could not mask a competitive element, Malinowski thought that kula might function as a substitute for war. Because he believed Trobrianders to be practical people, the absence of clear utility for the valuables or *vaygu'a* puzzled him. When he read **Marcel Mauss**'s comparison of the kula with other forms of ceremonial exchange such as the Kwakiutl potlatch that were all based on the quasi-legal and religious principle of reciprocity he thought he had found an answer to his questions.

The first 100 pages or so of *Argonauts* was devoted to an exposition of fieldwork methodology, stressing the importance of surveys, maps, synoptic charts as well as the dos and don'ts of participant observation. Fieldwork in natural sciences such as zoology clearly supplied a model. The kula was compared to other forms of exchange such as mortuary feasts and competitive distributions (*kayasa*) as well as barter. There was a description of kula mythology and of an actual kula voyage, although Malinowski himself was able to complete only part of the circuit.

Utilitarianism was the main constituent of Malinowski's functionalism: among Trobrianders and all other peoples social and cultural institutions satisfied species, individual, and social needs. Evolutionary theories of intellectual growth were cast aside. A primary target was Frazer's idea of a progression in thought from magic, based on illusions of unlimited control of nature, through religion to modern science based on limited but demonstrable control of specific forces. Malinowski also attacked his contemporary Lucien Lévy-Bruhl who insisted that primitive thought was 'prelogical' and dominated by 'mystical' representations. In the Trobriands, magic, religion, and common-sense knowledge (proto-science) co-existed. In *Magic, Science and Religion* (1948 [1925]), Malinowski emphasized that magic was eminently practical. Knowledge and skill were needed to plant, tend, weed, and harvest yams, and to build canoes, but they ensured success neither in gardening nor in kula. Health and illness were also beyond control. Some individuals were fortunate and others were not. Because of such uncertainties magic played a large role in people's lives and was constantly employed in garden work, in kula, and in love. Its purpose was to put food on the table, make people safe, and to secure their social relationships, to relieve anxiety and promote success. Totemic religious observances were explained all too simply in a mundane fashion: 'the road from the wilderness to the savage's belly is an indiscriminate background against which there stand out the useful, primarily the edible, species of plants and animals' (Malinowski 1948: 44). The reduction of complex social institutions to the fulfilling of biological, emotional, or social needs may seem somewhat prosaic and unsatisfactory to the twenty-first century reader but this strategy was designed to counteract the exoticizing explanations that were all too common in those days. A systematization of Malinowski's functional theory appeared in the posthumous *Scientific Theory of Culture* (1944).

Malinowski's knowledge of Trobriand gardening and garden magic was immense and published in two volumes as *Coral Gardens and their Magic* (1935). His ideas about magic went beyond common ideas concerning sympathy ('like affects like') and contagion. Spells often contain strange 'meaningless' words such as 'abracadabra,' but they are effective performances: Within magic, 'the meaning of any significant word, sentence or phrase is the effective change brought about by the utterance within the context of the situation to which it is wedded' (Malinowski 1935 (2): 214). These ideas anticipate later ideas concerning 'performative utterances.'

Malinowski tended to generalize from the particularities of Trobriand custom. Applying Mauss's ideas, he stated that Trobrianders demonstrated that effective social control without courts and police depended on the sanction of denial of reciprocity (1926). Sometimes he also used the particular to demolish older generalizations.

Accordingly he attacked evolutionary theories of primitive communism and primitive individualism by demonstrating that neither extreme corresponded with the institution of ownership in Trobriand law. He also attacked persistent notions of primitive matriarchy. It is therefore puzzling to some that Malinowski continued to believe in the notion of primitive ignorance or *nescience* of physiological paternity which evolutionists believed was the natural concomitant of primitive promiscuity and primitive matriarchy. He insisted that Trobrianders believed quite literally in the idea that sexual intercourse merely opened the way for the entry of reincarnated spirit beings (children) belonging to the mother's clan, a dogma that legitimated matriliny. Paradoxically, he turned nescience of physiological paternity into an argument that demonstrated the strength of the family among the Trobrianders inasmuch as strong family bonds and loving, paternal care existed among them despite their failure to recognize the father's biological connection with his child. Furthermore, Trobriand children regarded the father as a source of affection and the mother's brother as a source of authority, thereby demonstrating that the Freudian family romance and the Oedipal stage were not universal (Malinowski 1927).

Premarital sexual experimentation and a form of trial marriage were institutionalized in the Trobriands. Malinowski believed that such experimentation could lead to sexual contentment after marriage took place. *The Sexual Life of Savages* (1929) contained extensive textual material on Trobriand lovemaking and ideas about sex as well as descriptions of marriage and the exchanges surrounding it. The influence of the sexologist, Havelock Ellis, who wrote a preface to the work, was very apparent.

In 1927 Malinowski became the first person to be awarded the title of Professor of Anthropology at the London School of Economics. His students included **Raymond Firth**, Audrey Richards, **Hortense Powdermaker**, Jomo Kenyatta, Francis Hsu, and **Edmund Leach**. Three other students, **Evans-Pritchard**, **Meyer Fortes**, and Isaac Schapera deserted the Malinowskian camp because they were influenced by the Durkheimian STRUCTURAL-FUNCTIONALISM of **A. R. Radcliffe-Brown**. For his part, Malinowski disdained Durkheimian ideas of the collective consciousness and ridiculed 'kinship algebra.' During the late 1920s and 1930s, Malinowski used Rockefeller funds to promote research in Africa. Although he was never an opponent of colonialism as such, he was worried about the effects of colonial interference there. Malinowski addressed two missionary conferences on the subjects of sexuality and polygyny in

Africa. He advocated a new applied anthropology as a more enlightened form of surveillance (Lyons and Lyons 2004: 175).

A fervent opponent of both fascism and communism, Malinowski
was strongly opposed to anti-Semitism, and was involved in a
successful bid to extricate the dying Freud from Vienna in 1938. That
same year he moved to the USA, where he had many friends,
including some of the disciples of **Franz Boas**. He took up a position
at Yale in 1938, and began new research in Mexico. He died of a
heart attack in May 1942.

Selected readings

Firth, R. (ed.) (1957) *Man and Culture: An Evaluation of the Work of Bronislaw
Malinowski*, London: Routledge & Kegan Paul.
Lyons, A. and Lyons, H. (2004) *Irregular Connections: A History of Anthropology
and Sexuality*, Lincoln: University of Nebraska Press.
Malinowski, B. (1916) 'Baloma: The Spirits of the Dead in the
Trobriand Islands,' *Journal of the Royal Anthropological Institute* 46:
353–430.
——(1922) *Argonauts of the Western Pacific*, London: Routledge &
Kegan Paul.
——(1926) *Crime and Custom in Savage Society*, London: Routledge & Kegan
Paul.
——(1927) *Sex and Repression in Savage Society*, London: Routledge &
Kegan Paul.
——(1929) *The Sexual Life of Savages in Northwestern Melanesia*, London:
Routledge & Kegan Paul.
——(1935) *Coral Gardens and their Magic*, 2 vols, London: G. Allen and
Unwin.
——(1944) *Freedom and Civilization*, New York: Roy.
——(1948) *Magic, Science and Religion, and other essays*, Glencoe, IL: Free
Press.
——(1963 [1913]) *The Family among the Australian Aborigines*, New York:
Schocken Books.
——(1967) *A Diary in the Strict Sense of the Term*, trans. N. Guterman,
London: Routledge Kegan Paul.
Young, Michael W. (2004) *Malinowski: Odyssey of an Anthropologist,
1884–1920*, New Haven, CT: Yale University Press.

ANDREW P. LYONS

MARCEL MAUSS (1872–1950)

Mauss's 'Essai sur le don' (*The Gift*) is still in print and widely read
despite being originally published in 1925. It is not the only work of

Mauss to which anthropologists remain indebted. Although he taught a course on fieldwork method from the late 1920s till he retired, he made only one brief field trip to North Africa. Mauss was arguably the last great armchair anthropologist.

Mauss was born in Épinal, Alsace-Lorraine. His university education took place in Bordeaux and Paris. His mother's brother was the great French sociologist, Émile Durkheim, and Mauss assisted and collaborated with him on a number of works, including the editing of Durkheim's journal, *L'Année sociologique*. After Durkheim's death in 1917 and the loss of some of his disciples in war, Mauss assumed the leadership of the remnant of the Durkheimian school. He taught in the École pratique des hautes études in Paris, and late in his career became a Professor at the Collège de France. With Paul Rivet, he created and led the *Institut d'Ethnologie* in Paris in 1925. His collaborators included Henri Hubert, Henri Beuchat, and other members of the *Année* group. Contemporaries and colleagues whom he influenced included Lucien Lévy-Bruhl, Maurice Leenhardt, Georges Bataille, Georges Dumézil, Michel Leiris, **Bronislaw Malinowski**, and **A. R. Radcliffe-Brown**. His students included Africanists such as Marcel Griaule and Denise Paulme, the Mesoamericanist and politician Jacques Soustelle, and Georges Devereux, ethnopsychiatrist and Mojave ethnographer. Later scholars who were influenced by him included **Claude Lévi-Strauss**, Louis Dumont, **Edward Evans-Pritchard**, **Rodney Needham**, and **Marshall Sahlins**. Respectful disagreement was evident in the writings of **Pierre Bourdieu** and Jacques Derrida. Although Mauss was a lifelong socialist, his students included right-wingers who later worked with the Vichy régime. This is possibly why he lost his apartment but survived the Second World War.

In Mauss's collaborative writings it is sometimes hard to discern his precise contribution. He took much from Durkheim, accepting that sociology (including anthropology) was a distinct discipline concerned with cross-cultural laws, and devoted to the study of distinct phenomena called 'social facts' and 'collective representations' that were irreducible to biological or psychological universals and differences (to 'instinct' or to 'race' for example). Like Durkheim, he searched for the commonalities in belief and practice that held societies together and accepted both his uncle's equation of religion with the sacred gathering or 'church' and the idea that religious practice always represented some sort of 'truth,' because the god/sacred being that was worshipped was society's projection of itself, most particularly in moments of communal ecstasy or *effervescence*. Durkheim's somewhat uneasy opposition between the 'sacred' (in place and time), marked by collective ritual, and the 'profane,' in which the collective was absent, was occasionally modified by his nephew. Mauss mastered the emerging ethnography of Australian Aborigines who were seen as exemplars of the earliest, least complex, and therefore clearest forms of religious expression.

In *Primitive Classification* Durkheim and Mauss discussed Australian, Zuni, and Chinese classification systems. 'Totemic' classifications of social groups (such as clans), the alignment of heavenly bodies, types of animals and plants, the moral order (sacred and profane), the cardinal points and the directions (such as up/down, center, North/South, West/East), are all constructed on parallel principles of binary opposition. They felt that such classifications required a physical, observable model. The template was the division of the horde or tribe, for example into twos and fours, which might be displayed on the sacred ground during times of ritual intensity. Symbolic classification of things was thus grounded in the social classification of people. Classificatory schemes increased in complexity as civilization advanced. These assumptions have been criticized for being ethnocentric, and even Mauss was later sceptical of such ideas of contemporary primitivity.

Binary classifications could be said to reflect social reality in another, literally down-to-earth sense. Mauss and his student Beuchat wrote an essay on the social morphology of the Eskimo (Inuit) people. For Mauss 'social morphology' included environment, demography, house building techniques, and aspects of social organization as it related to all the preceding facts, and so on. Mauss and Beuchat contrasted winter, when walruses and other sea mammals were hunted, with summer, when the Inuit subsisted by hunting caribou and other land animals. In winter people lived communally and engaged intensively in rituals. Summer in contrast, was profane with little ritual intensity as people dispersed in pursuit of migratory game.

Food taboos were linked to hunting practice. Caribou meat was banned in winter, and walrus meat was banned in summer. There are echoes of Mauss's concern with transhumance in Evans-Pritchard's account of the Nuer in equatorial Africa (1940), and Mauss's insistence on the practical grounding of classification systems is revived in Bourdieu's account of the Kabyle agricultural calendar.

Durkheim's absolute distinction between religion as collective and sacred and magic as individual and profane was modified by Mauss in *A General Theory of Magic* (1904). He noted that in practice the two categories occupied the ends of a continuum. Both involved harnessing MANA, or unusual power. The ideas behind any magical system were collective representations, just like those in ritual. One difference between magic spells and prayers is that the former are supposed to have automatic results, whereas prayer is often addressed to a superior being who might grant the request, and it might not be performed with respect to a specific object. In his unfinished work on prayer (Mauss 2003 [1909]), Mauss noted that, although it resembled a spell or a curse in its primitive forms, there was evidence that prayer existed in all societies. It encompassed both talk and action, begging the question of the priority of myth/narrative/speech versus ritual. Mauss distinguished between four kinds of speech acts – spell, curse, oath, and prayer.

One of Mauss's (and Hubert's) earliest essays, *Sacrifice* (Hubert and Mauss 1981 [1898]), was based largely on Semitic, Vedic, and classical sources. *Sacrifice* dismisses early theories which relied too heavily on single ideas that did not apply to all cases. These include **Tylor**'s theory that sacrifice is a form of gift exchange with a deity, and Robertson Smith's theory that clans ate their totemic animal in order to consume the substance of the ancestor that it represented. Hubert and Mauss noted that sacrifice could involve animals, plants, people, and things as victims and offering. The *dramatis personae* might include the person(s) for whose benefit the offering was being made, the performer of the ritual, the audience, the victim or offering, the instrument of sacrifice, and the divinity/spirit receiving the offering. They describe a three-stage process in sacrifice; similar to those outlined later by **Arnold van Gennep** in his work on rites of passage and Robert Hertz in his essay on death. In the central stage of the ritual of blood sacrifice, the victim acts as a conduit for communication between divinity, sacrificer, and the community. All ritual action leads to and away from this moment.

Mauss's concern with the sociology of practical and physical action is evident in a late paper on techniques of the body. The different ways American and French women walk, the ways in which different peoples use implements, make gestures, dance, handle food, drink, swim, are all social facts. Mauss labeled the process (custom, habit, physical molding) which produced such techniques of the body, *habitus*, a word later familiar to readers of Bourdieu.

In his last essay on the concept of the person (1985 [1938]) Mauss examined distinctions between legal and moral ideas of personhood in traditional and contemporary societies. In societies like aboriginal Australia, the NW Coast, and early Rome people were identified with their social roles. In modern societies *the individual* is the moral and legal focus.

Jacques Derrida said that Mauss discussed everything in *The Gift* but 'the gift' in the familiar sense of a spontaneous act of generosity which is instantaneously over; perceived as non-binding by the recipient and with no expectation of a return. This is an ideal type which might inspire some forms of giving in our society, but is remote from what Mauss describes, which is a variety of customs involving compulsory, planned exchanges. Mauss's first accomplishment in *The Gift* was to compare customs which had never been compared before. In *Argonauts of the Western Pacific* (1922), **Bronislaw Malinowski** compared KULA valuables to the British Crown Jewels but could not initially think of equivalents in the ethnographic record. The POTLATCH of the Kwakiutl, Haida, and Tlingit in British Columbia was competitive in ways very unlike kula. Potlatches could mark rites of passage but they were also held to validate rank and status. Huge quantities of food were consumed. Chiefs vied with each other to give away valuables. Potlatches might involve the destruction of property as a form of shaming. At potlatches, dancers impersonated sacred animals by wearing elaborate masks. The British Columbia Government found the institution incomprehensible and banned it. Mauss compared kula with potlatch and also with forms of ceremonial exchange in Samoa, New Zealand, prehistoric Germany, ancient Rome, and Iceland. He noted that there was a tripartite system of obligation – to give, to receive, and to repay – and that there were sanctions enforcing these obligations.

Mauss's central argument concerned differences between ceremonial gift exchange and the commercial transactions of a market economy. He did not deny that there was an economic side to ceremonial exchange. However, economics, politics, rituals, myth and folklore, feasting, drinking, and sociability were all elements in the picture. Each was imbricated in the other. Gift exchange was therefore a *total social fact*. In its pure form, ceremonial exchange did not exist in Western society, but exchanges at rites of passage and Christmas partially preserved the spirit of the gift. Mauss saw some of the best aspects of the exchange ethos in the modern co-operative movement which he supported.

Note that in Mauss's view societies that performed gift exchange were not seamless social wholes, held together by organic solidarity, as Durkheim postulated. Rather they needed rituals of exchange to repair cracks in the social body. In an essay published shortly after *The Gift* Mauss attributed a similar function to joking relationships.

Mauss thought of the power of the gift as an aspect of mana. Gift objects reflected the personality of the giver and indeed of all who had given and received them. In his search for an indigenous, spiritual concept of the mana type, Mauss discovered the *hau* of the gift – a spiritual force which would come to haunt the recipient who neglected the obligation to repay. As Sahlins has noted, Mauss misinterpreted a Maori text from which he derived the notion of *hau*.

In traditional societies, Mauss remarked, everything is stuff to be given away – objects, words, animals, and people. This model inspired Lévi-Strauss's analysis of marriage exchanges in *Elementary Structures of Kinship*. Although Mauss's work on exchange has been well received by those who believe that market forces are not a historical and cross-cultural universal, he has been criticized by those who believe in the universality of rational economic action, including Raymond Firth and the adherents of formalist economics, as well as cultural materialists and utilitarians such as the late **Marvin Harris**.

Selected readings

Durkheim, E. and Mauss, M. (1967 [1903]) *Primitive Classification*, translated and with an introduction by R. Needham, Chicago: University of Chicago Press.

Hubert, H. and Mauss, M. (1981 [1898]) *Sacrifice: Its Nature and Function*, translated by W. D. Halls, Chicago: University of Chicago Press.

James, W. and Allen, N. J. (eds) (1998) *Marcel Mauss: A Centenary Appreciation*, London: Guilford Press.

Mauss, M. (1972 [1904]), with Henri Hubert, *A General Theory of Magic*, translated by R. Brain, London: Routledge & Kegan Paul.

——(1973 [1935]) 'Techniques of the Body,' translated by. B. Brewster, *Economy and Society* 2: 70–88.

——(1979 [1904/1905]) with Henri Beuchat, *Seasonal Variations of the Eskimo. A Study in Social Morphology*, translated by. J. J. Fox, London: Routledge & Kegan Paul.

——(1985 [1938]) 'A Category of the Human Mind: The Notion of Person; the Notion of Self,' in *The Category of the Person: Anthropology, History, Philosophy*, M. Carrithers, S. Collins, and S. Lukes (eds), pp. 1–25, Cambridge: Cambridge University Press.

——(1990 [1925]) *The Gift: Forms and Function of Exchange in Archaic Societies*, translated by W. D. Halls, foreword by M. Douglas, London: Routledge.

——(2003 [1909]) *On Prayer*, edited and with an introduction by W. S. F. Pickering, translated by S. Leslie, New York: Berghahn.

ANDREW P. LYONS

MARGARET MEAD (1901–78)

When she died Mead was the world's most acclaimed anthropologist. No anthropologist has achieved her level of international fame. From the time of her first book, *Coming of Age in Samoa* (1928), Mead was in the public eye as a widely roving and highly articulate commentator on American culture. A public intellectual with impeccable scholarly credentials, she addressed the problems of her era in plain and cogent language, occasionally laced with flashes of wit. Whether it was nuclear power plants, abortion, breast-feeding, civil disobedience, euthanasia, or pre-marital sex, Mead had a pithy point of view.

An eloquent and engaging speaker, she was in great demand as a public lecturer, traveling frequently and widely to lecture, attend conferences, and carry out research. Skilfully utilizing the mass media of newspapers, magazines (she wrote a monthly column for *Redbook* from 1965 until her death), radio, film, and television, she set forth her often challenging and controversial views. When she championed the legalization of marijuana in 1969, the governor of Florida called her 'a dirty old lady,' an epithet that amused her. Her own anthropological colleagues sometimes scorned her, usually more privately than publicly, because of her provocative pronouncements or advice on almost any topic of social concern.

Born in Philadelphia she was the eldest of five children of Edward Sherwood and Emily Fogg Mead. Her father taught at the Wharton School at the University of Pennsylvania; her mother, a Wellesley graduate, suffragette, and sociologist, conducted research among Italian immigrants for her Master's thesis. Mead's father's widowed mother, a college graduate and former teacher, also lived with the family and was a strong positive influence in her life. Although both of her parents were secular agnostics, Mead elected to be baptized when she was eleven in her local Episcopal Church. Throughout her life she maintained ties to organized religion, serving on ecumenical committees and involved in both the National and World Council of Churches.

For one unhappy year, Mead attended DePauw University, her father's alma mater, and then transferred to Barnard College in New York City where her fiancé, Luther Cressman, was studying at Union Theological Seminary. Majoring in psychology, Mead took a course in her senior year with **Franz Boas** where she befriended his teaching assistant, **Ruth Benedict**. Made aware that many societies were rapidly disappearing and convinced by

Benedict of the relevance of anthropology to human problems, she decided on a career in anthropology. In 1923, Mead graduated from Barnard, married, kept her maiden name, and began work on her anthropology doctorate while completing her Master's in psychology.

Boas wanted Mead to do fieldwork on American Indians but she preferred a remote French Polynesian island. It was finally agreed that in 1925 she could go to Samoa to study female adolescence. The problem he proposed was to examine the extent adolescent upheavals in American society are biologically determined and the degree they were modified by the adolescent's culture. *Coming of Age in Samoa* is Mead's most famous book and her findings came down on the side of culture. Documenting adolescent sexuality and tropical love, it catapulted the idea of culture into the parlance of the general populace where today it is an essential concept to educators, politicians, and advertisers alike.

After her death Mead's account of Samoa was challenged by Derek Freeman's controversial book, *Margaret Mead and Samoa: The Making and Unmaking of an Anthropological Myth* (1983). Taking the position that there can be only one version of Samoa, even though the time, place, and conditions of their observations differed significantly, Freeman's rigidity found little sympathy from fellow anthropologists.

Back in New York, Mead began her first job as Assistant Curator of Ethnology at the American Museum of Natural History; her primary professional affiliation until her death. Her main responsibility was for the South Pacific artifact collections but there were public outreach expectations as well. Mead's office for her entire career was in the top of the lofty northwest tower of the original building and she delighted in its remoteness, working on the collections and writing undisturbed. Besides *Coming of Age in Samoa*, she wrote *Social Organization of Manua* and in 1929 obtained her PhD with the library dissertation *An Inquiry into the Question of Cultural Stability in Polynesia*.

Although Museum based, she also was an active and dedicated teacher. Except for the years 1968–70 when she chaired the social science division of Fordham University, her teaching position was usually that of a 'visiting professor' at various universities including Yale, Vassar, New York University, and Emory. Her major teaching commitment, however, was to Columbia University where she taught from 1940 onwards, usually as an adjunct professor.

Throughout her career, Mead welcomed the theories and data of other human disciplines and cultivated a large network of collaborators and friends in the fields of education, social work, psychology, sociology, psychiatry, and paediatrics, among others. She was especially close to the psychiatric profession and regularly lectured to psychiatry departments.

Divorcing Cressman, Mead married Reo Fortune, a New Zealand anthropologist whom she had met while returning from Samoa, in 1928 and began fieldwork in the Admiralty Islands north of New Guinea. Her resulting book, *Growing Up in New Guinea* (1930) was the first anthropological study of childhood and inaugurated the field of childhood socialization. Back in New York Mead was given a small summer grant by the Museum in 1930 to study Indian women, about whom little had been written. Fortune accompanied her to the Omaha Reservation in Nebraska where they found the people poor and demoralized. Mead worked diligently with the women and published a compelling picture of *The Changing Culture of an Indian Tribe* (1932), one of the first studies to look specifically at culture change.

Mead and Fortune intended to leave for New Guinea in early 1931 but a review of *Growing up in New Guinea* alleged that Mead did not know the kinship system. This so irritated her that they postponed their departure to write *Kinship in the Admiralty Islands* (1934), the most detailed monograph of kinship up until then. Mead, still intrigued with Boas's problem of innate attributes, intended to research the way sex roles are stylized in different cultures as a precursor to any study of innate difference between the sexes. Studying three different societies in New Guinea's Sepik Basin, she wrote one of her most influential and controversial books, later translated into ten languages (*Sex and Temperament in Three Primitive Societies*, 1935). Examining the stereotyped sex roles of the Arapesh, Mundugumor, and Tchambuli, Mead described how male and female temperament was culturally patterned and not an innate factor of one's gender.

Much has been written about the meeting in a Sepik River village of Mead and Fortune with Gregory Bateson, who was studying the Iatmul. The tangled love triangle that ensued generated the next stage of Mead's field research. In the spring of 1933, their research concluded, the three sailed together to Australia, and then each went their separate ways. Mead would not see Fortune again until after their divorce in 1935.

Mead and Bateson were married in Singapore in 1936. They then sailed to Bali, and spent the next two years there studying childhood socialization and personality development while pioneering new and more comprehensive field methods with the intensive use of tape recordings, film, and, especially, photography. Their joint publication was the path breaking, *Balinese Character: A Photographic Analysis.* They then returned to the Sepik River in Papua New Guinea where they worked with the Iatmul utilizing their new field methods in a comparative setting. While they were still in the field, the first of Mead's six-volume ethnography of the Arapesh was published. Mead returned to New York in early 1939; her only child, Mary Catherine Bateson, was born that December.

During WWII Mead took a leave from the Museum and became Executive Secretary of the National Research Council's Committee on Food Habits whose studies were directed toward national policy decisions such as food rationing. From 1947 to 1951, Mead was closely involved with the innovating multidisciplinary project, Columbia University Research in Contemporary Cultures, inaugurated by Ruth Benedict, and subsequently, after Benedict's death in 1948, convened by Mead. It was the largest study of its kind, some 120 social scientists and clinicians participated in work on seven cultures studied 'at a distance' that is, temporally or spatially inaccessible, with a research focus on national character structure. Its imaginative methods are detailed in *The Study of Culture at a Distance* edited by Mead and Rhoda Metraux in 1953. During this period, Mead maintained her interest in gender roles and in 1949 published *Male and Female,* using the seven South Pacific societies she had studied to make her comparative points.

In 1950, Mead and Bateson were divorced, and in 1953 she returned to Manus to record the cultural transformation generated by WWII. In her earlier fieldwork, she stated that change took place first in adult society before it could impact the lives of children. Now she found that it was the children who were the main transforming agents in the society and were influencing the adults. She reported her findings in *New Lives for Old* (1956). Although she continued to make short field trips, visiting the Iatmul in 1967 and returning several times to Manus, this was her last sustained fieldwork.

When Mead died shortly before her seventy-seventh birthday, it was the same day that the *World Almanac* cited her as one of the twenty-five most influential women in the world. Much honored, Mead received twenty-eight honorary degrees from around the world and more than forty awards, including the coveted Viking Medal in anthropology and, posthumously, the Presidential Medal of Honour. Among the professional organizations to which she was elected president are the American Anthropological Association, the American Association for the Advancement of Science (the first anthropologist in forty-four years since Boas), the World Federation of Mental Health, and the Society for Applied Anthropology.

Mead published forty-four books (eighteen co-authored) and over 1,000 articles, reports, prefaces, and book reviews. Her archived material at the Library of Congress is one of the largest for a single individual. Loyal to friends and family, Mead wrote hundreds of letters that not only trace her own life, but are a vivid chronicle of anthropology in the twentieth century. Mead was always careful to protect her personal reputation and, while she rarely dissembled, she withheld information in biographical accounts that would establish her bisexuality. That Mead was fully comfortable with her sexual orientation is indicated by the fact that her archived materials are available to researchers.

In reviewing Mead's long and astonishingly productive career, it is significant that she entered anthropology at the age of twenty-three when the discipline itself was just beginning to find its way. Thus, she was in a strategic position to help define and implement research on anthropology's problems as it evolved during the twentieth century, a fact of which she took full advantage. Her pioneering contributions include theoretical work in the sub-fields of CULTURE AND PERSONALITY and national character, recognition and use of photography and film as methodological tools, use of projective tests in the field, relating the uses of anthropology to other disciplines, and developing concepts for the fields of applied anthropology and culture change.

Although Mead herself was not an activist feminist, her pathmaking research on gender roles and socialization helped to fuel the 1960s' sexual revolution. In many ways Mead herself was an agent of cultural change in shaping our contemporary world. It was a role she consciously sought, cherished, and labored diligently at until the end of her life.

Selected readings

Bateson, M. C. (1984) *With a Daughter's Eye: A Memoir of Margaret Mead and Gregory Bateson*, New York: William Morrow and Company.

Lutkehaus, N. (2008) *Margaret Mead: The Making of an American Icon*, Princeton, NJ: Princeton University Press.

Mead, M. (1928) *Coming of Age in Samoa: A Psychological Study of Primitive Youth for Western Civilization*, New York: William Morrow.

——(1930) *Growing Up in New Guinea: A Comparative Study of Primitive Education*, New York: William Morrow.

———(1935) *Sex and Temperament in Three Primitive Societies*, New York: William Morrow.

———(1949) *Male and Female: A Study of the Sexes in a Changing World*, New York: William Morrow.

———(1956) *New Lives for Old: Cultural Transformation in Manus, 1928–1953*, New York: William Morrow.

WILLIAM E. MITCHELL

LEWIS HENRY MORGAN (1818–81)

Perhaps the author of the first ethnography, *League of the Ho-de-no-sau-nee or Iroquois* (1851), certainly the initiator of kinship studies exemplified in *Systems of Consanguinity and Affinity* (1871), clearly the first social EVOLUTIONIST in anthropology to relate the development of the family to the ways people made their living, Lewis Henry Morgan was also a lawyer, a politician (New York State Assemblyman and State Senator), a naturalist, and an occasional advocate of indigenous rights.

Morgan was raised in western New York State where his family farmed land that had belonged to Native Americans in the days before the War of Independence. He studied law at Union College, Schenectady. The syllabus at Union included the Classics and some relatively contemporary thinkers, including Lord Kames, the Edinburgh philosopher who surmised that humanity had passed through four stages of development, from hunting through pastoralism and farming to commerce.

Morgan possessed a strong interest in natural history. An early essay, 'Mind and Instinct' (1843) demonstrates a belief in the continuity of nature, rejecting any sharp divide between animal instinct and human intelligence. This theme recurs in his study of that very social creature, *The American Beaver and His Works* (1868).

Like many young men of his day, Morgan joined a 'secret' society, founding the Order of the Gordian Knot in Aurora, New York. After Morgan changed the name of his association to the *Grand Order of the Iroquois*, he embarked on a serious quest for authentic Iroquoian knowledge. He contacted Henry Schoolcraft, the foremost authority on Native American custom, and then had a chance encounter which was to alter the course of anthropology's history. In an Albany bookstore, he encountered a brilliant young Seneca, Hasaneanda (otherwise Ely Parker). Parker, who was later to become a Brigadier General in the US Army and, briefly, Commissioner of Indian Affairs, was privately educated by his people in the hope that he would represent their interests against the land companies and other colonizers who were depriving them of their land. He became Morgan's friend and was his guide on half-a-dozen visits to Seneca communities in places like Tonawanda, which is now part of Buffalo in New York State. Morgan could hardly be said to have done systematic fieldwork, but he did learn quite a lot in a short time. Parker contributed his own work to *League of the Iroquois*, although he was well aware of the power inequalities which led to the disclosure of sacred knowledge and to the decision by the Tonawanda community to put up with the 'adoption' of Morgan and two of his lodge members. The *League of the Iroquois* traces the seventeenth-century creation and subsequent development of the five nation confederacy of the Seneca, Mohawk, Cayuga, Onondaga, and Oneida (the Tuscarora joined later on), a political and military alliance. Fifty chiefs served at the will of the people. Clan mothers played an important role in the selection of chiefs. Morgan described: the matrilineal family; the exogamous clans (initially called 'tribes') which were based on the same matrilineal principle – like a huge, extended family; the two phratries in each tribe consisting of four clans apiece which existed for ceremonial purposes; and the six nations themselves. He noted the importance of the clan longhouses, communal dwellings for as many as twenty families, and the role of the clan mothers in their governance. There were descriptions of traditional horticulture, technology, and clothing. There were accounts of the main events in the traditional ceremonial calendar as well as the newer religion of Handsome Lake. Morgan admired the Seneca and for a brief period became their advocate in their legal battles against the Ogden Land Company. In the 1850s expanding business interests in Upper Michigan caused him temporarily to cease his study of the Iroquois and put an end to his work in their behalf. His interest resumed in the late 1850s after he attended a meeting of the American Association for the Advancement of Science.

Morgan had married Harriet Steele, his mother's brother's daughter. Harriet Morgan's priest was the Rev. Joshua Hall McIlvaine. The latter, along with Morgan and Martin Anderson, the first president of the University of Rochester, and several local notables, was a member of an informal group known as 'The Pundit Club,' which met to hear presentations by amateur and professional scholars. McIlvaine and Anderson were interested in comparative philology, and McIlvaine was also interested in ethnology. In one of his presentations to the Club Morgan discussed the well known work of Louis Agassiz at

Harvard who had taken strong positions on some controversial issues of the day. Agassiz believed in polygenesis, the creation as separate species of Europeans, Chinese, African, Amerindians, and so on. This position made Agassiz popular with Southern slavery advocates and unpopular with abolitionists and defenders of scientific and biblical monogenesis, the doctrine that all humanity is one species. Agassiz and other polygenists rejected the hypothesis that the ancestors of Amerindians had crossed the Bering Straits from Asia.

By way of contrast, it was the belief of the philologist Friedrich Max Müller, whom Morgan and McIlvaine admired, that the languages of the world would ultimately be shown to have a common origin. Following Müller, Morgan classified Eurasian languages into three groups – Aryan, Semitic, and Turanian. He added a fourth term, Ganowanian, for North American peoples. Morgan suspected that 'classificatory' kinship terminologies such as the one he had found among the Iroquois might provide a better answer than philology to the question of origins.

Until thirty years ago the comparative analysis of relationship terminologies and discussion of their social significance were core activities of anthropologists, thanks in part to Morgan. Some kin terminologies, such as the Hawaiian, are more concerned with relative age and/or generational status than blood ties. Terminologies may or may not reflect marriage systems past or present. They may lump an individual's close blood-kin together with people who may be more distant biological relatives or may not be related at all.

The Seneca relationship terminology represented a puzzle to Morgan because it seemed to be built on a different principle from that prevalent in Western societies. Among the Seneca, father and father's brother were called by the same term; mother and mother's sister were not distinguished. One's sister was called by the same term as one's parallel cousins – mother's sister's daughter and father's brother's daughter – but cross-cousins (mother's brother's daughter, father's sister's daughter) were distinguished from them. Siblings, as well as parallel and cross-cousins, were divided by sex (in English the term 'cousin' is not gendered). Morgan was later to talk of the Iroquois case as an exemplar of 'classificatory' (as opposed to 'descriptive') systems that failed to distinguish lineal from collateral relatives. One's mother's sister is 'collateral' because she is not in one's direct line of descent.

By 1858 Morgan had discovered that the Ojibwa had a terminology that was in some ways similar to the Iroquois. With the help of the new Smithsonian Institute Morgan sent out questionnaires all over the world. He also traveled to the American West, journeying as far as New Mexico and Montana, between 1859 and 1862. He concluded that 'classificatory' terminologies were widespread, and that the resemblances between Iroquoian and South Asian (e.g. Tamil) terminologies, supported both the ideas of monogenesis and direct migration from Asia to the Americas. Kinship terminologies, being naturally conservative, supplied evidence which the rest of language could not provide, often pointing to past stages in institutional development.

Morgan's conclusions were published in *Systems* in 1871. The vast book contained diagrams and data concerning 200 kinship terminologies worldwide. The last chapter contained some speculations about family origins which Morgan had developed in the mid-1860s. The kin terminologies of Malayo-Polynesian peoples did not differentiate between father, father's brother, or mother's brother, or between mother, mother's sister, or father's sister. McIlvaine suggested to Morgan that they might reflect a former sexual code which banned parent–child incest but permitted unions between siblings. Hawaiians no longer permitted sibling incest, but there was supposedly a rare custom of group marriage (Punalua) whereby two brothers from Group A might jointly marry two sisters from Group B. Such a practice would be consistent with the Iroquoian or Dravidian terminology. Thomas Trautmann (1987) has noted that Morgan did not pay much attention to McIlvaine's second suggestion, that such terminologies might be consistent with cross-cousin marriage.

Morgan now assumed that there had been a moral evolution from primitive promiscuity to Victorian monogamy, from early disorder through matriliny to patriliny and Victorian modernity, and that Iroquoian institutions emerged at an intermediate stage. The 1860s and 1870s were the highpoint of such social evolutionary theories which were legitimated by the recent scientific acceptance of an expanded time-scale for human development, following the triumph of uniformitarian geology and the confirmation of palaeontological finds and discoveries concerning the rise of lithic technology. Darwin was only part of this picture, inasmuch as natural selection barely figures in Morgan's writing. Morgan's British rivals, J. F. McLennan and John Lubbock, shared with him the idea of progression from a period of sexual chaos through matriliny toward moral order, but they employed different institutional fossils to advance their arguments – the ceremonial capture of brides played a role in the work of McLennan and Lubbock similar to that of kin terms in Morgan. Sir Henry Maine argued that the patriarchal family was primary and that there was no preceding stage of matriliny. All four men, including Maine, agreed that kinship, family, and the clan (whether matrilineal or patrilineal) were the building stones of most contemporary primitive societies which differed from civilized societies based on territory and commerce.

In *Ancient Society* (1877) and *Houses and House-Life among the American Aborigines* (1881), Morgan hypothesized that social evolution had developed in parallel fashion everywhere, albeit at a varying pace, through the unfolding of primal 'germs of thought.' The three primary stages of evolution – savagery, barbarism, and civilization – and their subdivisions (or 'ethnical periods') were characterized by parallel movements in technology, the family, political institutions, property ownership, and house type. The period of savagery saw the invention of fire, fishing, hunting, foraging, the spear, and the bow. This was accompanied by the development of the matrilineal family out of promiscuity, and the move from social isolates to the band (as we would now call it) to the matrilineal clan (or *gens* – the Roman term). Property remained communal throughout this stage. The invention of pottery heralded the development of horticulture and village settlement, ushering in the lower 'status of barbarism.' Marital unions were sometimes monogamous, sometimes polygamous, but were easily dissolved. There was a degree of sexual equality, and communalism in property still largely prevailed.

The matrilineal clan flourished among groups like the Iroquois whose communalism was marked by the building of longhouses. The advent of patriarchy was accompanied by the invention of irrigation agriculture and the domestication of animals in the middle stage of barbarism. Inequality of all kinds increased, and communalism declined. The progress of culture in the Americas and Eurasia diverged, because there were few animals domesticated in the Americas. The greater availability of animal protein in the Old World led to an increase in brain size among the Aryan and Semitic peoples (a kind of Lamarckian evolution) which enabled them to progress to the last stage of barbarism marked by the introduction of the iron plough and to civilization marked by the emergence of writing systems. At the end of the book Morgan expressed the hope that a 'mere property career' would not be the destiny of mankind.

These last thoughts appealed to Karl Marx, who made detailed notes on *Ancient Society* and found support for his own evolutionist ideas in Morgan's notion of primitive communalism. Engels's work, *The Origin of the Family, Private Property and the State* (1891), is largely a précis of Morgan. In the early twentieth century **Franz Boas** and **Robert Lowie** saw Morgan as the epitome of all the faults of unilinear evolutionism. The Kwakiutl, despite their splendid art and elaborate potlatches, were relegated by him to upper savagery because they were not farmers. The Aztecs were assimilated to the Iroquois, inasmuch as the distinctive features of state formation were downplayed. In Britain, Edward Westermarck and **Bronislaw Malinowski** disproved the notion of primitive promiscuity. From the 1930s to the 1960s **Leslie White** labored to rehabilitate Morgan's reputation and to develop a version of his grand ideas without the ethnocentrism which had embarrassed the Boasians. In the twenty-first century Morgan's work still inspires the minority of anthropologists who conduct kinship studies and believe in the comparative method.

Selected readings

Engels, F. (2001 [1891]) *The Origin of the Family, Private Property and the State,* Honolulu: University Press of the Pacific.

Morgan, L. H. (1963 [1877]) *Ancient Society,* with an introduction by Eleanor Leacock, Cleveland, OH: World Publishing Company.

——(1965 [1881]) *Houses and House-Life of the American Aborigines,* Chicago: University of Chicago Press.

——(1966 [1851]) *League of the Ho-de-no-sau-nee or Iroquois,* New York: Franklin.

——(1970 [1868]) *The American Beaver and His Works,* New York: Franklin.

——(1997 [1871]) *Systems of Consanguinity and Affinity of the Human Family,* with an introduction by Elisabeth Tooker, Lincoln: University of Nebraska Press.

Resek, C. (1960) *Lewis Henry Morgan, American Scholar,* Chicago: University of Chicago Press.

Trautmann, T. R. (1987) *Lewis Henry Morgan and the Invention of Kinship,* Berkeley: University of California Press.

ANDREW P. LYONS

GEORGE PETER MURDOCK (1897–1985)

George Peter Murdock was born in rural Connecticut. His father was an educated farmer, involved in politics and banking, and George and his siblings were raised in an atmosphere fostering New England notions of free inquiry, individualism, and agnosticism. He was educated at the Phillips Academy, Andover and then studied American History at Yale, with a leave to briefly serve in the First World War, then returning to Yale to earn his BA in 1919.

After attempting to study law at Harvard, and some travels in Asia, Murdock settled on pursuing doctoral studies at Yale under Albert G. Keller. At Yale, Murdock studied geography, and a hybrid mixture of sociology, psychology, and anthropology that was conjoined with the academic traditions of William Graham Sumner and Keller. This milieu was counter to the Boasian tradition of historical particularism that was then dominating American academic anthropology at Columbia University, but also at other universities being populated with **Franz Boas**'s students. These studies led Murdock to incorporate much more positivist research methods than the Boasians adopted when they conducted cultural rather than biological inquiries, and led Murdock to incorporate Boas's critique of unilineal evolution while pursing models of multilinear evolution. This drive to collect, operationally sort, and positivistically analyze cultural data would guide the development of much of Murdock's professional life. Even as **Leslie White** struggled to resurrect strands of **L. H. Morgan**'s cultural evolutionary theory, Murdock translated Julius Lippert's *The Evolution of Culture* (1931) into English (as part of his doctoral work), and his 1934 text, *Our Primitive Contemporaries*, illustrates how his cultural evolutionary views influenced his categorizations of different societies.

From 1928 to 1960, Murdock was a professor of anthropology at Yale. He came late to fieldwork, having studied anthropology outside of the Boasian tradition. With the assistance of **Edward Sapir**, Murdock studied a Haida village in 1932 and lived with the Tenino of Oregon during the summers of 1934 and 1935. While this fieldwork impressed on Murdock the importance of field data collection and analysis, his life's work was decidedly confined to libraries and research institutions rather than the field.

Murdock was associated with Yale's Institute of Human Relations (IHR), which combined the work of anthropologists, psychologists, sociologists, and psychiatrists, though prior to the late 1930s most of the work produced by this group tended to focus more on psychological than cultural analysts. After 1937, Murdock's IHR work focused on the creation of a 'cross-cultural survey' designed to present comparable data from what was seen as a stratified sample of human societies. These efforts to distil quantitative ethnographic data to be analyzed using statistical methods pioneered new analytical techniques and theories in American anthropology. Murdock explicitly rejected Boasian notions that cultures or cultural traits could not be meaningfully compared, and that such comparisons could not be used to generalize scientific statements or regularity or causality. Prior to America's entry into the Second World War, the collection and analysis of such data had progressed to a very basic level, but with America's entry into the war Murdock and his 'culture bank,' a collection and catalog of disjointed cultural information, suddenly were in high demand by the United States military.

Murdock, who joined the Navy Reserve as an officer, held multiple positions during the war. With the assistance of John Whiting and Clellan Ford he adopted the preliminary cross-cultural index work he had completed at Yale to the wartime purpose of supplying the Office of the Chief of Naval Operations with a series of twenty *Civil Affairs Handbooks* that described the historical, cultural, geographical, administrative, and economic features of island groups of the South Pacific of importance to the American war effort. Elements of Murdock's prewar organizational structure were apparent in the organization and presentation of information in these books.

What would be Murdock's strength in wartime, the standardization of cultural information in a simplified, locatable, and usable form, would later provide the basis of critique. But the uniform collection and presentation of cultural data in wartime was extremely useful to US armed forces, and the success of Murdock's war work in informing military and intelligence work directly paved the way for his post-war cross-cultural research, and provided clear rationalizations for funding his post-war, Ivory Tower academic research. Murdock and the team at IHR developed a standardized report format that organized specific culture traits on topics as diverse as economic systems, etiquette, marriage patterns, fishing, or land use. Each report used an almost identical organizational format and trait categories, and different information was provided for each island group; this organizational format was suited to the Navy's needs (of conquest and occupation), and used an organizational methodology and structure that would later be expanded in Murdock's Human Relations Area File (HRAF). Murdock's ability to make these different cultures legible, in the sense described by James Scott (1998), made his work of high value to the military during the war, and brought HRAF funding in the post-war period.

His 1949 book *Social Structure* established Murdock as the premier cross-cultural methodologist and theorist. *Social Structure* was an ambitious effort to use positivist methods to identify and distinguish elements of social structure, with the hope of identifying specific elements of culture (e.g. forms of kinship, marriage, religion) that could be linked with other traits or other culture complexes. This was a library-based, as opposed to field-based, research project. Murdock began by compiling and sifting through published materials on eighty-five societies; with time he expanded this sampling of societies to a total of 250.

In *Social Structure*, Murdock used the available ethnographic literature to identify and codify information on: familial organization, kinship, clans, community, determinants of kinship terminology, the evolution of social organization, and the social organization and regulation of human sexuality. Rather than advancing an aggressively universalist theory accounting for specific forms of social structure, Murdock instead advanced and tested a number of smaller ideas and 'theorems.' For example, in his chapter on 'determinants of Kinship Terminology,' he used the data compiled from his sample of 250 societies to test and confirm: '*Theorem 22*: Exogamous moieties tend to be associated with kinship terminology of the bifurcate merging type' (Murdock 1949: 169). With some notable exceptions Murdock mostly linked specific elements of social structure with other structural components – thus, his statistical analysis sought to correlate terminologies like our own with neolocal residence, but he did not correlate the presence of matrilineal descent with specific forms of economic organization.

Murdock established the Human Relations Area File (HRAF) in 1949 at Yale as a non-profit consortium devoted to codifying and indexing cultural traits in ethnographies so that it could later be retrieved by other scholars using HRAF's indexing system (found in the *Outline of Cultural Materials* [1939]) to conduct cross-cultural research on these traits. Originally five research universities formed the HRAF consortium, but the list of sponsoring universities later expanded, and other agencies, including the Central Intelligence Agency, funded directed research projects. From 1949–58 HRAF data was organized on five by eight inch pieces of paper that were cataloged and organized in large file cabinets at member universities and institutions. Each entry was duplicated and filed under its *Outline of Cultural Materials* trait heading and under the specific culture it referenced. From 1958 until the late-1980s (when computer versions of HRAF were developed) records were produced on microfiche.

In 1960, Murdock left Yale to be appointed the Andrew W. Mellon Professor of Anthropology at the University of Pittsburgh's newly established anthropology department. At Pittsburgh he founded the journal *Ethnology*, and remained editor of the journal until 1973. In 1967 he published *Ethnographic Atlas*, a statistical compendium of eighty-nine traits culled from HRAF on 1,170 societies that provided researchers with summaries of data to be examined for correlations. Murdock's 1981 *Atlas of World Culture* divided the world into six geographical conglomerates, summarized cultural features with generalized narratives, and provided coded ethnographic data.

Throughout his career, Murdock was an intense political actor engaging in academic and personal disputes with colleagues. At Yale and Pittsburgh he fought with colleagues over resources, patronage, and research, and in his disputes within the larger anthropological community he mixed politics, theory, and personality.

In 1947 anthropologist Melville Jacobs was subjected to an investigation by the Washington State Legislature and the University of Washington's Committee on Tenure and Academic Freedom to determine if he was Communist; the following year archaeologist Richard Morgan was subjected to a similar Red Hunt investigation and fired from his job at the Ohio State Museum. At the 1948 business meeting of the American Anthropological Association, concerned members spoke out against a climate of fear that seemed to be building towards an anti-Communist fever; a dozen anthropologists spoke forcefully in favor of the creation of an AAA committee protecting academic freedom. Later that week, as a reaction to this movement, Murdock wrote a four page, detailed letter to FBI Director, J. Edgar Hoover recounting the details of the meeting and identifying (and providing specific information on) a dozen anthropologists who spoke out against these witch hunts, and in favor of an AAA committee investigating such affronts to academic freedom.

Not only did Murdock present Hoover with a sinister narrative account of a meeting focusing on academic freedom and civil rights, but he gave the FBI dossiers of a dozen of his enemies – and the passages from this letter were later reproduced in the FBI files of these targets. Here's what Murdock wrote about Jacobs:

Melville Jacobs, University of Washington, Seattle, Wash. Has publicly admitted (after an original denial) that he has been a party member. There is good evidence that he is an extremely important figure, a genuine big shot in the organization. He appears to be the only one of the twelve who has the unusual authority to express minor criticisms of Russia or of Communist activities when these are adjudged to be tactically or strategically useful. Characteristically, he remained completely in the background during the Toronto meeting, though observed in conference with the active leaders just prior to the important discussion.

(Price 2004: 74)

Murdock's letter presented Hoover with similar damaging profiles of eleven other civil libertarians who had spoken up for establishing AAA support for scholars under attack. The fear of Hoover's power was so widespread that it is inconceivable that Murdock did not know how much damage he would cause, but, as if to assuage some guilt, Murdock closed his letter claiming: 'I have been in some personal conflict as to whether to write this letter or not, and I very strongly hope that nothing I have said will be used in any way to damage the purely academic and scientific careers of the persons I have named' (Price 2004: 75). The ironic outcome of the AAA's vote to establish a Committee on Scientific Freedom was that Murdock was soon appointed to this committee. That Murdock did not recuse himself from this appointment, given his role as an FBI informer, provides some measure of his commitment to political maneuvering within the discipline.

Murdock left an enduring legacy in American anthropology. Many graduate students passed through his hands including Leopold Pospisil, Ward Goodenough, Rich Scaglion, and Melvin Ember. He served as president of the three most prominent American anthropological societies: the American Anthropological Association (1955), the Society for Applied Anthropology (1947), and the American Ethnological Society (1952–53). Murdock was a methodological visionary insofar as his efforts to cross-index and retrieve massive collections of texts in a pre-computer, pre-internet world pushed data-retrieval to the very limits of the technology of his era.

Selected readings

Murdock, G. P. (1934) *Our Primitive Contemporaries*, New York: Macmillan.
——(1949) *Social Structure*, New York: Macmillan.
——(1954) *Outline of World Cultures*, New Haven, CT: Human Relations Area Files Press.
——(1967) *Ethnographic Atlas*, Pittsburgh, PA: University of Pittsburgh Press.
——(1981) *Atlas of World Cultures*, Pittsburgh, PA: University of Pittsburgh Press.
Price, D. (2004) *Threatening Anthropology: McCarthyism and the FBI's Surveillance of Activist Anthropologists*, Durham, NC: Duke University Press.
Scott, J. (1998) *Seeing Like a State*, New Haven, CT: Yale University Press.

DAVID PRICE

RODNEY NEEDHAM (1923–2006)

Needham was born in Kent. He served as a Captain in the Gurkha Rifles during the war and subsequently studied Chinese at London University and Social Anthropology at the University of Oxford, where he taught for almost his entire career, after a brief stint at the University of Illinois. He became Professor of Social Anthropology in 1976, retiring in 1990. For most of his time as Professor he taught and researched at All Souls College, rather than at the Institute for Social Anthropology, because of collegial disagreements.

Needham changed his name from Green in 1947, after a conflict with his father. Also in 1947 he married Ruth Brysz, later known as Claudia Needham, who collaborated with him on translations of French scholars. In the 1950s Needham conducted fieldwork in Indonesia. While most of his influential work was theoretical, his Indonesian experience was important, insofar as it led him to an appreciation for several important Dutch scholars and to a long term commitment to the study of systems of prescriptive marriage, for which a number of Indonesian societies are particularly important test cases.

In *Remarks and Inventions: Skeptical Essays about Kinship*, Needham encapsulates a quest which occupied him for much of his career:

A true theory would call in the first place for a vocabulary of analytical concepts that were appropriate to the phenomena under consideration but would not be merely derived from them.

(Needham 1974: 16)

Much of Rodney Needham's work was concerned with two things: the categories which anthropologists use to order their data and the categories by which ethnographic subjects order their lives. He hoped that improvements in defining anthropologists' analytical categories would lead to more accurate and elegant mappings of the cosmologies and taxonomies employed by the people they study. Another passion of Needham's was the translation, editing, and uncovering of earlier, often forgotten work which, he believed, had contributed to these projects.

Needham's students in the 1960s were introduced to their teacher's enthusiasms in tutorials, for which the assignments were likely to include the work he had brought to the attention of British anthropologists: the writings of Hertz and others on the symbolism of right and left, A. M. Hocart's suggestion that the anthropological 'problem' of classificatory kinship was largely an artifact of mistranslation, and **Arnold van Gennep**'s acerbic short stories exposing some of the idiocies of academic life (van Gennep 1967). He frequently made the point that some hoary subject of anthropological analysis, such as the incest taboo, was not a 'useful analytical notion' in itself, though it might be dissolved into some other notion such as 'rules governing the distribution of women.' Needham was not alone in his ardor for this activity; **Edmund Leach** too dismissed such categories as 'butterfly collecting.'

The monograph which cemented Needham's reputation, *Structure and Sentiment: A Test Case in Social Anthropology* (1962), contained all of the elements described. The book was a critique of *Marriage, Authority and Final Causes: A Study of Unilateral Cross-Cousin Marriage*, (1955), George C. Homans's and David Schneider's application of the work of **A. R. Radcliffe-Brown** to the problem of prescriptive alliance, the compulsory marriage of men in certain societies to the daughters of their real or classificatory mothers' brothers. Radcliffe-Brown had argued that in strongly patrilineal societies, fathers are disciplinary figures while a man's mother's brother is often an object of strong affective bonds. Homans and Schneider suggested that the daughter of such a beloved relative would be a desirable marriage partner. Needham argued that the reasons for mother's brother's daughter marriage were logical and social, not emotional, and that in societies which practiced prescriptive alliance the systems of classification governing relatives, domestic space, the body, and the cosmos formed interrelated systems articulated around the rules governing marriage.

Structure and Sentiment, along with the contributions of Leach and **Mary Douglas**, established a British version of STRUCTURALISM. For the British structuralists, society could be analyzed as a system of classification in which the distance between socially imposed categories of things, people, animals, plants, and features of the landscape and the cosmos was regularly mitigated by exchanges of women, property, sacrifices, and assistance, as well as by ritual which enabled movement from one category to another. This version of structuralism, while inspired by **Claude Lévi-Strauss**'s work, was perhaps even more grounded in a direct reading of earlier sources in French: **Marcel Mauss**'s essay on gift exchange, van Gennep's essay on rites of passage, Robert Hertz's essays on the symbolism of right and left and on the rituals surrounding death, and Durkheim and Mauss's *Primitive Classification* which postulated an equivalence between the ordering of the natural world and that of the social world in primitive societies. Indeed, Needham had translated Hertz's work as well as the essay on primitive classification. It is probably more useful to speak of different versions of structuralism which emerged in England and France than to argue about which version was 'true' structuralism.

Key to his reading of prescriptive alliance was Needham's lifelong search for universal patterns of thought, which could be demonstrated unequivocally by ethnographic fact. The binary classifications of societies practicing prescriptive alliance, in which left and right handedness, broader spatial categories, social groupings, and moral concepts could be said to be symbolic equivalents, suggested binarism as just such a universal pattern. At the time he wrote *Structure and Sentiment*, Needham was attracted to the work of Lévi-Strauss, who appeared to share these views about prescriptive alliance, and he had translated Lévi-Strauss's seminal essay *Le totemisme aujourd' hui*. This work featured analytic strategies Needham favored: the deconstruction of an anthropologically defined 'social institution' (totemism) and its replacement by a system of logical relationships (the mirroring of the classification of animal species by the classification of human groups linked by the exchange of women). However, by the time Needham edited and oversaw the translation of Lévi-Strauss's 1949 classic, *The Elementary Structures of Kinship* (Lévi-Strauss 1969) disagreements had developed between them, and Lévi-Strauss used the volume's preface to publicly distance himself from Needham's understanding of key aspects of his work.

Lévi-Strauss accused Needham of overstating the difference between prescriptive and preferred alliance. Lévi-Strauss argued that both systems created an opposition between 'wife givers' and 'wife takers' around which an entire regime of exchange and obligations could be ordered. Needham took Lévi-Strauss's use of two separate terms as denoting two separate types of marriage system, and had written about the much more orderly alignment of social organization and collective representations found in societies with prescriptive alliance, compared to societies which recommended, but did not prescribe, a particular class of relatives (real or classificatory mother's brothers' daughters) as marriage partners.

For Needham the fact that prescriptive systems seemed to provide a near perfect, ethnographically demonstrable, example of congruence between collective representations and social organization was of central importance. He was fond of quoting George Dumézil's assertion that systems of thought were truly 'in the facts' and existed at the conscious, not merely the unconscious, level. However, Needham acknowledged that the orderliness of prescriptive alliance was an exception, and that empirically demonstrable patterns in human thought and society were elusive, and in human emotion even more so.

Many scholars regard *Belief, Language and Experience* (1972) as Needham's most important work. In it, Needham, following

Wittgenstein, argues that there is no feature common to all instances of 'belief' that would render 'belief' a universal experience. Indeed, he argued, there is no evidence for the existence of any interior state to which the label 'belief' might refer, in such a way that a human hearing the word about another human would know what the person said to 'believe' was actually experiencing. Needham suggested that 'belief' was one of many 'odd job words' describing aspects of human experience that posed difficulties for the comparative method.

In an important 1975 essay, 'Polythetic Classification: Convergence and Consequences' Needham discussed what he believed to be appropriate and inappropriate categories for comparative analysis in anthropology. 'Odd job words' like marriage might be useful in describing the customs of individual societies, so long as one made clear what range of meanings they had in such cases, but as foci of comparison, particularly where that comparison was intended to identify universal human behaviors or capabilities, they were useless, as there was no possibility of arriving at a common meaning. However, he suggested that conceptual relationships such as 'symmetry' or 'complementarity' might provide more useful topics for comparison than apparently morphologically similar 'institutions' that gave the illusion of being monothetic classes.

In works published during the 1970s and 1980s Needham explored several such relationships and recommended to readers a number of thinkers whose work he considered exemplary. He republished Charles Staniland Wake's neglected rethinking of the premises of nineteenth century social EVOLUTIONISM (Wake, edited by Needham 1967 [1889]). In *Exemplars* (1985) Needham discusses an eclectic range of thinkers, including Locke, Swedenborg, Wittgenstein, and Dumezil. In *Primordial Characters* (1978), Needham took up the question of whether something akin to Jung's archetypes, supposedly universal, inherited germs of human thought, existed, and found that common, emotionally laden images, such as 'the witch' could be dissolved into a few logical relationships. In the case of witchcraft, the relationship was the 'inversion' of 'normal' categories, altogether less romantic than the concept of the witch that his readers had likely brought to the encounter. In *Counterpoints* (1987) he took up the subject of 'opposition' in broad, comparative terms.

What of the early polemics on kinship, which had seen Needham involved in such strident debates? By the mid-1970s, kinship had, for Needham, become one of those illusory monothetic categories fit only for dissolution. Interestingly, his early adversary, David Schneider, seems to have undergone a similar transition, coming ultimately to regard kinship not as a 'thing' based on the facts of mating and birth, but as a series of metaphors such as 'blood' and 'love,' though Schneider attempted to have the last word by arguing that he himself had gone farther than Needham in rejecting the category of kinship as a useful analytical notion (Schneider 1984).

The British and French structuralists wrote at a time when old categories were breaking down, although arguments ensued between them over exactly what was to replace them. The truly radical and exciting nature of this era should not be forgotten.

Selected readings

Durkheim, É. and Mauss, M. (1963) *Primitive Classification*, trans. and with an introduction by Rodney Needham, London: Cohen & West.

Hertz, R. (1960) *Death and the Right Hand*, trans. R. Needham and C. Needham, Aberdeen: Cohen & West.

Homans, G. C. and Schneider, D. M. (1955) *Marriage, Authority, and Final Causes; a Study of Unilateral Cross-Cousin Marriage*, Glencoe, IL: Free Press.

Leach, E. (1966) 'Rethinking Anthropology,' in *Rethinking Anthropology*, London: The Athlone Press.

Lévi-Strauss, C. (1964) *Totemism*, trans. R. Needham, London: Merlin Press.

——(1969) *The Elementary Structures of Kinship*, trans. J. H. Bell, J. R. von Sturmer, and R. Needham (ed.), London: Eyre and Spottiswoode.

Mauss, M. (1954 [1925]) *The Gift: Forms and Functions of Exchange in Archaic Societies*, trans. I. Cunnison, London: Cohen & West.

Needham, R. (1962) *Structure and Sentiment: A Test Case in Social Anthropology*, Chicago: University of Chicago Press.

——(1972) *Belief, Language and Experience*, Chicago: The University of Chicago Press.

——(1974) *Remarks and Inventions: Skeptical Essays about Kinship*, London: Tavistock Publications.

——(1975) 'Polythetic Classification: Convergence and Consequences,' *Man*, N.S. 10(3): 349–69.

——(1978) *Primordial Characters*, Charlottesville: University of Virginia Press.

——(1985) *Exemplars*, Berkeley: University of California Press.

——(1987) *Counterpoints*, Berkeley: University of California Press.

Radcliffe-Brown, A. R. (1924) 'The Mother's Brother in South Africa,' *The South African Journal of Science* 21: 542–55.

Schneider, D. M. (1984) *A Critique of the Study of Kinship*, Ann Arbor: University of Michigan Press.

van Gennep, A. (1960) *The Rites of Passage*, London: Routledge & Kegan Paul.

——(1967) *The Semi-Scholars*, trans. R. Needham, London: Routledge & Kegan Paul.

Wake, C. S. (1967 [1889]) *The Development of Marriage and Kinship*, edited and with an introduction by R. Needham, Chicago: University of Chicago Press.

HARRIET D. LYONS

SHERRY B. ORTNER (1941–)

Even at the apex of professional accomplishment as Distinguished Professor of Anthropology at the University of California, Los Angeles (2004–Present), Sherry Ortner continues aspiring to 'define directions at certain moments in the discipline.' Throughout her career Ortner has made a habit of challenging convention and starting conversations to critically engage the human condition theoretically and socially. Whether it is attempting to get at the nature of symbolic action through Sherpa rituals or playing a major role in the beginning of feminist anthropology, Ortner seeks to produce 'pieces that make a difference.'

Born in Newark, New Jersey in 1941, Ortner traces her interest in anthropology to her father's 'magic suitcase' containing exotic items brought home from his extensive travels. Ortner graduated from Weequahic High School in 1958 and went on to Bryn Mawr College. In an introductory anthropology course, childhood curiosity was met by tantalizing images of cultural otherness and the romance of conducting research in faraway places. The image of **Margaret Mead** and the Pacific Islands led her to the University of Chicago for graduate school. Initially she worked with David Schneider but found him overly critical and eventually found a mentor in **Clifford Geertz**. Geertz's work on religion and the interest in Buddhism within anthropology at the time led Ortner to Nepal where she studied Sherpa religious practices. After graduating in 1970 Ortner took a position at Sarah Lawrence College and embarked on a distinguished career as a professional anthropologist, holding positions as Professor of Anthropology (1977–95), Department Chair (1986–89), and Sylvia L. Thrupp Professor of Anthropology and Women's Studies (1992–94) at the University of Michigan; Professor of Anthropology at the University of California, Berkeley (1994–96); and Professor of Anthropology at Columbia University (1996–2005, Department Chair 2003–4).

To her contemporaries Ortner may be a 'conversation starter,' as she describes her multiple seminal works. However, within an historical context commentators note an emphasis on bridge making between theoretical and methodological divisions within anthropology. Rather than feeding crises Ortner's efforts at creatively combining competing viewpoints and her foreshadowing of important moments in anthropology are apparent in her earliest work. 'On Key Symbols' (1973) reflects a turn from 'ethnoscience' toward an informant-centered elaboration of symbols, but also maintains a firm footing in the structural elements of cultural analysis. This mixed approach guides *Sherpas through their Rituals* (1978), Ortner's first major ethnographic work. *Sherpas* asserts that some symbols used by societies are of particular importance, and if understood they can contain the understanding of the whole culture. Ortner uses an interpretive framework to argue for an analysis that privileges local categories and illustrates the ways in which Buddhist ritual is connected with daily Sherpa social life. *Sherpas* moves beyond standard interpretive anthropology to account for the relationship between anthropological categories and structural inequalities embedded in local knowledge/experience. Ortner privileges textual understandings among villagers and people disenfranchised by kin relations, as well as the reinforcement of social stratification through status, foreshadowing the developing concern over representation and agency that would occupy 1980s and 1990s anthropology.

Concurrent with publishing on Sherpas and interpretive anthropology, Ortner, along with others in the 'anthropology of women' movement, began to address a three-fold problem: the lack of women-centered ethnographic accounts and analysis, the ubiquity of women's subordination cross-culturally, and the overwhelming sexism within the field of anthropology. 'Is Female to Male as Nature is to Culture,' an essay in the first book on feminist anthropology, *Women, Culture, and Society* (1974), is a thoughtful critique of male-centered anthropology. Ortner uses a **Lévi-Strauss**ian structural analysis to propose that a woman's body and its functions, such as childbirth, appear to be closer to nature. Because men do not bear children they are more involved in the reproduction of culture. Ultimately culture is intended to rise above and control nature and thus men's association with culture accounts for the universal subordination of women. Given that she has been heavily criticized for her analysis by subsequent writers in feminist anthropology, one must look at the context of her argument, at what is particularly 'Ortner' about 'Is Female to Male … .' The ultimate act of radicalization in the essay is Ortner's use of Lévi-Straussian **STRUCTURALISM** to account for and critique universal male domination. Ortner seized the social and intellectual moment to transform a paradigm in and of itself a product of male-centered anthropology to begin the debate of anthropology's study of sexuality, gender, and sex as well as initiating the creation of feminist anthropology.

Ortner again attempted to reorient the discussion of sex, sexuality, and gender toward issues of hierarchy with the publication of *Sexual Meanings* (1981) co-edited with Harriet Whitehead. This collection of essays takes varied approaches to the relationship between prestige hierarchies and gender. In the introduction, Ortner and Whitehead propose looking at sexuality and reproduction as embodied with meanings that have the potential to generate social asymmetry. Asymmetries at the site of sexuality and gender are rendered political in ways comparable cross-culturally. Rather than retreating to an extreme CULTURAL RELATIVISM or strict political economy, Ortner again brings discussion of status and sex/gender constructions back to the internal logic of culture as an analytical category.

In *High Religion: A Cultural and Political History of Sherpa Buddhism* (1989), Ortner turned to history and practice theory, an approach based on the 'logic' of culture and placing politicized subject positions at the center of analysis to help resolve the struggle within anthropology over the relevance of the culture concept. In examining the founding of the first celibate Buddhist monasteries in Northeast Nepal, Ortner maintains a commitment to her roots in hermeneutic understandings of cultural schemata, but innovates by placing this schema within the structural constraints generated by the politics of inheritance and the moral economy among Sherpas. The founding of celibate monasteries has cultural origins in centuries' old schemata which framed the realignment of social relations caused by opportunities for the accumulation of wealth outside traditional Sherpa fraternal inheritance and political intervention by the Nepalese state. The founding of monasteries provided avenues for the expression of fraternal rivalry through sponsorship of monasteries as well as opportunities for small people to gain prestige by entering celibate monastic life. Continuing to emphasize the importance of practice, Ortner edited the volume *Culture/Power/History* (1994) that featured some of the most prominent thinkers working on issues of practice in social theory.

In the 1990s Ortner contributed to the intense reflection in anthropology with multiple works concerning the culture concept and the analytical use of resistance, domination, and agency, with the edited volume *The Fate of 'Culture'* (1999) as well as essays in journals. However, it is in her J. I. Staley Prize-winning book, *Life and Death on Mt. Everest* (1999) that we see a culmination of Ortner's mastery of

Nepalese culture paired with an accessible critique and creative use of some features of 1990s anthropological thought. She proposes that cultural encounters on Everest come from 'the embodiment of other forms of difference'; differences that each group, the sahibs (the non-Sherpa mostly European climbers) and Sherpa porters and guides, bring to their encounters with each other and the mountain. Ortner proposes that sahibs and Sherpas are engaged in 'serious games' – the ways in which individual action is not the result of 'cultural scripts' or 'material necessity' – but rather an individual's intentional and purposeful negotiation of the 'constant play of power' in matters of human relationships (Ortner 1999: 23–24).

By Ortner's own account her transition in the late 1990s from researching Nepalese Sherpas to American society was an overwhelming experience. After three books and a film on the Sherpas, Ortner turned to the issue of class in America. Conducting fieldwork on the Weequahic High School Class of 1958 in Newark, New Jersey, Ortner spent years retooling her ethnographic understanding of American culture. When asked about giving up the comfort of being the foremost authority on Nepalese Sherpas to conduct ethnographic research in the US, Ortner spoke of the disorientation and felt as if 'I were a graduate student again.' Working in the US and researching laterally across lines of socio-political structure has traditionally been looked down upon by American anthropology. When queried, Ortner said, 'there are a lot of anthropologists "studying-up" with their fieldwork on American culture,' modestly unaware that her work paved the way for a transition in attitudes for the discipline.

In *New Jersey Dreaming: Capital, Culture and the Class of '58* (2003), Ortner continues to address the relationship between culture and materiality by focusing on high school as a 'social game' where multiple forms of capital intersected in the lives of the Class of '58 to formulate paths to future successes and failures, what she characterizes as 'boy tracks' and 'girl tracks' which intersect the material realities of individual students. Turning her attention to class structure in America, Ortner again addresses the tension between structure and agency by drawing our attention to the changing shape of the socio-economic landscape. Ortner argues that the 'hidden injuries of class' experience are embodied in a post-war America where the class structure looks more like an hour glass, bulging at the top and bottom, and constricted in the middle.

Ortner's concern for the fate of culture in anthropology continues in her attempts to reconcile the culture concept with shifts in social theory that find culture as a somewhat nebulous 'moving object.' In *Anthropology and Social Theory* (2006) Ortner proposes that practice theory should adapt to contemporary critiques of the 'old' culture concept by examining culture as a set of 'public texts' 'analyzed for the kinds of ideological work they [do]' (2006: 13) and as a set of discourses that are spatially mobile through socio-economic flows of late capitalism. Concurrently, she argues for the need of an understanding of culture that is temporal through formations and possibilities of constraint.

These latest theoretical formulations are the basis of Ortner's 'Hollywood' project, which began as an examination of the culture industry of Hollywood and morphed into an ethnographic project with independent filmmakers. Finding Hollywood personalities and studios unwilling to cooperate, Ortner turned to the UCLA film school where she found a welcoming culture that celebrates itself as the anti-Hollywood. She is currently 'in the field' among the producers, writers, and directors of the independent film community. Ortner sees this as a return to her 'interpretive days' but with the goal of 'upgrading the interpretive process.' Her inevitable goal is to use the culture industry to illustrate a more 'fluid concept of culture' that can reveal how 'texts move into complicated relationships with people's lives.'

Select readings

Ortner, S. (1973) 'On Key Symbols,' *American Anthropologist* 75: 1338–46.
——(1978) *Sherpas through their Rituals,* Cambridge: Cambridge University Press.
——(1984) 'Theory in Anthropology since the Sixties,' *Comparative Studies in Society and History* 26(1): 126–66.
——(1989) *High Religion: A Cultural and Political History of Sherpa Buddhism,* Princeton, NJ: Princeton University Press.
——(1995) 'Resistance and the Problem of Ethnographic Refusal,' *Comparative Studies in Society and History* 37(1): 173–93.
——(1996) *Making Gender: The Politics and Erotics of Culture,* Boston, MA: Beacon Press.
——(1998) 'Generation X: Anthropology in a Media-Saturated World,' *Cultural Anthropology* 13(3): 414–40.
——(1999) *Life and Death on Mt. Everest: Sherpas and Himalayan Mountaineering,* Princeton, NJ: Princeton University Press.
——(2000) 'Some Futures of Anthropology,' *American Ethnologist* 26(4): 984–91.
——(2002) 'Subjects and Capital: A Fragment of a Documentary Ethnography,' *Ethnos* 67(1): 1–24.

——(2003) *New Jersey Dreaming: Capital, Culture, and the Class of '58*, Durham, NC: Duke University Press.

——(2006) *Anthropology and Social Theory: Culture, Power, and the Acting Subject*, Durham, NC: Duke University Press.

Ortner, S. B. (ed.) (1999) *The Fate of 'Culture': Geertz and Beyond*, Berkeley: University of California Press.

Ortner, S., Dirks, N. B., and Eley, G. (eds.) (1994) *Culture/Power/History: A Reader in Contemporary Social Theory*, Princeton, NJ: Princeton University Press.

Ortner, S. and Whitehead, H. (eds.) (1981) *Sexual Meanings: The Cultural Construction of Gender and Sexuality*, Cambridge: Cambridge University Press.

BRIAN JOSEPH GILLEY

HORTENSE POWDERMAKER (1896–1970)

A British-trained American anthropologist, Powdermaker broke new ground in terms of topical focus and contexts for fieldwork. Her writings are so insightful about a wide range of issues – from the role of women in a non-Western society, the psychology of racism in the US South, and power dynamics in contemporary media to social change in Africa and the ethics and epistemology of fieldwork – that her career deserves serious attention. Indeed, judging by a number of recent reassessments of her work she has recently been 'rediscovered,' especially in the subfield of media anthropology.

Powdermaker was born in Philadelphia and raised in Reading, Pennsylvania and Baltimore in a Jewish-German business family in a family environment she later described as materialistic and sterile. She studied history and humanities as an undergraduate at Goucher College, and while there was exposed to Baltimore's slums and the labor movement. It was a political consciousness-raising experience, and after graduation she moved to New York and began work for the Amalgamated Clothing Workers of America. Her work as a union organizer in New York and other cities such as Rochester and Cleveland introduced her to elements of fieldwork – listening, recording stories, and connecting those stories to broader political and economic dynamics – that she enjoyed and in which she succeeded.

Seeking a change of scenery and lifestyle, she moved to London, and in 1925 out of curiosity began taking anthropology courses at the London School of Economics and Political Science (LSE). Here a group of students was coalescing around **Malinowski**, including

Evans-Pritchard, Isaac Schapera, and Audrey Richards. In this setting Powdermaker discovered that 'anthropology was what I had been looking for without knowing it' (quoted in Silverman 1989: 291). She began research for a PhD under Malinowski on leadership in primitive societies. Lack of funds meant that her PhD was library based. In 1929 after receiving her doctorate, the Australian National Research Council funded her to conduct pioneering fieldwork on Lesu, a New Ireland island outlier in New Guinea. The resulting monograph, *Life in Lesu* (1933), offered a FUNCTIONALIST analysis, albeit with more emphasis on women's roles than was then common. In the field, Powdermaker identified herself as sociologically female and did not seek to participate in men's rituals and politics, a strategy that was not necessarily unique since women anthropologists had focused on the lives and roles of women since the 1880s. But it contrasted somewhat with other female anthropologists of her time, such as **Mead**, Richards, and **Benedict**, who had involved themselves in both men's and women's activities.

Although Malinowski was an inspiring teacher, he was not a mentor in the sense of actively sponsoring Powdermaker's career, and she never gained a position in a British university. Returning to the US after her Lesu fieldwork, Powdermaker obtained a fellowship from the National Research Council and an affiliation with the Institute of Human Relations at Yale University. At Yale she worked with **Edward Sapir**, becoming, as Sapir claimed, one of his protégés, together pursuing shared interests in psychology, perception, and individual experience within the frameworks of 'CULTURE AND PERSONALITY' and psychoanalysis.

During this period, Powdermaker decided to pursue research in the US using ethnographic fieldwork methods, which up to that point had only been used in non-industrial societies. In 1932, she began fieldwork focusing on the psychological dynamics of race relations and racism in the deeply divided black and white community of Indianola, Mississippi. It was watershed research. It represents not only the first ethnographic study of a 'modern' community; it was one of the first studies ever to analyze racial tensions and prejudices from both white and black perspectives. She paid particularly close attention to the psychological costs of racism for both blacks and whites, as well as the adaptive strategies individuals in each group employed to avoid repressive action, or, as the case may be, maintain the social advantages that accompanied racial inequality. During fieldwork, Powdermaker was acutely aware of the suspicion her research generated in both communities. Her research among whites was thus covert, telling them she was studying Negroes. Although she was more open in the black community about her research, she was careful not to be seen with black men in public (lest they be threatened by whites) and tended to rely heavily on her relationships with certain trusted black women.

The important publications that emerged from this research, *After Freedom* (1939) and an article entitled 'The Channeling of Negro Aggression by the Cultural Process' (1943), mark significant early contributions to the empirical study of race relations. Committed to reaching a broader audience, she authored a short book, *Probing Our Prejudices: A Unit for High School Students* (1944), that was used in anti-racism programming in New York City schools for several decades. This accessible book was based on a simple premise: just as prejudices are learned – largely through enculturation and poor reasoning derived from individual experience – they can be unlearned through careful thought and a commitment to ideals of fairness and justice.

During the Mississippi research, Powdermaker became attuned to the role of mass media in providing audiences with behavioral and cognitive models as they relate to race and race relations. During 1946–47, seeking to better understand how these models are constructed and whose interests they serve, she conducted fieldwork in Hollywood among film producers. The book that resulted from this endeavor, *Hollywood, the Dream Factory* (1950), is perhaps her best known book outside of anthropology, and one of the only close studies of Hollywood filmmaking in existence in the social sciences. In it she views media production as a process of totalitarian control in which producers exercise power over those who work under them, and whose final product exercises powerful control over the minds of audiences through the mass production of 'pre-fabricated day-dreams.' Although the book was heavily criticized and Powdermaker later admitted that her tone of moral outrage at the unequal power relations within film studios generated too rigid an analysis, her insights parallel the analyses of Frankfurt School media theorists such as Theodor Adorno, and anticipate critiques commonly found in media studies today. This work has also been appropriated as an 'ancestral' text by the subfield of media anthropology that coalesced in the 1990s.

Powdermaker's long-standing desire to conduct research in Africa led her in 1953–54 to Guggenheim-funded fieldwork in the Copper Belt town of Luanshiya in Northern Rhodesia (now Zambia). *Copper Town* (1962) examines the rapid transition from tribal to urban life, uniting anthropological theories of social change with psychological theories of individual change, demonstrating her ongoing concern for 'the extension of the areas of self awareness, of perception, of action, and of the range of identifications.' It received mixed reviews, the most negative coming from Africanist anthropologists skeptical of her psychological orientation and her lack of background in the region. As a result, this work is not as influential as her ethnographic studies of Lesu, racism, and Hollywood, each of which maintain their status as classics in their respective areas of anthropological literature.

Powdermaker was deeply committed to the methodology of ethnography, not simply as a scientific tool for gathering information, but as a humanistic endeavor characterized by highly rewarding, and sometimes deeply unsettling, practical, philosophical, and psychological challenges. She explores these themes in her final book, the autobiographical *Stranger and Friend* (1966), which is part intellectual history, part discussion of the principles of fieldwork gleaned from her particular ethnographic experiences. A key discussion centers on the characteristic mode of anthropological research, which requires converting the close personal proximity of friendships gained in the field into the detachment of the scientist-stranger. She observes:

Anthropology is a profession in which it is an asset for the practitioners to be somewhat outside of their own society and of the ones they study, and yet be able to step into them and relate to people. Certain personality types carry this dual role of involvement and detachment more easily than do others and even enjoy it.

(Powdermaker 1966: 303)

Another critical discussion focused on how she managed the tensions that exist between being a social critic – of American racial attitudes and Hollywood film production, for example – and the anthropological commitment to avoid ethnocentric judgments. Noting that anthropological training cultivates acquired defenses against ethnocentrism, she asserts that anthropologists nevertheless still hold values to which they must be true. Powdermaker understood that these values may be more diffuse than hegemonic values, but their intensity and taken-for-grantedness means they cannot be readily discounted.

A major part of Powdermaker's professional life was as an undergraduate teacher at New York's Queens College. Powdermaker was among the first faculty, and she spent thirty years there as a highly regarded teacher and mentor, retiring in 1968. (During World War II, she also taught two days a week at the Army's Specialized Language Program at Yale, in which she trained army units in local languages and cultures of the Southwest Pacific.) Powdermaker taught and mentored a number of students at Queens who achieved anthropological prominence including **Eric Wolf**, Erika Bourguignon, and Nancy Scheper-Hughes. After retiring, she moved to Berkeley where she obtained a research associateship at the University of California, with a plan to study youth culture on campus, work that ended with her death in 1970.

Powdermaker was well aware of the social and occupational limitations she confronted as a woman, a Jew, and a feminist, a point that makes her accomplishments and the professional honors she received more salient. Chief among these were her presidency of the American Ethnological Society (1946–47); vice presidency of the New York Academy of Sciences and Chair of the Anthropology section (1944–46); an honorary doctorate from her alma mater Goucher College (1957); and 'Teacher of the Year' award from the Alumnae Association of Queens College (1966).

One minor puzzle about Powdermaker is her lack of relative prominence in the history of the discipline vis-à-vis other early and mid-century contemporaries, especially those first students of Malinowski with whom she studied at LSE. Several possible factors present themselves, and are open to discussion. One of these may be related to the fact that her British training but American career meant that she stood somewhat separate from the construction of a distinctly American anthropology (notwithstanding her relationship with Sapir), and as a result could not rely as solidly on the social networks that may have furthered her career had she remained in Britain. Another possibility is that, being primarily a teacher of undergraduates, she did not have a coterie of graduate students to carry on her legacy. She was also not a theoretical innovator, but in the Kuhnian sense, a practitioner of 'normal' science, especially in her use of psychological theory. Perhaps she was also in certain respects 'ahead of her time' in her commitment to applying ethnographic methods in the settings and themes of contemporary industrial society at a time when the mainstream of the discipline was more focused on non-Western village level societies. Whatever the case, Powdermaker was nothing if not a dynamic anthropologist. Throughout her career, she was committed to addressing the intersections of individual experience and structures of power and social inequality, and in the process she opened exciting new topics and settings for ethnographic investigation.

Selected readings

Powdermaker, H. (1933) *Life in Lesu: The Study of a Melanesian Society*, New York: W.W. Norton and Company.

——(1939) *After Freedom: A Cultural Study in the Deep South*, New York: The Viking Press.

——(1943) 'The Channeling of Negro Aggression by the Cultural Process,' *American Journal of Sociology* 48: 122–30.

——(1944) *Probing Our Prejudices: A Unit for High School Students*, New York: Harper and Brothers.

——(1950) *Hollywood, the Dream Factory: An Anthropologist Looks at the Movie-Makers*, London: Secker & Warburg.

——(1962) *Copper Town: Changing Africa; The Human Situation on the Rhodesian Copperbelt*, New York: Harper & Row.

——(1966) *Stranger and Friend: The Way of the Anthropologist*, New York: W.W. Norton and Company.

Silverman, S. (1989) 'Hortense Powdermaker,' in *Women Anthropologists: Selected Biographies*, U. Gacs, A. Khan, J McIntyre, and R. Weinberg (eds.), pp. 291–95, Urbana: University of Illinois Press.

Wolf, E. (1971) 'Hortense Powdermaker, 1900–1970,' *American Anthropologist* 73: 783–86.

LUIS VIVANCO

A. R. RADCLIFFE-BROWN (1881–1955)

A person of immense, if sometimes distant, charm and arrogance, but with a surprisingly sparse publication record, Radcliffe-Brown is one of the most significant anthropologists in the history of the discipline, given his key role in the establishment of anthropology in South Africa, Australia, the United States, and the United Kingdom.

Born in Birmingham into a family of modest means, Alfred Reginald Brown won a scholarship to Trinity College Cambridge. He intended to focus on the natural sciences but eventually wound up doing moral sciences (psychology, philosophy, and political economy). Here he became W. H. R. Rivers's first anthropology student and also worked with A. C. Haddon, both of whom became important sponsors of his work and career. A College Fellowship enabled him to do fieldwork in the Andaman Islands in 1906–8 for what was to be his Masters thesis. It is unclear why he chose this site and his thesis is largely a reconstruction of Andaman life and customs.

Still supported by his Trinity Fellowship, he first visited Australia in 1910–11 to join E. L. Grant-Watson and Daisy Bates on an expedition to the northwest to study remnants of Aboriginal tribes. Controversially, some Australianists, along with **Rodney Needham**, claim he stole the latter's field-notes. He returned again in 1914 to participate (along with **Bronislaw Malinowski**) in the British Association for the Advancement of Science meetings. The outbreak of the First World War forced him into teaching high school in Australia before being appointed Director of Education in Tonga.

Being tubercular, he moved to the healthier climate of South Africa in 1918 to stay with his elder brother and followed his lead in signing himself Radcliffe Brown, and in 1926 changed his name by deed poll to Radcliffe-Brown. Initially employed at the Transvaal Museum he successfully applied for the foundation Chair of Social Anthropology in the newly created Department of African Life and Languages at the University of Cape Town. Here he helped inaugurate a series of vacation schools focused on the 'native problem.' D. D. T. Jabavu, later a leading African intellectual, reported that the star of these schools was Radcliffe-Brown:

> As a lecturer he wields a versatile combination of the scholarly gifts of facile oratory, graphic illustration and unlimited comparison, with resourceful erudition … he possesses a sense of humour and 'joie de vivre' in his subject, investing his discourse with reality and fascination … he marshals the attention of his hearers even more effectively by the practical and constructive conclusions he constantly deduces from his minutiae of information.

Jabavu was especially impressed by his scientific approach since the banes of the 'Native Question' were the 'ubiquitous self-styled amateur authorities' who claimed 'omniscience' (*Cape Times* 24 March, 1924). The most important protégé to emerge from this period was Isaac Schapera.

Funding insecurity and a desire to go back to an area where he had worked led him to accept the Rockefeller-funded chair of Anthropology at Sydney where he taught from 1926 to 1931. A major legacy was his founding of the journal *Oceania*. Radcliffe-Brown's arrogance and air of superiority apparently did not sit well with egalitarian Australians and he only produced one serious student, Ian Hogbin (who attended Malinowski's famous seminar with **Meyer Fortes**). However, he did have an impact on W. Lloyd

Warner, as well as several Melanesianists like **Margaret Mead**, Reo Fortune, and Gregory Bateson who transited Sydney. Intellectually he worked through his Australian material and developed a comparative method for understanding variations in social structure among the different Aboriginal groups. The applied anthropology model he deployed in South Africa was not as successful in Australia and with the decline in Rockefeller Foundation research funding and the Depression adding to the general stress, he left in 1931 to teach at the University of Chicago, where for six years he had a number of prominent graduate students including Fred Eggan and Sol Tax. Finally in 1937 he accepted the first chair of Social Anthropology at Oxford where he worked closely with **E. E. Evans-Pritchard**, Fortes, and **Max Gluckman**. When the Association of Social Anthropologists was founded in 1946, the model for the association came from the informal pub-tutorials led by Radcliffe-Brown in Oxford before the war. Financial exigencies forced him to take visiting appointments in Yenching (China), Alexandria (Egypt), and Rhodes (South Africa) after his retirement in 1950. Such was his impact that he was presented with two *Festschrifts* (Eggan 1937, Fortes 1949).

Intellectually the first significant influence on Radcliffe-Brown was Kropotkin's anarchism. Indeed as an undergraduate he was known as 'Anarchy' Brown. From Kropotkin Radcliffe-Brown derived the notion of society as a self-regulating system and that anthropology was best conceptualized as a natural science of society. However the lasting influence was to be Durkheim, especially *The Elementary Forms of Religious Life* which he studied closely on his return from the Andaman Islands, and this theoretical focus eventually led to his *Andaman Islanders* being heralded as a masterpiece of Durkheimian interpretation. Compared, however, to other ethnographies of the era it is a rather sparse and anaemic volume. Instead Radcliffe-Brown's reputation rests on a number of essays that were reprinted later in two volumes.

'How does society exist?' was the key question underlying his quest, and eventually he conceptualized it as consisting of a social structure of juridical roles (derived from Maine through Durkheim), and norms and statuses which shaped behavior and existed independently of individual actors. While he used the term 'function' in a variety of ways, the one most closely associated with him is as a 'recurrent activity, which makes for structural continuity.' Of key importance here was kinship (emphasized by Rivers), which was a significant organizing feature of the social structure and frequently had a corporate quality, and this emphasis led easily into the notion of a self-sustaining organically integrated entity. Unlike Rivers, who saw kinship as reflecting ancient social facts, and **Alfred Kroeber** who saw it as reflecting language and psychology, for Radcliffe-Brown the importance of kinship was its relation to existing social facts. One important consequence was that for about a decade kinship studies were the centrepiece of social anthropology and indeed some of Radcliffe-Brown's seminal essays concern joking relations and the significance of the mother's brother. Both these pieces focus on tensions between familiarity and authority created by the rules of kinship and marriage. In the patrilineal societies of South Africa the mother's brother indulged the sister's son who was able to take liberties at his expense, while offering compulsory respect to his father. Perhaps one of his major contributions was to 'descent theory' which argued that patri- and matrilineal descent groups formed the driving force of many tribal societies, a position that was later challenged by **Lévi-Strauss**ian 'alliance theory' which argues that marriage *exchanges* between descent groups were significant building blocks of society in their own right.

Radcliffe-Brown felt that culture was not a particularly useful mode of investigation. What was important was not what indigenes were thinking or believed, but how they behaved and what structural features shaped this. This derived from his positivism, that is to say he stressed observable social facts rather than abstract ideas. Social structure was the network of 'actual social relations.' Given his attempt at scientific rigor his anthropology was a nomothetic inquiry. The search for laws and generalizations was paramount and it is not surprising that he launched telling attacks on what he called 'conjectural history,' the mode of reconstructing cultural history so popular among theorists who sought to explain non-functional customs as 'survivals' from an earlier epoch. Radcliffe-Brown believed that employing an inductivist and supposedly empiricist approach could develop natural laws of society – he made much of verifiable facts and observations – and comparison. Such an approach he believed could lead to a single unified social science. His articulate espousal of positivism, done with exceptional economy and clarity at a time when many believed that a scientific anthropology was attainable, led to a cult-like status. Indeed he did much to ingrain the notion that fieldwork was of a lower status than the comparative analysis of other people's ethnographies of which he had an outstanding knowledge. His closest immediate intellectual heir was probably Fortes.

In order to break with this older mode of anthropology, and as a tribute to Durkheim's influence, he labeled his interests comparative sociology rather than anthropology. Together with some of the ideas propounded by Malinowski this approach is often seen as the basis for what became known as STRUCTURAL-FUNCTIONAL anthropology. This very abstract theoretical formulation displayed a number of characteristics. All customs served a function or purpose. Its key metaphor was the organic analogy that compared a society to a biological organism, which was derived from Spencer and Durkheim. Everything was interrelated and changing one part would result in a ripple effect. Except at such times of change, it was assumed that society existed in equilibrium. Ultimately, distortions would self re-adjust, and following from this it was implied that societies were normally static. More than Malinowski, he seemed aware of the potential flaws of FUNCTIONALISM. Certainly he did not naively believe that every custom had a positive function, noting that people could be bonded together by shared hatred as much as by shared love, and in later life he proved to be quite amenable to historical studies. His theoretical musings had a significant influence beyond anthropology on sociologists such as Kingsley Davis and Robert K. Merton.

While Radcliffe-Brown did not distinguish himself doing fieldwork, he nevertheless emphasized this as a method of data collection that was necessary to provide for classification of data and generalizations which were achieved through undertaking comparisons. The comparative method, he believed, was essential and this was later refined by anthropologists like Adam Kuper who undertook controlled comparisons among societies which were broadly similar ecologically and culturally, and attempted to examine variations.

Radcliffe-Brown's ideas were developed in particular socio-cultural milieux that undoubtedly had an impact on the way in which he framed his arguments. His signature paper, 'The Methods of Ethnology and Social Anthropology' (1923, republished in 1952) was written while Radcliffe-Brown was dealing with a racist, segregationist society. He paid tribute to the sterling lead given to anthropology by earlier scholars but rejected conjectural history, especially about racial and cultural origins, in favor of a search for synchronic laws of society. More importantly, he argued that South Africa was already so interconnected and complex that segregation was unworkable. Inspired by Durkheim, he claimed that the task of anthropology in South Africa was not to interpret or translate between different cultural groups but to treat blacks and whites as part of a single social system and accordingly study both.

Radcliffe-Brown's distinction between pure and applied research flowed logically from his concept of social anthropology as a natural science like chemistry or physics, and mirrored then conventional views of the task of science. It was to become one of the most famous lines of cleavage between him and Malinowski. Radcliffe-Brown was unequivocal on the relationship of anthropology to policy-making and repeatedly stated that social anthropologists were not to get involved in policy, as this would make the elimination of prejudice and bias even more difficult. Asked to respond to the government's proposed Colonial Development and Welfare Act during his Presidency of the Royal Anthropological Institute, he emphasized the role of universities in leading anthropological research activities. Framing the problem in scientific terms served to place it above the ordinary level of intellectual gymnastics and academic doctrine that characterized the local 'Native Experts.' While few anthropologists nowadays claim to follow Radcliffe-Brown, and his ideal of a 'natural science of society' proved illusory, his key insight that social anthropology is about relationships is still one of the defining characteristics of contemporary anthropology.

Selected readings

Eggan, F. (ed.) (1937) *Social Anthropology of North American Tribes*, Chicago: University of Chicago Press.
Fortes, M. (ed.) (1949) *Social Structure: Studies presented to A. R. Radcliffe-Brown*, Oxford: Clarendon Press.
Gordon, R. J. (1990) 'Early Social Anthropology in South Africa,' *African Studies* 49(1): 15–48.
Radcliffe-Brown, A. R. (1922) *The Andaman Islanders: A Study in Social Organization*, Cambridge: Cambridge University Press.
——(1952) *Structure and Function in Primitive Society*, London: Cohen and West.
——(1957) *A Natural Science of Society* (based on a series of lectures at the University of Chicago in 1937 and posthumously published by his students), Chicago: University of Chicago Press.
——(1958) *Method in Social Anthropology: Selected Essays by A.R. Radcliffe-Brown*, M. N. Srinivas (ed.), Chicago: University of Chicago Press.

ROBERT GORDON

PAUL RADIN (1883–1959)

Unlike most anthropologists discussed in this volume, Paul Radin did not spend an extended period of time as a faculty member at any single university and did not mentor protégés. He was primarily interested in ritual, myth, folklore, cosmology, and ethnolinguistics and is best known as the author of some influential books, one of which, *The Trickster*, is still a staple of the curriculum in courses on folklore and myth. Radin was born in Lodz in the Russian-administered part of Poland but shortly after his birth the family emigrated to the United States. Radin's father was a Reform rabbi and the Radin children were raised in a somewhat secular post-Enlightenment brand of Judaism.

Before becoming an anthropologist, Radin studied a variety of subjects including zoology and history at New York's City College and Columbia University. He intended to become a zoologist, but changed when he studied in Berlin and Munich in 1907 and 1908, and he became interested first in physical and latterly in cultural anthropology. Returning to New York, he began fieldwork with the Winnebago people of Nebraska, Iowa, and Wisconsin in 1908 and obtained his doctorate at Columbia University in 1911 under **Franz Boas**. For the rest of his career, despite studying other people, Radin was primarily identified with the Winnebago. Shortly after he received his doctorate he took a position under the direction of **Edward Sapir**, at the Canadian National Museum in Ottawa, and stayed there during the period of the First World War, studying the Ojibwa of SE Ontario and the Nootka of British Columbia. Radin also visited the Zapotec in Mexico and a number of peoples in California including the the Patwin and the Achumawi. He wrote a monograph on Wappo, a Californian language which is now extinct.

As a teacher and scholar Radin moved from institution to institution, never staying in a single place for more than five years. His places of employment included Cambridge University, the University of Chicago, Kenyon College, Mills College, Berkeley, Black Mountain College, the C. G. Jung Institute in Switzerland, and Brandeis University. Radin had some very influential friends including John Dewey, the educational philosopher, John Crowe Ransom, the literary critic, C. G. Jung, the psychoanalyst, and Karl Kerenyi, the classicist and scholar of comparative mythology. Among anthropologists his friends included Sapir, Alexander Goldenweiser, and Cora DuBois. Stanley Diamond invited him to his last position at Brandeis and edited a Festschrift, *Culture in History*, which appeared in 1960. This peripatetic career obviously raises questions. Diamond (1981) remarks that Radin was an unworldly and impractical person who could not change an electrical plug and wrote in longhand because he could not learn to use a typewriter. He appears to have had a somewhat 'difficult' temperament. His socialist politics tended toward anarchism. Recently David Price (2004) has revealed that the FBI kept a file on Radin for nearly twenty years, suspecting him of communist sympathies and Communist Party membership. They were probably unaware that Radin's anthropology was anything but systematically Marxist. They were concerned that he gave public lectures about racism during the Second World War. His contract at Black Mountain College was not renewed by the administration after he defended two female students who were accused of prostitution by suggesting that class disadvantage might have explained their association with dubious elements in the local black community. Radin shared his dislike of racism with Franz Boas and Boas's other students. Like them he deplored the implicit or even explicit ethnocentrism of nineteenth and early twentieth century theories of social evolution and rejected Lucien Lévy-Bruhl's notion of the prelogical mentality of primitive peoples.

As Regna Darnell (2001) has demonstrated, the integration of linguistics and cultural anthropology was a key aspect of Boasian methodology and theory. Boas was not an advocate of prolonged PARTICIPANT OBSERVATION, but he was insistent on the value of repeated visits by anthropologists who acquired fluency in indigenous tongues for which no written grammar existed. A substantial number of Radin's publications were in linguistics, and he accumulated a substantial number of texts from his informants.

For all that he had in common with Boas and his disciples, Radin personally disliked Boas and the dislike was reciprocated. Both Boas and **Alfred Kroeber** regarded Radin as unreliable and thought of him as an indifferent scholar (Lindberg 2000, Leeds-Hurwitz 2005). For his part Radin thought that Boas was too obsessed with the relative merits of evolution and diffusion in the history of cultures. He was bored by the accumulation of statistical data, so beloved by Kroeber, concerning the spread of cultural traits such as styles of basket-weaving. Although his earliest work in anthropology concerned net-making, Radin was not particularly interested in material culture. He deplored Kroeber's idea of the 'superorganic' which reified the social and wilfully ignored subjectivity. Within a few years of obtaining his doctorate Radin expressed his belief that anthropologists should study the individual in culture and focus on the subjective elements in the lives of primitive peoples, something which Boas and his students wrongly neglected. This was a direction which Boas, Sapir, and Ruth Bunzel would partially endorse later on, but Radin was the pioneer. He expressed his disagreements with fellow Boasians in 1933 in *Method and Theory in Ethnology*. Radin advocated the collection of indigenous autobiographies because they were a route to understanding the experience, knowledge, and feelings of the makers of rituals and the narrators of tales in primitive cultures. Few anthropologists could ever hope to obtain such an understanding by participant observation, because time, willingness, and funds were all lacking. No questionnaire could arrive at such answers and indigenous informants were unaware of anthropological categories and unable to conceptualize the structures of their cultures. Radin's first, brief Winnebago autobiography was published in 1913. In 1920 he published 'The Autobiography of a Winnebago Indian,' the life history of Sam Blowsnake whose brother was the subject of the 1913 article. The essay was later presented to the general public as *Crashing Thunder: The Autobiography of an American Indian*. Radin's remarkable account is based on Blowsnake's written narrative in a special syllabary. It is a story of an actor who participates in a swift and often traumatic process of cultural upheaval. The young Blowsnake learns to gather cranberries, court girls, hunt with bow and arrow, fast in order to receive visions which he only pretends to experience, and participate in the medicine dance. As a physically mature man he marries a number of times and has several sexual partners. He joins a road show as a living exhibit of his culture, drinks far too much and becomes dissipated. After participating as accessory to the murder of a man from another tribe, he is arrested and spends some time in jail before acquittal. Subsequently he follows the example of members of his family and enjoys a calmer life after undergoing conversion to the peyote religion. Since Radin's time there has been much debate about issues of authenticity in the gathering of life histories as well as questions about the very Western nature of the genre with its intrinsic notion of emplotment and the constructed life. Radin saw no problem with such texts, claiming that the narration of life histories was something that came naturally to articulate informants.

Primitive Man as Philosopher (1927) was crafted as a response to Lévy-Bruhl, whose theories on primitive mentality were partly misunderstood by Radin and some of his contemporaries. The French philosopher did not mean to say that primitive thought was in any way *illogical*, but rather that it was based on different premises from our own. Connections which we would presume to be impossible were assumed a priori. Thus a West African might be taught from infancy that all shadows *were* souls, so that the disappearance of the shadow at noon implied danger to the soul. Witchcraft and magic were built on similar connections and *participations*. Primitive thought was pre-eminently *mystical*.

In response, Radin noted (as also did **Malinowski**) that primitives were pre-eminently pragmatic, that a lot of magic was extremely practical in its aims and limited in its effects, and that in all societies people differed in their religiosity and degree of belief. Furthermore, as in our own society, there were differences in all primitive societies between men of action and intellectuals (such as shamans and priests). The latter were often the initiators of elaborate cosmologies and sophisticated codes of ethics. Because it was not based on the written word, primitive thought did not rely almost exclusively on the visual sense, thereby fostering a cult of 'objectivity,' nor was it obsessed by reifications. Maori, Hawaiian, Ba-Ila (African), Ojibwa, and Winnebago texts provided supporting evidence. The existence of a preliterate mode of thought was not called into question, albeit Radin's primitives were closer to us than Lévy-Bruhl's.

Radin felt that moral ambiguity in the cosmos was realistically addressed in the cosmologies of indigenous peoples (Radin 1953 and 1971). The Winnebago trickster, Wakdjunkaga, is a being who defies all categories in ways that are often farcical. As a chief he goes on the warpath himself after breaking sexual taboos, discarding his companions and wandering away from home. He makes his right arm fight his left. He carries his penis in a box and it appears to assume a separate existence. He orders his anus to guard the geese he has just killed and cooked, while he gets some sleep. When foxes arrive and steal the geese, the anus farts in vain. On waking Trickster is enraged and burns the anus in order to punish it. He is quite surprised when he experiences pain. After many comical episodes including the events following his wilful consumption of a laxative bulb, Trickster returns to his own village to pursue family life. Although still the perpetrator of tricks, he can now use his trickery to defend his community.

The Trickster appeared during Radin's stay at the Jung Institute, and contained essays by Kerenyi, Jung, and Radin himself, as well as the texts of the Wakdjunkaga cycle, the Winnebago Hare Cycle dealing with an animal trickster, and summaries of the Assiniboine and Tlingit trickster myths. The achievement of Radin and his distinguished collaborators was to bring into juxtaposition stories of animal tricksters from all over the world (hare, rabbit, raven, coyote, spider), stories of trickster beings with human or semi-divine attributes, trickster deities, and culture heroes who are at first sight the diametrical opposite of tricksters but can be melded into them.

Wakdjunkaga can be compared and contrasted with Anansi, Hermes, Prometheus, Eshu, Raven, and so on. Trickster may indeed be 'the spirit of disorder, the enemy of boundaries,' as Kerenyi stated, but Radin interprets the Winnebago cycles as narratives that trace the building of social and moral categories out of primal confusion, inasmuch as Trickster is shown to be slowly learning from his mistakes. The socialization process is the subject of the cycle. At the same time, the satirical element is always present. And the tenuous nature of the social bond is always evident. Within a decade, essays on liminality by **Edmund Leach** and **Victor Turner** were to fit more pieces into the puzzle Radin so brilliantly set.

Selected readings

Darnell, R. (2001) *Invisible Genealogies: A History of Americanist Anthropology*, Lincoln: University of Nebraska Press.

Diamond, S. (1981) 'Paul Radin,' in *Totems and Teachers*, S. Silverman (ed.), pp. 51–73, New York: Columbia University Press.

Diamond, S. (ed.) (1960) *Culture in History: Essays in Honor of Paul Radin*, New York: Columbia University Press.

Leeds-Hurwitz, W. (2005) *Rolling in Ditches with Shamans*, Lincoln: University of Nebraska Press.

Lindberg, Christer (2000) 'Paul Radin: The Anthropological Trickster,' *European Review of Native American Studies* 14(1): 1–9, accessed at http://web.telia.com/~u40211489/PDF/Texter/RADIN.PDF.

Price, D. (2004) *Threatening Anthropology: McCarthyism and the FBI's Surveillance of Activist Anthropologists*, Durham, NC: Duke University Press.

Radin, P. (1920) 'The Autobiography of a Winnebago Indian,' *University of California Publications in American Archaeology and Ethnology* 16: 381–473.

——(1933) *Method and Theory in Ethnology*, New York: Basic Books.

——(1953) *The World of Primitive Man*, New York: Henry Schuman.

——(1957 [1927]) *Primitive Man as Philosopher*, New York: Dover.

——(1971 [1956]) *The Trickster: A Study in American Indian Mythology*, with Commentaries by K. Kerenyi and C. G. Jung, with a new Introduction by Stanley Diamond, New York: Schocken.

——(1999 [1926]) *Crashing Thunder: The Autobiography of an American Indian*, Ann Arbor: University of Michigan Press.

ANDREW P. LYONS

RENATO ROSALDO (1941–)

Both an anthropologist and a poet, Renato Rosaldo contributed to several prominent trends in post-1960s anthropology. Most notable is his leading role during the 1980s and 1990s in the critical reassessment of ethnographic truth and authority, his promotion of methodological self-reflexivity, and his understanding of culture as a moving process rather than a timeless structure. He has also been at the forefront of studies of multiculturalism, Chicano identity and politics, citizenship, and globalization. Rosaldo is deeply committed to anthropology's humanistic and interpretive mission, as well as to the potential of intellectuals to reshape cultural politics.

A Chicano, Rosaldo grew up in Tucson, Arizona. A 1959 graduate of Tucson High School, he returned there some forty years later to discuss his work as a writer and poet. In one of the poems read for the occasion (Rosaldo 2001), he reflected on his teenage years as a Pachuco (the Mexican-American youth subculture in the US Southwest). Rosaldo attended Harvard as an undergraduate, where he realized the academic inadequacies of his previous schooling and experienced the pain of ethnic stereotyping (Rosaldo 2001). He majored in Spanish History and Literature, and decided to pursue a PhD in social anthropology in Harvard's School of Social Relations. While there he dated and subsequently married Michelle ('Shelly') Zimbalist, a student several years behind him in the same program, who would herself gain prominence as an influential figure in feminist and psychological anthropologies. It would be a close professional partnership. They conducted dissertation fieldwork between 1967 and 1969 in the Philippines among the Ilongot, slash-and-burn agriculturists who had historically practiced headhunting. Explaining that choice of field site – both of them had been involved previously with Mexico-focused research – one colleague notes that like many young graduate students they wanted to work in a faraway 'primitive' place.

The focus of Rosaldo's Ilongot research, which culminated in his highly regarded book, *Ilongot Headhunting, 1883–1974* (Rosaldo 1980), was on understanding the history and structure of Ilongot society. It examined the centrality of headhunting to Ilongot social organization, marriage, notions of male adulthood, and kinship practices. Social structure was not a static all-encompassing phenomenon, but intertwined with and shaped by historical circumstances. As he noted, 'I stress not just the given nature of society, but also the way human beings continually construct, manipulate, and even recast the social worlds into which they were born and within which they will die' (1980: 23). More than just a challenge to then dominant ahistorical STRUCTURAL-FUNCTIONALIST accounts, this approach reflected an ethnographic sensibility for Ilongot ways of knowing, for 'one of the most deeply held Ilongot values is that their lives unfold more through active human improvisations than in accord with socially-given plans' (1980: 23). Rosaldo was also writing against ethnocentric accounts of Ilongot society; especially those based on lurid stereotypes of bloodthirsty headhunters, and those of scholars whose interpretations of Ilongot history ignored Ilongot perspectives and historicity.

On a research trip to study the neighboring Ifugao in 1981, Shelly accidentally slipped on a trail and fell to her death, a profoundly disruptive event for Rosaldo and their two young sons. In a watershed essay published initially in 1984 and expanded as the introduction to *Culture & Truth: The Remaking of Social Analysis* (Rosaldo 1989), Rosaldo discussed the impact of Shelly's death on his life and professional career. He also wrote about how her death helped him better grasp one aspect of Ilongot society that he could never truly understand, which was the Ilongot explanation for headhunting. Ilongots explained that they would kill a victim after a loved one died. They said that that the act of severing a head helped a man to vent his rage – a rage born of grief – that released him from his anger and allowed him to get on with life. Until Shelly's death, Rosaldo wrote, he had dismissed this explanation, searching for a 'deeper' cultural truth, in exchange theory, for example. But his own devastating loss, which generated similar rage-in-grief, helped him move beyond his scientistic detachment to understand the emotional force to which Ilongots referred, and, more importantly, to better appreciate the cultural force of emotions without reducing them to what he describes as the 'brute abstractions' promoted by anthropological norms of objectivism (Rosaldo 1989: 2).

Drawing on various intellectual currents including post-structuralist theory, INTERPRETIVE ANTHROPOLOGY, postcolonialism, and feminism, Rosaldo insisted that this kind of analysis – interweaving personal insight and ethnographic knowledge – had broad significance for the production of anthropological knowledge and authority. His argument came to full fruition in *Culture & Truth*, the book that established his reputation as a prominent figure both in and beyond the discipline. In it, he criticized classic ethnography's indifference to human emotions in support of a stance of detached objectivism. He argued that the ethnographer's own life experiences, structural location, social relations, and shifting positionality powerfully influenced what the ethnographer learns, and continued to shape ongoing revisions of ethnographic knowledge long after the fieldwork was completed. Instead of trying to hide the open-endedness and relationality of ethnographic knowledge and the positioned subjects that produced it, he argued for recognizing their methodological and epistemological significance. Yet he was just as wary of the tendency of reflexive ethnography to be self-absorbed and politically vacuous. His position was, he argued, indicative of an ongoing sea change in cultural studies, in which:

> the truth of objectivism – absolute, universal, timeless – has lost its monopoly status. It now competes, on more nearly equal terms, with the truths of case studies that are embedded in local contexts, shaped by local interests, and colored by local perceptions.
>
> (1989: 21)

He insisted that this shift was not just an outcome of processes and debates internal to academia, but was forced by the decolonized objects of research, because they 'are also analyzing subjects who critically interrogate ethnographers – their writings, their ethics, and their politics' (1989: 21).

In *Culture & Truth*, Rosaldo also critically re-evaluated notions of culture as a bounded entity or as a timeless and static social structure, emphasizing instead that culture is based on fluid and relational social processes. This was a timely and articulate analysis that converged with others arguing for such processual approaches to culture. For Rosaldo, this argument emerged at least partly from his theoretical leanings, but also from his position as a Chicano intellectual. (Since the early 1970s, Rosaldo had been researching and teaching on Chicano culture and politics, co-editing two anthologies, *Chicano: The Evolution of a People* (1973) and *Chicano: The Beginnings of Bronze Power* (1974), and at Stanford University, where he taught beginning in 1970, he had served as Director of the Center for Chicano Research. When his Philippines research effectively ended with Shelly's death, he refocused more on Chicano issues and multiculturalism.) Throughout the 1980s, Chicano intellectuals were fascinated with borderlands, which most scholars had viewed as analytically empty transition zones. Borderlands were instead regarded as strategically useful geographic, philosophical, methodological, and political locations to explore themes of power and social inequality, and validate themes of hybridity and difference. Rosaldo drew from ethnographic research, Mexican-American folklore studies, and the works of artists like Southwest border lesbian poet Gloria Anzaldúa to argue that borderlands are characterized by processes of creative cultural production, mixing, and mediation that undermine any notion of culture as an 'autonomous, internally coherent universe' (1989: 217). Insisting that such insights apply beyond the geographical space of border zones, Rosaldo justified a shift away from investigating culture as a unified entity toward investigating processes of cultural production and mediation in everyday life.

One feature that distinguishes Rosaldo's processualism is its interpretive orientation, which is as interested in the production of meanings as it is in social and structural dynamics. (Rosaldo's interpretive orientation developed in personal dialogue with **Clifford Geertz**, and he has clearly explained and endorsed Geertz's defiance of CULTURAL RELATIVISM. See Rosaldo 2007.) Although Rosaldo's work was greeted with skepticism by some, a processual and meaning-centered view of culture was embraced widely in the discipline during the 1980s and 1990s, not simply because of Rosaldo but certainly influenced by him. *Culture and Truth* was enthusiastically read in the interdisciplinary field of Cultural Studies, and Rosaldo became one of the most recognizable anthropologists in that field while also explaining Cultural Studies' possibilities to skeptical anthropologists.

Rosaldo also did pioneering work in the emerging subfield of the anthropology of globalization where he emphasized processes of cultural mixing and hybridization, and promoted the work of Argentine-Mexican hybridization and globalization theorist Néstor García-Canclini, and co-edited an influential reader on *The Anthropology of Globalization* (2002).

An enduring concern for Rosaldo has been the issue of citizenship in culturally pluralistic societies. Noting that 'second-class citizen' status gets imposed on immigrant and minority groups because of their variation from dominant cultural norms, which then justifies their exclusion from the public sphere, Rosaldo has sought ways to reconceptualize citizenship so as to recognize the cultural distinctiveness and ethnic consciousness of minority groups. In articles and co-edited volumes Rosaldo has elaborated the concept of 'cultural citizenship' as an alternative approach to citizenship because it promotes a sense of belonging, inclusion, and enfranchisement in the public sphere for minority groups without forcing them to deny their unique cultures and identities. In support of this work, Rosaldo and his students conducted long-term ethnographic research in San José, California throughout the 1990s among Chicanos, refugees from Vietnam, and immigrants from Mexico and other Latin American countries. Their research documented the ways members of these communities made sense of their second-class status, but also fought for citizenship in ways that allowed them to maintain their specific cultural identities.

In the public sphere and on campus, Rosaldo has been a strong defender of his intellectual positions on multiculturalism and anthropology. In the late-1980s he fought against Stanford's 'Western Civilization' requirement, a course required of first year students in which they studied canonical Western literature, arguing that the designated canon did not include women and non-Europeans, and promoting curricular reforms to cultivate critical thinking about increasing global interdependencies. He has also publicly challenged political scientist Samuel ('Clash of Civilizations') Huntington, describing him as nativist for his assertions about the corrosive effects of Latino immigration on US culture (Rosaldo 2004). Rosaldo was also at the heart of a storm in the Stanford anthropology department during the 1990s which led to a split into two departments, one defining anthropology as a scientific field, and the other as humanistic and interpretive. Rosaldo stepped down as chair when he suffered a stroke in late 1996, which he attributes to the stresses of chairing the department. In 2003 he retired from Stanford, and took a visiting position at New York University where his wife, literary scholar Mary Louise Pratt, also teaches.

After the stroke Rosaldo began writing poetry in English, Spanish, and sometimes both. Viewing writing poetry as a key aspect of his recovery (he calls it 'cognitive therapy'), Rosaldo has dedicated tremendous energy to it. His poetry has won numerous awards, including an American Book Award in 2004. A self-styled 'anthropoeta' (anthropologist-poet) because some of his poetry treats issues raised by his ethnographic research, Rosaldo continues to challenge and create new forms of a humanistic anthropology he cares deeply about.

Selected readings

Flores, J. and Rosaldo, R. (eds.) (2007) *A Companion to Latina/o Studies*, Malden, MA: Wiley-Blackwell Press.

Inda, J. X. and R. Rosaldo (eds.) (2002) *The Anthropology of Globalization: A Reader*, Malden, MA: Blackwell.

Rosaldo, R. (1980) *Ilongot Headhunting, 1883–1974*, Stanford, CA: Stanford University Press.

——(1984) 'Grief and a Headhunter's Rage: On the Cultural Force of Emotions,' in *Text and Play: The Construction and Reconstruction of Self and*

Society, E. Bruner (ed.), pp. 178–95, Washington, DC: American Ethnological Society.

——(1989) *Culture & Truth: The Remaking of Social Analysis*, Boston, MA: Beacon Press.

——(1994) 'Whose Cultural Studies?,' *American Anthropologist* 96(3): 524–29.

——(2001) 'Guardian Angel: Lessons of Writing Poetry,' *Rhetoric Review* 20 (3/4): 359–67.

——(2003a) (ed.) *Cultural Citizenship in Island Southeast Asia: Nation and Belonging in the Hinterlands*, Berkeley: University of California Press.

——(2003b) *Prayer to Spider Woman / Rezos a la Mujer Araña*, Gobierno del Estado de Coahuila: Instituto Coahuilense de Cultura (ICOCULT)

——(2004) 'The Return of the Nativist: An Anthropologist's Duty to Respond,' Lecture presented at the New York Academy of Sciences, September 27.

——(2007) 'Geertz's Gifts,' *Common Knowledge* 13 (Spring): 206–10.

LUIS VIVANCO

JEAN ROUCH (1917–2004)

Jean Rouch, savant extraordinaire, was a forerunner of the French New Wave movement and a re-inventor of ethnographic cinema. From the 1940s he explored spirit possession, migration, and colonialism in West African society. He introduced the 'ciné-gym' method to train students to film hand-held as part of the doctoral programs at the Sorbonne. In the 1970s, he introduced young indigenous African filmmakers to Super-8mm filmmaking techniques. In 1987, he was elected President of the Cinémathèque Française.

A rebel 'zazou' – a term derived from youths of the 1930s in Paris who wore American or English clothes and listened to Swing music – and a Surrealist of Catalan origin, Rouch used cinema as a way of continuously proposing new interpretations of the world. Nothing was sacred to him, neither authority nor himself. Those who challenged his claim that one can laugh about everything frequently criticized his humor, both cruel and tender, inspired by the African notion of joking relationships. Like the Dogon people with whom he worked for many years, Rouch seemed to think that progress emerged through chaos.

Son of a naval officer, Rouch was born in Paris in 1917 and grew up in a family of artists in Algeria, Germany, Morocco, and later Athens and Istanbul. He described seeing *Nanook of the North* (1922) and *Robin Hood* (1922), and reading accounts of Marcel Griaule's

Dakar-Djibouti Mission (1933) as formative experiences of his child-hood. While training as a civil engineer in Paris, he attended Griaule's lectures at the Musée de l'Homme and Langlois's screenings at the Cinémathèque, rare places of freedom in wartime Paris of 1941. Rouch claimed his uncle, Gustav Gain, painter and photographer, taught him to 'see.' The latter's son, André, critic and painter, intro-duced Rouch to intellectuals including De Chirico, André Breton, Gérard de Nerval. Dance, theatre, cinema, and jazz influenced by the Surrealists were a part of his everyday life.

To escape from occupied France, Rouch accepted a post as an engineer in Niger. On a construction site, he met Damouré Zika, a Sorko fisherman with whom he would make films for the next fifty years. When lightning killed ten of his workers, Damouré took Rouch to his grandmother, who called on the ancestral spirits. She accused Rouch of angering the Thunder God by constructing a road without permission. Jean and Damouré sent notes and images of the grandmother's interpretation to Griaule in Paris. Germaine Dieterlen replied by sending Rouch a questionnaire, encouraging him to con-tinue. In 1942, the administration sent Rouch to Dakar, where he studied with Théodor Monod. Back in Paris after the war, Rouch continued his studies with Griaule and **Marcel Mauss**, the founder of Modern French Anthropology.

In 1946, Rouch returned to Africa with a Bell and Howell 16mm camera. With Jean Sauvy and Pierre Ponty, he paddled the Niger River from source to mouth, a trip in part financed by articles and images sent to France Presse in Paris. Actualités Françaises presented his footage of the trip as exemplary of an ageless Africa under the title of *Pays des mages noirs* (In the land of the black magi) (1946/47). Dismayed by this distortion, Rouch nonetheless retained a lesson from the experience: during the trip his tripod fell overboard. He continued to film hand-held, discovering a freedom of expression hitherto unknown. At the time 16mm cameras had hand-cranked motors that could film only twenty-five-second silent shots. Rouch learned to film only the salient moments of the action, counting on the subsequent voice-over recordings to create a sense of continuity, as can be seen in *The Magicians of Wanzerbe* (1948) and *Circumcision* (1949). He subsequently entered the world of the spirits with *Initiation à la danse des possédés* (Initiation into possession dance) (1949), which won first prize at the 'Festival du Film Maudit,' orga-nized by Cocteau and Langlois.

Profoundly influenced by Flaherty's use of feedback techniques, showing his rushes to Inuit during the filming of *Nanook of the North*,

Rouch screened a first cut of *Bataille sur le Grand fleuve* (Battle on the Grand River) (1951) to the Sorko fishermen and hunters who provided suggestions included in subsequent versions of the film. Rouch believed: 'This type of participatory research, as idealistic as it may seem, appears to me to be the only morally and scientifically feasible anthropological attitude today' (2003: 44). He acknowledged that the filmmaker's involvement is a catalyst that can *make* things happen. Rouch was also influenced by the Russian filmmaker Dziga Vertov's analyses of Cinéma Vérité, a term used to describe films shot hand-held with synchronous sound and no formal script. Frequent misinterpretations of this concept as a positivist claim to truth led Rouch to use the term Cinéma Direct, which differed from the American idea of Direct Cinema in which filmmakers attempted to make themselves *invisible*. Rouch's claim to truth was poetical rather than positivist.

In 1954/55 Rouch made *Les maîtres fous* (The mad masters), showing Hauka men possessed by their colonizers, with rolling eyes and foaming at the mouth, eating a sacrificed dog and burning their own bodies. One is drawn into a 'ciné-trance' by the subjects of his film, filmed close-up on an altar dripping with blood, including a colonial Governor-General presented as a fetish statuette, all of which was accompanied by wild marching parodying British military protocol. Rouch's voice-over informs that 'Commandant Mugu' is the wicked major, 'Gomno' is the Governor-General, and 'General Malia,' General of the Red Sea. The next day, Rouch shows the men back at work in great shape, suggesting the healing nature of the ritual in helping them cope as migrant workers. The film ends with an official military parade showing the real soldiers in full regalia.

In Paris, the film provoked an outcry and Griaule insisted that it be destroyed. Rouch had broken the rules by filming a 'degenerate ritual.' The British authorities in Ghana banned the film and Rouch did not show the film to the Hauka, since they could be plunged back into trance if they saw themselves. *Les maîtres fous* went on to win a prize at the Venice Film Festival. The film appealed to the Surrealists and inspired both Jean Genet's *Les nègres* and Peter Brook's *Marat/Sade*. Rouch completed his doctorate with a study on ritual possession to accompany the film and subsequently became a member of the National Centre for Scientific Research (CNRS).

In 1952, Jean Rouch and André Leroi-Gourhan founded the Comité du film ethnographique (CFE) at the Musée de l'Homme to promote the relationship between social science and cinema. Henri

Langlois, Rouch's counterpart, directed the French Cinémathèque and their unspoken partnership soon became notorious. While Langlois organized one of the most impressive film archives of the history of the cinema, Rouch pursued the mysteries of life, making his first ethno-fictions, *Jaguar* (1955) and *Moi, un noir* (Me, a black) (1958). Rouch filmed fiction as he filmed reality: without knowing what was going to happen next, using 'creative license to "capture" the texture of an event, the ethos of lived experience' (Stoller 1992: 143). Jean-Luc Godard acknowledged that much of his cinema was influenced by *Moi, un noir* and that his classic *A bout de souffle* could have been called 'Moi, un blanc.'

In 1960, Rouch and Edgar Morin made *Chronique d'un été* (Chronicle of a Summer), a social fresco of Paris dealing with key contemporary issues such as the war in Algeria. Rouch started filming with an Arriflex camera but changed to an Éclair-Coutant with a ten-minute magazine. A portable Nagra tape recorder that could record sound on long reels was adapted for the sound. Several cameramen worked on the film, including Raoul Coutard, who shot the Renault factory with a hand-held 35mm camera, telephoto lens, and ultra sensitive film. Michel Brault, who had done hand-held synchronous work for the Canadian Film Board, introduced a Lavalière microphone for the shots he filmed at the Place de la Concorde featuring Marceline Loridan, at the time a student film-maker and concentration camp escapee. Marceline was carrying the Nagra as she recorded memories of her father who died in Auschwitz. Later in the film, at Les Halles in Paris, she whispered a few words to her late father. Both scenes were real, yet their impact lay in the fact that they were filmed as continuous large wide-angle synchronous sound shots that added to Marceline's sense of desolateness. *Chronicle of a Summer* was one of the first Cinéma Direct films with an urban theme, showing people in improvised scenes based on their real lives. The film won the International Critics Prize at the Cannes Film Festival in 1961.

After 1966, Rouch returned to Africa periodically to film the Sigui funeral ritual of the Dogon, performed every sixty years over a period of seven years. He had read Griaule and Leiris's descriptions of a ritual they did not attend in 1907–17 but which was described in detail in oral tradition. Rouch likened this to being the first spectator of an opera whose libretto he knew before the curtain rose. One of the first Sigui sequences he filmed with synchronous sound, was a scene of a row of men with white bonnets and horse-tail fly whisks dancing to the rhythm of drums beating and the elders singing: 'The Sigui has flown on the wings of the wind.' In 1972 he reconstituted parts of the rites that he was unable to film previously in an Islamic village, providing completion to the ritual. Rouch screened the seven phases of the Sigui film to some of the participants in Sangha, who had not attended all the consecutive years' rites. Rouch's way of filming these rituals went beyond a mere recording of reality. He reshaped the rituals to his point of view, his sense of rhythm and editing, and a mise en scène of which he had read the libretto before the action started. The Dogon imaginary universe was congenial to his desire to invest the ethnographic image with aesthetic intensity. Rouch did not publish research papers on his work with the Dogon, but his films contributed widely to the international reputation of the region since 'film is a means of total expression for me, and I do not see the necessity for me to write before, during, or after filming' (2003: 273).

In 1969 Rouch made another landmark film, *Petit à petit* (Little by little). Damouré Zika, director of Petit à petit Imports, a company created in *Jaguar*, arrives in Paris on business but ends up studying the ways of the natives, hence reversing anthropology. It is not always clear whether Rouch's films are pure fictions or ethno-fictions. However, it is evident that he considers anything related to humans to be anthropological or ethnographic. In films like *Dionysos* (1984), *Enigma* (1986), *Folie ordinaire d'une fille de Cham* (Ordinary Folly of a Girl of Cham) (1987), *Liberté, égalité, fraternité et puis après* (Liberty, Equality, Fraternity ... and Then After) (1990/1989), and *Moi fatigué debout, couché* (Tired Standing Up and Lying Down) (1997), he shows that there is no encounter without fiction. This is most apparent in *Les maîtres fous* where Rouch *dances* with his camera into the heart of the action, recording fictionalized biographies told in multiple tongues, and inspired by the everyday reality of immigrants in colonial Africa.

A lifelong rebel always demanding the impossible, Jean Rouch remained curious and joyful throughout his life. In 2004, he died in a car accident in Niger, on his beloved African soil. Appropriately he has been commemorated in several documentary films.

Select readings

Rouch, J. (1997) *Les hommes et les dieux du fleuve: Essai ethnographique sur les populations Songhay du Moyen Niger, 1941–1983*, Paris: Editions Artcom, Collection Regard d'Ethnographie.
——(2003) *Cine-Ethnography*, trans. and ed. by S. Feld, Minnesota: University of Minnesota Press.

——(2008) *Alors le Noir et le Blanc seront amis: Carnets de mission. 1946–1951*, Paris: Mille et une nuits.
Stoller, P. (1992) *The Cinematic Griot: The Ethnography of Jean Rouch*, Chicago: University of Chicago Press.
Ten Brink, J., (ed.) (2007) *Building Bridges: The Cinema of Jean Rouch*, London: Wallflower Press.

Select filmography

Bregstein, P. (1986) *Jean Rouch and His Camera in the Heart of Africa*, filmed for Dutch Television, color, 74 min.
Meyknecht S., Nijland, D., Verhey, J. (dirs.) (1998) *Rouch's Gang*, color, 70 min.
Sylvestre, C. (dir.) (1960) *Entretien de René Lévesque avec Jean Rouch, anthropologue et cinéaste*, Quebec, n/b, 27 min., v.o.

RINA SHERMAN

GAYLE RUBIN (1949–)

Sex is often a difficult subject, and in anthropology, it is difficult to solicit information about something that the human animal does largely as a concealed activity. Unlike her predecessors, Rubin approaches sex with directness, even a measure of defiance. 'The time has come to think about sex' are the words that open one of her signature works. Her mark in the discipline is subtle, but pronounced.

Born in 1949, Rubin grew up in South Carolina, graduating from the University of Michigan with a BA in 1972 with high honors. She was the first individual to graduate with an independent major in Women's Studies. She received her MA in anthropology from the University of Michigan in 1974. In 1978, Rubin moved to San Francisco to study the gay leatherman culture. She received her doctoral degree, also from Michigan, in 1994, and currently holds an appointment there in both Anthropology and Women's Studies.

It was in the late stages of her undergraduate studies that the first version of one of her better-known works took shape. 'The Traffic in Women: Notes on the "Political Economy" of Sex' was at once a pointed critique of the limits of Marx and an opening salvo in a nascent war within feminist thought. It first appeared in Rayna Reiter's 1975 collection *Toward an Anthropology of Women*.

'The Traffic in Women' examines women in society through multiple lenses. The essay is informed by her reading of Marx, Freud,

Claude Lévi-Strauss, and Jacques Lacan and by the teaching of her mentors at Michigan including **Marshall Sahlins**. Rubin argues that while the domain of classical Marxism – the examination and analysis of labor and capital – serves as an excellent look at the oppression of women, it does so *only* in the context of capitalist societies. But as Rubin points out, there are innumerable cases of societies which are, in her words, by 'no stretch of the imagination' (1975: 163) capitalist societies, and yet the oppression of women is severe. Rubin further notes that for Marx, the *entire* domain of sex, sexuality, and sex oppression is subsumed under 'historical and moral elements' (in a comment found in *Capital*, Vol. 1, Chap. 6).

It is within this opening framework that she proposes a 'sex/ gender' system. All societies, she argues, have a sex/gender system. In considering the nature of this system, Rubin suggests that sex is itself a social product insofar as desire and its expression are subject to strong social influence. To better understand the nature of the sex/ gender system, Rubin turns to anthropology, specifically kinship. Drawing on the work of Claude Lévi-Strauss, Rubin argues that kinship systems are 'observable and empirical forms of sex/gender systems' (1975: 169). Lévi-Strauss, she suggests, looks at marriage on a grand scale, suggesting women as a medium of exchange. Here Rubin introduces another key idea: women and their relation to the gift. She argues that kinship systems demarcate the boundaries of sexual exchange, genealogical status, and the like in a system of social relationships. There is an 'economy' of sexual systems to be found in ethnographies and other anthropological writing. What is needed, Rubin argues, is a *political* economy of sexual systems. She goes on to suggest that the division of labor itself creates gender systems which reproduce the labor force and constitute women as objects of exchange. Lévi-Strauss is criticized for taking women's 'object' status for granted, without further interrogation. Through the exchange of women, non-normative sexuality is not simply marginalized, but completely obscured. The major result is compulsory heterosexuality. Variations are suppressed. Anthropology, she argues, fails to explain the conventions by which children are ultimately 'engraved with the conventions of sex and gender' (1975: 183).

At this point, Rubin considers feminism. She contended that a serious feminist revolution would liberate all forms of sexual expression, rather than simply liberating 'women' as we have been taught to understand that term. Sex/gender systems, she argues, are the products of human activity, not rooted in some form that is 'natural.' Ultimately, the study of sex/gender systems must be comprehensive:

the real study and understanding of such systems, Rubin suggests, must include *everything* in the system.

While conducting her doctoral research in San Francisco, Rubin, along with many others including Pat Califia, founded *Samois* in June 1978. This was one of the earliest known lesbian groups devoted to community support of women who engaged in sadomasochism (S/M). *Samois* appeared during what are often called the 'feminist sex wars' and seems to have shaped much of Rubin's approach toward her study of sexuality and gender. After *Samois* disbanded in 1983, Rubin and others formed another support and social group, *The Outcasts*. Much of Rubin's later work is informed by the immersion in these experiences and her extended fieldwork.

Almost a decade after 'The Traffic in Women,' Rubin's next major work appeared. 'Thinking Sex: Notes for a Radical Theory of the Politics of Sexuality' delved more deeply into sex itself, stepping past the usual conventions about sexuality and gender. Much had shifted within feminism during the intervening time. Much of what western society understood by 'sex' was subsumed under theories of 'gender oppression,' leading to ongoing controversies around such issues as pornography. The essay appeared in Carole Vance's 1984 volume *Pleasure and Danger: Exploring Female Sexuality*, a collection of papers delivered at a 1982 conference at Barnard College which had been opposed by anti-pornography feminists. Rubin's activism in San Francisco had already exposed her to attacks by such groups.

Rubin suggested that only within sexology was the kind of work being done that really considered sex itself rather than relegating it to a subtopic of gender or history. 'Thinking Sex' begins with what is a remarkably timely series of observations. Rubin notes that:

> Contemporary conflicts over sexual values and erotic conduct have much in common with the religious disputes of earlier centuries. ... Disputes over sexual behavior often become the vehicles for displacing social anxieties, and discharging their attendant emotional intensity.
>
> (1993a [1984]: 3)

Rubin spends considerable effort examining sex laws. Here she not only builds a compelling case for better scholarship, but also opens herself up to criticism from outside academe. Sex laws are deeply embedded in society. In 1873, the US Government enacted the first Federal law aimed at obscenity, the Comstock Act. This led, in turn, to many laws designed not simply to suppress obscenity, but also to suppress *any* non-normative, that is non-heterosexual, sexual expression. It was not until 1975, nearly a hundred years later, that the US Supreme Court struck down a Texas law restricting sodomy. Rubin demonstrates the manner in which non-normative sex, especially homosexuality and, later, sadomasochistic practices is demonized, a process leading to an increasingly intolerant attitude about sex and sexuality.

Rubin argues for a radical theory of sex that 'must identify, describe, explain and denounce erotic injustice and sexual oppression' (1993a [1984]: 9). Those who denounce sexuality in the forms deemed non-normative often invoke nature: sex is a 'natural' force, one that exists outside of institutions. Some academic studies of sex have reproduced this kind of sexual essentialism. Rubin attempts to simultaneously avoid both essentialism and the dissolution of sex in other discourses, not an easy task.

Sexual politics must be considered in larger terms than the body. Sex is a matter of neighborhoods, settlement patterns, social contexts, and even migration. Sex is too often seen as suspect, dangerous, and a threat to the well being of society. Sex negativism permeates much of US society, leaving most individuals with the sense that heterosexual marriage is the only acceptable way to be sexual. In the end, Rubin suggests, sex is a 'vector of oppression' (1993a [1984]: 22).

Feminism did not escape the 'moral panic' problem. Rubin argues that so-called 'second wave' feminism assumed that 'sex' could be explained through the analysis of gender. Sex and gender, she argues, are simply not interchangeable. This conflation has led to a profound polarization in feminist thought. In distinct contrast to 'The Traffic in Women,' she now considers it essential to separate sex and gender in order to attain greater clarity in the analysis of either one. 'In western culture, sex is taken all too seriously' (1993a [1984]: 35) but sexual persecution is not taken seriously enough. There is little social significance to the various *acts* of sex. Why are they so strongly persecuted?

Much has changed since Rubin wrote 'The Traffic in Women' and 'Thinking Sex.' Same-sex marriage has become thinkable, and, in some jurisdictions, doable. The status of the transgendered person has received some social recognition. Both of these facts indicate that the 'sex-gender' system is to some degree malleable. Nonetheless, political interests still exert a tenacious hold on ideologies that are easily used to generate moral panics. Children are typically the center of these efforts.

The zealousness of Rubin's detractors is nearly the stuff of legend (or at least a good television soap opera). In some cases, pseudo-academic research attempts to paint her as a supporter of paedophilia, a pressing issue for many, regardless of political affiliation. Words from Rubin's writings that are likely to elicit a strong reaction are placed in quotes to draw the reader to the author's idea about what is 'wrong.' There is often no distinction made between consensual sex between persons who might be quite close in age and the forcible abduction of children by adults. Many attackers insist that their own thoughts and feelings about sex are in harmony with nature, whereas Rubin's perspective is outside of nature, ergo unnatural. These critics thus rely on the same stigmatizing mechanisms that Rubin so brilliantly elucidates.

Rubin's influence is rather remarkable in that it extends well outside the field of anthropology. Feminism, queer theory, sexology, and gender studies all draw from her work. Equally powerful is her influence within the larger community that she studied as well as those individuals whose sexual identities are under fire. Numerous individuals have told this author that her keen wit, character, and unwavering support played a significant and positive part in their lives.

It is instructive that Gayle Rubin has chosen a subject that elicits so much vilification. The ideologies which she considers in her work are firmly in place; sexual minorities, of which she herself is a member, are widely reviled. The experience of living as queer in any form in the United States, indeed in many western and non-western countries, can be a sobering, often painful, sometimes fatal experience. That we have the beginnings of an attempt to challenge and document the degree of pain combined with a adroit analysis of its causes is notable.

Selected readings

Rubin, G. (1975) 'The Traffic in Women: Notes on the "Political Economy" of Sex,' in *Toward an Anthropology of Women*, R. Reiter (ed.), pp. 157–210, New York: Monthly Review Press.

——(1982) 'The Leather Menace,' *Body Politic* April: 33, 34.

——(1991) 'The Catacombs: A Temple of the Butthole,' in *Radical Sex, People, Politics, and Practice*, M. Thompson (ed.), pp. 119–41, Boston, MA: Alyson Publications.

——(1993a [1984]) 'Thinking Sex: Notes for a Radical Theory of the Politics of Sexuality,' in *The Lesbian And Gay Studies Reader*, H. Abelove, M. A. Barale, and D. M. Halperin (eds.), pp. 3–44, New York: Routledge; originally published in *Pleasure and Danger: Exploring Female Sexuality*, C. Vance (ed.), London: Routledge and Kegan Paul.

——(1993b) 'Misguided, Dangerous and Wrong: An Analysis of Anti-Pornography Politics,' in *Bad Girls and Dirty Pictures*, A. Assiter and C. Avedon (eds.), pp. 18–40, London: Pluto Press.

——(2000) 'Sites, Settlements, and Urban Sex: Archaeology and the Study of Gay Leathermen in San Francisco 1955–95,' in *Archaeologies of Sexuality*, R. A. Schmidt and B. Voss (eds.), pp. 62–88, London: Routledge.
——(2002) 'Studying Sexual Subcultures: the Ethnography of Gay Communities in Urban North America,' in *Out in Theory: The Emergence of Lesbian and Gay Anthropology*, E. Lewin and W. Leap (eds.), pp. 17–68, Urbana: University of Illinois Press.

DAVID L. R. HOUSTON

MARSHALL SAHLINS (1930–)

Marshall David Sahlins was born on December 27, 1930 in Chicago, Illinois, where, at the time of writing he was still the remarkably productive Charles F. Grey Distinguished Service Professor of Anthropology Emeritus at the University of Chicago. Though his name has become indelibly linked to that institution and city, he earned his PhD at Columbia University (1954) and his Bachelors and Masters degrees at the University of Michigan, where he also taught for a number of years before his return to Chicago in 1973. Among his major early intellectual influences were the evolutionary theories of **Leslie White** at Michigan and the views of economic historian Karl Polanyi and environmental anthropologist **Julian Steward** (both at Columbia). Their ideas were reflected in Sahlins's early writings of a historical materialist and NEO-EVOLUTIONIST bent. After a period in Paris in the late 1960s, however, he experienced something of a mid-career 'conversion' to a cultural theory that eschewed any strict determination by material or biological constraints. The major influence on him at that time was the STRUCTURALIST movement inspired by **Claude Lévi-Strauss**, though Sahlins has also acknowledged ideas from French classical historians such as Georges Dumézil. Despite this changing theoretical trajectory, throughout his career he has consistently maintained a left-wing political stance, both speaking out against the Vietnam War in the 1960s and becoming one of the few senior anthropologists to take a strong public stand against the invasion of Iraq in 2003, to take just two widely spaced examples. Indeed he has even drawn astute parallels between present-day American imperialism and its counterparts in the earlier histories of Europe and the Pacific.

His political stance may explain why he appears distinctly ambivalent about another stream of French theory that was emerging during his time in Paris, the 'power/knowledge' approach most famously exemplified by Michel Foucault. Sahlins has often expressed his distaste for views that seemingly 'reduce' culture to relations of power (as in certain strains of postmodernism and postcolonialism that imply resistance is either futile or the product of the power it opposes). This is not to say that he belittles power and oppression as factors in human history but rather that he retains a belief in some forms of transformative human action and political opposition.

Unusually, Sahlins's PhD dissertation was based not on ethnographic fieldwork but on library research. Published as his first book, *Social Stratification in Polynesia* (1958), it applied the comparative and evolutionist frames of his Michigan and Columbia training to documentary sources in order to formulate an explanation for the variations of kind and degree of hierarchy in traditional Polynesian societies. By the time the book appeared, Sahlins had undertaken field research on the Fijian island of Moala, work that resulted in a monograph of that title (1962). In between these two publications he co-edited a volume with Elman Service, *Evolution and Culture* (1960) and shortly after the Fiji monograph produced one of his most seminal essays, 'Poor Man, Rich Man, Big-Man, Chief' (1963), in which he famously contrasted the simple modes of Melanesian leadership systems with the supposedly more advanced and complex Polynesian ones. These writings represent the highpoint of his evolutionism – a historically nuanced version but evolutionism nonetheless.

A co-edited volume of essays on economic anthropology dedicated to Polanyi's memory came out in 1965, and this interest continued with a collection of his own papers, *Stone Age Economics* (1972). Its best known essay, 'The Original Affluent Society,' questioned conventional evolutionary thinking about the hardship and privations of hunter-gatherer existence, arguing that Australian Aborigines in fact derived a full subsistence lifestyle from less time and effort than most other forms of social organization and technological development.

By now, the influence of the Paris sojourn was beginning to make itself felt, culminating in Sahlins's first clearly structuralist book, *Culture and Practical Reason* (1976). Rather than seeing culture as a succession of ways in which people have adapted to nature over time, he was starting to articulate nature and history as phenomena that have always been 'culturalized.' Another outcome of this reorientation was his stinging critique on sociobiology, *Use and Abuse of Biology* (1977), which dissected the bourgeois economism and conservative ideology underpinning that theory.

While these theoretical interventions gained public attention, behind the scenes Sahlins was spending time in archives in Fiji, Hawai'i, and New Zealand, preparing a major revision of Pacific historiography. Paradoxically, the products of this areal specialization have come to the attention of a wider audience than the more general works and have consolidated his reputation as one of the leading anthropologists of his day. The new approach was signaled by two talks given in 1979, a distinguished lecture to the Association for Social Anthropology in Oceania that expanded into the brief monograph *Historical Metaphors and Mythical Realities* (1981), and a keynote address to the Congress of the Australian and New Zealand Association for the Advancement of Science, 'The Stranger-King: Dumézil among the Fijians' (1981). The latter provided a term for his approach, 'processual structuralism,' while *Historical Metaphors* launched his most controversial analytical case study, a detailed reworking of the literature surrounding the initial welcome and subsequent killing by Hawai'ians of Captain Cook in 1779. Cook's reception by the locals as an embodiment of one of their pre-eminent deities, Lono, had previously been seen as an interesting and exotic footnote in most commentaries on his explorations. Sahlins now turned it into the central point for understanding this cultural encounter, one in which Cook's arrival, conduct on land, departure, and return all fitted within Hawai'ian cosmology as expressed through the annual ritual cycle of Makahiki when an agricultural god was killed with promise of future resurrection. Instead of seeing the reception of Cook/Lono as just another instance of irrational natives deferring to Westerners' military power or succumbing to the allure of their shiny trinkets, Sahlins powerfully demonstrated the logic by which Hawai'ians encompassed the strangers and recruited them to the service of their own culture. The essay on Fiji meanwhile reinforced the message by posing the idea that Polynesian systems of leadership depended on periodic intrusions by outsiders and their eventual domestication by locals. This essay was reprinted along with others in a new collection, *Islands of History* (1985).

Much of the remainder of the decade of the 1980s was spent by Sahlins in preparing a detailed historical ethnography of a Hawai'ian valley, *Anahulu* (1992), a project undertaken in collaboration with an archaeologist, Patrick Vinton Kirch. He also engaged in clarifying and elaborating the argument proposed in *Historical Metaphors*, often in the context of replying to critics who questioned his grasp of the historical sources or of Hawai'ian culture. By and large, he managed to bat away most of the objections convincingly.

The best-known critique of his thesis, however, was to come from an unexpected direction. Gananath Obeyesekere of Princeton University is an anthropologist of Sri Lankan origin, well respected in the discipline for his research on Buddhism and its place in South Asian cultures. Like Sahlins, he is a senior scholar and emeritus professor but until 1992 he was not known for any interest or expertise in Oceania. In that year he mounted a double-pronged assault on Sahlins's interpretation of the encounter between Cook and the people of Hawai'i. The more important of these was a book, *The Apotheosis of Captain Cook: European Mythmaking in the Pacific*, in which he claimed historical accounts showed that the Hawai'ian motives for treating Cook as Lono were explicable purely in universal rational and utilitarian terms, not in terms of a local cultural logic. Sahlins in short had bought into a longstanding Western fantasy about how Westerners were perceived by 'natives.' The other prong of Obeyesekere's assault was an essay denying the veracity of Western accounts of cannibalism in the Pacific, again attributing the stories to fantasies and projected fears about 'savages.' As an academic whose primary expertise lay elsewhere, Obeseyekere based his critique on published and secondary sources, claiming that even a scholar without Sahlins's specialized knowledge could see the holes in his argument.

Sahlins's riposte was the book *How 'Natives' Think: About Captain Cook, For Example* (1995). Once more he demonstrated his unsurpassed command of the primary source material and his ability to defend his theoretical position. These strengths later enabled him to demolish Obeyesekere's denial of the reality of cannibalism in two brief articles published in *Anthropology Today* (2003).

In recent years, Sahlins has issued a magisterial overview of his approach to culture and (or as) history, *Apologies to Thucydides* (2004), as well as a stream of essays arguing forcefully against the imposition of ethnocentric cultural logics on non-Western cultures, especially in respect of debates over (under)development and dependency. In so doing, he stands in an anthropological tradition that questions not only the spread of a hegemonic Western monoculture but, more profoundly, even the very existence of such a homogeneous world system. Sahlins tries to practice what he preaches and has revived the old form of political consciousness-raising – the pamphlet. He publishes and edits a pamphlet series appropriately called *Prickly Paradigm* which seeks to promote public debate on pressing issues by making publicly accessible longer essays on contentious issues of the day.

In the restless refashioning of his theoretical repertoire, Sahlins has become perhaps the best-known practitioner of a new kind of historical anthropology, one that he has done more than anyone else to create. The impact of his rethinking of Cook's encounter with Hawai'i, as well as the subsequent controversy generated by

Obeyesekere's critical attack, have helped propel his ideas into spheres well beyond the usual territory for an anthropologist. These include cultural studies, philosophy, history, comparative literature, and literary theory.

Selected readings

Obeyesekere, G. (1992a) *The Apotheosis of Captain Cook: European Mythmaking in the Pacific*, Princeton, NJ: Princeton University Press.
——(1992b) '"British Cannibals": Contemplation of an Event in the Death and Resurrection of James Cook, Explorer,' *Critical Inquiry* 18(4): 630–54.
——(1993) 'Anthropology and the Cook Myth: A Response to Critics,' *Social Analysis* 34: 70–85.
——(1994) 'How to Write a Cook Book: Mythic and Other Realities in Anthropological Writing,' *Pacific Studies* 17(2): 136–55.
Sahlins, M. (1958) *Social Stratification in Polynesia*, Seattle: University of Washington Press.
——(1962) *Moala: Culture and Nature on a Fijian Island*, Ann Arbor: University of Michigan Press.
——(1963) 'Poor Man, Rich Man, Big-Man, Chief: Political Types in Melanesia and Polynesia,' *Comparative Studies in Society and History* 5(3): 285–303.
——(1972) *Stone Age Economics*, Chicago: Aldine-Atherton.
——(1976) *Culture and Practical Reason*, Chicago: University of Chicago Press.
——(1981a) *Historical Metaphors and Mythical Realities: Structure in the Early History of the Sandwich Islands Kingdom*, Ann Arbor: University of Michigan Press.
——(1981b) 'The Stranger-King: Dumézil among the Fijians,' *Journal of Pacific History* 16(3/4): 107–32. (Reprinted in M. Sahlins [1985] *Islands of History*, Chicago: University of Chicago Press.)
——(1985) *Islands of History*, Chicago: University of Chicago Press.
——(1992) *Anahulu: The Anthropology of History in the Kingdom of Hawaii. Vol. 1: Historical Ethnography*, Chicago: University of Chicago Press.
——(1993) 'Goodbye to Tristes Tropes: Ethnography in the Context of Modern World History,' *Journal of Modern History* 65(1): 1–25.
——(1995) *How 'Natives' Think: About Captain Cook, For Example*, Chicago: University of Chicago Press.
——(1999) 'What is Anthropological Enlightenment? Some Lessons of the Twentieth Century,' *Annual Review of Anthropology* 28: i–xxiii.
——(2000a) *Culture in Practice: Selected Essays*, New York: Zone Books.
——(2000b) 'On the Anthropology of Modernity; or, Some Triumphs of Culture over Despondency Theory,' in *Culture and Sustainable Development in the Pacific*, A. Hooper (ed.), pp. 44–61, Canberra: Asia Pacific Press.

——(2000c) '"Sentimental Pessimism" and Ethnographic Experience; or, Why Culture Is Not a Disappearing "Object",' in *Biographies of Scientific Objects*, L. Daston, (ed.), pp. 158–202, Chicago: University of Chicago Press.

——(2002a) *Waiting for Foucault, Still*, Chicago: Prickly Paradigm Press.

——(2002b) 'An Empire of a Certain Kind,' *Social Analysis* 46(1): 95–98.

——(2004) *Apologies to Thucydides: Understanding History as Culture and Vice Versa*, Chicago: University of Chicago Press.

MICHAEL GOLDSMITH

EDWARD SAPIR (1884–1939)

Edward Sapir, the most distinguished linguist among the first generation of **Franz Boas**'s students, was born January 26, 1884, in Lauenberg, Pomerania. His parents, Eva Segal and Jacob David Sapir, were Lithuanian Jews. His father's profession of cantor took the family to England and eventually to the United States. In 1890, the family settled in Richmond, Virginia, but Sapir grew up on New York City's Lower East Side. He used a city-wide Pulitzer scholarship for promising immigrant children to attend Columbia University where he received a BA in 1904 and an MA in 1905, both in Germanics. His PhD in Anthropology, under the tutelage of Boas, was awarded in 1909.

Sapir's initial professional positions were interspersed with field-work. In 1907–8, he was a research fellow at the University of California. From 1908–10, he held a Harrison fellowship at the University of Pennsylvania, before moving to Ottawa as the first director of Canada's Division of Anthropology, under the auspices of the Geological Survey of Canada, a position he held for fifteen years. In Ottawa, Sapir built up collections at the Victoria National Museum and assembled a staff to survey the Aboriginal cultures and languages of the Dominion. Diamond Jenness and Marius Barbeau, both British-trained, held permanent positions, but Sapir also hired fellow Boasians Wilson Wallis, **Paul Radin**, Alexander Goldenweiser, and Harlan Smith on short-term contracts for field-work. These men formed the core of the emergent professional anthropology in Canada.

In 1910, Sapir married his distant cousin, Florence Delson, with whom he had three children. Florence died in 1924 after some years of illness. Family difficulties coincided with cutbacks in research funding during World War I. Sapir, like Boas, was a pacifist who placed the priorities of science above those of national politics.

During these years, Sapir frequented Ottawa literary circles, published poetry and literary criticism, and transposed his fascination with psychoanalysis to the anthropological problem of personality and culture.

In 1925, Sapir was called to the University of Chicago as the superstar expected to revitalize the Department of Anthropology, which became independent of Sociology in 1929, and to link American Indian ethnography and linguistics to Rockefeller Foundation-sponsored interdisciplinary social science. He served as the key mediator between Chicago sociology and psychology, establishing collaborations especially with interactional psychologist Harry Stack Sullivan and political scientist Harold Lasswell. He developed a cohort of students at the intersection of linguistics and anthropology but increasingly wrote for interdisciplinary audiences. He married Jean Victoria McClenaghan in 1926 and had two more children.

In 1931, despite warnings of anti-Semitism, Sapir could not resist the invitation to move to Yale University where the Rockefeller Foundation underwrote a research and training program for invited foreign fellows on 'the impact of culture on personality.' Sapir soon clashed with the Institute of Human Relations, however, and found his position increasingly stressful. He trained students both in linguistics and in personality and culture. After his first heart attack in 1937 forced cancellation of a planned sabbatical in China, his health deteriorated rapidly. Boas read his presidential address to the American Anthropological Association in the fall of 1938, and he suffered a fatal attack on February 4, 1939.

Throughout his career, alongside his academic appointments and interdisciplinary commitments, Sapir continued to prepare grammars, dictionaries, and texts of American Indian languages, based primarily on his first-hand fieldwork. He worked on more than thirty different languages, taking full advantage of opportunities to interview Native representatives visiting Ottawa, to explore other languages spoken by his primary informants, and to make brief visits to Algonquian and Iroquoian communities located within easy distance of Ottawa, often in the company of fellow Boasian Frank Speck. His most linguistic-intensive fieldwork was with Southern Paiute, Nootka, and Navajo. His principal consultants, Tony Tillohash, Alex Thomas, and Albert 'Chic' Sandoval, respectively, led him to consider the 'psychological reality' of sound patterns. He invented the concept of the phoneme independently of European linguistic developments in 1925, combining his preoccupation with language as understood by its speakers with his concurrent concern about the impact of culture on the individual and the creativity of the individual.

Sapir's fieldwork is inseparable from his theoretical contributions. In 1916, he provided Boasian anthropology with *Time Perspective in Aboriginal American Culture: A Study in Method*. This seminal monograph rendered linguistics, in the absence of useful archaeological dating methods, indispensable to historical reasoning by students of culture. Regular sound change in language on the Indo-European model, Sapir argued, demonstrated properties of coherence and predictability that other domains of culture lacked. Therefore, distant relationships of groups and their interactions could be derived directly from the methods of historical linguistics. Sapir built his model on the Boasian insight that, in the absence of written records, geography held the key to historical migrations and borrowings.

Despite this theoretical reasoning on behalf of his non-linguistic colleagues, however, Sapir's own historical linguistics was devoted primarily to consolidating the fifty-five linguistic families in America north of Mexico as defined in 1891 by John Wesley Powell for the Bureau of American Ethnology. In 1921, he posited only six major stocks for all of North America. This breakthrough drew largely on his own work and that of **Alfred Kroeber** and Roland Dixon in California for the Hokan-Siouan and Penutian families. Sapir was fascinated by tone in the Na-Dene languages, including Navajo, and thought that this linguistic family offered the possibility of links to Asian languages. His Aztec-Tanoan family incorporated his early work on Ute and Southern Paiute. Algonquian-Ritwan linked some California and Northwest Coast linguistic diversity to the long-known and closely related Algonquian languages of central and eastern North America. Eskimo-Aleut was so clearly independent of anything else that its unity was unquestioned.

Colleagues, both then and now, have quibbled with particular attributions and remained unconvinced of the genetic or historical (as opposed to regionally diffused) nature of some relationships that Sapir fully accepted. Nonetheless, his linguistic intuitions were universally admired, and his suggestions were taken seriously in the interpretation of past ethnographic and historical relationships, even when further demonstration of relationship was desired. Evidence of relationship at great time depth was necessarily fragmentary and required inference and comparison of multiple related languages. Even for those who preferred a more conservative intermediate classification, however, Sapir's insistence that language could shed light on the movement of peoples in the past and the past relationships of contemporary groups guided their interpretations.

Sapir's only book, *Language*, appeared in 1921. Designed for the general as well as specialist reader, this brief and highly accessible volume combined insights on linguistic structure from a variety of American Indian languages with others from familiar Indo-European languages. His purview encompassed the uses of language, the cultural specificity of meanings, and the importance of literature and expressive aesthetics. Sapir's linguistics was firmly grounded in the humanities, in contrast to the more behaviorist and scientific structural linguistics that developed after his death under the leadership of Leonard Bloomfield. Beginning in the 1960s, however, Noam Chomsky's transformational linguistics returned questions of psychology and meaning to linguistics. This contributed to the revitalization of a Sapirian perspective toward language in relation and culture.

The so-called Sapir-Whorf hypothesis has been misrepresented dramatically. Its strongest forms are associated with Sapir's Yale student and protégé Benjamin Lee Whorf, but Sapir himself wrote frequently about the influence that linguistic structures had on the habitual thought of native speakers of a language. Although such structures could be transcended by training in linguistics, by what Whorf called 'multilingual awareness,' or by the experience of bilingualism, Sapir believed that the speakers of different languages lived in fundamentally different worlds. Translation, whether of language or culture, required suspension of familiar grammatical and semantic categories. Sapir was a STRUCTURALIST in the sense that he expected coherence in the linguistic patterns of a single language and contrast across languages.

Sapir's immediate successors tried to apply this line of reasoning as a deterministic influence of linguistic structure on culture in a way that would have made little sense to Sapir or Whorf. The hypothesis was considered generally disproven until the emergence of post-Chomskian cognitive linguistics. Although the assumptions underlying this work attend more to universals than to Sapir's contrasts in the patterning of particular languages, his influence on the emergent paradigm remains substantial.

The breadth of Sapir's interests makes a unitary summary of his influence virtually impossible. A festschrift organized by his students after his death attempted to represent his work in psychology, linguistics, and ethnology. Another memorial collection of grammars of American Indian languages illustrated his processual, meaning-oriented approach.

The CULTURE AND PERSONALITY papers he published in the 1920s and 1930s remain individually influential. A selection of Sapir's own papers, including most of the significant culture and personality essays, was edited by his former student David Mandelbaum in 1949 (reissued in 1963 and 1989). Notes from his culture and personality courses were preserved by various students and have been edited by Judith Irvine. A sixteen-volume edition of Sapir's collected works is being issued by Mouton De Gruyter. The centennial of Sapir's birth in 1988 produced a spate of conferences and reassessments, including a biography.

Sapir's legacy has evolved somewhat independently in linguistics and anthropology. Linguistics was emerging from its Indo-European and anthropological roots as an autonomous discipline. Sapir was a key figure in the founding of the Linguistic Society of America and its journal *Language* in 1925. For the first time since his graduate training in Indo-European linguistics, Sapir was able to write for a linguistically sophisticated audience. Indeed, he returned to some small problems of Indo-European in the last years of his life. Sapir's work on the phoneme and his meaning-oriented grammars defined one pole of the discipline of linguistics, while simultaneously, within anthropology, challenging Boas's more ethnographic and descriptive linguistic methods. In the short term, Bloomfieldian structuraliam predominated, but Sapir remained as a model for the potential breadth of linguistics as the general study of language.

In anthropology, Sapir was the exemplar of Boas's insistence that students of American Indian ethnology must also be linguists. Indeed, many of them produced the requisite texts, grammar, and dictionary of their dissertation field languages. Little was known about many of these languages when Boas and his students began their systematic fieldwork. Boas insisted that grammars should seek out the categories of the languages being described in order to capture 'the native point of view.' Sapir was alone among his students in his formal linguistic training and his sheer talent for this work. Sapir switched from Germanics to anthropology because of the urgency of recording rapidly changing and often disappearing Native languages. The quality of Sapir's linguistic work guaranteed its continued theoretical as well as descriptive salience in both anthropology and linguistics. The position of his work between the two disciplines solidified linguistics as one of the four subdisciplines of Americanist anthropology, even though few anthropologists defined themselves primarily as linguists.

Sapir's efforts to develop an interdisciplinary social science during the interwar years were largely abortive, at least in institutional form.

The Rockefeller Foundation cut back on its social science funding, and post-war research funding came increasingly from the federal government. Sapir's theory of culture, however, drew on his collaborations across disciplines. Culture for him was about the individual. Perhaps from the sociologists, he learned to incorporate society as a third term between culture and the individual. He drew on several schools of psychology and psychoanalysis in his thinking about individual creativity in different cultures. His synthesis of these perspectives provided an alternative to the culture-as-a-whole and national character studies of **Margaret Mead** and **Ruth Benedict**. The Sapirian perspective on language and meaning re-emerged in the ethnoscience of the 1960s and 1970s.

Sapir's contemporaries often referred to him as a 'genius.' He left few institutions to the disciplines he practiced, but his students developed his ideas and passed them on to their own students. Contemporary linguistic anthropologists regularly return to Sapir's original work and continue to build upon it. In the post-positivist climate of contemporary social science, he is increasingly singled out as a precursor and exemplar of the theory of culture.

Selected readings

Darnell, R. (1990) *Edward Sapir: Linguist, Anthropologist, Humanist*, Berkeley: University of California Press.

Hymes, D. and Fought, J. (1975) *American Structuralism*, The Hague: Mouton.

Sapir, E. (1916) *Time Perspective in Aboriginal American Culture: A Study in Method*, Geological Survey Memoir 90: No. 13, Anthropological Series, Ottawa: Government Printing Bureau.

——(1921) *Language: An Introduction to the Study of Speech*, New York: Harcourt Brace.

REGNA DARNELL

JULIAN STEWARD (1902–72)

Julian Haynes Steward saw anthropology as science, and his strong identification as a scientist had roots that reached back to his childhood in Washington, DC. His father, a career federal employee, became Chief of the Board of Examiners of the US Patent Office. His maternal uncle was a meteorologist and chief of the US Weather Bureau. The two men counted other government scientists as close associates, both at work and as members of the Cosmos Club, a private men's club founded by John Wesley Powell for Washington's intellectual elite. Powell served as a director of the US Geological Survey before founding and directing the Smithsonian's Bureau of American Ethnology. Steward would eventually join the ranks of government scientists as an employee of the Bureau.

Educated in public schools until the age of sixteen, Steward was recruited to attend an innovative college preparatory school, a working ranch in Deep Springs Valley, California that enrolled about twenty male students. They spent mornings in class and afternoons doing ranch work. Some of the hired ranch hands were Indians, mainly Paiute from the region.

During his three years at the school (1918–21) Steward had experiences that were unusual for his social class and urban eastern origins. He learned to work with his hands, often as part of a male work group. These experiences later informed some of his theoretical ideas about the environment, technology, and the organization of work. He would undertake his first ethnographic fieldwork with Paiute Indians just thirty miles from his old school.

In 1921, when Steward entered the University of California at Berkeley, he happened to enrol in an introductory anthropology course taught by **Alfred L. Kroeber, Robert H. Lowie**, and Edward W. Gifford (1887–1959). In 1922 he transferred to Cornell University, where many of his fellow classmates from Deep Springs were students. Cornell did not offer courses in anthropology, and Steward earned a bachelor's degree in geology and zoology in 1925. He considered a career in law, history, or a natural science, but eventually decided on anthropology.

In fall 1925 he returned to the University of California at Berkeley for graduate study. He took courses with Kroeber, Lowie, and others, including geographer Carl Sauer. In 1928, before completing his dissertation, he began to teach at the University of Michigan. He received a PhD in 1929, and resigned from the University of Michigan in 1930 in order to accept a position at the University of Utah. His fiancée Dorothy B. Nyswander (1894–1998), an educational psychologist, was one of the few women on the faculty of the University of Utah. They had met in Berkeley as graduate students. Nyswander, a committed behaviorist and experimental scientist, was Steward's intellectual ally and sounding board for seven years, between 1925 and 1932.

The couple married in 1930 and separated two years later. Steward resigned from the university in 1933. In the same year he married Jane

Cannon, whose family was prominent in Utah. With the Great Depression still underway, Steward spent the next two years in a series of temporary jobs and in fieldwork. In 1935, he joined the Bureau of American Ethnology in Washington, DC as a research ethnologist. Eleven years later he left the BAE for a professorship in anthropology at Columbia University (1946–52). He spent the longest portion of his career (1952–69) on the faculty of the University of Illinois, Urbana.

Steward had a distinctive voice in mid-twentieth-century anthropology. His environmental perspective on culture and his use of data from archaeological as well as ethnographic fieldwork were unusual for the time. He undertook his first fieldwork in the 1920s as a graduate student, working at archaeological sites in California and in Oregon. During 1927 and 1928 he also spent several weeks in ethnographic research with Owens Valley Paiutes in eastern California.

The faculty position in archaeology that Steward accepted at the University of Utah in 1930 led to work at various sites in the state. His intensive archaeological fieldwork ended when he left the university in 1933. Over the course of several months in 1935–36, Steward carried out ethnographic research in the Great Basin of the western United States. Along with his wife, Jane Cannon Steward (1908–88), he traveled through four states – California, Nevada, Utah, and Idaho – seeking out dozens of Paiute and Shoshone elders to interview about how they had lived as hunter-gatherers before American conquest and settlement in the mid-nineteenth century. He saw this work as the first step in what he termed his 'twenty-year plan' for research. It called for studying cultural change by starting with small societies of hunter-gatherers and then moving on to larger, more complex societies (Kerns 2003).

Both types of fieldwork, archaeological and ethnographic, contributed to Steward's general goal of reconstructing the past, a historical orientation that he shared with archaeologists and most American cultural anthropologists of the time. But he departed from the prevailing cultural historicism of **Franz Boas** and his students, including Kroeber and Lowie, by developing a theoretical approach that was environmentally oriented, materialist, and, although he never acknowledged it, thoroughly behaviorist. His major ideas were the antithesis of relativistic and humanistic trends in cultural anthropology, as represented by the work of his colleague at Columbia University, **Ruth Benedict**.

Steward consistently focused on what was external and observable: environmental resources, particularly those important for subsistence (such as wild game, edible plants, water); technology (primarily tools used in the food quest); and behavior (especially subsistence-related work). These elements comprised what he termed the *cultural core*. He defined this key concept as 'the constellation of features that are most closely related to subsistence activities and economic arrangements' (Steward 1955: 37).

Another foundational concept, the *patrilineal band*, figured in what he regarded as his 'first major theoretical work,' his 1936 essay on bands. Steward defined the patrilineal band as an exogamous and politically independent group of male kin who own land and defend exclusive rights to that territory. He hypothesized that this type of band developed in arid regions and others where hunting centered on small numbers of non-migratory game, and where food resources were generally limited and scattered. This kept human population density low and the size of bands small. He conceived of this type of band later as a *culture type*, or *cross-cultural type*. It presumably occurred under certain ecological conditions, and other types, under other conditions.

Steward's search for the patrilineal band motivated nearly all of his ethnographic fieldwork. He found no evidence in the field that hunter-gatherers in the Great Basin had formerly lived in patrilineal bands (Kerns 2010). His ethnography, *Basin-Plateau Aboriginal Sociopolitical Groups* (1938), focused instead on how environmental conditions in different localities varied, how people in each place adapted culturally, and how this affected the varying size and structure of local groups. In 1938 he traveled to South America with his wife, planning to do fieldwork in Chile with Araucanian Indians, whom he thought might have lived in patrilineal bands. He returned to the United States before reaching Chile. He carried out his last ethnographic fieldwork in 1940 in western Canada with Carrier Indians, and again found no evidence of patrilineal bands.

Over the course of twenty years, between the mid-1930s and mid-1950s, Steward wrote a series of articles later included in a collection titled *Theory of Culture Change* (1955). In one of those articles, 'Cultural Causality and Law: A Trial Formulation of the Development of Early Civilizations' (1949), he used archaeological reports to argue that the first civilizations developed in arid and semi-arid environments; and that they showed a uniform sequence of development, including the use of irrigation in agriculture. The article illustrates one of Steward's key questions: What causes cultural change, such as the independent development of early civilizations? It also illustrates one of his key premises, drawn from the natural sciences: that it is possible to formulate cultural laws, akin to natural laws.

Steward came to use the name *cultural ecology* for his approach, and he included an essay on his method in *Theory of Culture Change*. Although he had not found evidence of the patrilineal band in his fieldwork, he included a slightly revised version of his 1936 essay on the topic. A few years later he quietly abandoned his concept of the cultural core, but continued to refer to the patrilineal band in his writings.

Steward's theoretical perspective, cultural ecology, had a direct impact on American cultural anthropology for decades and proved to have an even more enduring influence on archaeology. During his six years at Columbia, Steward worked with a generation of male graduate students, World War II veterans attending Columbia on the GI Bill, who were drawn to materialist perspectives. Many of them – including Stanley Diamond (1922–91), Morton Fried (1923–86), Sidney W. Mintz (1922–), Robert F. Murphy (1924–90), Elman R. Service (1915–96) and **Eric Wolf** – achieved prominence in academic anthropology. **Marvin Harris**, who was also a post-war student at Columbia, later promoted Steward's ideas – notably his materialist, nomothetic approach – in a widely read book, *The Rise of Anthropological Theory* (1968).

Beginning in the 1950s, Steward was often compared to **Leslie White**, who had replaced him at the University of Michigan in 1930. The two men were seen as fellow EVOLUTIONISTS, although White's brand of cultural evolutionism differed in many respects from Steward's. Steward always rejected White's approach, and he adopted the term 'multilinear evolution' to distinguish his ideas from what he called White's 'universal evolution.' He evidently turned to cultural evolution because he had found it difficult to 'sell' cultural ecology, as he put it. Despite the new name, the basic ideas of multilinear evolution came from cultural ecology. Steward's primary interests from the early 1930s until the end of his career remained constant. He focused on environmental resources and conditions, technology, the organization of work, and cultural change. He developed the concept of *levels of socio-cultural integration* to help analyze change in sociopolitical complexity, a topic of great interest to him.

Cultural ecology, the name Steward preferred for his approach, proved to be the one that endured. Attention to multilinear evolution waned in American anthropology, and cultural ecology gained ground among some. Steward's ideas influenced researchers, such as Richard B. Lee (1937–) and June Helm (1924–2004), who undertook long-term ethnographic fieldwork with hunter-gatherers; and a far greater number of archaeologists, beginning with Gordon Willey

(1913–2002) who assisted Steward with a major editorial project in the 1940s and 1950s: the seven-volume *Handbook of South American Indians*, a work that reflected Steward's theoretical interests. His environmental perspective later helped spawn a variety of ecological approaches, including those of Roy Rappaport.

Steward's founding role in Great Basin anthropology and his work as a witness for the federal government in several Indian Claims Commission trials have made him a figure of controversy. Some have questioned how he represented Great Basin Indians, both in his scholarly works and as an expert witness (e.g., Clemmer et al. 1999; Blackhawk 2006). His role in founding environmental anthropology has received growing recognition. Since 2002 the Anthropology and Environment Section of the American Anthropological Association has annually given the Julian Steward Award to the best work in ecological/environmental anthropology.

Select readings

Blackhawk, N. (2006) *Violence over the Land: Indians and Empires in the Early American West*, Cambridge, MA: Harvard University Press.

Clemmer, R. O., Myers, L. D., and Rudden, M. E. (eds.) (1999) *Julian Steward and the Great Basin: The Making of an Anthropologist*, Salt Lake City: University of Utah Press.

Kerns, V. (2003) *Scenes from the High Desert: Julian Steward's Life and Theory*, Urbana: University of Illinois Press.

——(2010) *Journeys West: Jane and Julian Steward and Their Guides*, Lincoln: University of Nebraska Press.

Steward, J. H. (1938) *Basin-Plateau Aboriginal Socio-Political Groups*, Bureau of American Ethnology Bulletin 120: 1–346, Washington, DC: Government Printing Office.

——(1955) *Theory of Culture Change: The Methodology of Multilinear Evolution*, Urbana: University of Illinois Press.

Steward, J. H. (ed.) (1946–59) *Handbook of South American Indians*, vols. 1–7, Bureau of American Ethnology Bulletin 143, Washington, DC: Government Printing Office.

VIRGINIA KERNS

DAME MARILYN STRATHERN (1941–)

Marilyn Strathern was the William Wyse Professor of Social Anthropology at Cambridge University from 1993 until 2008, after leaving the position of Head of Department and Professor of Social Anthropology at the University of Manchester, which she had held since 1985. She began her career in Cambridge as an undergraduate (BA 1963), conducting fieldwork in Mount Hagen, New Guinea Highlands from 1964 to 1965 for her doctorate (Cambridge PhD 1968), and returned to the country in 1973 when her then husband Andrew headed the Department of Anthropology at the University of Papua New Guinea in the years leading up to the nation's independence in 1975. After leaving Papua New Guinea, she held visiting positions at the Australian National University and the University of California at Berkeley. In 2001, Strathern was knighted for her services to the discipline of anthropology.

The strength of her contribution to anthropology was forged in two stages. The earlier stage included an extended period of ethnographic research in the young nation of Papua New Guinea; the later years were marked by the creation of a distinctive form of anthropological argument which made cultural critique vital to the work of ethnographic description. The links between the first part of her career and the latter show the nature of her unique approach to anthropological research.

Her career is marked by incisive studies of gender and personhood as the key entry points to understanding society and social life. Her doctorate, published as *Women in Between* (1972) forwarded an early criticism of kinship, both of alliance and descent theories, by making the women's lives – as sisters, wives, and daughters – central to the study of relatedness in society. Following her doctorate, Strathern researched and published several books and book-length reports while living in Port Moresby, and working as a consultant to the Papua New Guinea Administration, and as a researcher with the New Guinea Research Unit. These titles include a book co-authored with Andrew Strathern, *Self Decoration in Mount Hagen* (1971), followed by the reports, *Official and Unofficial Courts: Legal Assumptions and Expectations in a Highlands Community* (1972) and *No Money on Our Skins: Hagen Migrants in Port Moresby* (1975). Each of these studies was undertaken as an independent piece of research, entailed a rigorous re-thinking of the terms of social analysis to incorporate the Melanesian perspective, and provided full qualitative studies of each of the anthropological themes expressed in their titles. The larger problem addressed in each was 'what is society?' which was a core issue for social science in these years of the later twentieth century when the work of decolonization was given serious intellectual (as well as political) priority by the Australian administration of the Territories of Papua and New Guinea. Strathern's work at this time can be read in the light of the movement towards independence for the territories; if Papua New Guineans were to be able to use that research to lead the nation, then it was simply necessary for the administration and new Melanesian elite to understand the nature of local society and its regeneration through the acts of men and women. Three edited volumes completed during her years in Manchester carry forward her concerns with the nature of the social under the themes of gender, leadership, and transitions of social life. These were *Dealing with Inequality* (1987), *Big Men, Great Men* (with M. Godelier, 1991) and *Shifting Contexts* (1995).

A pivotal text, *The Gender of the Gift: Problems with Women and Problems with Society in Melanesia* (1988) marked a transition in her primary interest from ethnographies of Melanesia to the critical status of anthropology's ethnographic method and theory. In this book Strathern denies that alienation in social life is the core social problem to be understood in Melanesia. She insists that gender relations are not best defined by the separation of women from men in relations of hierarchy or alienation, but advocates the study of gender com-plementarity as it is expressed as a kind of 'symbolic operator.' Instead of a historically grounded study such as that by Gregory in *Gifts and Commodities* (1982), Strathern advances the comparative method as a triangulation of approaches to 'the problem of women and the pro-blem of society.' *The Gender of the Gift* stands on an ideational tripod to make its argument. It consists of incommensurable fields of knowledge that she delineates from three sources: a wide-ranging account of Melanesian culture, abstracted general concepts in political economy from its nineteenth century formulation in property theory, and outlines of the feminist politics as the cause of the day. The book unfolds in a succession of critiques of two of each of the three legs – Melanesian ethnography, political economy, and feminist politics – from perspective of the remaining one. Anthropologists are familiar with her critiques of political economy from the viewpoint of Melanesia and with her critiques of Melanesian ethnography for carrying ethnocentric western assumptions in its underpinnings; however they have written less frequently of Strathern's critique of feminism.

Strathern argues that gender is better understood in terms of social complementarity, rather than as a form of estrangement between male and female. This is a profound claim if it is correct that gender marks the primary division of labor in all societies. Strathern's feminist critiques challenge anthropologists to reconsider what gender com-plementarity signifies as a form of social action, whereas her con-temporaries, **Ortner** and Weiner, take political stances on the subordination of women and women's work both as it was and ought to be valued. In a series of essays published throughout the early 1980s, Strathern argued that the anthropologist should consider how gender as a symbolic operator problematizes dichotomies like 'public' and 'private life,' 'domestic work' and 'labor,' with the aim of doing away with the distinction between 'nature' and 'nurture.' In *The Gender of the Gift* the reader perceives Strathern's disquiet with the assumption shared by many of her colleagues that gender politics should be the cause of the day and the core of new understandings of a new feminist social theory. In this book she seeks 'a place in the feminist debate' to raise the possibility that the most compelling questions of the late twentieth century may be those that recognize that human freedom is a capacity to move with and beyond conventional constraints on thought and action. That this may be especially so in later years of decolonization remains unstated in her work, but it is a view that is concomitant with the history of her earlier and later research.

In *The Gender of the Gift* Strathern made a new departure in anthropology by deploying general ethnographic insights about Melanesian social life to destabilize the underpinning assumptions about the character of society. She deploys these insights in a career of polemical arguments which she uses against the shared, often implicit, assumptions held in scholarship on gender politics, political economy, cultural property, biotechnology (especially scientifically assisted conception), and public policy. Her critique parallels that of Marcus and Fischer's (1986) *Anthropology as Cultural Critique.* Whereas they advocated the uses of localized ethnography to critique global knowledge, Strathern defined ethnography in terms of its inherently critical relationship to scholarly academic thought, as a kind of partial connection to the fieldwork community made from the anthropologist's office through specific and shared political struggles. Rather than a richly descriptive narrative or a positivist account of other societies, Strathern writes ethnography as an illustrative mirror of social theory with the effect of unsettling scholarly politics of the day.

Gender of the Gift ushered in *After Nature* (1992), which Strathern wrote immediately afterwards as an analysis of expressive culture in Britain, charting the long rise of the concept of the individual and individualism. Her career continued with a series of critiques of core cultural assumptions underpinning the common wisdom of western social life, and now built upon observations about English life. Very early as a student at Cambridge, she had been introduced to the possibility of conducting research 'at home' in the anthropologist's own society. An early study of a 'proper village' in Essex in which students of Audrey Richards had learned PARTICIPANT OBSERVATION appeared as *Kinship at the Core: An Anthropological Study of Elmdon in the 1960's*. Later, with the rise of concerns with scientifically assisted reproduction Strathern published a collection of essays, *Reproducing the Future* (1992), which analyzed the terms of regenerative social life at the nexus of policy and popular debates in British popular culture, and a related co-authored volume, *Technologies of Procreation* (1993). In these collections of Strathern's later writing she broadened her study from English cultural traditions to the more general expressive culture of Anglo-American society of the last part of the twentieth century, which she described as 'Euro-American,' especially as that distinctive form of social life is comprised by a set of assumptions shared by people, policy makers, and the popular media on each side of the Atlantic. Among other points, she shows that the self cannot be owned by an individual or that kin might be unknown to each other as relatives. These are both examples of ways shared Euro-American assumptions can constrain scholarly thought and social action.

Her later work demonstrates that ethnography can free anthropologists to intervene in debates about social life. Strathern advanced a set of critiques about accountability in bureaucracy, which were influenced by her experience as Head of Department at Manchester, and published these in her introduction to the edited collection, *Audit Culture* (2000). In it, she makes the important point that accountability does not ensure critical engagement in the analysis of the complexity of social life. At about the same time, in a collection of essays, *Property, Substance, Effect: Persons and Things* (1999), she addresses the limits of theories of political economy for understanding the ownership of human bodies and expressive culture in the late twentieth century, and later turns attention explicitly to cultural property in *Transactions and Creations: Property Debates and the Stimulus of Melanesia* (co-editor E. Hirsch, 2004). Strathern argues that social anthropology's ethnographic method offers one of the best ways to understand the complexity of new reproductive technologies, regimes of bio-ethics, cultural property, public policy, as well as the audit culture of bureaucracy. In *Commons and Borderlands* (2004) she describes the different forms of social property assumed by those who practice interdisciplinary study. Her most recent book, *Kinship Law and the Unexpected: Relatives are Always a Surprise* (2005) continues that line of inquiry into the interstices of human action and social constraint, with specific reference to biotechnology and the assumptions underpinning public policy as these might affect the ownership of human bodies.

Anthropological knowledge in Strathern's terms rarely comes with the exposure of inequality, or the theory of how it comes into the world, rather it is 'the exploration of relations through relations.' As a result, anthropological research is necessarily reflexive if it is to generate a critical theory of social life. Concerning Strathern's distinct style in anthropology and her sense of an intellectual vocation more broadly it can be fairly said that her first fieldwork in Melanesia shaped her scholarly contribution to the discipline throughout her career: one academic capacity developed through analysis of contemporary social theory, the other developed in the conduct of ethnographic fieldwork. Although the combination is apparently paradoxical for scholars of other disciplines, Strathern's work shows that anthropologists might develop such a unique approach because they must reflect upon the personal encounter in fieldwork and challenge common wisdom in the critical essay.

Select readings

Strathern, M. (1972) *Women in Between: Female Roles in a Male World*, London: Academic Press.

——(1988) *The Gender of the Gift: Problems with Women and Problems with Society in Melanesia*, Berkeley: University of California Press.

——(1992) *After Nature*, Cambridge: Cambridge University Press.

——(1992) *Reproducing the Future. Essays on Anthropology, Kinship and the New Reproductive Technologies*, Manchester: Manchester University Press.

——(1999) *Property, Substance and Effect*, London: Athlone Press.

——(2005) *Kinship, Law and the Unexpected: Relatives are Always a Surprise*, Cambridge: Cambridge University Press.

Strathern, M. (ed.) (2000) *Audit Cultures, Anthropological Studies in Accountability, Ethics and the Academy*, London: Routledge.

KAREN SYKES

VICTOR W. TURNER (1920–83)

Victor Turner was born in Glasgow in 1920 and died in Charlottesville, Virginia in 1983. He received his PhD from the University of Manchester in 1955. He is best known for his concept of 'liminality,' which greatly expanded on **Arnold van Gennep**'s analyses of rites of passage, and for his use of drama as a model for social processes, inspired in part by the literary critic Kenneth Burke, which offered a way of interpreting social facts that was squarely grounded in the humanities.

Turner conducted fieldwork among the Ndembu of Zambia (then Northern Rhodesia) between 1950 and 1954, under the auspices of the Rhodes-Livingstone Institute. The exceptional quality of this research established the foundation for many of Turner's theoretical contributions. Supervised by **Max Gluckman**, Turner's doctoral research for the University of Manchester was concerned with mechanisms of conflict resolution. The thesis, and the resulting book, *Schism and Continuity in an African Society* (1957), broke new ground beyond the paradigms that have come to be associated with the 'Manchester School.' Gluckman was interested in the ways in which social order and social hierarchy were maintained despite tension and dissatisfaction, and saw ritual as one mechanism by which this was accomplished, insofar as it allowed for 'rebellion' without revolution. Turner's work did not disconfirm this, but as his career progressed he came to see ritual as both more complex and more meaningful in itself, apart from its role in social engineering, than his training under Gluckman would have led him to expect. He suggested that social life among the Ndembu (and elsewhere) followed predictable plots, in which conflicts might be resolved, be aired without resolution, or lead to social schism. He argued that society was better seen as a process than a machine or organism. Rituals were vital parts of this process.

Turner identified stages in the dramas of social life which resembled the acts of a play. Between outbreaks of overt conflict, which, among the Ndembu, might concern such things as witchcraft accusations or inheritance, social life proceeded from day to day with a number of potential fault lines embedded in the social structure. Among the matrilineal Ndembu an important fault line was the conflict between men's ties to their fathers and their duty to their mothers' brothers. The first act in a typical social drama might involve the illness of an important figure, in connection with which his nephews and his sons might mumble rumors of witchcraft, taking sides with an eye toward their inheritance. The climax might involve outright accusations, in which villages might split, suspect persons might go into exile, or the matter might be at least temporarily resolved, often with the aid of ritual. Turner found that this sequence of tolerated conflict, growing tension, outbreak of overt conflict, and resolution, involving either schism or some adjustment, was regularly repeated: this is what constituted the social drama.

The Ndembu invested a considerable amount of their time and resources in ritual, and Turner was accordingly led to consider ritual's meaning beyond its social utility. In a series of essays and monographs, Turner argued that symbols in ritual had multiple meanings, linking together disparate domains of experience. Sometimes ritual brought conflicts to light: a ritual performed to cure bad luck in hunting might air grievances about the apportionment of game between a man's father and his mother's brother, for example. In *Chihamba: the White Spirit* (1962, republished in Turner 1975: 37–203) and in several essays which were gathered in the collection *The Forest of Symbols* (1967), Turner examined the ways by which the human body, features of the natural world, the social order, and moral concepts were linked together by ritual symbols.

The *mudyi* tree, a tree with a white latex sap, figured in many Ndembu rituals. The sap of the *mudyi* tree could stand for mother's milk or semen, visibility and moral uprightness (as opposed to the things people do under cover of darkness, like witchcraft), as well as the matrilineal ideal encapsulated in nursing mothers. The *mukula* tree, which had a red gum, stood for blood, which was shed in both positive and negative contexts: childbirth and menstruation, hunting and homicide. Red stood for the conflicts inherent in adult social relationships, and, at the philosophical level, for ambiguity itself. Symbols like these (along with other plant materials, and red, black, and white chickens, earths, and dyes) were manipulated in rituals to convey meaning and issue guidance to people suffering from illness or misfortune, or going through initiation or other rites of passage.

Turner pointed out that *chijikijilu*, the Ndembu word which he translated as 'symbol,' literally meant a marker in the forest to guide people on their way, usually placed at the boundary between familiar and unfamiliar territory. By deploying symbols which were both abstract and highly concrete the Ndembu went well beyond the maintenance of social boundaries and social functioning ascribed to ritual by van Gennep and Gluckman. They expressed an entire cosmology and philosophy and negotiated the boundary between people and the supernatural. Moreover, Turner argued, some symbolic meanings might be part of a universal psychobiological repertoire: red, white, and black, for example, figured in many cultures with meanings similar to those found among the Ndembu.

Turner came to believe that the Ndembu possessed in their rituals a form of experience which filled an inherent human need. For himself, he filled this need by conversion to Catholicism. He left Manchester and moved to the US, teaching at Cornell University, the University of Chicago, and the University of Virginia.

During his years in the US, Turner was associated with a number of scholars interested in symbolism, drama, and religion including **Clifford Geertz**, Mircea Eliade, and Richard Schechner, with whose work, particularly Schechner's, there were parallels and mutual influences. Turner was a major figure in the movement called SYMBOLIC ANTHROPOLOGY, which attempted to understand culture through its symbols. Through Cornell University Press, he initiated a series of books by authors like Barbara Myerhoff and Barbara Babcock which became foundation texts in this field.

Turner concluded from his own experience, his encounters with the work of others, and his research among the Ndembu that ritual was the product of inbuilt human capacities, giving it a status independent of its social function. He worked toward developing a hypothesized actor he labeled 'ritual man,' akin to the 'economic man' used by economists to predict people's behavior with regard to money and commodities. If 'economic man' would, all things being equal, seek to make a profit, a characteristic goal of 'ritual man' was the experience Turner called 'liminality.' The concept derives from van Gennep's description of the middle (or 'liminal') stage of rites of passage, named after the Latin word for threshold, *limen*. This stage followed a stage of separation from one's old status and preceded incorporation into the new one. During this stage normal social rules, such as those governing gender, hierarchy, and decorum, might be suspended or inverted. For van Gennep this acted as a marker of the fact that during this period of transition the ritual 'passenger' was symbolically without status. Turner's innovation was to describe liminality as a positive good in itself, an experience which humans performed rituals to achieve.

In *The Ritual Process* (1969), Turner expanded his description of liminality and compared various settings in which liminality might be experienced. He developed the notions of 'anti-structure' and *'communitas'* which acted as correctives and commentaries with regard to the divisive effects of social status. They also gave opportunities for heightened emotion, feelings of oneness with the supernatural and one's fellow celebrants, and enhanced creativity. It had long been conventional to argue that ritual enhanced social solidarity, but 'social solidarity' was defined in ways that did not distinguish between social bonding and social structure. Turner pointed out that these dimensions of society were by their nature in conflict with each other. Ritual foregrounded *communitas*, an existential connection between individuals, at the temporary expense of structure, or *societas*.

In *The Ritual Process* Turner branched well beyond the Ndembu to explore contexts in which states of liminality might be achieved, as well as delving further into Ndembu ritual. He discussed Hindu myths about dairy maids leaving their families to follow Lord Krishna. He described suspensions of hierarchy in the Indian festival of *Holi* and the Christian and secular observance of Halloween. He described people who seemed to be invested with liminality on a long term basis, outside of specific ritual contexts, including Gandhi, St. Francis and 1960s folksingers. Citing Max Weber, he described processes of routinization, such as that which took place among the Franciscans, in which the characteristics of liminality gave way over time to structure and hierarchy.

After *The Ritual Process*, Turner continued to explore diverse modes of liminality, including pilgrimage (with Edith Turner: 1978), historical and contemporary mysticism, and political protest. One controversial piece (Turner 1974: 50–97) suggested that St. Thomas Becket, the Archbishop of Canterbury murdered in his Cathedral in 1170, in choosing martyrdom rather than capitulation to the King, was enacting a set of universal 'root' paradigms (e.g. the 'red' paradigm of blood symbolism) which were available to him as part of the human heritage – and which helped to account for his appeal as a subject of legend and literature. Some anthropologists were uncomfortable with the idea of universal symbols not grounded in specific ethnographic facts. There were also criticisms that the Turners cast liminal experience, especially Christian pilgrimage, in too joyous a light.

Insofar as it appeared to have applications in many different areas, from circuses to liturgies, Turner's work attracted notice from anthropologists concerned with topics ranging from tourism to children's play, and from non-anthropologists such as experimental dramatists, literary critics, historians, and designers of church ritual. Notions of carnival and celebration, associated with liminality, were appealing to many people. To some degree Turner welcomed this; however, he came to insist that some of his would-be followers pushed the notion of liminality further than he intended. He tried to impose a distinction between truly liminal events, which involved multiple layers of meaning, including supernatural ones, and 'liminoid' creations, like some aspects of the mass media, which were both secular and relatively shallow in meaning, though they drew on some of the same human capacities and needs. Many of Turner's admirers nonetheless continued to use liminality in a broader sense than Turner might have liked.

Together with Edith Turner, who had always been involved in his work, Turner explored the notion that anthropologists needed to concentrate on internal human experience, rather than categories external to that experience. After Turner's death, Edward M. Bruner ensured that a co-edited volume on the topic, begun during Turner's lifetime, appeared (Turner and Bruner 1986). As a widow, Edith returned to the Ndembu and published a controversial volume in which she attempted to analyze Ndembu rituals in a way which accepted the Ndembu experience of them as 'real.'

Turner inspired deep admiration and loyalty in many students, colleagues, and others, many of whom went on to expand and develop symbolic anthropology. Liminality has become a core analytical concept, deployed in many fields. Many contemporary writers do not feel a need to know its origins. Like that of **Claude Lévi-Strauss**, Turner's influence may, in part, be assessed by the degree to which his ideas are taken for granted.

Selected readings

Turner, E. with Blodgett, W., Kahona, S., and Benwa, F. (1992) *Experiencing Ritual: A New Interpretation of African Healing*, Philadelphia: University of Pennsylvania Press.

Turner, V. W. (1957) *Schism and Continuity in an African Society*, Manchester: Manchester University Press.

——(1967) *The Forest of Symbols: Aspects of Ndembu Ritual*, Ithaca, NY: Cornell University Press.

——(1968) *The Drums of Affliction: A Study of Religious Processes Among the Ndembu of Zambia*, Oxford: Clarendon Press.

——(1969) *The Ritual Process: Structure and Anti-Structure*, Chicago: Aldine Publishing Company.

——(1974) *Dramas, Fields and Metaphors: Symbolic Action in Human Society*, Ithaca, NY: Cornell University Press.

——(1975) *Revelation and Divination in Ndembu Ritual*, Ithaca, NY: Cornell University Press.

Turner, V. W. and Bruner, E. M. (eds.) (1986) *The Anthropology of Experience*, Urbana: University of Illinois Press.

Turner, V. W. and Turner, E. (1978) *Image and Pilgrimage in Christian Culture*, New York: Columbia University Press.

HARRIET D. LYONS

SIR EDWARD BURNETT TYLOR (1832–1917)

Edward Tylor was a leading social EVOLUTIONIST in England from the 1860s to the first decade of the last century. He was an advocate of psychic unity, used the 'doctrine of survivals' as a mode of proof of social progress, and employed the concept of 'animism,' which he believed to be the first stage in the development of religion. In 1883 Tylor was the first anthropologist to be appointed to a position at Oxford, becoming a professor in 1896. He was instrumental in encouraging early anthropological fieldwork despite his posthumous reputation as an 'armchair anthropologist.' Lastly, Tylor was the first individual to coin an anthropological definition of 'culture' although his famous words have evolutionary overtones that the modern reader can easily ignore.

Because Tylor was a Quaker and not an Anglican, he was denied entry to Oxford or Cambridge as an undergraduate. Instead his brothers planned for him to enter their business, a brass foundry. However, in 1855 Tylor set off for the United States while convalescing from a suspected bout of tuberculosis. He then proceeded to Cuba. By chance he encountered an older Quaker businessman, Henry Christy, on a bus in Havana. Christy was a devotee of the new science of archaeology, and also interested in ancient history and ethnology. He quickly converted Tylor to these interests, and the two traveled together by stagecoach and on horseback from Vera Cruz to the Valley of Mexico.

Tylor's travel book, *Anahuac*, appeared in 1861. It is not a work of anthropology in the strict sense, but it does provide many glimpses of Tylor's developing knowledge. Christy and Tylor visited sites where obsidian tools had been discovered. They went to Teotihuacan. They also observed contemporary Mexican customs including Easter celebrations. They visited sugar plantations and textile factories. Tylor noted some interesting cross-cultural similarities. For example, he noted the burning of effigies of Judas during Easter ceremonies, and compared the custom with the burning of effigies of Guy Fawkes in England on November 5th. Tylor also deplored the mistreatment of Mesoamerican peoples, just as he condemned slavery in the Caribbean and the USA. However, he thought that Mestizos were more excitable than the full-blooded Aztecs and indigenous peoples he admired. Furthermore, some anti-Catholic prejudice is evident in the book.

By the time *Anahuac* appeared Tylor was committed to anthropology. Although his primary interest was in linguistics, mythology, and folklore, he was increasingly stirred by a wave of theoretical changes and discoveries in geology, palaeontology, and archaeology which convinced the British scientific community of the reality of technological and social evolution over an extended time scale, finally putting paid to the 6,000 year chronology of Archbishop Ussher.

In 1858 the British Association received reports validating Boucher de Perthes's Palaeolithic finds in the Somme Valley and the discovery of ancient fauna and late Paleolithic tools at Kent's cavern in Devon. The Swiss Lake dwellings of the La Tène culture had recently been unearthed, and excavations were undertaken by Édouard Lartet and Tylor's friend, Christy, in the caves of the Dordogne and Vézère. Darwin's *Origin of Species* appeared in 1859 and in 1863 his views were endorsed by the dean of uniformitarian geology, Charles Lyell. Darwin's young neighbor, the anthropologist John Lubbock, invented the word 'Neolithic' in 1865.

Accordingly, the idea that humans had evolved from a state of savagery to civilization through the Palaeolthic, Mesolithic, and Neolithic stages of the Stone Age and had then passed through the ages of Copper, Bronze, and Iron, became common currency.

Many Victorian scholars assumed that there had been a corresponding progress in mental ability, in morality, religion, economic and social institutions, and confidently assumed that their culture was the pinnacle of civilization.

Such ideas were not uncontested. Polygenists who viewed different human races as different species contested the idea of a single narrative of human progress. Degenerationists such as Richard Whately disputed the inevitability of progress, claiming rather that human sin had resulted in cultural decline. This was why a Mayan peasant might stare, supposedly without comprehension, at the temples of his ancestors. In 1865, John Lubbock published *Prehistoric Times*, a book which boldly stated the findings of the new archaeology and anthropology and attempted to refute the degenerationists. This was also the year in which Tylor's first important book appeared. It was called *Researches into the Early History of Mankind and the Development of Civilization.*

In this work, archaeological and historical research from all portions of the world, concerning successive modes of tool-making, the manufacture of bows, the development of guns, and the evolution of fire-making techniques, is deployed in order to demonstrate that the tide of progress is rarely reversed. Once the manufacture of iron axes becomes commonplace, people are unlikely to return to stone tools. Simple fire-making devices which involved the manual twirling of a pointed stick in a groove were replaced by more complicated fire-drills that utilized the technology of the longbow and the crossbow to pull on a thong that was twirled round the drill. Once matches were invented the drill became an anachronism. Tylor was highly skeptical about reports that there were peoples who failed to utilize fire, but he did see real cultural differences in fire-making technology which reflected different stages in technological development. In modern European countries, peasants occasionally made use of more antiquated technology such as fire-sticks in calendrical ceremonies, such as midsummer eve.

Like technology, language had evolved from early origins in gesture language to the more abstract signs of civilized discourse. In general, primitive thought, like the thought of modern children, was concrete rather than abstract, blurring boundaries between self and other, and between image and object. Magic (e.g. putting pins in a doll or effigy to cause injury to the person it represents) was based on such childlike logic. In *Researches* Tylor noted the parallel evolution of technology and modes of thought throughout the world. This was proof of psychic unity and the existence of a single narrative of progress. Most cultural parallels were the product of independent invention by like minds, but many cultural similarities were due to diffusion, the spread of custom through trade or migration. Myths, for example, were often transmitted from one people to the other. However, if the hosts were too dissimilar, the grafts would not take.

Degenerationists such as the Duke of Argyll were not convinced by Tylor's arguments. They argued that technological progress could not be simply equated with moral and intellectual advancement. Tylor and Lubbock may have made a case for the former, but they had not proven the case for intellectual and moral evolution. Tylor's two-volume masterpiece, *Primitive Culture* (1871), was intended to be a convincing riposte to such arguments. It traced the development of religious thought from *animism* through polytheism to monotheism (and implicitly humanism), from religious forms which depended on anthropomorphism and concrete rituals to the more refined and abstracted religious practice of Victorian Protestants. Tylor used the comparative method, producing hundreds of examples from every part of the world to demonstrate the existence of psychic unity as it was manifested in each stage of religious and cultural evolution. The different stages in social evolution were explicitly modeled on the distinct strata (each containing flora and fauna at a certain stage of evolution) which were being uncovered by geologists and naturalists. Peasant folklore often contained links to the primitive past. Modern culture contained a share of *survivals* which were the equivalent of fossils inasmuch as they linked the present to the past. Saying 'Bless You,' when someone sneezes, may appear to be a meaningless custom but it links us to past beliefs about possession by external spirits which resemble those of contemporary primitives. Such beliefs are animistic.

Animism arose from the primitive's attempts to answer a number of important questions, such as the meaning of life and death, whether or not there was life after death and reincarnation, what was the relationship between reality and dream, why the dead appear in dreams and why we ourselves wander to strange places during them, what our personality is composed of, and so on. Tylor felt that the notion of the 'soul' (*anima*) and the 'ghost soul' were the products of early speculation in which the interpretation of the dream experience played a major role. If I see my deceased uncle in my dream, that's because I have a soul and he has a ghost soul. Ancestor worship, the belief in reincarnation and the worship of guardian spirits are logical developments from such beliefs. Furthermore, if we have souls, is it not logical that animals, plants, and the heavenly bodies possess something similar? In that way we can reduce the whole world to a more human scale. Polytheism arises when an attempt is made to order humanity and nature into hierarchies and divisions. It involves a degree of abstraction, but monotheism, for Tylor represented a more advanced mode of thought. Even monotheistic societies displayed anachronisms – Tylor thought that there were many survivals of animism in Victorian society, revivals of animism such as spiritualism, and further that some mainstream religions such as Catholicism deliberately retained primitive practices.

Tylor's theory of animism was based on an understanding of religion as a form of erroneous, albeit logical, folk philosophy. The emotional component of religion is missing from Tylor's account. Critics of his own time such as Andrew Lang noted that elements of monotheism could be found in many primitive societies. The ethnocentrism of his account distances him from us. Nonetheless the notion of animism has been revived in some recent anthropology, for example the writings of Stewart Guthrie, not as a putative first step in religious evolution but rather as an element in all religious and some secular thought.

The first page of *Primitive Culture* contains his definition of our most important concept: 'Culture, or civilization, taken in its broad, ethnographic sense, is that complex whole which includes knowledge, belief, art, morals, law, custom, and any other capabilities and habits acquired by man as a member of society.' Some forty years ago George Stocking noted that it is very easy for modern anthropologists to underestimate the distance between our notions of culture and Tylor's. He was talking of the culture of all humanity in evolutionary progression rather than the culture of a specific people in our time. He believed in psychic unity but, unlike **Franz Boas**, he was never a relativist.

In *Primitive Culture*, Tylor had little to say about diffusion, but he returned to the theme in a paper written in 1879, noting that resemblances between the Mexican game of *patolli* and the Indian *pachisi*, both of which resemble *lotto*, are so detailed that they could conceivably result from diffusion rather than independent invention. In 1888 Tylor made a single foray into statistical, cross-cultural analysis, foreshadowing the later work of **George Peter Murdock**. For example, he noted a correlation between matrilocal residence, mother-in-law avoidance, and teknonyms (naming men after their children).

Tylor came to believe that fieldwork was an essential part of anthropology. He encouraged the work of Lorimer Fison and A. W. Howitt, and later Baldwin Spencer and F. J. Gillen, in Australia, and supported the efforts of Rev. E. F. Wilson and Horatio Hale in Ontario as well as the young Franz Boas in British Columbia.

Selected readings

Stocking, G. W. (1968) *Race, Culture and Evolution*, New York: The Free Press.

Tylor, E. B. (1879) 'On the Game of Patolli in Ancient Mexico, and its Probably Asiatic Origin,' *Journal of the Anthropological Institute* 8: 116–29.

——(1889) 'On a Method of Investigating the Development of Institutions; applied to Laws of Marriage and Descent,' *Journal of the Anthropological Institute* 18: 245–69.

——(1958 [1871]) *Primitive Culture*, two volumes, New York: Harper.

——(1964 [1865]) *Researches into the Early History of Mankind and the Development of Civilization*, edited and abridged from the third edition by Paul Bohannan, Chicago: University of Chicago Press.

——(1970 [1861]) *Anahuac, or Mexico and the Mexicans*, New York: Bergman.

ANDREW P. LYONS

ARNOLD VAN GENNEP (1873–1957)

Arnold van Gennep stands out as an early proponent of ethnography as a distinct discipline separated from anatomy, archaeology, and sociology. He is well known for his criticism of the dominance exercised over sociology and much of the humanities in France by Durkheim and **Mauss** through their journal *L'Année sociologique* (tr. 'Sociological Yearbook'). His approach disparaged the separation between the man-on-the-spot and the metropolitan scholar and produced an anthropology that stressed the importance of fieldwork and that called for linguistic competence. Van Gennep believed theory should emerge out of the encounter with field informants, in contrast to the dogmatic approach of professionals based in government institutions. He is most famous for his study of folklore and for his work on rites of passage.

He was born in Ludwigsburg, in the kingdom of Württemberg. His parents divorced when he was six and his Dutch mother (whose name he adopted) moved with him to France where she married a doctor with a summer practice in Savoy. Van Gennep's ties to this part of France date from his early youth. He acquired a fluency in French, German, and Dutch at this time and would later claim an ability to work in eighteen languages. He studied at the École des langues orientales in Paris with a view to entering the diplomatic service and also at the École pratique des hautes études (EPHE) where he studied linguistics, Egyptology, and, under Léon Marillier, the science of religion. In 1897 he married, became a naturalized French citizen, and took up a position as a French teacher in Poland where he learned new languages and translated Frazer's classic essay on totemism. On his return to France in 1901 hopes of an academic career were dashed when Mauss replaced Marillier at the EPHE. This led van Gennep to become chief translator at the Ministry of Agriculture for the next seven years. During this time he worked under Mauss and produced a thesis on *Tabou et totémisme à Madagascar* in 1904 and a dissertation on *Mythes et legends d'Australie* three years later.

This position on the edge of academic life allowed van Gennep to develop new and critical ideas about the practice of ethnology, particularly when, in 1906, he started to write a quarterly column in the leading French literary journal, the *Mercure de France*. Called on to write under the headings of 'ethnography' and 'folklore,' van Gennep turned the study of these topics in new directions. He developed a cosmopolitan approach to ethnography that drew on the works of British, American, and German scholars. In ethnology he called for a greater emphasis on direct observation. This led him to downplay the importance of the community and to stress the individual's contribution to social behavior. It led to emphasizing empirical evidence including material artifacts and folklore. Van Gennep also argued for ending the distinction between the amateur in the field, who gathered facts, and the professional, armchair anthropologist in the metropole, who analyzed them. Instead he called for linguistically competent investigators to enter into extended dialogue with their informants. He also criticized writings that distinguished between 'civilized' and 'non-civilized' peoples, 'inferior' and 'superior' races, or gave credence to racist ideas. He opposed the notion that 'folklore' should deal with the material culture and social organization of European communities while 'ethnography' should deal with non-European, generally colonized, peoples. Importantly, van Gennep argued that ethnology could be harnessed to serve the cause of an enlightened colonial administration.

In 1909 *The Rites of Passage* was published. It remains an important work in anthropology. Its influence was manifest in the writings of **Victor Turner, Edmund Leach, Rodney Needham, Mary Douglas,** and many others. One could say that van Gennep provided a universal grammar or syntax of ritual, resting on a comparison between the human body, the social body, and the demarcation of ritual (and non-ritual) space both in the domestic and the greater world. The book begins with a discussion of territorial rites that ensure safe passage from home to abroad and back, from the secure internal space of the house to the world of neighbors and non-kin. Such transitions may be dangerous, particularly in between destinations, and rituals ensure safe transit. There are rites of separation, rites of transition, and rites of incorporation to mark successful returns. Thresholds (Latin *limen*) were often ritually marked because of potential ritual danger. Brides were carried over them. Jews touched the *mezuzahs* that were placed on them when entering and leaving a house. Van Gennep noted that life crisis rituals (otherwise rites of passage) such as birth, marriage, burial, and initiation, often enact a metaphor of territorial transition. There are wedding marches and funeral marches and the same three stage process of separation, transition, and incorporation. Parts of the body (such as the nose) or its accoutrements such as clothing might be ritually altered to reflect a change of state. The penis might be circumcised; clothing might be shredded. Lastly van Gennep noted that many calendrical rituals, such as Christmas and New Year celebrations, were comparable processes with a similar tripartite structure or process. Van Gennep was aware of some of the symbolic properties of the liminal stage, such as role reversal, which were to play a major role in the work of Turner. It should be noted that he derived many of the specifics of his theory from predecessors and contemporaries in France. The notion of physical boundaries and their ritual importance could be derived from the mid-nineteenth century historian Fustel de Coulanges. Henri Hubert and Marcel Mauss had noted a comparable ritual grammar in their work on sacrifice (1898) and Robert Hertz had observed a three-stage process in death rituals. What made van Gennep's work unique was that he sought to establish a universal pattern in all or most ritual processes and that he did so by a masterly exercise in the comparative method, drawing on cases from all over the world in order to sustain the argument.

Van Gennep extended his professional influence geographically when, in 1908, he founded the *Revue des etudes ethnographiques et sociologiques*. His approach to ethnology was global although, because Asia was covered by the École française d'Extrême-Orient, he concentrated on sub-Saharan Africa. Nevertheless, Europe and the Maghreb also received extensive coverage. In 1910 he played a leading role in the establishment of the Institut ethnographique international de Paris. This provided a research community for individuals with colonial experience to discuss and debate their findings and encouraged the development of a problem-oriented ethnography. Van Gennep continued to stress the importance of direct observation and in 1911 and 1912, undertook research trips to Algeria. His first-hand experience of researching indigenous communities would exercise a strong influence on his development as an ethnographer.

This approach to ethnography marginalized him in a field increasingly dominated by journals and institutions run by university professors. He virulently opposed Durkheim's view of ethnology as just a sub-branch of sociology and, through his publishing and networking, attempted to provide ethnography with a methodological base and an independent status. He moved closer to this objective when in 1912 he was offered a chair in 'the anthropology and comparative history of civilizations' at the University of Neuchâtel. Two native Neuchâtelian friends engineered this position, the first chair of social anthropology in Switzerland and one of the first in the world: the missionary-ethnographer Junod and the Egyptologist G. Jéquier who had known van Gennep at the EPHE in Paris.

From this institutional base, van Gennep set about establishing ethnography as an independent, professional discipline. On the eve of the Great War he organized the First International Congress of Ethnology and Ethnography which drew a large number of participants to Neuchâtel from a wide range of countries. Ethnography dominated proceedings as van Gennep tried to establish the subject's independence from archaeology and physical anthropology. But the major tension at the conference emerged as van Gennep struggled to free ethnography from the hold of the Durkheimians and from the overlordship of sociology. This tension was manifested in a debate over Junod's study of the husband's relationship to his mother-in-law among the Ronga people of southern Mozambique. Mauss criticized the missionary for turning to a native informant for the reasoning behind the rituals governing the relationship between the husband and his wife's mother, and for accepting a somewhat individualistic interpretation. He also defended Durkheim against Junod's criticism of his doctrinaire approach to religion. The absent Junod served as a substitute for van Gennep in this debate. In 1912 van Gennep had produced a review critical of Durkheim's division of societies into a hierarchy stretching from simple to complex.

Van Gennep was interested in the significance of rites rather than in their compilation; his concern lay with uncovering the pattern of rites that could be distinguished in the behavior of people and groups. Mauss expressed some criticism of van Gennep's book on rites of passage as too close to the generalized compilations of fact gathered by Sir James Frazer. But at van Gennep's conference in Neuchâtel in 1914 the debate between the representatives of the different approaches to ethnography held by the editors of *L'année sociologique* and the (renamed) *Revue d'ethnographie et de sociologie* turned around the differences raised by Mauss and Junod.

Van Gennep's stay in Neuchâtel came to an abrupt end in 1915 when his criticism of the support extended to Germany during the First World War by a large part of the Swiss population led to his expulsion from the country. Back in France he found it difficult to regain a footing. His parody of the French academic community, *Les demi-savants* (1911, translated by Rodney Needham as *The Semi-Scholars*), had raised the ire of many of his contemporaries and the nationalist sentiments fanned by the war left little space for his notion of a cosmopolitan scholarship. Marginalized once again from academic life, he worked as a translator and, in 1922, undertook an extensive lecture tour of the United States. After this he moved to Bourg-la-Reine, a commune in the southern suburbs of Paris where he devoted his time to the study of folklore, a topic that he defined as 'ethnography of the rural populations of Europe, and nothing else.' This also set him against the Durkheimians who ignored folklore as they felt they had nothing to learn from the cultural vestiges of European peasants. Van Gennep survived on his translations, and on payments received for lectures and articles. He produced many works on the folklore of France, most notably *Le Manuel de folklore français contemporain* (1947–58).

Arnold van Gennep is remembered as 'the creator of French ethnography' and 'the master of French folklore.' To anglophone anthropologists he is primarily the author of *Rites of Passage*. His reputation is at least in part due to a romantic concern with the individual's confrontation with the 'system' created by the academic establishment in France. It is also based on a voluminous bibliography amounting to 437 titles. He stands out as a free-thinker who challenged a set of ideas and practices regimented by professionals ensconced in government institutions. A non-conformist and an amateur, van Gennep described himself as 'caste-less' (*hors-caste*). In his preface to the English translation of *The Semi-Scholars* (1967) Rodney Needham called his treatment 'an academic disgrace.' Van Gennep lived on until 1957, just a few years before he finally received the international recognition he deserved.

Selected readings

Belier, W. (1994) 'Arnold van Gennep and the rise of French Sociology of Religion,' *Numen* 41: 41–162.
Belmont, N. (1979) *Arnold van Gennep: the Creator of French Ethnography*, trans. D. Coltman, Chicago: University of Chicago Press.
Gluckman, M. (1962) *Essays on the Ritual of Social Relations*, Manchester: Manchester University Press.
Sibeud, E. (2004) 'Un ethnographe face à la colonisation: Arnold van Gennep en Algérie (1911–12),' *Revue d'histoire des sciences humaines* 10(1): 79–103.
van Gennep, A. (1960 [1909]) *The Rites of Passage*, trans. M. Vizedom and G. L. Caffee, Chicago: University of Chicago Press.
——(1967 [1911]) *The Semi-Scholars*, trans. and ed. R. Needham, London: Routledge & Kegan Paul.
Zumwalt, R. (1988) *The Enigma of Arnold van Gennep (1873–1957): Master of French Folklore and Hermit of Bourg-la-Reine*, Helsinki: Suomalainen Tiedeakatemia.

PATRICK HARRIES

ANTHONY WALLACE (1923–)

Anthony F. C. Wallace was born in Toronto, Ontario, on April 15, 1923. Both his father and grandfather were professors. Wallace's career-path within anthropology was strongly influenced by the academic career of his father, Paul A. W. Wallace, who was head of the English Department at Lebanon Valley College in Annville,

Pennsylvania and possessed a life-long fascination with folklore and history. He employed his eldest son, Anthony, as a research assistant, initially collecting tales of witches and other 'Pennsylvania Dutch' folklore from his school mates (Wallace 1966: v), and later searching and copying archival materials for a monumental biography of the eighteenth-century Pennsylvania Indian agent and interpreter, Conrad Weiser (Paul A. W. Wallace 1945). At age thirteen the younger Wallace accompanied his father on a research trip to the Six Nations Reserve near Brantford, Ontario (on the career of Paul A. W. Wallace, see Smith 1997).

Anthony Wallace served in the European theater late in World War II, where he carried a one-volume edition of Sir James Frazer's *Golden Bough* for reading matter. After his military service, Wallace returned to Pennsylvania. He received a BA in history (1947) and both an MA (1949) and PhD (1950) in anthropology from the University of Pennsylvania (Grumet 1998: 105). Wallace's entire career has been spent in Philadelphia. After an initial teaching appointment in sociology at the University of Pennsylvania, Wallace joined the Eastern Pennsylvania Psychiatric Institute in 1955, becoming Director of Clinical Research in 1960. Ties between anthropology and clinical psychology were strong in this decade. Wallace notes that at this time 'one out of every six anthropologists in the United States was supported by psychiatric research grants and fellowships.' The National Institute of Mental Health played a major role in funding anthropological research, including Wallace's ethno-historical investigations of religious movements (Wallace 2003a: 144). In 1961 he returned to the University of Pennsylvania as Chair of Anthropology. Wallace has testified that a factor in his resignation from the Eastern Pennsylvania Psychiatric Institute was the objections of researchers to requiring informed consent from participants in experiments. 'Disgusted by what appeared to me (as administrator) to be self-interest cloaked in protestations of principle, I resigned a Director of Clinical Research and at Loren Eiseley's invitation returned to teaching in the anthropology department at the University of Pennsylvania' (Wallace 2003a: 148; see also Grumet 1998: 112). There he remained until his retirement in 1988. He served as President of the American Anthropological Association during the tumultuous year of 1972, when that body was involved in the debate over the Viet Nam War and anthropological participation in that conflict.

As a graduate student Wallace came under the influence and tutelage of A. Irving Hallowell and Frank G. Speck, both legendary for their field abilities in investigating the cultures of Native North Americans. From Speck, Wallace received inspiration to develop his longstanding interest in historical aspects of the cultures of eastern North America. From Hallowell, he received inspiration to examine the relationship between the individual and culture, including personality and its response to stress in times of cultural deprivation and change.

Wallace's initial research involved the cultures and history of Native Peoples of north-eastern North America. Field trips with his father and later tutelage under Speck and Hallowell demonstrated the influence of the past on contemporary communities. After writing (and publishing) his master's thesis, a cultural and psychological biography of the Delaware 'king,' Teedyuscung (Wallace 1949 – it remains in print, see Wallace 1990), Wallace went on to examine and determine the 'modal personality' of the residents of the Tuscarora Reservation in western New York (Wallace 1952). The Tuscarora were the sixth nation of the famed Iroquois Confederacy, and the Iroquois have been important in the anthropological canon since the classic pioneering ethnography of **Lewis Henry Morgan** (1851).

The Tuscarora Reservation was a nominally Christian community. Wallace moved on to conduct field research among another member of the Iroquois Confederacy, the Seneca, who like their brethren on the Six Nations Reserve in Canada, included a segment of the community which followed the calendrical ceremonial cycle of the traditional religion. While they might be said to practice a 'traditional' Native American religion, the Seneca and other Iroquois considered themselves followers of the historic prophet, Handsome Lake. This led Wallace to consider issues involved in the rise of prophets and the founding of religions (Wallace 1956a).

Coming from the American anthropological tradition, Wallace sees culture as his subject matter, but for Wallace culture is a set of mental rules, conscious or unconscious. He frequently uses the term *mazeway* to refer to this map of the surrounding world. Wallace has dealt with his personal *mazeway*, describing his journey to work each morning and his role as an academic bureaucrat in his day at the office (Wallace 1965b, 1971, 1972).

Carrying this concept of *mazeway* into his discussion of origins of religions, Wallace sees revitalization movements in psychological terms, when the *mazeway* is no longer satisfactory and is reformulated to provide a new and improved *Gestalt*. The basic process involved movement from (1) a steady state to (2) a period of increased individual stress to (3) a period of cultural distortion to (4) the period of revitalization. Revitalization involved *mazeway* reformulation by the founder or founders of the movement, communication of the new way to the larger community, organization and adaptation by the larger community, and finally cultural transformation, routinization, and a new steady state.

Wallace developed his ideas about the temporal process of revitalization through an examination of the career of Handsome Lake, whose visions experienced in 1799 led to a revitalization of Iroquois religion. Handsome Lake's message and the events surrounding his preaching have been preserved both in Seneca oral traditions and a rich record of historical documentation. A detailed ethnohistoric analysis of the story of the Seneca prophet and his teachings became a monograph (Wallace 1970a), described as a classic study of a Native American culture in time.

For Wallace, understanding the *mazeway* of an individual is a key to constructing his or her personality. He notes, however, significant variation in the *mazeways* among participants in a culture. This explains variation of personality within a given society and leads Wallace (like **Sapir** and Hallowell, both of whom he cites) to champion 'the uniqueness of the individual' (Wallace 1970b: 128). It follows from this that culture as seen by the social scientist is something greater than any individual's *mazeway*. Culture is constructed by the student and observer. 'Descriptions of culture will include statements of relations between behaviour patterns that no informant has given or is able to give: cultural descriptions need not be "psychologically real" to the informant' (Wallace 1970b: 129).

Wallace's view of culture as a map in the mind of its participants led him to play a leading role in the approach to the investigation of culture which came to be known as componential analysis. This approach grew out of the American anthropological tradition which emphasized both the mental aspect of culture and the importance of linguistics and language. Wallace and Atkins provided an analysis of kinship terms as revealing the 'cognitive processes in culturally organized behavior' (Wallace and Atkins 1960: 79). He published an important article in *Science* on 'Culture and Cognition' (Wallace 1962) and his discussion of the psychological validity of componential analyses had a wide impact (Wallace 1965a).

A less well appreciated part of Wallace's career was his pursuit of research into communities which had faced major disasters with the implication that the results of these studies would facilitate the more effective meeting of similar disasters in the future. The Cold War led to the funding of this applied research since a primary goal was to aid planning for a civic response to a nuclear attack (see Wallace 1956b). Wallace developed a model of behavior, 'the disaster syndrome,' exhibited by survivors of the event. He reported three stages – the isolation period or random movement stage in which survivors exhibit dazed, apathetic, and stunned behavior; the rescue period or the suggestible stage when survivors respond readily to directions from outsiders arriving to help; and the rehabilitation period or euphoric stage involving intense identification with and willingness to cooperate with fellow survivors (Wallace 1956b:125–26).

Despite the hostility toward ideas of cultural evolution displayed by his **Boas**ian teachers at the University of Pennsylvania, Wallace continued in his admiration of Sir James Frazer and later expressed admiration for the writings of **Marvin Harris** which were 'modifying Marxist doctrine to give elegant expression to this view of the primacy of economic change in his formulations of cultural materialism'(Wallace 2003b: 123). Thus Wallace's approach to religion includes an evolutionary dimension. Wallace sees varieties of cult institutions: individualistic cult institutions, shamanistic cult institutions, communal cult institutions, and ecclesiastical cult institutions. The first two are found in nearly all human societies, and are the only religious institutions found in the least complex societies. More complex societies see the addition of communal cult institutions, while still more complex societies add ecclesiastical cult institutions. Those societies with ecclesiastical cults practice either Olympian (with numerous high gods) or Monotheistic (with one high god although other supernatural beings are also invariably present) religion. This religious typology has allowed Wallace to posit thirteen religious culture areas in the world (Wallace 1966).

Wallace has noted that 'cultural and social anthropology tended – and still tends – to neglect the Industrial Revolution ... [which] appears to be located in the turf of library-bound historians' (Wallace 2003b: 122). Wallace chose to deal with the topic, bringing to his investigations his interest in the individual mind and his sympathy toward the primacy of economic institutions. The result was two lengthy monographs dealing with the impact of nineteenth century industrial development on two small Pennsylvania communities (Wallace 1978, 1987). Even more recently, Wallace has published on policies of the early American republic toward its indigenous population, research which perhaps harkens back to Wallace's early role as an expert witness for the Sac and Fox case before the Indian Claims Commission of the United States (Wallace 1993, 1999; for his land claims work see Grumet 1998: 111; Wallace 1970c).

Wallace's many-faceted contributions to anthropological thought have been built upon a foundation of American cultural anthropology. Long before Wallace, anthropologists in the American tradition dealt with historical topics, religious movements, and issues of cognition and CULTURE AND PERSONALITY. What Wallace brought to the examination of these topics was exceptional scientific rigor and clarity of thought. He was recently invited to present the Distinguished Lecture to the Society for the Anthropology of Consciousness at the Annual Meeting of the American Anthropological Association (on December 2, 2005). He discussed various views of time including references to his own findings among the Tuscarora and those of his teacher A. Irving Hallowell among the Berens River Ojibwa. Perhaps appropriately, Wallace concluded this paper with a reference to the point where his anthropological journey at least partially began, Sir James Frazer's *Golden Bough* (Wallace 2005).

Selected readings

Darnell, R. (2002) 'Anthony F. C. Wallace, 1972,' in *Celebrating a Century of the American Anthropological Association: Presidential Portraits*, R. Darnell and F. W. Gleach (eds.), pp. 221–24, Lincoln: University of Nebraska Press.

Grumet, R. S. (1998) 'An Interview with Anthony F. C. Wallace,' *Ethnohistory* 45(1): 103–27.

Morgan, L. H. (1851) *League of the Ho-dé-no-sau-nee or Iroquois*, Rochester, NY: Sage.

Smith, D. (1997) 'Biographical Sketch of Paul A. W. Wallace and How *The White Roots of Peace* Came to be Written,' in *The White Roots of Peace* by Paul A. W. Wallace, pp. 6–23, Ohsweken, ON: Iroqrafts.

Wallace, A. F. C. (1949) *King of the Delawares: Teedyuscung*, Philadelphia: University of Pennsylvania Press.

——(1952) 'The Modal Personality Structure of the Tuscarora Indians as Revealed by the Rorschach Test,' *Bureau of American Ethnology Bulletin* 150, Washington: US Government Printing Office.

——(1956a) 'Revitalization Movements: Some Theoretical Considerations for their Comparative Study,' *American Anthropologist* 58: 264–81.

——(1956b) *Tornado in Worcester: An Exploratory Study of Individual and Community Behavior in an Extreme Situation*, Disaster Study Number 3. Committee on Disaster Studies, Division of Anthropology and Psychology. National Academy of Sciences – National Research Council Publication 392, Washington: National Academy of Sciences – National Research Council.

——(1958) 'Dreams and Wishes of the Soul,' *American Anthropologist* 60: 234–48.

——(1962) 'Culture and Cognition,' *Science* (New Series) 135(3501): 351–57.

——(1965a) 'The Problem of the Psychological Validity of Componential Analyses,' in *Formal Semantic Analysis*, E. A. Hammel (ed.), *American Anthropologist*, Special Publication 67(5), pt. 2.

——(1965b) 'Driving to Work,' in *Context and Meaning in Cultural Anthropology: Essays in Honor of A. Irving Hallowell*, Melford E. Spiro (ed.), pp. 277–92, New York: Free Press.

——(1966) *Religion: An Anthropological View*, New York: Random House.

——(1970a) *The Death and Rebirth of the Seneca*, New York: Knopf.

——(1970b) *Culture and Personality*, 2nd edn (1st edn 1961), New York: Random House.

——(1970c) *Prelude to Disaster: The Course of Indian–White Relations Which Led to the Black Hawk War of 1832*, Springfield: Illinois State Historical Library.

——(1971) *Administrative Forms of Social Organization*, Module 9, Reading, MA: Addison-Wesley.

——(1972) 'A Day at the Office,' in *Crossing Cultural Boundaries: The Anthropological Experience*, S. T. Kimball and J. B. Watson (eds.), pp. 193–203, San Francisco, CA: Chandler.

——(1978) *Rockdale: The Growth of an American Village in the Early Industrial Revolution*, New York: Knopf.

——(1987) *St. Clair: A Nineteenth-Century Coal Town's Experience with a Disaster-Prone Industry*, New York: Knopf.

——(1990) *King of the Delawares: Teedyuscung 1700–1763*, Syracuse: Syracuse University Press.

——(1993) *The Long, Bitter Trail: Andrew Jackson and the Indians*, New York: Hill and Wang.

——(1999) *Jefferson and the Indians: The Tragic Fate of the First Americans*, Cambridge, MA: Harvard University Press.

——(2003a) *Revitalizations and Mazeways: Essays on Culture Change, Volume 1*, ed. by R. S. Grumet, Lincoln: University of Nebraska Press.

——(2003b) *Modernity & Mind: Essays on Culture Change, Volume 2*, ed. by R. S. Grumet, Lincoln: University of Nebraska Press.

——(2005) 'The Consciousness of Time,' *The Anthropology of Consciousness* 16(2): 1–15.

Wallace, A. F. C. and Atkins, J. (1960) 'The Meaning of Kinship Terms,' *American Anthropologist* 62(1): 58–80.

Wallace, P. A. W. (1945) *Conrad Weiser, 1696–1760: Friend of Colonist and Mohawk*, Philadelphia: University of Pennsylvania Press.

THOMAS S. ABLER

LESLIE WHITE (1900–75)

It is perhaps fitting that Leslie White spent his most productive scholarly years in Michigan, a state then renowned for cutting edge technology, as he saw energy or, more accurately the mode of harnessing it and putting it to human use, as the key component in how societies evolved and changed. Moving from food gathering to food production, then on to the use of fossil fuels, culture was transformed – *evolved* – from primitive to modern. Culture was made possible by the ability to symbol, but for White material inventions were the most important product of such symboling. His famous formula stated: '*As the amount of energy harnessed per capita per year increases, culture will advance.*' In White's scheme of things technology was the key driver of Cultural change, but he distinguished between Culture and specific cultures. That is, while he believed that Culture developed generally toward states of higher complexity and greater harnessing of energy, he acknowledged that individual cultures developed in response to a variety of particular factors. His interest was in all human Culture rather than in particular cultures.

Initially the human species had lived in small societies that depended on hunting and gathering to survive, using their own energy, augmented by tools. In time, humans learned to farm, planting cultigens and using the energy of domesticated animals. This led to larger communities and more complex societies, some of which used water power in irrigation and milling, as well as wind power. Then came the harnessing of fossil fuels, the industrial revolution, and the advent of modern civilization. White was writing as nuclear energy was increasingly being heralded as the energy source of the future, and he believed that we were entering a new era that would lead to still more complexity.

White taught that attempts to understand this progress in terms of biology or psychology were misguided. Human biology and human nature had been a constant. Change lay in the dynamic nature of culture itself. Culture was a process, a process *sui generis*, as he was fond of saying. White argued that the scientific study of this process was the proper goal of anthropology. He proposed that this study be called *Culturology* and proclaimed himself a *Culturologist*. In his lectures and writing White promoted his conviction that anthropology was a science, and advanced a view of the role of culture as *the* determinant of human behavior. He vigorously challenged those who thought differently. His response to colleagues who challenged him could be forceful and withering. However, students who rose to question him in class could be treated more gently. If the query were in the form of a question and seemed to be seeking clarification, White would be helpful and thorough. But if he was challenged or denounced, which seemed to happen about once a semester, the student could experience the full force of his wit and oratorical power. While this approach served as a powerful alternative to the dominant Boasian and 'STRUCTURAL-FUNCTIONALIST' paradigms, White's ideas now largely provide powerful conceptual tools for archaeologists to analyze their material finds.

Born in 1900 in Colorado, Leslie Alvin White grew up in the Midwest and served briefly in the US Navy during the closing years of the Great War. After studying at Louisiana State University he moved and switched majors from physics, ending up in psychology, majoring in that subject in 1923 at Columbia University. The following year he obtained a Masters in Psychology from Columbia but at the same time discovered anthropology, courtesy of Alexander Goldenweiser at the New School. He then moved to the University of Chicago and enrolled in the joint Sociology-Anthropology Department. There, funded by Elsie Clews Parsons, he was able to undertake fieldwork in the Keresan Pueblos on secret medicinal societies, and obtained his doctorate in 1927.

White had developed his perspective mainly in the 1930s and 1940s. In the early decades of the twentieth century, **Franz Boas** and his students had dominated anthropology in the United States. Initiated by Boas, they established an intellectual tradition that has come to be called *historical particularism*. These 'Boasians' saw anthropology as the description of the cultural practices of particular peoples and of the extent to which particular cultural practices were shared among different cultures, the process of *cultural diffusion*. They offered this approach as an alternative to the earlier EVOLUTIONARY anthropology of the nineteenth century, which they dismissed as purely speculative.

As a student in the 1920s, White had absorbed this perspective. He initiated research among the indigenous populations in the American Southwest, an effort pursued through most of his career. While his theoretical perspective was to undergo a radical transformation, his ethnographic research remained true to the Boasian tradition. He offered no ethnographic methodology to accompany his theoretical stance. In fact, he explicitly held that there was no connection between ethnographic research and theoretical work. Today, the disconnection between his field research and his theoretical pursuits seems strange and difficult to understand.

White was fond of sharing an anecdote with his students about his conversion to evolutionism. He explained that early in his career right after Chicago, he had been hired at the University of Rochester where his teaching was very much in the Boasian mode. This included a dismissal of the work of the nineteenth century American evolutionary anthropologist, **Lewis Henry Morgan**. However, Rochester was Morgan's hometown, and some of White's students were moved to read Morgan's work. Questions they raised in class about Morgan, White claimed, led him to read Morgan's opus for the first time. A visit to the Soviet Union the following year further solidified his interest in Morgan, because Engels had used his schema extensively in developing his views of society. White's reading and experiences had convinced him that socialism was the future of society.

As a result, he explained, he came to accept Morgan's project and to reject the Boasian approach. He became, in effect, Morgan's champion. He claimed that neither Boas nor any of his students ever actually engaged Morgan's ideas, but simply dismissed them out of hand. A standing challenge in White's classes was to find a place where any specific passage of Morgan's had actually been cited and discussed in the writings of Boas or any of his students.

In 1930 he was hired to replace **Julian Steward** at the University of Michigan and he was to remain there until his retirement. For many years it was a one person Department and he remained there, much to the chagrin of the university administration who reluctantly gave him tenure and promotion because of his outstanding teaching and publications. White was a superb teacher and among his students were Fred Eggan, Robert Carneiro, David Aberle, Lewis Binford, **Marshall Sahlins**, Elman Service (as an undergraduate), Napoleon Chagnon, Beth Dillingham, John W. Cole, and Mischa Titiev, although they and others such as **Marvin Harris** used his ideas in synthesis with other concepts, frequently Steward's multilinear evolution. White was also a wordsmith of exceptional and rare ability and recognized as such by no less a figure than Thomas Mann.

It was common among White's contemporaries to refer to his approach as 'NEO-EVOLUTIONISM' and to contrast it with the evolutionism of the nineteenth century. White rejected this label and maintained that his evolutionism was fully consistent with nineteenth century evolutionists such as Lewis Henry Morgan and **Edward Burnett Tylor**. White is unique among anthropologists in claiming that he had nothing new or original to say, claiming only some slight innovation in how he presented the ideas of others.

White was, of course, well aware that he had few supporters in championing cultural evolutionism. Not only did he face the hostility of the Boasians, but also across the Atlantic British SOCIAL ANTHROPOLOGISTS and French STRUCTURALISTS were committed to synchronic studies of primitive social life. However, he predicted that the centennial of the publication of Charles Darwin's *Origin of Species* in 1959 would usher in a revival of interest not only in biological evolution but in cultural evolution as well.

Notions of cultural evolution had expanded to include the way in which specific cultures fit into the overall process. Moreover, the interaction of different cultural types with particular environmental settings had attracted much interest. At the same time, White's rather sweeping generality of cultural progression had given way to more precise delineation of the specific characteristics of particular evolutionary stages – the familiar sequence of Bands, Tribes, Chiefdoms, and States.

Yet, while appreciative of White's intellect and well aware of what might be called his progressive influence on anthropology in the past, his students, especially the later ones, looked elsewhere for inspiration. In the course of the 1960s anthropology's contemplation of the civil rights movement, the Cold War, and liberation struggles taking place in the so-called 'Third World,' had led to profound transformations in where anthropologists found their subjects, in how they viewed them, and in how they viewed their discipline. Led inter alia by White's erstwhile colleagues **Eric Wolf** and Marshall Sahlins, anthropologists increasingly focused on culture at home as much as in exotic locations, tending to see all existing populations as interlinked rather than viewing some as modern and others as surviving 'primitive contemporaries.'

While White consistently claimed that he was not interested in founding a 'School,' as the Boasians or structural functionalists had, Michigan became renowned for its ecologically based anthropology, and his grateful students published a well-received *Festschrift*.

Outside of anthropology, White was an accepted figure within the scientific community. He was a frequent contributor to the journal *Science*, and served on its editorial board, and was a member of *The American Society for the Advancement of Science*. His 1947 article, 'The Locus of Mathematical Reality' was reprinted several times, most famously in the four volume work, *The World of Mathematics* in 1956. Championed by the Michigan mathematician R. I. Wilder, White's view of mathematics as a cultural rather than a natural phenomenon gained a following among mathematicians. Later in life, appreciation for White's scholarship led to numerous accolades, including election to the presidency of the American Anthropological Association, and two honorary doctorates.

However, outside of the academy, White was rather a pariah. There was no place for the supernatural in his Culturology and this upset certain leaders of organized religion who actively sought to have him fired at Michigan. His views also made him vulnerable to the anti-communist hysteria of the 1950s. However, he weathered these threats and continued on at Michigan until his retirement in 1967. His political writings for the socialist periodical *The Weekly People*, written under the pseudonym John Steel, were unknown even to his students and colleagues until after his death in 1975.

Selected readings

Dole, G. E. and Carneiro, R. (eds.) (1960) *Essays in the Science of Culture in Honor of Leslie A. White*, New York: Thomas Y. Crowell.

Peace, W. J. (2004) *Leslie A. White: Evolution and Revolution in Anthropology*, Lincoln: University of Nebraska Press.

White, L. A. (1949) *The Science of Culture: A Study of Man and Civilization*, New York: Farrar and Strauss.

——(1956) 'The Locus of mathematical reality,' in *The World of Mathematics*, J. R. Newman (ed.), vol. 4, pp. 2348–64, New York: Simon & Schuster.

——(1959) *The Evolution of Culture: The Development of Civilization to the Fall of Rome*, New York: McGraw-Hill.

——(1966) *The Social Organization of Ethnological Theory*, Monograph in Cultural Anthropology, Vol. 52, No. 4, Houston, TX: Rice University Studies.

——(1975) *The Concept of Cultural Systems: A Key to Understanding Tribes and Nations*, New York: Columbia University Press.

White, L. A. and Dillingham, B. (1987) *Ethnological Essays*, Albuquerque: University of New Mexico Press.

White, L. A., Carneiro, R.L., Urish, B. and Brown, B. J. (2008) *Modern Capitalist Culture*, Walnut Creek, CA: Left Coast Press.

JOHN W. COLE

MONICA HUNTER WILSON (1908–82)

Described as 'the most distinguished anthropologist to have lived and worked in South Africa' (Hammond-Tooke 2001: 85), Wilson's reputation rests primarily on five monographs: *Reaction to Conquest* (1936); the 'Nyakyusa Trilogy', including *Good Company*, published in the 1950s; and a final ethnography on the Nyakyusa, *For Men and Elders* (1977). This work made a substantial contribution to anthropological understanding of religion, ritual, symbolism, social change, and generation in South and Eastern Africa. She is also remembered as the co-editor and main contributor to the inter-disciplinary two-volume *Oxford History of South Africa*, widely seen as a capstone of liberal scholarship.

Her lifelong friend Audrey Richards, another of the pioneering generation of woman anthropologists, reflected that Wilson was unique in anthropology because of her ability to 'pursue her own way.' Wilson's way was the result of an unusual combination of circumstances in her personal life and her intellectual career, as well as the preference of a highly private person for following her own instincts without regard for fashion or fame.

The first elements contributing to this distinctive way were her deeply religious and racially liberal upbringing at Lovedale in the Eastern Cape Province of South Africa where she was born to Scottish emigrant missionary parents. Here she absorbed a deep-seated lifelong religious commitment. From the multiracial Lovedale Mission School she developed an interest in African culture and history, which she would trace to informal debates over bride-wealth with her Xhosa friends and classroom debates about the biased treatment of the Xhosa–British frontier wars in textbooks that insultingly dubbed them 'Kaffir Wars.' However, it was the tragic death of her only sibling Aylmer when she was six years of age, which contributed to a deep sensitivity to suffering, that informed her intellectual and political work in later life.

Monica Hunter's undergraduate training at Cambridge University between 1927 and 1930 also shaped her career in important ways. Here she chose to specialize in social anthropology, while retaining a passionate interest in history. This dialogue between anthropology and history would emerge as one of the distinctive features of her contribution to African studies. While Cambridge taught her critical skills and introduced her to FUNCTIONALISM, the colonial, official-style ethnography of her Cambridge tutors (Hodson and Driberg) provided little by way of the induction in fieldwork methodology that **Malinowski** offered contemporaries like Richards and Schapera. She did later attend the famous LSE seminar, but remained on the margins of Malinowski's magic circle.

There is therefore a distinct sense of invention and adaptation when reading her Pondoland and Eastern Cape field-notes of the 1930–32 years, which provided the raw data for her 1934 Cambridge doctoral thesis that would be published in significantly reworked form as *Reaction to Conquest* in 1936. Hunter recorded her information on sheets or even scraps of paper, which she would later cut-and-paste, rearrange, and loosely archive in folders under broad thematic headings. Her idiosyncratic aversion to the notebook continued during her 1935–38 fieldwork among the Nyakyusa.

The need to invent, innovate, and adapt also accounts for her pioneering multisited fieldwork approach in a period when village-based or island-based ethnographies were the norm. In order to explore the extent of social change in Pondo society, Hunter selected sites where the Pondo (or Xhosa-speakers more broadly) had varying degrees of cultural contact with Europeans. These ranged from remote villages in the heart of the Pondoland reserve to settler farms in the Eastern Cape and then African locations in East London and Grahamstown.

Reaction to Conquest was immediately recognized as being among the best anthropological studies of its generation, not least by Malinowski and **Radcliffe-Brown**. It not only offered one of the most meticulously detailed accounts of the traditional life of an African people, but presented an incisive analysis of social change in the sections on African workers on farms and African town life, giving it a claim to the status of the pioneering contribution to urban anthropology in southern Africa. The book's political significance went beyond the laudatory preface by the then South African Prime Minister Jan Smuts. In the concluding section on 'Tendencies,' it presented an incisive and highly current analysis of the rising tide of African nationalist ideology manifested in political organizations, trade unions, and independent churches.

Indeed, it was for a study of African independent churches that Monica Hunter was awarded an International African Institute Fellowship in 1934. She was now engaged to Godfrey Wilson, only son of the Shakespearian scholar Dover Wilson. Godfrey had gone from studying Greats (Classics) at Oxford to becoming one of Malinowski's favored sons. The Wilsons struck upon the Nyakyusa as their subjects of study based, as Monica later recalled, on a rather arbitrary combination of the knowledge of Imperial Airways links with Africa, a sense that studying the Ibo (as Margery Perham had suggested) would simply be too uncomfortable in the heat of West Africa, and some inkling from the volume of a resident colonial official about their relatively high degree of cultural and geographical isolation.

What ultimately emerged from this chance decision, however, was one of the most intensive ethnographic studies ever done by a remarkable husband-and-wife team. Collectively the Wilsons spent fifty-one months in the field, again adopting a multisited ethnographic strategy from their three primary fieldwork bases as well as tracking the movements of labor migrants to the nearby Lupa goldfields. They saw their fieldwork as two sides of a coin, with Godfrey focusing on tradition through interviews with Nyakyusa men, and Monica on social change through interviews with Nyakyusa women at schools and churches.

In January 1938, when Godfrey Wilson took up his prestigious appointment as the first director of the Rhodes-Livingstone Institute in Northern Rhodesia, they envisaged publishing two books on the Nyakyusa with a separate volume of case studies as an appendix. Their plan was substantially delayed, first by Monica's pregnancy and the demands of motherhood after the birth of their sons in 1939 and 1943, then by the challenges and frustrations associated with Godfrey's new study of Bemba migrant laborers in the mining town of Broken Hill (Kabwe).

They also worked on the jointly authored *Analysis of Social Change, based on Observations in Central Africa*, which was only published a year after Godfrey's suicide in 1944 as a result of a war-induced recurrence of depression. Here the Wilsons sought to refine the concept of social scale, arguing that the differences between 'primitive' and 'civilized' societies are best conceptualized in terms of differences in the extent and intensity of social relations (both real and imagined). While this theoretical contribution initially received a lukewarm reception, the major and under-acknowledged achievement of their study was its prognosis about the deep underlying contradictions between capitalist development and racial segregation in a rapidly modernizing Central African context. Written in the shadow of the Holocaust (and perhaps Godfrey's war-time depression), there is a darkly predictive quality about their laying bare of white settler racism and its volatile implications for the development of an urban African working class and a struggling African peasantry. This was an attempt not only to merge Malinowski and Marx but, like **Gluckman**'s 'Analysis of a Social Situation in Modern Zululand' (1940, 1942), to bring Europeans and Africans under a single ethnographic lens.

Monica Wilson saw the publication of her 1950s Nyakyusa Trilogy as 'a sacred trust and a labour of love' in memory of her late husband who continued as an active imaginative presence in her life. As such her Trilogy was concerned much more with the traditional life of men that Godfrey had explored in his extended periods of fieldwork than with the changes brought by Christianity and education that she had attempted to chart. The trilogy addressed two primary research problems: first, explaining what the Wilsons considered to be the most distinctive feature of the social structure of the Nyakyusa – their unique system of age-villages – and, second, understanding the complex ritual cycles of kinship and community. In *Good Company* (1951) Monica Wilson related the age-village system to its primary social function, that of maintaining social separation between generations, and explored the forms of 'social pressure' that maintained order in age-villages: economic reciprocity, moral values, and notions of mystical interdependence associated with the fear and threat of witchcraft. The most incisive section of the book is its complex analysis of the core moral values that bound Nyakyusa age-mates together, including dignity, decency, and hospitality (the 'good company' of the book's title).

Rituals of Kinship among the Nyakyusa (1957) is perhaps the most tightly structured and densely detailed of the Trilogy in its tracking of ritual practices and associated symbolism from the elaborate and emotional funerals through the puberty and marriage rituals, which include the careful applications of medicines to the dangerously fertile parents in twin births. The third study (*Communal Rituals of the Nyakyusa* [1959]) extended Wilson's exploration of 'the genius of Nyakyusa religion' through an analysis of 'coming out' rituals, cleansing the country, rain-making, and sacrifices at the groves of chiefs. There were some concluding reflections on the Nyakyusa Christian community and on the social changes of the intervening two decades which she had observed when she returned for a three-month fieldtrip in 1955.

By this time Wilson had established a career, having progressed from a position as lecturer in Social Anthropology at Fort Hare Native College between 1944 and 1946 to Chair of Social Anthropology and the first woman professor at Rhodes University College from 1947 to 1952, finally succeeding Schapera as Chair of Social Anthropology an the University of Cape Town, where she remained until retirement in 1973. Again she was the first woman to be appointed as a full professor and later the University's first dean of the Faculty of Arts. Wilson had now achieved a secure international scholarly reputation, as confirmed by a host of academic awards including the inaugural Rivers Medal for Fieldwork in 1952, and courageously chose to stay in South Africa. Despite an active involvement in church, university, and liberal politics during her UCT years, she was often exhausted and depressed about the volume of teaching and the increasingly bleak political landscape.

In these years she turned increasingly to history as a way to challenge the political mythologies of the apartheid government, from myths of the empty land to white mythologies about static African societies and the putative connections between biology and culture that the *Oxford History* sought to overturn. It was, however, 'the continuous teaching in South African universities,' Richards recalls, that she deemed 'her special contribution to the fight for the African cause' (1975: 1). The roll-call of prominent former students includes **Victor Turner**, Max Marwick, Bengt Sundkler, Peter Rigby, Colin Murray, **Jean Comaroff**, **John Comaroff**, Peter Carstens, Martin West, Pamela Reynolds, and Archie Mafeje, whose insider ethnography served as the basis for their co-authored *Langa: A Study of Social Groups in an African Township* (1963). These former students have presented an overwhelming confirmation of the extraordinary success of her mission to contribute to social change through teaching and their works are further testimony to her anthropological legacy.

Selected readings

Hammond-Tooke, D. (2001) *Imperfect Interpreters: South Africa's Anthropologists, 1920–1990*, Johannesburg: Witwatersrand University Press.

Richards, A. (1975) 'Monica Wilson: An Appreciation,' in *Religion and Social Change in Southern Africa: Essays in Honour of Monica Wilson*, M. G. Whisson and M. West (eds.), pp. 1–13, Cape Town: David Philip.

Wilson, G. and Wilson, M. (1945) *The Analysis of Social Change based on Observations in Central Africa*, Cambridge: Cambridge University Press.

Wilson, M. (1936) *Reaction to Conquest: Effects of Contact with Europeans on the Pondo of South Africa*, London: Oxford University Press.

——(1951) *Good Company: A Study of Nyakyusa Age-Villages*, London: Oxford University Press.

——(1957) *Rituals of Kinship among the Nyakyusa*, London: Oxford University Press.

——(1959) *Communal Rituals of the Nyakyusa*, London: Oxford University Press.

——(1977) *For Men and Elders: Change in the Relations of Generations and of Men and Women among the Nyakyusa-Ngonde People, 1875–1971*, New York: Africana Publishing Company.

Wilson, M. and Thompson, L. (eds.) (1969–71) *The Oxford History of South Africa*, Oxford: The Clarendon Press.

ANDREW BANK

ERIC R. WOLF (1923–99)

'Anthropology at its best,' said Wolf (1999: 134) 'is analytic, comparative, integrative, and critical, all at the same time. It is a mode of knowledge like no other.' A PARTICIPANT OBSERVER in a volatile global village, he sought to explain and understand power in society – its uses and abuses, political organization, and ideological mystification across the globe and through history. What moved him to pioneer a critical anthropology of power? The answer is embedded in his biography as it unfolded in an unstable world transfigured by the contradictory forces of expanding capitalism and reactionary nationalism.

Eric Robert Wolf was born into an assimilated Jewish middle-class family in 1923 in Vienna, the moribund center of a convulsing Europe. The break-up of the Austrian-Hungarian Empire in the aftermath of World War I created new international state boundaries, unsettling millions of people and reconfiguring their ethnic iden-tities and historical connections. That war also united Eric's parents. His father had been captured and imprisoned in Siberia but in the mayhem of the 1917 Communist Revolution found his way to Novosibirsk where he met his future wife.

In 1933, the Wolf family relocated to Czechoslovakia where Eric's father managed a factory in a Sudetenland town inhabited by ethnic Germans and Czechs. Eric enjoyed mountaineering and became intrigued by peasants. In 1937, he and a friend bicycled to Munich and witnessed a Nazi mass rally. Appealing to angry emotions of wounded German pride Hitler envisioned a megalomaniac project of pan-German nation building and led his extremist movement into creating a racist totalitarian state. Ideologically reclassified as belonging to an inferior race, the Wolf family fled to England in 1938 and Eric was sent to a boarding school. A year later World War II broke out and most aliens were interned, and in this camp seventeen year old Eric had his first serious exposure to Marxian theories (Wolf 1977: 30).

Sponsored by his mother's aunt who had emigrated to the US, the family sailed to New York in July, 1940. At Queens College, he studied biochemistry – later stumbling on anthropology – but in 1943 enlisted with the 10th Mountain Division, married Kathleen Bakeman, and became a US citizen. Wolf was promoted to the rank of sergeant. His regiment saw service in Italy where he was seriously wounded. He recovered, spending the rest of the war debriefing German captives.

A decorated Wolf returned to New York and completed his undergraduate degree in 1946 under **Hortense Powdermaker**. That summer, prior to entering graduate school, he read Wittfogel's his-torical study of China's ecology and political economy. Supported by the GI Bill, Wolf enrolled in Columbia's anthropology graduate program, joining a brilliant cohort of veterans and progressive students, including Sidney Mintz, Stanley Diamond, Morton Fried, and Elman Service who banded together as the Mundial Upheaval Society. Although Wolf enjoyed **Ruth Benedict**'s lectures on 'CULTURE AND PERSONALITY,' his budding interest in historical materialism meshed with the cultural ecology of **Julian Steward** who was also influenced by Karl August Wittfogel. Of special interest was Wittfogel's interpretation of the revolutionary potential of peasantry, controlled by and periodically rebeling against the state, as in the case of the political mobilization of the rural masses in the 1940s, which proved to be decisive in China's civil war between the victorious Communists, backed by the Soviet Union, and the US-backed Nationalists.

Exploring a Marxian approach, which encouraged a convergence between anthropology and history, Wolf joined Steward's multi-sited research team studying changing systemic relations between environment, technology, and the socio-economic organization of Puerto Rico as a complex society. After fieldwork in a highland community of coffee-growing peasants, Wolf completed his doctoral dissertation in 1951, later published in *The People of Puerto Rico* (1956). Wolf then left for Mexico where exiled German Marxist anthropologist Paul Kirchoff had introduced Wittfogel's 'hydraulic hypothesis' regarding large-scale irrigation in the pre-Hispanic state formation process to Spanish Civil War exiles Pedro Armillas and Angel Palerm. With Palerm Wolf returned to the highlands and co-authored influential publications on irrigation agriculture in pre-Hispanic Mexico.

After publishing his model on levels of socio-cultural integration, Steward obtained multi-year funding for a team project, 'Research on Cross-Cultural Regularities of Change,' and moved to the University of Illinois, hiring Wolf as the project's first Research Associate (1952–55). Wolf analyzed how peasant communities are interlinked and systemically integrated within larger polities, especially the state. Departing from the study of rural communities as microcosms, he focused on their structural relationships to regional and national institutions and analyzed social webs of relatives, neighbors, friends, brokers, patrons, and fictive kinsmen institutionally bonded by means of *compadrazgo* (ritual co-parenthood). Defining communities in complex societies 'as the local termini of a web of group relations which extend through intermediate levels from that of the community to that of the nation,' Wolf emphasized 'that the exercise of [economic and political] power by some people over others enters into all of them, on all levels of integration. … Group relationships involve conflict and accommodation, integration and disintegration, processes which take place over time' (1956: 1065, 1066).

In 1955, Wolf joined the University of Virginia, where he completed several publications based on fieldwork and archival research in Mexico, including his now classic article on the country's national symbol *The Virgin of Guadelupe*, followed by a semi-popular book on the cultural history and ecology of Mesoamerica titled *Sons of the Shaking Earth*. In 1960, after briefly teaching at Yale and the University of Chicago, Wolf left for fieldwork among peasants in the Tyrolean Alps, an unstable contact zone between Germanic-speaking peoples and their Romance-speaking neighbors. Choosing two villages on this long-contested Austrian-Italian frontier, he compared how neighboring communities sharing the same mountainous environment historically constructed different national identities.

Leslie White recruited Wolf in 1961 to Michigan where, welcomed by Service and **Marshall Sahlins**, he enjoyed a productive decade publishing the highly acclaimed books *Anthropology* (1964), *Peasants* (1966), and *Peasant Wars of the Twentieth Century* (1969). Periodically returning to research in Italy, Wolf also established a Mediterranean Studies group guiding students into doctoral research projects, including John W. Cole, with whom he co-authored a pioneering study in political ecology titled *The Hidden Frontier: Ecology and Ethnicity in an Alpine Valley*.

In 1965, with the waning of European colonialism, the growing momentum of the US civil rights movement, and the escalation of the Vietnamese war, Wolf and Sahlins were leaders in the country's first anti-war 'teach-in.' That summer, an international social science project code-named Camelot became a scandal when it emerged that it was covertly funded by the US Defense Department. Project Camelot forced the American Anthropological Association (AAA) to draft a code of professional ethics in 1967. Chairing the AAA's Ethics Committee and motivated by anti-war activism, Wolf blew the whistle on unethical professional behavior by colleagues involved in overt and covert counterinsurgency research in Thailand two years later.

Described by Aram Yengoyan (2001: xvi) as 'an anguished humanist,' Wolf was aware that Marx was anathema in American academia until the mid-1960s. Now radically rethinking the discipline and seeking a way out of 'the impasse' in anthropology, he argued that anthropologists must commit themselves to the writing of:

a critical and comprehensive history of the modern world [in] which we spell out the processes of power which created the present-day cultural systems and the linkages between them [which] would provide us with the intellectual grid needed to order the massive data we now possess on individual societies and cultures engulfed by these phenomena.

In 1971, Wolf accepted an appointment as Distinguished Professor at Lehman College and the Graduate Center of the City University of New York. The following year a divorced Wolf married fellow anthropologist Sydel Silverman. He proceeded to develop a critical anthropology of power in the modern world. His analysis showed how the rise of global capitalism was predicated on the penetration and ensuing cataclysmic transformation of band and tribal societies, chiefdoms, and kingdoms drawn into its orbit, forging regimes of exploitation and fomenting violent conflicts.

Analyzing capitalism as a dynamic political-economic force in world history since the fifteenth century, Wolf structured his ambitious project in two major phases, beginning with the infrastructure of world capitalism, as it historically impacted tribal and peasant peoples. He used the Marxian concept of mode of production (m.o.p.), distinguishing three types: kin-ordered, tributary (comprising feudal and Asiatic m.o.p.), and capitalist. Arguing that 'peasants and primitives' have been misrepresented as isolated and timeless peoples Wolf gave his next book, recognized as his magnum opus, the ironic title *Europe and the People without History* (1982).

In the early 1980s, Wolf embarked on the second phase of his ambitious project, exploring the superstructure of unfolding global capitalism. Developing his three m.o.p types, Wolf (1984: 398) explained: 'These modes of mobilizing social labour are not only ... [means of] governing the human relation with nature through social organization. They also impart a characteristic directionality, a vectorial force to the formation and propagation of ideas.' In search of explanations, Wolf reconsidered basic anthropological concepts such as culture and society, and most crucially, power, turning to 'Frankfurt School' critical theory and left-wing European intellectuals who were seeking a rapprochement between Marx and Weber. Of singular importance was Gramsci's concept of cultural hegemony as an ideology deployed by ruling elites in establishing and maintaining dominance in a society. Wolf distinguished four modes of power, including tactical and structural power. Whereas tactical power indexes the ways in which actors or 'operating units' in a social field of force circumscribe or impose their will on 'the actions of others in determinate settings,' structural power 'organizes and orchestrates the settings themselves [and] shapes the social field of action so as to render some kinds of behaviour possible, while making others less possible or impossible' (Wolf 1990: 586, 587). Embedded in a norm-setting worldview, this power structures the political economy and appears to actors as naturally given or divinely ordained. Regarding the three m.o.p. types distinguished earlier, Wolf observed that in 'these concepts and in the bodies of signification associated with them we note a common phenomenon, the displacement or projection of the real contradiction underlying each mode upon an imaginary screen of belief and ritual' (1984: 397). His final monograph, *Envisioning Power: Ideologies of Dominance and Crisis* (1999), analyzed structural power by examining historical ideology-making in three societies, each representative of a distinctive and yet – due to Europe's expansionism – structurally interlocking m.o.p.: Kwakiutl (kin-ordered), Aztec (tributary), and Nazi Germany (capitalist). Wolf selected Germany as his final case study because he had personally witnessed the rise and demise of total power, and because its brutal dehumanization seemed to defy explanations.

In a lifelong search for explanations of asymmetrical power, Wolf turned to ethnographic case studies, comparative history, and critical theory. Although he found Marxian concepts and perspectives particularly useful, he was nuanced and eclectic in his theoretical explorations. Introducing a political economical perspective to anthropology, Wolf has been lauded for his comparative historical research on peasantry in complex societies. His explorations of structural power – the more challenging half of his grand project – have puzzled many. Committed to the holistic and integrative perspective, he tried to work toward a synthesis of both parts that make up his total oeuvre, but a diagnosis of cancer in 1996 slowed him down. In addition to high honors from all over the world, several of his books become international bestsellers and were translated into over a dozen languages. Eric Wolf left an impressive legacy that continues to provoke more critical thinking and responsible action in a world that desperately needs both.

Selected readings

Cole, J. W. and Wolf, E. R. (1974) *The Hidden Frontier: Ecology and Ethnicity in an Alpine Valley*, New York: Academic Press.

Wolf, E. R. (1956) 'Aspects of Group Relations in a Complex Society: Mexico,' *American Anthropologist* 58: 1065–78.

——(1959) *Sons of the Shaking Earth*, Chicago: University of Chicago Press.

——(1964) *Anthropology*, Englewood Cliffs, NJ: Prentice-Hall.

——(1966) *Peasants*, Englewood Cliffs, NJ: Prentice-Hall.

——(1969) *Peasant Wars of the Twentieth Century*, New York: Harper & Row.

——(1977) 'Encounter with Norbert Elias,' in, *Human Figurations: Essays for Norbert Elias*, Peter Gleichmann et al. (eds.), pp. 28–35, Amsterdam: Amsterdams Sociologisch Tijdschrift.

——(1982) *Europe and the People without History*, Berkeley: University of California Press.

——(1984) 'Culture: Panacea or Problem?,' *American Antiquity* 49(2): 393–400.

——(1990) 'Distinguished Lecture: Facing Power – Old Insights, New Questions,' *American Anthropologist* 92: 586–96.

——(1999) *Envisioning Power: Ideologies of Dominance and Crisis*, Berkeley: University of California Press.

——(2001) *Pathways of Power: Building an Anthropology of the Modern World*, Berkeley: University of California Press.

Wolf, E. R. and Hansen, E. C. (1972) *The Human Condition in Latin America*, New York: Oxford University Press.

Yengoyan, A. (2001) 'Foreword: Culture and Power in the Writings of Eric R. Wolf,' in *Pathways of Power: Building an Anthropology of the Modern World*, Eric Wolf, Berkeley: University of California Press.

HARALD E. L. PRINS

APPENDIX 1

Some key anthropological terms

The COMPARATIVE METHOD which involved the listing of parallel and similar customs, folklore, ritual practices, and marriage institutions in different societies throughout the world was employed by social **evolutionists** such as **Tylor** and **Morgan** in the late nineteenth century in order to sustain theories of the independent, parallel evolution of culture in different parts of the world. It assumed that similar practices, for example burying the dead with their possessions, wearing masks in rituals, reflected similar ideas ('psychic unity of mankind'). **Franz Boas**, a historical particularist, was sceptical about such theories because they took for granted what had to be proven, and preferred instead to look for proven historical connections over shorter distances. **Structural-functionalists** and **French structuralists** also used a version of the comparative method in their search for synchronic laws or regularities in human action and thought. In the last thirty years, the theoretical pendulum seems to have swung back to particularism, a trend exemplified by some of the later writings of **Clifford Geertz** and the work of anthropological **post-modernists.**

CONFLICT THEORY refers to positions in anthropological theory which view conflict rather than equilibrium or consensus as the fundamental reality of social life. Such views were often influenced by Karl Marx's idea that the struggle over access to economic resources was the driving force of history. Within **social anthropology** the Manchester school of **structural-functionalists** (such as **Gluckman** and early **Turner**) adopted this general position to suit specific ethnographic realities, mainly in Africa. They were particularly interested in mechanisms for resolving or containing conflict. Since the 1970s the most important advocates of conflict theory within anthropology have been critics of capitalism such as **Eric Wolf** and his disciples who have written about power relations in European, colonial, and postcolonial history. This is the contemporary Marxist position known as anthropological **political economy**.

CULTURAL MATERIALISM   is a body of theory and a research strategy associated with **Marvin Harris** and with the early work of Royf (particularly the ecological variety developed by **Julian Steward**), **functionalism** and Darwinism. It is materialist inasmuch as it rejects explanations of customs that are based on beliefs, ideas, and doctrines inside the heads of anthropologists or their informants, and favors explanations based on the fulfilment of survival needs. Accordingly, Harris explained the so-called 'sacred cow' complex in India by noting that it was economical to allow cows to live out their natural lives, because oxen were valuable beasts of burden, because the dung was used for fuel, because milk and cheese were important nutrients, and cows (unlike pigs) primarily consumed grasses that humans couldn't eat. For these reasons vegetarianism and avoidance of meat on the part of higher castes persisted. Indigenous Hindu explanations for such customs were discounted.

CULTURAL RELATIVISM   is the idea that each culture is characterized by its own worldview and practices, and that customs that might seem absurd or wrong to Westerners at first glance make sense within the terms of that worldview. Relativists such as **Boas** and **Herskovits** condemned the ethnocentrism of **evolutionism**. Cultural relativism does not necessarily imply full-scale ethical relativism: to understand why some groups justify human sacrifice doesn't mean you are endorsing the practice. In short many argue that cultural relativism calls for the researcher to suspend judgment while studying the phenomenon at hand.

CULTURE AND PERSONALITY   was the tradition of psychological anthropology that was begun by **Ruth Benedict, Edward Sapir**, and **Margaret Mead**. It assumed that cultures differed in the type of personality they favored, and that cultural differences were perpetuated by the socialization process. One culture (e.g. Zuni) might favor peacefulness and discourage aggression; another might favor frenetic activity and encourage aggression (e.g. Kwakiutl).

DIACHRONIC VERSUS SYNCHRONIC a diachronic analysis or explanation is evolutionary or historical (the Greek roots mean 'through time'), for example how state societies originated, or when the peoples of the North American Plains were introduced to the Arabic horse and how this development affected their cultures. A synchronic analysis or explanation concentrates on one particular point in time – you can analyze how a custom such as compulsory mother-in-law avoidance works among the Cheyenne without needing to know who introduced the custom to whom.

EVOLUTIONISM IN VICTORIAN SOCIAL ANTHROPOLOGY used the **comparative method** to develop theories of the parallel development of institutions such as the family, technology, and religion through identical stages in different parts of the world. Evolutionists assumed that parallel development was the result of psychic unity, that all people everywhere thought alike. Primitive peoples, like children, were yet to go through the more advanced stages of development. It is commonly assumed that evolutionary anthropologists were influenced by Darwin, but in fact most of them were not very interested in notions like the 'survival of the fittest.' What they shared with him was a belief that human culture had developed over a very long time.

FUNCTIONALISM the name given to theoretical approaches that flourished in British anthropology between the 1920s and 1960s. Functionalists explained social institutions and cultural practices in terms of the needs they fulfilled at the present time. Such institutions and practices were interconnected parts of a social or cultural system. Functionalists did not usually focus on the history or evolution of social systems. Anthropologists today distinguish between two varieties of functionalism: one was associated with **Malinowski**, the other was associated with **Radcliffe-Brown**.

1. MALINOWSKIAN FUNCTIONALISM Bronislaw Malinowski believed that the primary concern of all social institutions was the fulfillment of basic biological and psychological needs that all humans shared, such as food, shelter, safety, and reproduction. Because we are social animals living in groups, we are organized so as to assist one another, and we therefore have a further, secondary need for norms, customs, and beliefs to support the frameworks of that organization. For example, Malinowski believed that gardening served the

basic need for nutrition, that rituals associated with planting organized people to get necessary work done, and that garden magic relieved people's anxiety about possible crop failure. This emphasis on utility was seldom found in some earlier evolutionary theories that portrayed 'primitive' peoples as irrational and bound by tradition.

2. STRUCTURAL-FUNCTIONALISM   the version of functionalism associated with **A. R. Radcliffe-Brown** and his disciples such as **Meyer Fortes** and **Sir Edward Evans-Pritchard** in Britain and Fred Eggan in the United States. Radcliffe-Brown, who was greatly influenced by the great French sociologist, Émile Durkheim, advanced a version of the organic analogy which involves a comparison between society and a mammalian body, inasmuch as social institutions (structures) were likened to the various organs that maintain the body as a working system. The actual meaning of religious practices was less important than the fact that they contributed to the solidarity of the group. Political and legal institutions, as well as more informal methods of social control, were explained in terms of their contribution to the maintenance of equilibrium in the system. Unlike **Malinowski**, structural-functionalists had little interest in speculations concerning biological, as opposed to social, needs. They believed that their mission was to discover universal, **synchronic** regularities or 'laws' relating to social structure by use of the **comparative method**. They rejected historical and evolutionary explanations. In sociology at Harvard, Talcott Parsons developed a version of structural-functionalism which synthesized ideas from both Durkheim and Weber.

The KULA   is a form of ceremonial exchange carried out by the Trobrianders and other island populations of the Massim Archipelago which is situated in the Pacific to the NE of New Guinea. The best known form of kula involves the trade of objects which must include white armbands (*mwali*) and red shell necklaces (*soulava*) that were worn as adornments but had no practical utility. The trade often involved long trips between islands in outrigger canoes. Visitors received gifts from hosts and returned with them. The necklaces and armshells, many of which had their own reputations and histories, traveled in opposite directions, 'clockwise' and 'counter-clockwise' around the 'kula ring.'

No haggling and no direct bargaining for specific valuables was allowed, and there was a strict rule of reciprocity. If you received a good soulava from your kula partner when you visited him, you should endeavor to give him an equivalent mwali when he visited you some years later. **Malinowski** was the first to describe the kula in detail. He thought it prevented warfare. He endorsed **Mauss**'s comparison of kula with **potlatch** and other forms of ceremonial exchange. The kula is still carried out in the Massim.

MANA   is a Polynesian word that may merely mean 'off limits.' A hundred years ago many anthropologists believed that belief in an awe-inspiring magical power (*mana*), possessed by kings, priests, and sacred animals or objects, was a common feature of primitive religion.

NEO-EVOLUTIONISM   is a term that was applied to the writings of **Leslie White**, **Julian Steward**, and their various followers. White saw the harnessing of increasing amounts of energy per capita as the key to cultural evolution. Unlike Steward, he was not very interested in specific adaptations to the environment. Steward was less concerned than White with universal schemes and more interested in tracing particular evolutionary patterns such as the development of state societies in areas where vast public works were required to distribute water to farming populations. Neo-evolutionism was a self-conscious return to the tradition of **Tylor** and **Morgan** (particularly in White's case), but it tried to avoid their ethnocentrism.

PARTICIPANT OBSERVATION   once described by James Clifford and **Clifford Geertz** as 'deep hanging-out,' necessitates the anthropological fieldworker's immersion for a period of several months or even a few years in the day-to-day details of the lives of the people who are being studied. As an informal, unstructured methodology it may be contrasted to more formal procedures such as the administration of questionnaires and structured interviews. It was advocated by **Malinowski**, who claimed it was much superior to quick, fieldwork surveys as a tool for understanding other cultures.

POLITICAL ECONOMY   See CONFLICT THEORY and essay on **Eric Wolf**.

POSTMODERNISM   is the term used to cover a variety of approaches that developed in American anthropology in the 1980s. The term originally referred to different movements in philosophy, literary criticism, and architecture. Anthropological postmodernism, as exemplified in the 1986 volume, *Writing Cultures,* combined some elements evident in other fields, such as scepticism of grand theories and a blurring of the barriers between disciplines and genres (e.g. between ethnographies and novels) with some of the concerns of French poststructuralist philosophers such as Michel Foucault about inequalities of power in relationships between therapists, educators, and/or social scientists and their subjects. Postmodern anthropologists stress that ethnography should ideally reflect negotiation and co-operation between anthropologists and subjects in the creation of texts.

The **POTLATCH** is a form of ceremonial exchange performed by the coastal peoples of Southern Alaska, British Columbia, and Northern Washington State, including the Kwakiutl whose customs were described by **Franz Boas**. It was performed to mark rites of passage, calendrical rituals, and accession to chiefly titles. The objects that were given included blankets, candlefish oil, food and drink in large quantities, elaborately decorated copper shields, and, later on, modern boats and consumer items. Recipients were expected to give their own feasts returning gifts of at least equivalent value or else lose status. In extreme cases, property might be destroyed to shame a political opponent. It is possible that the competitive element in potlatch was enhanced by the fur trade. The government of British Columbia banned the potlatch for more than half a century because they viewed it as wasteful and destructive. **Mauss** noted both the differences and the resemblances between **kula** and potlatch.

STRUCTURALISM (French structuralism) is the method and theory closely associated with the name of **Claude Lévi-Strauss**, who was influenced by such linguists as Ferdinand de Saussure and Roman Jakobson. It was based on the assumption that there are universal cognitive rules and patterns underlying and sustaining diverse human institutions in different cultures. Structuralism depends on the linguistic analogy, inasmuch as language is a specialized cultural form which is in all cases everywhere based on grammatical rules whereby sounds (which in themselves have no meaning) and meaning elements (words, and parts of words) can be combined and contrasted. Whatever their differences, all languages have this grammaticality. Most individuals are only partly aware of the grammar they acquire; some aspects of grammar are unconscious. Binary contrasts, for example map/ nap, tell/told, are a key feature of these grammars. Lévi-Strauss applied the insights of structural linguistics to the analysis of different marriage systems, the strength of patterned relationships between kin (e.g. mother's brother vs. sister's son as opposed to father/son, brother/sister as opposed to husband/wife), and most memorably to the analysis of myth. Myths are broken down into mythemes (episodes) which encapsulate various principles, such as overvaluation of kin (Oedipus sleeps with his mother) versus undervaluation of kin (Oedipus kills his father).

SUBSTANTIVISM VERSUS FORMALISM IN ECONOMIC ANTHROPOLOGY Formalists (such as **Firth**) believe that the same economic principles, which could include the law of supply and demand and the endeavor to maximize rewards with the minimum expenditure of resources, underlie trade and economic relations in all societies. Substantivists (**Mauss**, Polanyi, **Sahlins**) believe that in traditional societies that have forms of ceremonial exchange, economic, political, and religious ideas are intertwined and there is no pure realm of economic action; rather economics is embedded in other institutions such as kinship.

SYMBOLIC AND INTERPRETIVE ANTHROPOLOGY is a movement in British and American anthropology that focused on the study of symbols in ceremonial, ritual, and daily life. It is particularly associated with **Mary Douglas**, **Victor Turner**, and **Clifford Geertz**. It foregrounds culture: for example industrialization does not determine household form, but rather it is the way people interpret industrialization that determines how they will construct households.

TRANSACTIONALISM was developed in the 1960s and 1970s by **Barth**, **Bailey**, Boissevain, and Paine as a reaction to some of the perceived excesses of **structural-functionalism**. Instead of focusing on the institutional mechanisms by which social structures were maintained, transactionalists concentrated on agency – the strategies and alliances developed by individual social actors in pursuit of their goals. The 'practice theory' of **Bourdieu** was also an attempt to develop ideas of agency, but without discounting the notion of structure.

APPENDIX 2

Timeline

1870–1890	**Classic Cultural Evolutionism**
1871	Tylor, *Primitive Culture*
1877	Morgan, *Ancient Society*
1890	Frazer, *The Golden Bough*, 1st Edition
1890–1925	**French Sociology**
1902	Durkheim and Mauss, 'Some Forms of Primitive Classification'
1909	Hertz, 'The Preeminence of the Right Hand,' later translated by Needham
1909	Van Gennep, *The Rites of Passage*
1924	Mauss, 'Essay on the Gift'
1896–1950	**Boasian School**
1896	Boas, 'The Limitations of the Comparative Method of Anthropology'
1912	Boas, 'Changes in Bodily Form of Descendants of Immigrants'
1920	Lowie, *Primitive Society*
1921	Sapir, *Language: An Introduction*
1923	Kroeber, *Anthropology*
1927	Radin, *Primitive Man as Philosopher*
1928	Mead, *Coming of Age in Samoa*
1934	Benedict, *Patterns of Culture*
1935	Hurston, *Mules and Men*
1942	Herskovits, *The Myth of the Negro Past*
1922–1944	**Malinowskian Functionalism**
1922	Malinowski, *Argonauts of the Western Pacific*
1929	Malinowski, *Sexual Life of Savages in Northwestern Melanesia*
1936	Firth, *We the Tikopia*
1937	Evans-Pritchard, *Witchcraft, Oracles and Magic Among the Azande*
1944	Malinowski, *A Scientific Theory of Culture*
1940–1960	**Structural Functionalism**
1923	Radcliffe-Brown, 'The Methods of Ethnology and Social Anthropology'
1940	Fortes and Evans-Pritchard, eds., *African Political Systems*
1940	Evans-Pritchard, *The Nuer*

1949	Fortes, *The Web of Kinship Among the Tallensi*
1950	Radcliffe-Brown and Forde, eds., *African Systems of Kinship and Marriage*
1951	Wilson, *Good Company*
1952	Radcliffe-Brown, *Structure and Function in Primitive Society* (collection of essays spanning Radcliffe-Brown's career)
1954	Leach, *Political Systems of Highland Burma* (transitional to British Structuralism)
1958	Goody, *The Development Cycle in Domestic Groups*
1959	Fortes, *Oedipus and Job in West African Religion*

1945–1965   **The Manchester School**

1955	Gluckman, *The Judicial Process Among the Barotse*
1957	Turner, *Schism and Continuity in an African Society*
1965	Gluckman, *Order and Rebellion in Tribal Africa*

1949–1972   **Neo-Evolutionism**

1949	White, *The Science of Culture*
1954	Leacock, *The Montagnais Hunting Territory and the Fur Trade*
1955	Steward, *Theory of Culture Change: the Methodology of Multilinear Evolution*
1959	White, *The Evolution of Culture*
1960	Sahlins and Service, *Evolution and Culture*
1972	Sahlins, *Stone Age Economics*

1949–1980   **Structuralism (France)**

1949	Lévi-Strauss, *Elementary Structures of Kinship*
1958	Lévi-Strauss, *Structural Anthropology*
1962	Lévi-Strauss, *Totemism*
1962	Lévi-Strauss, *The Savage Mind*
1964	Lévi-Strauss, *The Raw and the Cooked* (This was Volume 1 of 4 of the *Mythologiques* series, which was published in French between 1964 and 1971 and in English between 1969 and 1981)

1960–1972   **Structuralism (UK)**

1961	Leach, *Rethinking Anthropology*
1962	Needham, *Structure and Sentiment*
1966	Douglas, *Purity and Danger*
1969	Douglas, *Natural Symbols*
1972	Needham, *Belief, Language and Experience*

1959–2001   **Transactionalism**

1959	Barth, *Political Leadership among the Swat Pathans*
1969	Bailey, *Stratagems and Spoils*
1969	Barth, *Ethnic Groups and Boundaries*
2001	Bailey, *Treasons, Stratagems and Spoils*

1968–1985   **Cultural Materialism**

1968	Harris, *The Rise of Anthropological Theory*
1974	Harris, *Cows, Pigs, Wars and Witches: The Riddles of Culture*
1977	Harris, *Cannibals and Kings: The Origins of Culture*
1979	Harris, *Cultural Materialism: The Struggle for a Science of Culture*

1967–1990	Symbolic/Interpretive Anthropology
1967	Turner, *The Forest of Symbols*
1969	Turner, *The Ritual Process: Structure and Anti-Structure*
1973	Geertz, *The Interpretation of Cultures*
1973	Ortner, *On Key Symbols*
1974	Turner, *Dramas, Fields and Metaphors: Symbolic Action in Human Society*
1978	Ortner, *Sherpas Through their Rituals*
1980	Geertz, *Negara: The Theatre State in Nineteenth Century Bali*
1980	Rosaldo, *Ilongot Headhunting, 1883–1974*
1983	Geertz, *Local Knowledge: Further Essays in Interpretive Anthropology*

1969–2010	Political Economy
1969	Wolf, *Peasant Wars of the Twentieth Century*
1982	Wolf, *Europe and the People Without History*
1991	Comaroff, J. and J. L., *Of Revelation and Revolution: Vol. 1, Christianity, Colonialism and Consciousness*
1997	Comaroff, J. and J. L., *Of Revelation and Revolution: Vol. 2, The Dialectics of Modernity on a South African Frontier*

1970–2010	Feminism/Sex and Gender Studies
1974	Ortner, 'Is Female to Male as Nature is to Culture?'
1975	Rubin, 'The Traffic in Women: Notes on a "Political Economy" of Sex'
1981	Ortner and Whitehead, eds. *Sexual Meanings*
1984	Rubin, 'Thinking Sex: Notes for a Radical Theory of the Politics of Sexuality'
1988	Strathern, *The Gender of the Gift*

1977–2010	Post Structuralism/Post Modernism/Post Colonialism
1977	Bourdieu, *Outline of a Theory of Practice*
1984	Bourdieu, *Distinction. A Social Critique of the Judgment of Taste*
1986	Clifford and Marcus, eds., *Writing Culture*, inc. Rosaldo's 'From the Door of His Tent'
1986	Appadurai, *The Social Life of Things*
1989	Rosaldo, *Culture and Truth*
1996	Appadurai, *Modernity at Large: Cultural Dimensions of Globalization*
2006	Comaroff, J. L. and Comaroff, J., eds., *Law and Disorder in the Post Colony*

INDEX

Note: entries in bold indicate glossary or biography items

Social and Cultural Anthropology: The Key Concepts

Second Edition

Nigel Rapport and Joanna Overing

Social and Cultural Anthropology: The Key Concepts is an easy to use A–Z guide to the central concepts that students are likely to encounter in this field.

Now fully updated, the second edition includes entries on:

- Power
- The State
- Human Rights
- Hybridity
- Alterity
- Cosmopolitanism
- The Body
- Violence
- Gender
- Cybernetics

With full cross-referencing and revised further reading to point students towards the latest writings in Social and Cultural Anthropology, this is a superb reference resource for anyone studying or teaching in this area.

ISBN: 978-0-415-36751-6 (pbk)

Available at all good bookshops
For ordering and further information please visit
www.routledge.com

Anthropology: The Basics

Peter Metcalf

Anthropology: The Basics is the ultimate guide for the student encountering anthropology for the first time. It explains and explores key anthropological concepts, addressing questions such as:

- What is anthropology?
- How can we distinguish cultural differences from physical ones?
- What is culture anyway?
- How do anthropologists study culture?
- What are the key theories and approaches used today?
- How has the discipline changed over time?

Providing an overview of the fundamental principles of anthropology, this user-friendly text is an invaluable resource for anyone wanting to learn more about a fascinating subject.

ISBN: 978-0-415-33120-3 (pbk)

Available at all good bookshops
For ordering and further information please visit
www.routledge.com